SECOND CUSTOM EDITION FOR JROTC
A CHARACTER AND LEADERSHIP DEVELOPMENT PROGRAM

CITIZENSHIP IN AMERICAN HISTORY AND GOVERNMENT

Taken from:

Civics: Participating in Government
by James E. Davis and Phyllis Maxey Fernlund

America: Pathways to the Present
by Andrew Cayton, Elisabeth Israels Perry, Linda Reed
and Allan M. Winkler

PEARSON
Custom
Publishing

PEARSON
Prentice
Hall

Images and text taken from the following unless otherwise noted:

Civics: Participating in Government
by James E. Davis and Phyllis Maxey Fernlund
Copyright © 2001 by Prentice Hall, Inc.
A Pearson Education Company
Upper Saddle River, New Jersey 07458

America: Pathways to the Present
by Andrew Cayton, Elisabeth Israels Perry, Linda Reed and Allan M. Winkler
Copyright © 2002 by Prentice Hall, Inc.

Excerpts from *Content Knowledge: A Compendium of Standards and Benchmarks for K-12 Education*, reprinted by permission of McREL. Copyright © 2003 McREL: Mid-Continent Research for Education and Learning, 2550 S. Parker Road, Suite 500, Aurora, CO 80014.

Excerpts (text, cartoons, and images) from *We the People: The Citizen and the Constitution*, (1995), reprinted by permission of the Center for Civic Education. Copyright © 1995 Center for Civic Education.

Printed in the United States of America

10 9 8 7 6 5 4 3 2 1

ISBN 0-536-81439-2

2005300016

EM/JS

Please visit our web site at *www.pearsoncustom.com*

PEARSON CUSTOM PUBLISHING
75 Arlington Street, Suite 300, Boston, MA 02116
A Pearson Education Company

Citizenship in American History and Government

Table of Contents

Citizenship in American History and Government

Chapter 1

You the People— Citizenship Skills

Lesson 1

The Preamble

Key Terms

beneficiaries
goals
Preamble
responsible parties

What You Will Learn to Do

- Examine the Preamble to the United States Constitution

Linked Core Abilities

- Do your share as a good citizen in your school, community, country, and the world

Skills and Knowledge You Will Gain Along the Way

- Classify the components of the Preamble to the United States Constitution
- Explain the goals of the Preamble
- Connect the principles of the Preamble to the United States Constitution to your personal values
- Define key words contained in this lesson

Introduction

The Preamble to the Constitution of the United States establishes the purpose of the Constitution. It served as a "mission statement" for the framers of the Constitution. In this lesson, you analyze the Preamble to determine the **goals,** the **beneficiaries,** and the **responsible parties.**

The U.S. Constitution and the Preamble

The Constitutional Convention of 1787 produced the most enduring written Constitution ever created by human hands. Though the United States existed prior to the ratification of the Constitution, it was a nation held together by the threads of the Articles of Confederation, a sometimes contentious and often ineffectual national government. The men who attended the Constitutional Convention in Philadelphia, usually referred to as the Framers of the Constitution, created a document that was the result of dozens of compromises and shaped by the failures of the United States under the Articles as well as the failures of European governments of the time.

The entire Constitution was written by several committees, but the committee most responsible for the final form recognized today is the "Committee of Style and Arrangement." This Committee was tasked with getting all of the articles and clauses into a logical order. On September 10, 1787, the Committee of Style set to work, and two days later, it presented its final draft. Heading the draft was the **Preamble.** Committee members included Alexander Hamilton, William Johnson, Rufus King, James Madison, and Gouverneur Morris. The actual text of the Preamble and of much of the rest of this final draft is usually attributed to Gouverneur Morris (see Figure 1.1.1).

The Preamble holds in its words the hopes and dreams of the delegates to the convention, a justification for what they had done. Its words are familiar to us today, but the words are not always easy to follow. The Preamble to the United States Constitution reads as follows:

Figure 1.1.1: Gouverneur Morris is credited with the final draft of the Preamble.

Courtesy of Hulton Archive/Getty Images.

We the people of the United States, in order to form a more perfect union, establish justice, insure domestic tranquility, provide for the common defense, promote the general welfare, and secure the blessing of liberty to ourselves and our posterity, do ordain and establish this Constitution for the United States.

Taking a look at the different parts of the Preamble can help you understand this important start to our Constitution.

We the People of the United States

The Framers were an elite group, among the best and brightest America had to offer at the time. But they knew that they were trying to forge a nation composed not of elite, but of the common man. This first part of the Preamble speaks to the common man. It puts into writing the notion that the people were creating this Constitution. It was not handed down by a god or by a king; it was created by the people.

In Order to Form a More Perfect Union

The Framers were dissatisfied with the United States under the Articles of Confederation, and were striving for something better. The Articles of Confederation had been a grand experiment that had worked well up to a point, but now, less than ten years into that experiment, cracks were showing. The new United States, under this new Constitution, would be more perfect. Not *perfect,* but more perfect.

Establish Justice

Injustice, unfairness of laws and in trade, was of great concern to the people of 1787. People looked forward to a nation with a level playing field, where courts were established with uniformity and where trade within and outside the borders of the country would be fair and unbiased.

Insure Domestic Tranquility

One of the events that caused the Convention to be held was the revolt of Massachusetts farmers known as Shays' Rebellion. The taking up of arms by war veterans revolting against the state government was a shock to the system. The keeping of the peace was on everyone's mind, and the maintenance of tranquility at home was a prime concern. The Framers hoped that the new powers given the federal government would prevent any such rebellions in the future.

Provide for the Common Defence

The new nation was fearful of attack from all sides, and no one state was really capable of fending off an attack from land or sea by itself. With a wary eye on Britain and Spain, and ever-watchful for Indian attack, no one could go it alone. They needed each other to survive in the harsh world of international politics of the 18th century.

Misspelled Words in the Constitution?

The Constitution was written in 1787 in the manner of the day—in other words, it was written by hand. According to the National Archives, the version we are most familiar with today was penned by Jacob Shallus, a clerk for the Pennsylvania State Assembly. In the document itself are several words which are misspelled. Far from the days of spell checkers and easy edits, these misspellings survive in the document today.

At that time, the American spelling of words was inconsistent at best, and several words are spelled in the British manner. These words are "defence," "controul," and "labour." In America, we would today write these words as "defense," "control," and "labor."

Most of the misspellings are in the original document, which was written hastily after the Convention concluded. Aside from one use of British spelling in the Bill of Rights, the amendments are all error-free. The authors of the latter amendments all had the benefit of a standardized American dictionary.

Promote the General Welfare

This, and the next part of the Preamble, is the culmination of everything that came before it—the whole point of having tranquility, justice, and defense was to promote the general welfare—to allow every state and every citizen of those states to benefit from what the government could provide. The framers looked forward to the expansion of land holdings, industry, and investment, and they knew that a strong national government would be the beginning of that.

> **NOTE**
>
> *Welfare* in today's context also means organized efforts on the part of public or private organizations to benefit the poor, or simply public assistance. This is not the meaning of the word as used in the Constitution.

And Secure the Blessings of Liberty to Ourselves and Our Posterity

Along with the general welfare, the Framers looked forward to the blessings of liberty—something for which they had all fought just a decade before. They wanted to create a nation that would resemble something of a paradise for liberty, as opposed to the tyranny of a monarchy, where citizens could look forward to being free rather than looking out for the interests of a king. And more than for themselves, they wanted to be sure that the future generations of Americans would enjoy the same.

Do Ordain and Establish this Constitution for the United States of America

The final clause of the Preamble is almost anti-climatic, but it is important for a few reasons—it finishes the "We, the people" thought, saying what we the people are actually doing; it gives a name for the document, and it restates the name of the nation adopting the Constitution. That the Constitution is "ordained" reminds us of the higher power involved here—not just of a single person or of a king, but of the people themselves. That it is "established" reminds us that it replaces that which came before—the United States under the Articles.

Components of the Preamble

Table 1.1.1 shows how the components of the Preamble can be broken down into three categories: the beneficiaries (those who benefit); the goals (what the Preamble sets out to do); and the responsible party (those who are responsible for attaining the goals).

Conclusion

The Preamble is the "mission statement" to the document known as the United States Constitution. It lays the framework for this ever-changing and growing

Table 1.1.1: Components of the Preamble

Beneficiary	Goals	Responsible Party
To ourselves and our posterity	promote the general welfare	We the people of the United States
	establish justice	
	provide for the common defense	
	in order to form a more perfect union	
	do ordain and establish this constitution for the United States of America	
	and secure the blessing of liberty	

roadmap for our democratic society. This lesson examined the various parts of the Preamble, and explained the beneficiaries of, the goals of, and the responsible parties for this document.

In the following lesson, you will learn about citizenship skills. You will learn the definition of the seven *You the People* citizenship skills, and will relate the seven *You the People* citizenship skills to the Preamble of the Constitution.

Lesson Review

1. Define what is meant by the beneficiaries, the goals, and the responsible parties regarding the Preamble.

2. Choose one component of the Preamble and discuss it.

3. Why was the Preamble written?

4. Who wrote the Preamble?

Citizenship Skills

Key Terms

balance
cooperation
fairness
patience
respect
strength
self-improvement

What You Will Learn to Do

- Hypothesize what our country would be like without the seven citizenship skills

Linked Core Abilities

- Do your share as a good citizen in your school, community, country, and the world

Skills and Knowledge You Will Gain Along the Way

- Define the seven *You the People* citizenship skills
- Relate the seven *You the People* citizenship skills to the Preamble of the Constitution
- Explain the relationship between the citizenship skills and effective teamwork
- Define key words contained in this lesson

Introduction

The Preamble to the United States Constitution sets the stage for the success of our nation. Individual values, which are also important to the success of our nation, are inferred from the Preamble and are called Citizenship Skills in the Cadet Citizenship Training Program. These Citizenship Skills are basic human values envisioned by

Chapter 1

the Founding Fathers when they drafted the Constitution. This lesson explores the relationship between the values described in the Preamble and the seven Citizenship Skills to which you will be introduced.

You the People Educational Programs are designed to train Americans to make their nation truly a country of the people, by the people, and for the people.

Within this overall mission, the *Cadet Citizenship Training Program* is designed to help cadets:

- **Better understand the development of the United States system of government**
- **Learn the mechanics of how government works in the United States through hands-on exercises and experiences**
- **Develop interpersonal skills that will assist them throughout their personal and professional lives**

The primary teaching tool for this training program is the Citizen Action Group Process. The purpose of this group is to help cadets become effective citizens while guiding the governmental activity in their school, town, state, and country as the Founders of the United States of America envisioned.

After completing this course, cadets will be better educated and trained to effectively participate in their local, state, and federal governments by voting and by other means (for example, attending meetings, communicating effectively with representatives, and invoking change in their community).

You the Citizen

The Declaration of Independence established the ideals upon which this nation is based: freedom, equality, and unity. These ideals provide our country with a common theme.

The Constitution was written so that every American citizen is given equal opportunity to pursue these ideals. Only by exercising our rights as citizens can we enhance our governmental ideals of freedom, equality, and unity.

After you have registered to vote, you hold the highest office in America. You are the one who elects those representatives who go to Washington, D.C. and administer the government (see Figure 1.2.1). It is your tax money those representatives decide how to spend.

The Constitution specifies that the people rule the American government. American citizens, on paper, hold the ultimate power in this nation. While it appears that the President holds the highest office in this nation, as American citizens we really do. The President works for us.

How will you use your power as a registered voter? Do you care about this responsibility? Will you vote regularly? In what other ways (in addition to voting) will you participate?

Your answers to these questions will determine what kind of life you will have as well as what quality of life you will pass to your children and your children's children.

How can you become a more effective citizen of this country? The best way is to educate yourself.

The *You the People* text is organized into two main sections, each with corresponding exercises and classroom activities:

- **Citizenship Skill Development. To become an effective citizen you must develop certain skills or values that were well known to the Founders of our nation. Most of us have forgotten or have never learned these skills. This section provides an overview of the skills.**

- **Citizen Action Group Process. This section forms the core of the *You the People* Educational Series: a pro-active group process known as the Citizen Action Group Process. This process may be the future of democracy in America. Several types of these groups are already developing through grassroots organizations in many communities across the nation, perhaps even your own. In this section, you will get a chance to practice being a member of a Citizen Action Group and address issues that may concern you or others in your school. With this knowledge and experience, you can then decide how you want to participate at the next level, in your own communities.**

The following section introduces you to Citizenship Skill Development.

Citizenship Skill Development

As you learned in the previous lesson, the Preamble to the United States Constitution sets the stage for the success of our nation. Individual values, which are also important to the success of our nation, are inferred from the Preamble and are called citizenship skills in this Cadet Citizenship Training Program. These citizenship skills are basic human values the Founding Fathers envisioned when they drafted the Constitution.

> **The Preamble to the United States Constitution**
>
> We the people of the United States, in order to form a more perfect union, establish justice, insure domestic tranquility, provide for the common defense, promote the general welfare, and secure the blessing of liberty to ourselves and our posterity, do ordain and establish this Constitution for the United States of America.

Our government is based upon seven main citizenship skills. These individual skills are also interdependent; that is, to practice one skill you will need to use the others as well.

The Seven Citizenship Skills

The seven citizenship skills include:

Skill 1: Cooperation—"We the people," not we the individuals; work together as a group.

Skill 2: Patience—A "more" perfect union; take progressive steps towards a better situation.

Skill 3: Fairness—"Establish justice;" consider the common good as well as individual desires.

Skill 4: Respect—"Insure domestic tranquility;" accept your fellow citizens.

Skill 5: Strength—"Provide for the common defense;" stand up for what is right, denounce what is wrong, and admit your mistakes.

Skill 6: Self-improvement—"Promote the general welfare;" seek knowledge and skills.

Skill 7: Balance—"Secure the blessing of liberty to ourselves and our posterity;" support our nation's ideals (freedom, equality, and unity) by harmonizing or compromising solutions to our problems.

Skill 1: Cooperation

The Preamble to the Constitution states "We the people," not we the individuals. The premise here is that we can rule more effectively if we cooperate as a group to solve problems. In some instances, this might mean looking out for the common goals of the group at the expense of personal desires.

Cooperation involves thinking, as a group with each person trying to help the group in whatever way is best given the time and circumstances involved. Properly done, cooperative efforts can be more efficient and more successful than individual efforts. To accomplish this, however, people need an attitude of working together to achieve a common goal.

For example, a new student joined a science class that was undertaking a major research project to monitor the water quality of a nearby river. The instructor asked the class to include this new student in their project. Because she was not trained in collecting and recording water quality samples, an easy solution would have been to assign her a minor role. However, a group of students offered to spend their own

> **Key Note Term**
>
> **cooperation**—the art of working together as a group towards a common goal; cooperation is shown in an attitude of group awareness and willingness to help each other reach a common goal

Figure 1.2.2: The Canada goose is an example of cooperation.

Courtesy of Chase Swift/Corbis Images.

time, after school, to train her. They knew their project would be enhanced if they had another trained sampler who could collect valid samples from an additional location along the river.

The students' efforts are an example of a cooperative attitude. They did this extra work to help the overall purpose of the class research project.

Cooperation does not mean, however, we give up our beliefs and opinions for the good of the group or to support a poor idea. Instead, cooperation uses individual talents to obtain the very best group results.

It follows the popular saying: The whole is greater than the sum of the parts. When we cooperate using everyone's best talents, the group is more powerful than all the individual efforts.

Cooperation is an important citizenship skill because any nation of, by, and for the people must work together. If we can truly govern ourselves, we have to be willing to subordinate some of our individual desires so that the whole (our country) operates efficiently and effectively.

Cooperation is an active skill based upon a common purpose and common goals to achieve that purpose. The students in the example above were aware of the common purpose of the research project (to collect valid data) and recognized this purpose could be enhanced if they had another trained person taking samples from an additional location. Their actions were in support of this purpose.

Cooperation is important to achieving the rights promised to us in the Declaration of Independence (life, liberty, and the pursuit of happiness). Cooperation also supports peaceful coexistence. Cooperation means, among other things, helping others to see your point of view or helping them to clarify their own point of view. Without cooperation, humans break down into bickering, small groups, constantly fighting each other, as many societies have done all too often. Sometimes, cooperation is necessary for survival.

For example, geese fly in a "V" formation for a specific reason (see Figure 1.2.2). Scientists have found that each goose receives uplift from the one in front. By flying this way, geese extend their flying distances by more than 70 percent. Whenever a goose falls out of formation, it quickly feels the drag of flying alone and joins the formation again. The honks from behind encourage the leader to maintain the pace. When the leader is tired, it moves to the rear and a goose near the front takes over. If a goose lands for a rest or is injured, two or three from the flock will land with it and wait until the tired goose is able to fly again or dies; then they will fly together in a smaller "V" formation until they catch up with a larger flock. The flock depends on each goose cooperating and working together.

Skill 2: Patience

The Founding Fathers' goal was to form a more perfect union. The Articles of Confederation were not working well at the time and the Founders wanted to improve this design of government in the Constitution. In so doing, they were working toward a more perfect situation in our government.

The **patience** citizenship skill illustrates this idea of progressing toward a more perfect situation. Patience is knowing when it is best to wait, when it is best to act, and how much action one should take based on the circumstances. It is both an active and a passive skill.

One example of the use of patience in our nation's history is the signing of the Declaration of Independence. Why was the Declaration signed in 1776? Why not after the Stamp Acts or the Boston Massacre?

The Founding Fathers had been preparing for independence for some years before 1776. Committees of Correspondence had been formed, ammunition and weapons were being stockpiled, and political discussions were ongoing.

These preparations helped the independence movement. The Founders knew that independence from England would probably mean war. War required soldiers and the new colonies did not have a draft. Anti-English sentiment had to be widespread among the people, not just the political leaders of that time. Enough American colonists had to feel so strongly about their freedom that they would fight for it.

The Founders' preparations encouraged the anti-English feelings in 1776. Before this time the Founders were unsure if enough American colonists were ready to fight. Waiting until after 1776, provided too many unknowns. The English oppressions might lessen, thereby reducing the colonists' strong desire for freedom, or English oppressions might escalate, making the colonists' desire for freedom even stronger.

Therefore, the Founders felt the time was "ripe" for declaring independence in 1776, and they acted accordingly. They were successful because they used the patience citizenship skill effectively.

Patience is not just waiting for something; it is knowing when is the right time to act. In other words, patience is knowing when to act and when to wait. You have probably been told sometime in your life to be patient, to wait. Practicing the patience citizenship skill means waiting for something, as the Founders did when they waited for the right time to declare independence from England.

> ### Key Note Term
>
> **patience**—the skill of knowing the proper timing for acting on an idea or decision

Patience is one of the most difficult skills to practice. Sometimes we do not like to wait because we have been programmed by our culture to receive instant gratification. In addition, sometimes we like to "tune out" the world and watch it go by. In both cases, we are not using the patience citizenship skill effectively.

Skill 3: Fairness

Establishing justice, which the citizenship skill of fairness is about, involves balancing individual desires with the common good. This is a tricky balance to maintain and why we have a unique Supreme Court. Our justice system is based on following the spirit of the law. In turn, the laws are based on the ideals of the Declaration of Independence.

We elect representatives and judges (in most cases) who then create and execute the laws of our country. A sense of **fairness** within ourselves is important if we are to pick the right people to make and enforce these laws.

The United States' ideal of "equality" is a good illustration of the fairness citizenship skill. Under our Constitution, we citizens are encouraged to grow as individuals, but we must also promote equality so that all people have an equal opportunity to grow as well.

The method our government has chosen to promote equality has some inherent conflicts. Similar to most methods, there are two ways of looking at the promotion of equality: Do we promote individual opportunity or do we focus on bringing everyone up to the same level? In other words, do we look at the "form" of a person (that is, their race, religion, economic status) or do we look at both the "form" and "substance" when promoting opportunity, where "substance" is how much education the person has, how qualified that person is for the job, and so on.

One way equality can be achieved is if there's balance between the two ways (form and substance), allowing equal opportunity while maintaining objective standards for promotion—balancing individual desires against the common good for the nation as a whole. That is where fairness comes in.

Fairness means we constantly measure our individual desires against what is in the best interest of others and the majority of people around us.

Skill 4: Respect

The Preamble to the Constitution states ". . . insure domestic tranquility. . . ." This can be a challenge in a diverse country like the United States. This nation has a wide mix of cultures, races, and religions. We have achieved togetherness within this diversity because we have common ideals (see Figure 1.2.3). The Constitution and the Declaration of Independence are based upon our common ideals of freedom, equality, and unity.

To work toward these ideals, our nation must learn to accept and incorporate the various differences in our society. To do otherwise is to resort to fighting wars over these differences.

Our institutions and laws are designed to ensure, as much as possible, that our government works together so that we rule as one unified body. To be unified, however, we must recognize each other as being equal and deserving of **respect.**

Key Note Term

fairness—the act of tempering individual desires with the needs of society as a whole

---

Key Note Term

respect—accepting the differences in others and honoring those differences

---

Chapter 1   You the People–Citizenship Skills

Figure 1.2.3: Common goals and ideals bind all cultures.

Courtesy of Steve Chenn/Corbis Images.

Think of respect as having acceptance of others, not necessarily love for each other. Nice though it may be, loving everyone is difficult to achieve. We all evaluate others. The difference is how we act on these evaluations. That is where respect comes in.

Respect is a critical citizenship skill for any nation with our ideals (freedom, equality, and unity). If we can respect each other with all our differences, we will feel secure enough to state our ideas and opinions to each other. Everyone's opinion matters and deserves to be heard no matter how much we may disagree with it.

Respect is especially important to the Citizen Action Group Process introduced in this Cadet Citizenship Training Program. Without it, this group process might be stymied or dominated by one person or a group of persons. Respect allows cooperative communication to take place.

As you practice the respect citizenship skill, you may need to evaluate those around you based on their skills rather than on any personal or preconceived judgments. Respect for each other encourages participation, and participation is needed to keep our country alive. Participation is also vital to the Citizen Action Group Process.

Skill 5: Strength

The Preamble included the need for common defense, which refers to national **strength.** To be strong nationally, we must have a nation of citizens with strong convictions.

The strength citizenship skill involves the ability to stand up for what you believe (based on factual evidence and/or your values) even in the face of strong opposition. Strength is the main skill in the drug awareness program, D.A.R.E.

Key Note Term

strength—the willingness of citizens to stand up for what they believe in, to denounce what's wrong, and to admit when they've made a mistake

Strength is saying "no" when you mean "no" and "yes" when you mean "yes." Strength is a skill that challenges all of us.

We humans, it seems, are born with a "fear of rejection" (among other fears) written on our birth certificates. Students and adults alike all want to be accepted and liked by others. In addition, it is precisely the fear of not being accepted that keeps us from standing up for what we believe in. We are afraid if we say something others disagree with, they will not like us.

Consequently we tend to do one of two things: either we say nothing or we go along with our friends even when we do not agree. This is the working definition of peer pressure. We want our friends to like us. This is human.

We are not using the strength citizenship skill when we buckle under to peer pressure that ultimately hurts others and ourselves. We can be so afraid of "making waves" we will do what the group wants even if we do not believe in it. To the extreme, this can become dangerous. In political terms, it can lead to a dictatorship.

Germany had a democratic government in the 1920's, but by the 1930's, it was ruled by a dictator who imprisoned and executed millions of men, women, and children simply because of their race, religion, or disability. What happened? Part of it was unwillingness for people to denounce what was wrong. Unfortunately, there are countless other examples like this throughout history.

For our government to succeed, we need a nation composed of people willing to stand up for what they believe in and to denounce what is wrong.

Stand by your beliefs. Do not be afraid to say what you think, even if it might be construed as uncooperative. If you do it in a way that honors those who are listening, you will not come across as uncooperative.

Try also to be strong enough to allow others the same freedom—to have and hold their own beliefs. The greatest strength in many cases is the strength to admit when you have made a mistake.

For example, suppose you have told a joke you think is funny to someone who felt insulted by your joke. This joke poked fun at a particular ethnic group. You find out that this person belongs to that ethnic group. It takes great strength to admit that you were wrong and your joke was in poor taste.

Skill 6: Self-Improvement

"Promoting the general welfare," as the Preamble states, gives all of us the freedom to learn and work as we want. The Founding Fathers hoped that this would create a prosperous nation; however, for our nation to be prosperous, we have to be willing to improve ourselves.

Self-improvement is the skill of educating and training yourself so that you can be the best at whatever you do. We tend to be a nation of achievers because most of us have had to work hard to be where we are today. In essence, this is part of our national personality. Thus, most of us want to be the best we can be at whatever we attempt, to pursue perfection without being perfectionists.

As humans, we are imperfect. We make mistakes. Mistakes and failures are part of self-improvement. Without mistakes, we might never know where we need to

> ### Key Note Term
>
> **self-improvement**—a desire to continually learn new skills and improve on others so that citizens can better serve themselves and those around them

improve. Being a perfectionist means being intolerable of mistakes. Although some of us tend to be perfectionists, this can be counter to the self-improvement citizenship skill.

Thomas Edison tried over 2,500 times before he was successful at inventing the light bulb. Each time he failed, he learned something that helped him on the next try.

That is what self-improvement is all about—looking at weaknesses and discovering where to improve. Weakness can be another term for challenges or obstacles. Self-improvement involves the willingness to overcome obstacles even in the face of hardships. It is looking at obstacles as opportunities for growth rather than as stopping places.

Our country gives everyone an equal chance for education through our public school system. This relates to the citizenship skill of self-improvement. Our country must have educated citizens to elect good representatives and participate in running the government.

The "American Dream" of becoming or doing what you want is also based on this self-improvement skill. If you want to change your career and/or go to college at age 40, you have the freedom in this country to make that choice.

Self-improvement means looking at everything you do, whether it is cleaning a toilet or writing a novel, and doing the very best you can at that task. To do this, you may need more education or training, or you may have to overcome some obstacles.

For example, if you want to be good at competitive sports you not only have to practice to become better, but you also have to overcome the obstacle of losing some games or matches and learn from those losses. From this learning, you then can become a more effective player.

Likewise, if you want to make good decisions on community or school issues, you need to educate yourself about those issues, be willing to make some mistakes (such as bad decisions), learn from those mistakes, and be willing to overcome the obstacle of interacting with others who might think differently than you.

Because self-improvement takes courage and perseverance (strength and patience citizenship skills), it can only be practiced when there is an overall ideal or purpose in mind.

The Declaration of Independence provided the overriding ideals for our country (freedom, equality, and unity). When we use the self-improvement skill as a citizen, we are helping our country work toward these ideals.

Skill 7: Balance

To secure the blessings of liberty (as mentioned in the Preamble), our nation must continue to follow the ideals of the Declaration of Independence. The key to following these ideals is to work through problems until we find the best solution for all involved. This requires **balance**—both nationally and individually.

Our nation, indeed our world, is made up of different people with differing ideas and ways. Throughout history, many wars have been fought over differences. To eliminate war, the world must find another way of resolving differences. That is where the citizenship skill of balance comes in.

Balance is accepting there are at least two sides to every issue, each with some truth. There is not a wrong and a right viewpoint, even though one might appear better initially. All sides can have some merit. All viewpoints can have some errors as well.

Balance plays a win/win game where both sides benefit from the process. Winning and losing are for debates and football games. Thus, in some ways, practicing the skill of balance can be contrary to everything we have been taught.

The skill of practicing balance involves using either compromise or harmony to achieve an agreement that works. The two are very different. Harmony means combining the best qualities of all sides and coming up with an entirely different but better solution that meets all sides' needs. Sometimes this is called a win/win solution.

Compromise, on the other hand, is a solution in which each side gives a little to come to a common ground. This can also be win/win if each side does not give up too much.

Probably the best example of using balance in history was the development of the Constitution. Both harmony and compromise were used in the drafting of this document. Take look at each of these, respectively.

Two strong factions had differing opinions about the balance of power in our government. Some Founders wanted the states to hold the primary power of the nation; others wanted the majority of power to be held by a federal government.

Both sides had valid points. To harmonize the two factions, the Founders came up with a third solution that satisfied both sides of the argument—sovereign state governments supplemented by a federal government that was given great power but only in certain specific areas such as foreign affairs, defense, and interstate trade. The federal government also was given the power to resolve differences between states if the states alone could not resolve them. All other powers not specifically wielded by the federal government were reserved for the states.

This design was based on the dual-sovereignty theme of the Native American Iroquois Council of Governments. For hundreds of years before our nation was formed, the Iroquois used a form of government that combined five separate nations—Mohawk, Onondaga, Seneca, Oneida, and Cayuga into one overall League of Nations.

Each nation elected representatives called sachems. Sachems held meetings (called councils) to discuss issues that concerned the internal affairs of each nation. Periodically the sachems from all five nations would meet together in a Grand Council to discuss issues that affected all five nations such as war, peace, treaties, and new members to the Grand Council.

Benjamin Franklin became intimately familiar with the Iroquois government because of his job as a diplomat for Pennsylvania and as a scholar of Native American literature. He was able to persuade the Founders to copy the Iroquois system in many ways. The most important way was the design of state governments with an overall federal government.

The Founders were able to design a system of government that satisfied the needs of both sovereign states and a federal government—a win/win solution.

The debate between state or federal control of power continues in Congress to this day. Control of power was really challenged in the Civil War, but the design envisioned by the Iroquois and used by the Founders works because it uses balance as a key element.

Another agreement that was needed, as part of the Constitution, is known as The Great Compromise. This agreement obviously used compromise as a way to achieve balance. Large states wanted representation based on population, but small states were afraid the heavily-populated states would dominate. Therefore, both a Senate and House were formed in our Congress.

Both sides had to give up something—the heavily populated states had to relinquish their power in the Senate and the sparsely populated states had to relinquish their power in the House.

You are probably more familiar with the use of compromise as a way to achieve agreement, but do not rule out using harmony, where a whole new solution can be used that solves the problem for both sides.

One place to practice balance is when reading or hearing news reports. Political campaigns have shown how influential the news media can be. Before we make up our minds on an issue, though, we need to look at more than one news source to understand all sides. From this balanced knowledge, we are better able to see compromising or harmonizing solutions.

Conclusion

From the signing of the U.S. Constitution to present day, the seven citizenship skills have played a major part in shaping and developing our country. The Preamble set the groundwork for the ideals of this nation, and also created a guide to what good citizenship should be.

The next lesson looks at small group meetings. You will examine the purpose and process of small group meetings, from choosing a meeting leader to presenting the meeting agenda. You will also learn to identify the small group meeting roles.

Chapter 1

Lesson Review

1. **List the seven citizenship skills.**
2. **Choose two of the skills and explain how they can work together.**
3. **How do the seven citizenship skills relate to the Preamble of the Constitution?**
4. **Explain how self-improvement can make you a better citizen.**

Lesson Review

Small Group Meetings

Key Terms

agenda
consensus
decision-making
ground rule
simple majority
small group leader
small group meeting
timekeeper

What You Will Learn to Do

- Use the small group meeting process in decision-making situations

Linked Core Abilities

- Do your share as a good citizen in your school, community, country, and the world

Skills and Knowledge You Will Gain Along the Way

- Compare simple majority and consensus decision-making processes
- Explain the impact of the small group meeting agenda
- Describe all *You the People* ground rules
- Identify the small group meeting roles
- Explain the small group meeting process
- Design a process for the role rotations
- Define key words contained in this lesson

Introduction

Citizens participate in two types of Citizen Action Group meetings: small group meetings that are covered in this lesson, and representative group sessions that are discussed in the next lesson. In this lesson, you examine the purpose and process of small group meetings, from choosing a meeting leader to presenting the meeting **agenda.** You also practice using the seven citizenship skills as you participate in small group meetings.

> **NOTE**
>
> Before the first small group meeting, it is recommended that you view the You the People Video. It is a three part series on citizenship. The video also contains segments that refer to the separation between church and state. Please review the following sidebar for one perspective on that topic.

Small Group Meeting

A **small group meeting** is a gathering of about five to nine cadets who use a process to discuss and decide issues (selected by you and/or your instructor). The overall purpose of these groups is to teach you how to become an effective citizen and how to guide the governmental activity in your school, town, state as the Founders of the United States of America envisioned. In practical terms, the small group meeting gives your group a forum to apply and practice the citizenship skills (see Figure 1.3.1).

Your instructor has pre-selected the members of your small group. Barring any unforeseen consequences (such as students moving away), members within your small group should not change.

One of the first things you will do as a group is to come up with a name or number for your group. Deciding and agreeing on this name or number may be the first opportunity you have to practice the citizenship skills as a group. This name or number will be used to identify your particular group when you meet with other small groups.

Choosing a Group Leader

After you have a group name or number, select your first group leader. A group leader runs a small group meeting. Every member of your group will have the chance to be a group leader. Ask a volunteer to be your first **small group leader.** If no one volunteers, your instructor will select a leader. This leadership role rotates around the small group with each meeting.

Key Note Term

agenda—a list of tasks or a schedule to be followed

Key Note Term

small group meeting— one of two types of Citizen Action groups where a small group of five to nine persons meets periodically to discuss and decide on various issues and actions

Key Note Term

small group leader— leads a small group meeting

Figure 1.3.1: Small groups gather to discuss and decide issues.

Courtesy of Image Source/ Corbis Images.

Group Leader Responsibilities

As a small group leader, you are responsible for conducting the small group meeting. You learn the skills necessary to be a group leader as you conduct a meeting. The first few meetings you lead may be difficult, but that is also part of the learning process. Your responsibilities include:

1. *Prepare in advance.* **Read over your worksheets and notes from the last meeting. Know what the old issues are. Write or type out an agenda and give it to the other group members before the small group meeting (at least two days before if possible). If this is the first small group meeting, your instructor will have an agenda prepared for you.**

2. *Start your meeting on time.* **Even if not all your group members are present, begin your meeting; otherwise,** you will be hard-pressed to finish on time. If you start on time, group members are more likely to be punctual.

3. *Distribute optional blank worksheets (group worksheet and decision making worksheet).* **Members of your group can decide whether or not to use these worksheets. Your instructor may also have guidance for you pertaining to these worksheets.**

4. *Keep the group focused on the agenda.* **Keep the group focused on the agenda by assigning someone in the group to be the timekeeper. When it is time to move to the next agenda item, the timekeeper will notify you. Quickly bring the discussion to a close and move on.**

5. *Distribute action assignments to all small group members.* **Make sure that you come up with specific assignments for each group member before your meeting is adjourned. Do not let one or two group members end up doing all the work.**

Being a group leader is a challenging job, but it is a great opportunity for self-improvement.

Small Group Meeting Process

Learning how to work together with other cadets and make real decisions on issues that affect all of you is a process; however, the process of making a decision will be as important as the final decision itself.

Key Note Term

timekeeper—an individual who keeps track of the time at a small group meeting

As you participate in these groups, you will find the need to develop group skills. The following section covers these skills that will come in handy when working in small groups.

Group Skill 1: Reaching a Simple Majority

Most of us are familiar with the skill of reaching a **simple majority.** It is the "show of hands" voting process. To have a simple majority, more than half of the votes must be in favor of a certain option. Your group can decide what to do with an issue using this voting process.

As an issue is raised, you will ask for a vote to see what to do with it (do we act on it, do we research it more, or do we drop it because we're not interested enough). After you have brainstormed ideas on how to act on an issue or research it further, you will also call for a vote to determine which idea to select.

The following shows an example of how a simple majority works.

Simple Majority Example

A member of your group has raised the issue of reducing the voting age from eighteen to sixteen years of age. As a group, you must first decide what you want to do with this idea.

There are seven members in your group and you call for a vote to decide: Do you research it further? Do you drop it? Or do you act on it? The vote is:

- **Research it further: 5**
- **Drop it: 2**
- **Act on it: 0**

More than half of the group supports exploring the issue further; however, if the vote were 2, 3, 2, you would not have a majority because more than half of your group (that is, four or more) was not in favor of one option. You would then have to continue discussing the issue until your group came up with a simple majority in favor of one option. They could decide to delay discussing the issue until a later meeting where it might be easier to come to a majority (sometimes called "tabling" the issue).

For now, assume your group agrees by a majority that this issue needs further research. You brainstorm ways to research it further, and two ideas are thrown out for the group to consider:

- **Find out what the voting age is in other democratic countries**
- **Take a survey of your school to see if other students your age are interested in having the voting age reduced to sixteen**

You call for another vote to see what your group wants to do:

1. **Find out voting age in other countries: 0**
2. **Take a poll of other students: 1**
3. **Do both 1 and 2: 5**
4. **Do neither 1 nor 2: 1**

By a majority, your group has decided to research both options.

After a week, members from your group who were assigned the tasks of exploring this issue give their reports. (Cadets who are practicing the cooperation citizenship skill may have found out more than they were asked to do.) Your group discusses the results, which show there is little interest in lowering the voting age among your peers. Your group votes on what to do now: act on this issue or drop it. The vote is:

- **Act on Issue: 3**
- **Drop Issue: 4**

By a majority, albeit a slim one, your group can now drop the issue if the entire group consents to the process it took to reach this decision. Consensus is the next skill you need to learn.

Group Skill 2: Reaching a Consensus

Consensus is coming to general acceptance on an issue. Consensus is a vital group skill. Without it, your groups may not function, and instead meetings may become squabbling matches and arguments.

The key to consensus comes from the word "consent." It can be more a passive skill than an active one. Consensus is the skill of perhaps not agreeing with the decision the group made, but accepting it anyway because the process used by the group allowed your needs and opinions to be heard and acknowledged.

Consensus is more of a feeling than an action. You consent to the group's decision and thus you ultimately support it or not actively oppose it even though it is not your idea of a great choice.

As a group, you will use the skill of reaching a consensus to evaluate the process your group went through to make a decision. In essence, you will determine whether the seven citizenship skills discussed in the previous lesson were sufficiently practiced by your group in reaching decisions. This is not to imply your group used the citizenship skills perfectly, but that your group did the best they could. Thus you can live with the decision you made together.

Consensus is critically important because the real test of whether we can govern ourselves is if we can work together toward our country's ideals of freedom, equality, and unity.

One of the best ways to come to a consensus is to practice the seven citizenship skills. If you feel your group successfully used the seven citizenship skills to reach a decision, your group is working together and exercising the power envisioned by the Founders when they drafted the Constitution.

Conversely, if you do not feel your group used the citizenship skills successfully, if you or another member of your group was not heard or given respect, or if your group was uncooperative, you can decide not to consent to the process after a decision has been made.

You have power when you do this because then you can veto the decision. This power must be used wisely, however, or the **decision-making** process breaks down.

The following shows an example of how your group might reach a consensus on the decision making process.

Consensus Example

Continuing with the example discussed under the simple majority example, imagine your group decided because of little interest, to drop the idea of trying to reduce the voting age from eighteen to sixteen. Also assume you were the one who raised the issue in the first place.

Now you are evaluating your group's performance at the end of the meeting. You feel that there were members of your group who ridiculed your idea, calling it stupid and foolish. Their behaviors were out of line and disrespectful, in your opinion.

Consequently, you feel your group did not follow the seven citizenship skills as best they could, and you do not consent to the group's decision process. Therefore, at the end of the meeting, you stand up and say, "I veto the decision," and give your reasons. Your group will now delay the decision and discuss it further at the next group meeting. In this instance a consensus was not reached.

A "veto" should be rarely used—only when a decision is reached with obvious and blatant disregard for the seven citizenship skills. It is important that every group member knows that he or she can use the "veto." It is also important that members learn to use it wisely; in other words, veto only when absolutely necessary.

The strength citizenship skill gives you the courage to be honest and indicate when you think your group did not work together. It serves no one, especially the group, if you remain silent when the purpose is to learn more about working together according to the seven citizenship skills.

Now imagine that you did raise the voting age issue, and your group listened to your thoughts and ideas without judging or ridiculing them. Your group went through the decision process considering this issue as objectively as possible and still decided to drop it after researching it further and finding little student support.

In this instance, as you evaluate your group's performance at the end of the meeting, you admit the seven citizenship skills were adequately addressed during the handling of this issue even though the final decision didn't go your way. Thus, you feel the decision was arrived at satisfactorily and so does the rest of your group. This is when a consensus is reached.

By now, you should understand why the process itself is as important as the final decision. Before you begin an actual small group meeting, there are a few ground rules to cover.

Group Skill 3: Following the Ground Rules

Rules are necessary to maintain fairness (Citizenship Skill 3) and give each participant an equal chance. Rules of conduct ensure the ideals of our nation (freedom, equality, and unity) are fulfilled for our citizens.

For this reason small group meetings have rules to ensure that everyone has an equal chance to participate fully and the group works together. The following are 13 **ground rules** to keep in mind during your small group meetings.

Key Note Term

ground rules—rules to ensure that everyone has an equal chance to participate fully and the group works together

- *Ground Rule 1:* Each group meeting will start and end on time. Group members need to be punctual.

- *Ground Rule 2:* A group leader will run each group meeting. This job will rotate among all group members so that everyone will have an opportunity to be a group leader. The group leader will be responsible for facilitating the group discussion, making sure everyone follows the ground rules, and for keeping the group on track and on time. He/she may assign someone else in the group to monitor the time.

- *Ground Rule 3:* Each group member will be conscious of the seven citizenship skills as well as the group skills of reaching a simple majority, reaching a consensus, and following the ground rules during all meetings. If group members start to label, judge, or blame other group members for problems, the group will review the seven citizenship skills again and find out why there are difficulties in the group.

- *Ground Rule 4:* At the end of each group meeting, each individual will evaluate the group's performance as well as his or her own individual performance.

- *Ground Rule 5:* Personal topics will be left out of group discussions. These groups are not meant to be therapy groups.

- *Ground Rule 6:* If a group member gets angry or emotional, he or she will be asked to leave the group for 5 to 15 minutes to cool off (the timing is up to the group leader and/or instructor, if necessary), but he or she must agree to return to the group after the cooling-off period.

- *Ground Rule 7:* Each group member will be allowed time to speak if he/she desires; however, shouting or screaming will not be allowed. The group leader (or instructor, if necessary) may ask a shouting participant to leave the room to cool-off. The group leader will also make sure that each member has voiced her or his views and participated in the process. An issue cannot be decided upon unless everyone in the group has spoken or has openly chosen not to speak.

- *Ground Rule 8:* An issue can be "tabled" by a simple majority of those present, if the following occur:

  - A person is absent from a meeting;

  - The right people are not there to make a decision

  - The group just cannot come to a simple majority for any reason (such as the need to take a break from a highly emotional topic or the need to further research a topic). This issue will then be delayed for discussion at a later meeting.

- *Ground Rule 9:* The person who vetoes a decision, will verbalize their reasons to the rest of the group. The issue will then be discussed at the citizenship skill portion of the following meeting.

- *Ground Rule 10:* An issue can only be discussed in a total of four meetings (counting the first meeting it was brought up) unless agreed to otherwise by your group (see next ground rule).

- *Ground Rule 11:* Any change in the group process will be approved by a simple majority vote of at least 75 percent of the group. For example, if an issue has been overdone and your group wants to stop discussing it before the normal limit (four meetings), 75 percent or more of your group must vote in favor of dropping the issue. If your group wants to continue discussing an issue past the four-meeting limit, 75 percent or more of your group must vote in favor of this.

- *Ground Rule 12:* Your group will agree to meet and work together as long as determined by your instructor.

- *Ground Rule 13:* Discussions within any group meetings are confidential. That is, each group member must agree to not discuss group topics outside the group meetings unless the entire group approves.

Helpful Hints for Running a Small Group Meeting

As the leader of a small group, there are a few hints that might make your job easier and more fulfilling:

1. To keep the group discussion on track, use gentle reminders such as:
   - "Can we get back on the subject?"
   - "Maria has a good point, let's listen to her and not talk among ourselves."
   - "If we stay on the subject, we will finish on time."

2. Do not worry if you do not know all the answers. You do not have to be the most knowledgeable one in the group. Your job is just to keep the discussion moving and on track.

3. You might have group members who do not like to talk in the group. If you haven't heard from a group member, ask them for their thoughts, ideas, or opinions with specific questions like:
   - "Chad, what do you think of Mary's idea to hold an assembly on citizenship skills?"
   - "Belize, do you like the idea of having a senior litter pick-up day?"
   - "Will, what's the best way you can see for us to present our opinions to the city council when they decide on the town's curfew?"

4. Avoid having one person talk all the time. Keep everyone's discussion brief so that all group members have an equal chance to talk. Tell each group member that he or she will have two minutes to talk and that the timekeeper will monitor the time. Then move on to the next person. If there is time at the end, you can come back to that person again.

5. You might have group members who want to help others with personal problems (such as parent and boyfriend/girlfriend issues). Gently remind those group members that this type of discussion must take place outside the group meeting after class and then get back on track. Keep personal problems out of the group discussion.

6. If you have a group member who seems to know a lot about a certain subject, he or she may monopolize the entire discussion. Acknowledge this person for his or her knowledge and then when time is up, move on to the next person. Your group can use this person as a resource for finding out more information on a certain issue. Be careful, though, of making this your only source. All issues have more than one side to them.

7. Group members will want to talk among themselves. Eliminate side talking by calling attention to it such as: "Mandela and Leo, could you share your ideas with the group?"

8. You may have members of your group competing for your job. Simply remind them that they had their turn or that their turn is coming. Ask them to help you out with this difficult job by letting you do it your way. Also, remind them that making mistakes is the only way you will learn. Perhaps they will show respect for your strong and weak points as a result. If you really have trouble, ask your instructor for help.

9. If you have uncooperative members, remind them of the ground rule stating that they can walk out of the room to cool off, but emphasize that they must return to the group. If their behavior persists, ask them to leave the room to cool off. Get your instructor's help if necessary.

10. If group members start to label, judge, or blame other group members for problems, talk within the group about the respect citizenship skill.

11. When asking questions of your group members, wait a few seconds for the answers. Be patient. Give others in your group time to think about their answers.

12. Finally, if you have major problems in the group you cannot resolve, ask your instructor for help.

Small Group Meeting Agenda

The Small Group Meeting flow chart (see Figure 1.3.2), shows the general small group meeting process. Through a systematic process, an issue is brought up, discussed, and decided upon.

At first, your group might struggle with this process. Anytime we try something new (like a new sport for instance), it takes practice to excel at it. The same is true for this small group meeting. Have fun experimenting with this group process. Focus on the process itself and observe yourself and other group members.

Detailed Small Group Meeting Agenda

This section discusses what happens in each portion of a small group meeting. The small group leader is responsible for conducting the meeting and ensuring that each portion is accomplished.

1. *Administrative Business:* Read the group purpose: The purpose of these groups is to help us become effective citizens, able to guide and/or monitor the governmental activity in our school, town, state, and country. Take attendance. Name those group members who had homework and what they will be discussing later in the meeting (this will help those people get prepared). Schedule the next meeting. Pick the next group leader.

2. *Citizenship Skills Discussion:* Spend a moment in silence. Ask group members to close their eyes and visualize themselves practicing the citizenship skills during this group's session. Talk about homework (usually an individual assignment working on a specific citizenship skill, like patience, at home, work, and school). Bring up next skill and open it up to brief discussion. Distribute and explain citizenship skill homework (which your instructor will give you). Discuss any issues that were vetoed in the previous meeting to see if there are simple solutions to the problems or if they should be discussed again under old issues. Focus your group's discussion on the use of citizenship skills and not on the various slants to the issue itself (this discussion occurs under Old Issues following).

3. *Old Issues:* Ask for reports on assignments. For example: Maria says, "I spoke with Mr. Dean, and he's open to having an assembly on citizenship skills if we give him an outline of what we would cover." Be sure that an issue is fully discussed but not overly so. Ensure everyone's participation and do not let one person dominate the discussion. Ask the group if there is enough information to act on this issue. If there is, call for a vote to decide on a course of action. If there is not enough information, ask group members for ideas on research assignments. For example, "Mike, can you and Maria brainstorm a rough outline for a citizenship skills assembly and present it to us at the next meeting?" Finally, if any issues cannot be resolved at this time (as will be the case with sensitive and highly emotional issues), delay the issue until the next meeting (when it will be first on the agenda under old issues). An issue can only be discussed in a total of four meetings (includ-

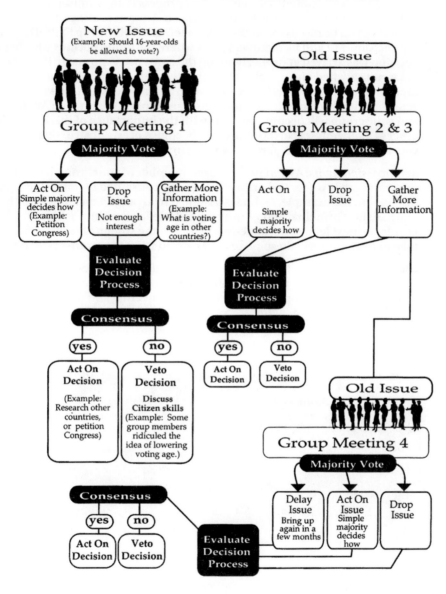

Figure 1.3.2: The Small Group Meeting flow chart.

Courtesy of US Army JROTC.

ing the first meeting it was mentioned) unless agreed to otherwise by your group. At this point, discuss any issue decisions that were vetoed to see if there are new grounds for agreement. Your group can also vote to drop an issue by a simple majority or to "table" it for later discussion, also by a simple majority.

4. *New Issues:* Ask the group members to bring up any new issues. Discuss each new issue briefly so you can decide to research it further, act on it, or drop it. Use a majority vote to decide what to do with this issue. If an issue cannot be decided on, it will be discussed under Old Issues at the next meeting. Occasionally, you will have issues with relatively simple resolutions. You can choose at this meeting to use a majority vote to handle these issues if there is not significant opposition within your group.

5. *Evaluation:* Spend a few minutes evaluating yourself and the group as a whole. The purpose of this evaluation session is for everyone to think about how well they participated in the group and how well they exhibited the citizenship skills. Except for the veto (which is stated), this evaluation process is anonymous. Use the group and individual evaluation forms for this purpose. Any poor ratings on the group's performance will be discussed at the next meeting's Citizenship Skills Discussion, but the decision will still be in force. This is where the group decides whether or not a decision was arrived at properly, using the consensus approach. If even one member is not satisfied and openly vetoes the decision, the problem becomes the first topic under the next meeting's Citizenship Skills Discussion. The decision remains vetoed until this discussion is completed and a new vote is taken. With time, you and your group will become familiar with the importance of this evaluation process. Remember also if this process becomes overly obstructive your group can vote to change it by a 75 percent or more majority.

6. *Action Assignments:* Assign tasks to each member of your group based on decisions the group made under Old or New Issues and consented to under the Evaluation discussion. For example, Joshua is assigned to arrange a meeting with the principal and assistant principal and go over the outline for the citizenship skill assembly. Jane is the next leader. Bernadette will attend the student government meeting and take notes. Tanya will do some research on an issue the group decided to continue.

7. *Closeout Details:* Take time to tie up any unfinished business—do group members have anything further to say? Remind people of their assignments for the coming week. Remind all group members of the next meeting and the name of the new group leader. Adjourn on time.

Quick Overview of the Small Group Meeting Agenda

1. Administrative Business

2. Citizenship Skills Discussion

3. Old Issues

4. New Issues

5. Evaluation

6. Action Assignments

7. Close-out Details

Conclusion

As with any process, there are rules and guidelines for holding and attending small group meetings. These rules and guidelines keep the meeting on track and enable those attending to know what's coming up in the current meeting as well as what's expected of them in the next meeting. Small group meetings are headed by a group leader, and that leader will change to another member of the group each time a meeting is held. All seven Citizenship Skills should be practiced at each small group meeting.

In the next lesson, you will learn about representative group sessions. A representative group session occurs when all the small groups merge into a larger assembly or class to discuss an all-class or all-school position on a specific issue.

Lesson Review

1. How is the small group meeting leader chosen, and what are the roles of the leader?

2. Choose one of the seven Citizenship Skills and explain how it pertains to small group meetings.

3. What are the three group skills that should be practiced at each meeting?

4. Explain what is meant by an action assignment.

Lesson 4

Representative Group Session

Key Terms

representative group session
representative group session agenda
small group representative

What You Will Learn to Do

- Participate in a Representative Group Session

Linked Core Abilities

- Do your share as a good citizen in your school, community, country, and the world

Skills and Knowledge You Will Gain Along the Way

- Identify the responsibilities of a small group representative
- Explain the impact of the representative group session agenda
- Describe the representative group session process
- Define key words contained in this lesson

Introduction

This lesson introduces you to representative group sessions, one of two types of Citizen Action Groups. A **representative group session** occurs when all the small groups merge into a larger assembly or class to discuss an all-class or all-school position on a specific issue. Representatives are elected from each small group. These representatives then hold a meeting, which is observed by all the small groups.

The purpose of the representative group session is twofold. In the beginning, these representative sessions are simply training sessions in which you will be addressing hypothetical issues, such as gun control or the United States' policy with China. These first few training sessions will help you become familiar with the representative process in general.

After you are familiar with the representative process, the second purpose of the representative group session is to address issues that need far-reaching action and cooperation from your class or school as a whole. Your **small group representatives** will be discussing and deciding on issues (such as a school-wide parking problem) and then coming up with action steps to resolve these issues.

This process can be expanded to the next level—to your school district—where small group representatives from other schools using the Student Citizenship Training Program, gather together in larger representative sessions (see Figure 1.4.1). Thus, the representative group session mirrors the current representative process of our local, state, and federal governments.

Before a representative session can be held, however, your small group needs to elect a representative. The procedure to elect a representative from your small group differs somewhat from the way you have elected class representatives for your school government.

Key Note Term

representative group session—one of two types of Citizen Action Groups in which small groups elect representatives to discuss and decide on issues in front of a class or other gathering

Key Note Term

small group representatives—a member of a small group who is elected to represent the group at the Representative Group Session

Selecting a Representative

Learning how to select an effective representative will not only help your small group, but also will help you select better representatives for your student government. When you are eligible to vote, this exercise will help you support the best person for political office.

Figure 1.4.1: Representatives from smaller groups gather to form larger representative group sessions.

Courtesy of Image Source/ Corbis Images.

To understand how to select the best representative, you can revisit the time when our government was being formed and look at the selection of George Washington as the Chairman of the Constitutional Convention.

He was the most obvious choice for Chairman, but not because of his knowledge of government. Almost all the Founders were better educated and knew more about the workings of a government than George Washington. However, Washington had a complementary set of skills that perfectly suited him as the chosen representative for the people in this new government.

Foremost, Washington had demonstrated his strength and leadership in the American Revolutionary War. Moreover, he had proven himself trustworthy over time. He

Figure 1.4.2: Because of his skills, Washington was the best choice for representative.

Courtesy of the Museum of the City of New York/ Corbis Images.

was open-minded, able to look at both sides of an issue, and make wise decisions. His cooperation skills were well developed and he always treated others with the utmost fairness and respect.

In essence, George Washington (see Figure 1.4.2) was the best at the citizenship skills you have learned so far. That is why he was the best choice as a representative.

When you choose your own representative, whether it is for this representative group session, your student government, city mayor, council member, or even the President of the United States, you begin by analyzing this person's grasp and practice of seven citizenship skills: cooperation, patience, fairness, respect, strength, self-improvement, and balance. You also look for a person who is trustworthy, intelligent, wise, and one who acts calmly under pressure; in other words, a person similar to George Washington.

Knowledge of the issues is a good trait for a representative to have, but it is not as important as these other skills. Any interested person can always learn about the issues. What helps is a person competent in the seven citizenship skills.

Recognize also that your small group's ability to pick a representative will be measured by the quality of the representative you pick. The other small groups will assume you have picked a worthy representative when she/he goes to the front of the class. Your other classmates will take what that person says as being representative of your small group's feelings and decisions, so choose wisely.

How to Select a Representative

There are three ways that you can select a representative for your small group. These steps include the following.

- **Ask cadets to volunteer if they are interested in becoming a small group representative. If no one volunteers, ask your instructor to select someone.**

- **Rate each potential candidate (hopefully you have more than one choice) on the representative rating sheet. Interviewing your prospective choices is a good way to gain more knowledge about them. Watching a debate between your choices (in a student or political election if these are held) also will give you information on a person's citizenship skills.**

- Hold an election for those in your small group who are interested in being a representative. Each group member votes for only one representative (usually the one who rated the best on the representative rating sheet). Write that person's name on a piece of paper and pass it to the group leader. The leader adds up the votes and the person with the most votes is your small group's representative. Your small group can choose to keep this representative for any period (a month, two months, semester, or year) or to elect a new representative at each representative group session.

Representative Group Session Agenda

If you are not an elected as the small group representative, you will merely observe this representative group session and then discuss it with your small group afterwards. Your instructor will give all the small groups the same issue to discuss. During the representative group session, your small group representatives will attempt to reach a class decision on the issue through a majority vote.

Detailed Representative Group Session Agenda

Similar to the small group meeting agenda, a **representative group session agenda** is necessary to keep the session on track. This agenda includes the following:

> **Key Note Term**
>
> **representative group session agenda**—a list of tasks or a schedule to be followed during a Representative Group Session

1. *Small Group Meeting:* Meet as a small group. Discuss the issue given to you by your instructor or decided upon by your class. Take a majority vote on what your group agrees is the best course of action for this issue. Elect your representative, if you have not already done so. Brief your representative on the thoughts and feelings of your small group.

2. *Representative Issue Discussion:* Small group representatives meet together in the presence of small groups and discuss the issue. Make sure each small group representative has had an opportunity to speak. Use a majority vote between the representatives to decide what to do with the issue. Call for a vote from the representatives to decide on a course of action (research it further, act on it, or drop it). If there is not enough information, decide what research is needed. If any issues cannot be resolved this time (as may be the case with sensitive and highly emotional issues), delay the issue until the next representative group session or ask your instructor for guidance. The issue also can be returned to the small groups for further research and/or discussion.

3. *Large Discussion (Class-wide, School-wide, or Larger):* With your instructor, discuss the results of the representative session with all the small groups (in the first few training sessions only). Did your small group representative present your group's ideas effectively and correctly? How was the conduct and quality of the representatives themselves? How well did the representative group session function? Were the seven citizenship skills used in the representatives' meeting?

4. *Action Steps:* Representatives then decide on the action steps needed to put their decision into effect. They will assign tasks to other students. These tasks might be as simple as writing a letter to the appropriate person(s) (congressmen/women, school board) or arranging a meeting between your principal and a few of your small group representatives. If you do not have enough data to make a decision on your topic, your action step might be to find out more information on this issue.

5. *Small Group Evaluation:* During the first few training representative group sessions, you will break into your small groups and fill out a group evaluation form to evaluate the representative process. Did your group's representative follow the citizenship skills while participating in the representative group session? Did your

small group do a good job of selecting a representative? How well did the representative process work? Any problems that come up during this evaluation step will be used for discussion at your next small group meeting.

6. *Homework Assignments:* If desired by your instructor, cadets (including small group representatives) are assigned various tasks determined by the representatives.

Quick Overview of the Representative Group Session Agenda

1. Small Group Meeting

2. Representative Issue Discussion

3. Large Discussion

4. Action Steps

5. Small Group Evaluation

6. Homework Assignments

Small Group Representative Responsibilities

Your duties and responsibilities as a small group representative include the following:

1. **Communicate accurately and effectively to the rest of the representatives your small group's majority feelings and opinions, not necessarily your own opinions and feelings.**

2. **Address other small group representatives as "the honorable representative from Group _____ (group's name or number)" rather than by name when he or she is participating in the representative group session.**

3. **Participate fully in the representative session by speaking when addressed and by ensuring the other representatives have heard your small group's ideas.**

4. **Be conscious of the seven citizenship skills and use them throughout the representative group session.**

5. **Work cooperatively with other representatives to reach a majority decision by the end of the representative session. (This decision does not necessarily have to be an action step.)**

6. **Contribute ideas and research needs to the other representatives. Help assign research or action steps to small group members.**

Evaluation

After your small group or representative group session has concluded a meeting, each member of your small group will be given time to evaluate the group's participation, especially the way the group arrived at certain decisions.

The primary purpose of this evaluation procedure is to evaluate your group's grasp of the citizenship and group skills and the Citizen Action Group Process itself. This evaluation process may be the most important learning you will take with you from this course. That is why this phase is so critical.

Take time to fill out the evaluation forms during each small group meeting or the first few training representative group sessions. After you have filled them out, your small group will discuss the results. If you do not reach a consensus that each decision was arrived at properly using the seven citizenship skills (that is, one person stands up and vetoes the decision), then that decision is vetoed and no action is taken. This problem is then discussed under the Citizenship Skills Discussion of your next small group meeting.

If, however, your small group agrees the decision was arrived at properly, you are free to go ahead and act on that decision.

After you understand the evaluation procedure, begin your first small group meeting or your first representative group session. After you have worked through two or three issues in a representative group session and understand how the representative process works, you will understand how our government currently works and how you can be more effective in getting your ideas and issues heard by your representatives (for example, by working in Citizen Action Groups and having your representative present issues to your school, city, state, or federal government representatives).

This is the process upon which our government was founded, and it is the way we make our government continue to work and improve. The process itself is as important as reaching decisions. Enjoy the learning in this Citizen Action Group Process. Take time to honestly evaluate yourself and your group and then look for areas where your representative can improve.

Conclusion

A representative group session takes place when many small groups combine into a larger group to share information about a specific issue. Representatives are elected from each small group, and these representatives then hold a meeting that is observed by all of the small groups. The representative reports back to the small group and discusses what was decided at the representative group session, and what action steps need to be taken.

Next, you will explore the United States Chief Justice game. Through this activity, you will gain an appreciation of the United States Constitution and of our democratic form of government.

Lesson Review

1. **What are the ways you can select a representative from your small group? What do you think is important when choosing a representative?**

2. **What is the main purpose of a representative group session?**

3. **What are the responsibilities of a small group representative?**

4. **Discuss why the evaluation step after a meeting is so important. What types of things would you evaluate?**

Chapter 1

Introduction to Chief Justice®

Key Terms

Chief Justice
cross examine
deliberations
forum
judge
jury
jury foreman
law firm
opening statements
trials
verdict

What You Will Learn to Do

• Explore the Chief Justice® process for debating constitutional and contemporary issue

Linked Core Abilities

• Do your share as a good citizen in your school, community, country, and the world

• Apply critical thinking techniques

Skills and Knowledge You Will Gain Along the Way

• Examine the purpose of the Chief Justice® game

• Explore the rules of the Chief Justice® game

• Identify how to render a verdict in a case

• Define key words contained in this lesson

Introduction

Chief Justice® is an educational game designed to give the cadets an appreciation of the United States Constitution and of our democratic form of government. The complete game contains 100 critical thinking questions that incorporate today's most important moral and ethical issues. The following five questions have been selected to be used by the U.S. Army Junior ROTC program for their curriculum.

- **Should the Ten Commandments be posted in classrooms in all public elementary and secondary schools?**
- **Should public school students be allowed to voluntarily participate in prayer before school sponsored sporting events?**
- **Should the news media be allowed to disclose the name of a felony suspect before a trial?**
- **Should post-conviction DNA testing be a right granted upon request to all inmates in state and federal prison?**
- **Should rap groups be allowed to include lyrics in their music, which advocate physical violence against law enforcement officers?**

> **NOTE**
>
> The game "Chief Justice®" was developed by Robert Aucone, Publishers Services, P.O. Box 2510, Novato, CA 94948; phone 415-883-3530; email chiefjustice2@yahoo.com. COPYRIGHT (1998 BY ROBERT AUCONE ALL RIGHTS RESERVED)

Chief Justice®

Chief Justice® is a game designed to engage the participants in a variety of debates on constitutional and contemporary issues. The purpose of the game is to:

- **Design a forum within which people, who hold opinions about various constitutional and contemporary issues, can come together and discuss those issues in an organized and effective manner**
- **Encourage each participant to give careful thought and consideration to his or her own views affecting our society and to express those thoughts in a meaningful and contemplative way**
- **Create a game in which each participant is motivated to learn and appreciate the United States Constitution**
- **Discover new ways of looking at constitutional issues and learn from other participants who may be able to share new insights on these issues**
- **Introduce a game that requires each player to use critical thinking skills**
- **Entertain the participants while at the same time create an environment for learning**

> **Key Note Term**
>
> forum—a place or opportunity for open discussion and participation

- Create a purpose for the players to extensively research their topics by using various search engines on the Internet

- Provide a forum in which players can develop their public speaking skills in a debate format

- Provide a forum that teaches ethics and values by using the United States Constitution as a moral compass

- Provide an opportunity for cooperative learning to take place

Game Contents

Nearly all games have various pieces for the players to use. Chief Justice® is no exception. This game contains:

- A game poster depicting the U.S. Supreme Court with six steps leading up to the court house. Each step is labeled and represents a career path for an aspiring law student from law school to the top step of Supreme Court and ultimately Chief Justice of the United States.

- A list of one hundred game questions for one hundred courtroom trials to be held in a classroom setting focusing on various constitutional and contemporary issues. (Five questions are available to Army JROTC at this time.)

- A supply of colored marker pins to identify where various teams are on the game poster during the course of the game. (Not available to Army JROTC at this time.)

- A copy of the U.S. Constitution.

- Game instructions and a suggested lesson plan for playing Chief Justice® in your class.

- A rubric to inform cadets as to the method of grading to be used and a guideline for the teacher to determine how to measure the cadets' performance and to issue an appropriate grade.

Rules of the Game

Game rules are important. Without rules, it would be hard to determine if players are playing fairly and if the winner actually won. The following sections detail the rules of the Chief Justice® game.

Setting

This game is most appropriate in a classroom setting (see Figure 1.5.1) but could be played in any forum where people choose to gather on an ongoing basis and debate constitutional and contemporary issues.

Number of Players

It is necessary that the participants be divided into small groups which are considered "law firms" with two players in each law firm. If you have an odd number of people

playing, it is allowable to have a law firm with three players participating. An unlimited number of people can participate in this game as jurors. The number of players participating as attorneys will depend on the size of the class and time constraints.

The Jury

A **jury** can be composed of any number of people who are not the attorneys in the present case. In a classroom situation, the remaining cadets not involved in the case are the jury (see Figure 1.5.2). These people listen to the opening statements presented by the attorneys, the cross examination and the closing arguments, and then privately deliberate the case and deliver a verdict.

Selection of a Judge

A **judge** is selected at the beginning of the game to keep order and have the players follow the rules of the game. In a classroom setting, this job normally would fall to the teacher.

Key Note Term

jury—a select group of individuals chosen to listen and render a verdict in a court case

Key Note Term

judge—a high-ranking court officer who supervises and gives a decision on an action or court case

Duties of the Judge

As in a real courtroom, the judge has specific duties. In the Chief Justice® game, the duties of the judge include the following.

> **Key Note Term**
>
> law firm—a group of lawyers

1. The first duty of the judge is to determine the players in each **law firm**. This can be done in a number of different ways, however it is recommended in a classroom setting that the cadets be allowed to choose their partners. Each law firm should include two attorneys; if there are an odd number of cadets in the class, some law firms may be made up of three attorneys.

2. Next, each cadet should read carefully the rules to the game and the rubric which will serve as a guideline for the grading process. The **trials** are expected to be held on a periodic basis over the course of a semester or perhaps the school year, with trial dates scheduled on a weekly basis or as time allows. A consistent pattern of scheduled trials works best, for example, every Tuesday could be used for the purpose of the courtroom trials. (Army JROTC will have five trials.)

> **Key Note Term**
>
> trials—examinations of facts and law in a court of law

3. The law firms are then directed to select a case from the first 20 questions listed from the Chief Justice® booklets. After the first series of trials have been concluded, the next set of questions from question 21 through 40 would be used for the second set of trials and so forth until the 100 questions have been explored and each law firm has had five chances to win a case and move up to the top step of Supreme Court on the game poster. (Army JROTC will have five trials.)

4. At the start of each series of trials it is necessary to determine which cases are to be heard. The judge will call two law firms to come forward with their one selection and on the flip of a coin will determine which of the two cases chosen by each law firm will be heard. The team winning the coin toss not only gets to have their case heard, but also gets to choose the side of the argument they wish to defend. The law firm that loses the toss will have to take the opposing view of that case and argue that side as effectively as possible. Good attorneys can argue either side of any case brought before them as will happen in the practice of law. This process will continue until all law firms have come forward and all the cases to be tried have been determined.

5. In a classroom situation, it is important to allow sufficient time for the law firms to research their cases and schedule court dates for sometime in the future. A minimum of two weeks might be necessary before the first case is heard. Following cases would be scheduled on an ongoing basis over the course of the following weeks as time permits. Cadets should be encouraged to use the Internet as an excellent source to gain material for their arguments.

6. During the day of the trial, the judge will call the attorneys to the front of the room where a sufficient number of chairs have been placed to seat them. It is recommended that a podium be placed between the two law firms if one is available and other props such as a gavel or a judge's robe (black choir robe) might be used to add authenticity to the setting.

7. The judge will then call for the opening statements from each side starting with an attorney representing the proponent's side of the question to be considered. For example: If the issue to be debated is "Should minors under the age of 18 who commit first degree murder be given the death penalty?", the side arguing that they should be given the death penalty would go first.

8. The attorneys are allowed to use their three-page written reports as reference, but they should engage the jury with direct eye contact and not read the report word for word. They should be prepared to speak on the issue and only occasionally use the prepared text for assistance.

9. Only one attorney from each side is allowed to give **opening statements** and should be limited to five minutes for this phase of the trial.

10. After the opening statements, the attorneys are allowed to **cross examine** each other. The law firm taking the opposing side of the issue would go first. In the example above that would be the side arguing against the death penalty for minors. Each side would be allowed up to five minutes each to cross examine the opposing law firm and to try to expose weaknesses in their arguments.

11. Closing arguments are then given by the attorney who did not give the opening statements. Five minutes are allowed for each side and the law firm opposing the question would begin. In this case, the side against the death penalty would give their closing arguments first and the proponents would present last.

12. At the end of the closing arguments, the judge (teacher) would collect the three page research material used by the attorneys and ask the attorneys to wait just outside the classroom with the door closed. The teacher will later administer a grade for their work based on the rubric provided.

Jury Deliberation

When the attorneys have given their closing arguments, it's time for the jury to begin their work. The steps for jury deliberation are:

1. The jurors (the remaining cadets in the class) then pick a **jury foreman**. This should not take much time and it is acceptable to have someone volunteer or have the judge, who is still sitting in the room, select someone to expedite this process. The foreman will take an initial vote on the case by reading the question to the jury and recording the number of jurors who raise their hands and are for the death penalty for minors and those that are against it.

2. The jurors are then asked by the foreman to comment on their positions on the case and try to influence the other jurors to vote with their side. The foreman is expected to keep order during this phase and to allow all jurors an opportunity to share their views on the case in an appropriate way. It is important to have selected a responsible cadet who can carry out these duties.

3. The foreman must conclude the **deliberations** and reach a final **verdict** by simple majority vote with at least five minutes remaining in the class. The verdict is kept secret and the attorneys are now asked to reenter the courtroom and take their seats at the front of the room.

4. The judge will then bang the gavel and call the courtroom to order. The foreman will stand and will be asked by the judge if the jury has reached a verdict. After answering in the affirmative, the foreman will then be asked to announce the verdict. The foreman will then announce the verdict.

5. The judge will then move the winning team's colored marking pin up one step on the Chief Justice® poster which has been hung on the bulletin board somewhere in the classroom. The judge will declare, "The court is now adjourned." (Poster is not available to Army JROTC at this time.)

The highest honor at the end of the game is to become **Chief Justice.** The game will come to an end when one law firm has reached the level of Supreme Court. The cadets are then asked to confirm a Chief Justice by secret ballot. Only one of the attorneys who has reached the level of Supreme Court will become Chief Justice. The Chief Justice should be chosen on the basis of his or her depth of knowledge of constitutional law, the amount of research of the various case laws used during the trials, and the degree of articulate persuasion of those moral and ethical principles the attorney has shared during the course of the game.

The final duty of the judge is to announce the name of the Chief Justice to the class and allow that cadet to move the colored marking pin representing his or her winning law firm to the star on the Chief Justice® poster. Applause is very appropriate at this time.

Time Frame to Conclude the Game

This game is designed to be played in a variety of time frames that suit a course curriculum or the schedule of any club or organization that wishes to provide a forum to debate current moral and legal issues. The time allocated for the Army JROTC program is five hours, one hour for each trial to be heard on a weekly basis.

Conclusion

It is believed by the author of this game that most of the time the collective wisdom of the majority of the people will determine the "right answer" given enough research, serious contemplation and open debate on any ethical or moral issue before them. Democracy works because "We the People" have inherent within us the collective wisdom and ability to govern ourselves. In this game cadets not only research what existing laws are relative to the questions before them, but also are asked to decide for themselves what the laws should be.

Chief Justice® is designed on the positive assumption that enlightened citizens are very capable of deciding what the laws should be. It is then the duty of all enlightened citizens to become actively engaged in the democratic process to ensure that our freedom is preserved.

The cadets are strongly encouraged to read the U.S. Constitution and interpret this historic document as a guide to finding the answers to as many questions as possible in this game.

This lesson concludes the You The People—Citizenship Skills chapter. The following chapters introduce you to the American political system, the Constitution, and the roles of citizens of the United States.

Lesson Review

1. What do Chief Justice® players learn about the U.S. Constitution? What is the purpose of the game?

2. What are five duties of the judge?

3. Explain the steps for jury deliberations.

4. How does a player get to be Chief Justice?

Chapter 2

Foundations of the American Political System

Lesson 1

Our Natural Rights

Key Terms

canton
civil rights
consent
constitutional government
democracy
equal protection
higher (fundamental) law
human nature
law of nature
legitimate

limited government
natural rights
political rights
private domain
republic
right of revolution
social contract
state of nature
unalienable (inalienable)
unlimited government

What You Will Learn to Do

- Examine the role government plays in protecting our natural rights

Linked Core Objectives

- Take responsibility for your actions and choices
- Apply critical thinking techniques

Skills and Knowledge You Will Gain Along the Way

- Explain the purpose of government based on the natural rights
- Explain the characteristics of a constitution and constitutional government
- Explain how the Founders' fear of abuse of power by government may have motivated them to establish a constitutional government
- Define key words contained in this lesson

Chapter 2

Key Note Terms

state of nature—the basis of natural right philosophy, state of nature is the hypothetical condition of people living together in a society

law of nature—in natural rights philosophy, the law of nature would prevail in the absence of man-made law, and contains universally obligatory standards of justice

natural rights—the doctrine of natural rights assumes that human beings had rights in a "state of nature" and create government in order to protect those rights

consent—agreement or acquiescence

social contract—the agreement among all the people in a society to give up part of their freedom to a government in return for the protection of their natural rights by that government

unlimited government—a government in which those who govern are free to use their power as they choose, unrestrained by laws or elections

limited government—in natural rights philosophy, a system restricted to protecting natural rights and that does not interfere with other aspects of life

constitutional government—a government in which the powers of government are limited in practice by a written or unwritten constitution which they must obey

Introduction

Natural rights philosophers such as John Locke explored ideas about the laws of nature and natural rights of all people. This lesson explores how the Founders' ideas of government supported Locke's philosophy of natural rights. Through discussion, reflection activities, and group work, you will identify how our government was developed to protect our natural rights.

This lesson introduces you to some basic ideas of the natural rights philosophy and theories of government that were of great importance in the development of our government. These major ideas include the **state of nature,** the **law of nature, natural rights, consent,** and the **social contract.** You learn about these ideas as they were developed by the English philosopher John Locke (1632–1704).

This lesson also introduces you to some basic ideas the Framers used in creating the kind of government they thought would best protect the natural rights of each individual and promote the good of all. When you finish this lesson you should understand the difference between and **unlimited** and **limited government,** the difference between written and unwritten constitutions, and how Americans have used the term **constitutional government.** You should be able to explain why a government with a constitution is not necessarily a constitutional government, and be able to identify alternative models of government that the Founders had to choose from.

When you finish this lesson, you should be able to describe how and why the natural rights philosophers used an imaginary state of nature to think about the basic problems of government. You should be able to explain some of the basic ideas of the natural rights philosophy.

Finally, you should be able to explain that the purpose of government based on the natural rights philosophy is to preserve our natural rights to life, liberty, and property.

Understanding the Natural Rights Philosophy

*We hold these Truths to be self-evident, that all Men are created equal, that they are endowed by their Creator with certain **unalienable** Rights, that among these are Life, Liberty, and the Pursuit of Happiness—That to secure these Rights; Governments are instituted among Men, deriving their just Powers from the Consent of the Governed, that whenever any Form of Government becomes destructive of these Ends, it is the Right of the People to alter or to abolish it, and to institute new Government.*

This excerpt from the Declaration of Independence includes some of the most important philosophical ideas underlying our form of government. They are ideas that had been familiar to almost everyone in the American colonies long before the Revolutionary War.

These ideas had been preached in churches, written in pamphlets, and debated in public and private. They had been developed and refined by political philosophers such as the Englishman John Locke, pictured in Figure 2.1.1, and others. Locke was the most important influence on the thinking of the Founders at the time of the Revolution. Locke's political philosophy is often called the natural rights philosophy.

The natural rights philosophy is based on imagining what life would be like if there were no government. Locke and others called this imaginary situation a state of nature. By this, Locke did not necessarily mean people living in a wilderness. A state of nature is a condition in which there is no government. For example, even with the existence of the United Nations, international relations between countries today operate in a state of nature. There is no superior power that can act effectively as a government over these individual states.

Thinking about what life would be like if there were no government was very useful to philosophers such as Locke in answering questions like these:

Figure 2.1.1: John Locke, 1632–1704.

Courtesy of Bettmann/Corbis.

- **What is human nature?**
  That is, what traits of personality and character, if any, do all human beings have in common? For example, are all people selfish or do they tend to care for the good of others?

- **What should be the purpose of government?**

- **How do the people running a government get the right to govern?**

- **How should a government be organized?**

- **What kinds of government should be respected and supported?**

- **What kinds of government should be resisted and fought?**

The natural rights philosophers' answers to these questions provided the foundation for many arguments the Founders made to explain and justify their decision to separate from Britain. They also used these ideas in writing state constitutions after the Revolutionary War and later in writing the Constitution of the United States and the Bill of Rights.

Taking the Position of A political Philosopher

To understand the natural rights philosophy, you should try to answer the questions it addresses. Some important questions are included in the following exercise.

Imagine that all the students in your school were transported to a place with enough natural resources for you to live well, but where no one had lived before. When you arrive, you have no means of communicating with people in other parts of the world. With this imaginary situation in mind, answer the following questions. Discuss your answers, and then compare your answers with those of John Locke, in the next section.

1. Upon arrival would there be any government or laws to control how you lived, what rights or freedoms you exercised, or what property you had? Why?

2. Would anyone have the right to govern you? Would you have the right to govern anyone else? Why?

3. Would you have any rights? What would they be?

4. What might people who were stronger or smarter than others try to do? Why?

5. What might the weaker or less sophisticated people try to do? Why?

6. What might life be like for everyone?

How do your answers compare with those of John Locke? Your answers may be similar to those developed by John Locke or they may differ. In this lesson you are focusing on understanding Locke's answers because they were widely shared by Americans living during the 1700s. They also played a very important role in the development of our government.

1. Locke believed that there were rules in a state of nature. He called these rules natural law or the law of nature. He said, "The state of nature has a law of nature to govern it which obliges every one. . . . No one ought to harm another in his life, health, liberty, or possessions. . . ." They were "the Laws of Nature and of Nature's God," as Thomas Jefferson called them in the Declaration of Independence. Jefferson believed they were laws made by a Supreme Being for the benefit of human beings.

Locke believed that most people understood this law of nature through the use of their reason and followed it because their consciences obliged them to do so. Not all humans were

According to Locke, how is personal property protected in a state of nature?

reasonable or good, however. There might even be disagreement about what the "laws of nature" were. If there were no government, there would be no one with the right to interpret or enforce these laws.

According to Locke, there would be no government because a government cannot exist until it has been created. A **legitimate** government cannot exist until the people have given their consent to be ruled by it. Thomas Jefferson included this idea in the Declaration when he wrote that "Governments are instituted among men, deriving their just powers from the consent of the governed. . . ."

2. No one would have the right to govern you, nor would you have the right to govern anyone else. According to Locke, the only way anyone gets the right to govern anyone else is if that person gives his or her consent. If the people to be governed have not consented to the creation of a government, there is no legitimate government.

3. Using his reason to determine what rights were provided for by the law of nature, Locke asked himself: "What are the things that all people always need and seek, no matter what they believe, no matter when or where they live?" His answer identified the following rights:

- Life. People want to survive and they want their lives to be as free as possible from threats to their security.

- Liberty. People want to be as free as possible from the domination of others, to be able to make their own decisions, and to live as they please.

- Property. People want the freedom to work and gain economic goods such as land, houses, tools, and money, which are necessary to survival.

These rights were called natural rights and you would have the right to defend them if other people threatened to take them away.

4. Locke believed that people are basically reasonable and sociable, but they are also self-interested. Since the only security people would have for the protection of their natural rights would be their own strength or cunning, people who were stronger or smarter would often try to take away the life, liberty, and property of the weak.

5. Weaker or less sophisticated people might try to protect themselves by joining together against the strong.

Key Note Term

legitimate—being in compliance with the law

Why did Locke believe it was necessary for people to create governments?

6. Since there would be no laws that everybody agreed upon, and no government to enforce them, everybody's rights would be very insecure.

What Do You Think?

1. Give examples of problems that might arise when one individual's rights to life, liberty, and property conflict with those of other individuals. What considerations might be used to resolve these conflicts?

2. Should some rights be given more protection than other rights? Why? Give examples.

3. The natural rights philosophy claims that government is based on consent. How do we give our consent and how do we withdraw it?

4. Many people today believe that the rights to life, liberty, and property include the right to public education and health care. Would the founders have agreed? Do you agree? Why?

Understanding the Significance of Locke's Definition of the Natural Rights to Life, Liberty, and Property

References to "human rights," "political and economic rights," "student rights," "consumer rights," "parental rights," and other terms using the word appear in the news every day. "Rights" is a word you are already familiar with. We have become so accustomed to the word, we don't often think about what it means.

A right may be described as a claim to have or obtain something, or to act in a way that is justified on legal or moral grounds. For example, you might claim the right to practice your own religion and justify it by appealing to the First Amendment of the Constitution. This is not, of course, the only justification you could give.

In describing the concept of natural rights, philosophers like John Locke were making a bold, new departure from previous uses of the term rights. Before the time of Locke and the other natural rights philosophers, the concept of rights had been applied in a very limited and selective way.

More often than not, rights were considered special privileges, enjoyed only by certain groups, classes, or nations of people. They were exclusive rights, not enjoyed by those outside the group. The natural rights philosophers disagreed with this interpretation. They believed that people's opportunities should not be limited by the situation or group into which they were born. These philosophers regarded the individual, rather than the class or group, as the most important social unit. They saw society as a collection of individuals, all of whom shared the same right to pursue his or her own welfare.

Locke, for example, defined natural rights in terms of life, liberty, and property because he considered them to be the essence of humanity. They are what make us human beings and what define our purpose in life. They are inclusive rights, belonging to every human being. These rights Locke also considered to be unalienable, the word that Jefferson used in the Declaration. This means they are so much a part of human nature that they cannot be taken away or given up. "The sacred rights of mankind," said another Founder, Alexander Hamilton, "are written, as with a sun beam in the whole volume of human nature, by the hand of the Divinity itself, and can never be erased or obscured by mortal power."

Governments and societies based on the natural rights philosophy guarantee specific rights to preserve our natural rights. Under the U.S. Constitution, for example, you possess **civil rights,** securing such things as freedom of conscience and privacy, and protecting you from unfair discrimination by government or others. You also possess certain **political rights,** like the right to vote or run for office (see Figure 2.1.2), which give you control over your government. Such civil and political rights serve to protect natural rights to life, liberty, and property.

Key Note Terms

civil rights— fundamental rights belonging to every member of a society

political rights—all of the implicit (constitutionally guaranteed) and implied (by natural laws) rights of a citizen in a free society

What Locke Meant by the "Social Contract"

Figure 2.1.2: One of your rights is the right to run for public office.

Courtesy of Szenes Jason/Corbis Sygma.

In an ideal state of nature, the law of nature would prevail. No one would have the right to interfere with your life and your freedom to acquire and hold property. Locke, however, realized that because not all human beings were rational or good, there would always be people who would try to violate your rights. Since there would not be any government, you and others would have to defend your rights on your own. The result would be that in the state of nature, your rights and their enjoyment would be insecure. You would be in constant danger of losing them.

For Locke and the other natural rights philosophers, the great problem was to find a way to protect each person's natural rights so that all persons could enjoy them and live at peace with one another. Locke said that the best way to solve this problem in the state of nature is for each individual to agree with others to create and live under a government and give it the power to make and enforce laws. This kind of agreement is called the social contract.

As in all contracts, to get something, you must give up something. In the social contract everyone promises to give up the absolute right to do anything he or she has the right to do in a state of nature. In return, everyone receives the security that can be provided by a government. Each person consents to obey the limits placed upon him or her by the laws created by the government.

Everyone gains the security of knowing that his or her rights to life, liberty, and property are protected. Government, then, is the better alternative to an imperfect state of nature where some people will not obey the laws of nature. Government's purpose is to protect those natural rights that the individual cannot effectively secure in a state of nature.

What Do You Think?

Give some thought to the following questions:

1. If the purpose of government is to provide security for the rights to life, liberty, and property, under what circumstances, if any, should government be able to limit these rights?

2. What criteria should be used to determine when, if ever, government should be able to limit an individual's liberty to

   - Believe as he or she wishes

   - Practice his or her beliefs

   - Use his or her property

   - Associate with whomever he or she wishes

3. Imagine yourself living in a community where all order and authority have broken down. Violent lawlessness is widespread. Do you think any government is better than none? Explain your answer.

4. It has been said that since people are not equal in their intelligence and character, it is unjust for everyone to have the same rights. Do you agree? Be prepared to defend your answer.

Examining Government Protection of the Basic Rights of the People

Key Note Term

equal protection—a requirement of the Fourteenth Amendment to the U.S. Constitution that states' laws may not arbitrarily discriminate against persons

Suppose you are not satisfied with living in a state of nature. You and others agree to enter into a social contract and a government to protect your natural rights. You must decide what kind of government you want and then establish it. Locke, Jefferson, and others knew that this is not an easy task. Throughout history governments have deprived people of their rights more often than they have protected them. Your problem is to design and establish the kind of government that will do what you want it to do, that is, protect your natural rights. This also means providing **equal protection** for the rights of everyone.

You and everyone else in your imaginary state of nature have agreed to live under a government. There are questions you must answer in deciding what kind of government to create.

1. **What in your opinion is the main purpose of government?**

2. **How should government get the authority or right to make laws telling people what they can and cannot do?**

3. **What should the people have the right to do if their government does not serve the purposes for which it was created? Why should they have this right?**

How do your answers compare with those of John Locke?

1. **Locke and other natural rights philosophers said that the purpose of government is to protect natural rights. Thomas Jefferson agreed and in the Declaration of Independence argued that the protection of rights is the main purpose of government.**

2. **Another of Locke's ideas that Jefferson stated in the Declaration of Independence is that government gets its right to govern from the consent of the people. Its powers are delegated to it by the governed. People give their consent in several ways. People can give explicit consent by:**

Under what circumstances would Locke agree that people have the right to take up arms against an established government?

- **Agreeing to the contract that establishes the society whose members then establish the government and choose its officers**

- **Joining a society that already is established People give implicit consent, also called tacit consent, by accepting the laws and services of the government and nation of their birth.**

3. **Locke believed that since the people give the power to the government, they have the right to take it away if the government is not serving the purposes for which it was established. They can then create a new government. Locke argued and the Founders agreed that if a government fails to protect the people's rights, the people have a right of revolution.**

Who is to judge if a government has failed? Locke and the Founders said that the people have the right to make that decision. This position is in the following words from the Declaration of Independence: "Whenever any Form of Government becomes destructive of these Ends, it is the Right of the People to alter or abolish it, and to institute new Government . . ." Revolution, however, is an extreme way in which to deal with bad government. Government should be designed or organized to limit its powers in order to protect individual rights and thus reduce the need for such extreme measures.

How Americans Express Consent to Their Government

The Americans, who ratified our Constitution in 1787, gave explicit consent to their new government. So did the many immigrants who came to America to seek a better life. Those who are born here have implied their consent by remaining in this country and living under its laws.

Every native-born American, as he or she grows up, has the choice of seeking the citizenship of another country. By remaining in this country, accepting its laws, and enjoying its benefits, you imply your consent to be governed by your federal, state, and local governments. You also affirm your consent every time you take the Pledge of Allegiance, participate in an election, or engage in other civic actions.

> ### Key Note Term
>
> **right of revolution—** "It is the foundation of consent of the governed and guarantees that you can take matters into your own hands if you must"

Understanding Constitutional Government

Limited governments have established and respected restraints on their powers, restraints such as laws and free and periodic elections. The opposite is unlimited government, in which those who govern are free to use their power as they choose, unrestrained by laws or elections. Tyranny, autocracy, dictatorship, and totalitarianism are other words to describe unlimited government.

What form of government was best suited to prevent the abuse of power in the newly independent states of America? From their reading of both history and the natural rights philosophers, the Founders believed that any government that served its proper ends would have to be a limited or constitutional government.

In a constitutional government, the powers of the person or group controlling the government are limited by a set of laws and customs called a constitution.

Defining a Constitution

A constitution is a set of customs, traditions, rules, and laws that sets forth the basic way a government is organized and operated. Most constitutions are in writing, some are partly written and partly unwritten, and some are not written at all.

Notice that according to this definition of the word, every nation has a constitution. Good governments and bad governments may have constitutions. Some of the worst governments have constitutions that include lists of the basic rights of their citizens. The former Soviet Union had one of the longest and most elaborate constitutions in history, but in reality its citizens enjoyed few of the rights guaranteed by it, as shown in Figure 2.1.3.

Figure 2.1.3: Despite the Soviet Union's constitution, many citizens still lived in oppression.

Courtesy of Peter Turnley/Corbis Images.

If you study the constitution of a government, you will be able to answer the following questions about the relationship between the government and its citizens:

- **What are the purposes of government?**
- **How is the government organized?**
- **How is the government supposed to go about doing its business?**
- **Who is considered to be a citizen?**
- **Are the citizens supposed to have any power or control over their government? If so, how is it to be exercised?**
- **What rights and responsibilities, if any, are the citizens supposed to have?**

It is very important to understand that having a constitution does not mean that a nation has a constitutional government. If a constitution provides for the unlimited exercise of political power by one, few, or even many—such a constitution would not be the basis of a constitutional government. If a constitution provides that the government's power is to be limited, but it does not include ways to enforce those limitations, it is not the basis of a constitutional government. In a constitutional government the constitution is a form of higher or fundamental law that must be obeyed by everyone, including those in power.

How the Founders Characterized Higher Law

According to the Founders, a constitution or **higher law** should have the following characteristics:

- **It sets forth the basic rights of citizens to life, liberty, and property.**
- **It establishes the responsibility of the government to protect those rights.**
- **It establishes limitations on how those in government may use their powers with regard to**
  - **Citizens' rights and responsibilities**
  - **The distribution of resources**
  - **The control of conflict**
- **It establishes the principle of a private domain.**
- **It can only be changed with the widespread consent of the citizens, and according to established and well-known procedures. This distinguishes the higher law from the ordinary law that governments regularly create and enforce.**

How does the principle of private domain protect you from government interference?

How Constitutional Governments Are Organized to Prevent the Abuse of Power

In constitutional governments powers are usually distributed and shared among several branches of government. This distribution and sharing of power makes it less likely that any one branch can abuse or misuse its powers. It is also less likely that any group will gain so much power that it can ignore the limitations placed on it by the constitution.

To prevent our government from abusing its powers, the Framers provided for distribution and sharing of powers among three branches of the national government. Each branch has primary responsibility for certain functions, but each branch also shares these functions and powers with the other branches. For example,

- **The Congress may pass laws, but the President may veto them**

- **The President nominates certain government officials, but the Senate must approve them**

- **The Congress may pass laws, but the Supreme Court may declare them unconstitutional**

It is this system of distributed and shared powers that provides the basis for checks and balances. Although each branch of the government has its own special powers, many of these powers are "checked" because they are shared with the other groups.

The complicated ways in which constitutional governments are organized often mean that it takes them a long time to get things done. It may seem strange, but this "inefficiency" was seen by the Framers as an advantage. They thought that these difficulties would help to prevent the abuse of power and make it more likely that when a decision was finally made, it would be a good one.

Does a system of checks
and balances guarantee
that power will not be
abused?

Examining Why the Founders Feared the Abuse of Power by Government

Given their knowledge of history and their experiences with the British government, it is not surprising that the Founders greatly feared the possible abuse of the powers of government. For example, read the following selections from some of their writings. Then discuss with the class your answers to the questions that follow.

Give all power to the many, they will oppress the few. Give all power to the few, they will oppress the many.

—*Alexander Hamilton, 1787*

There are two passions which have a powerful influence on the affairs of men. These are ambition and avarice; the love of power and the love of money.
—*Benjamin Franklin, 1787*

From the nature of man, we may be sure that those who have power in their hands . . . will always, when they can . . . increase it.
—*George Mason, 1787*

1. **Explain the view of human nature expressed in each of these quotations.**

2. **If you agreed with the views of human nature expressed in the quotations, what kind of safeguards to prevent the abuse of power would you include in your government?**

3. **Do you think the Founders' fear of government is as valid today as it was in the 1700s? Explain your answer.**

What Kinds of Governments May Be Constitutional Governments?

The Founders knew that constitutional government can take many forms. It is possible to have a constitutional government with one ruler, a group of rulers, or rule by the people as a whole, so long as those in power obey the limitations placed on them by the "higher law" of the constitution.

Historically, constitutional governments have included monarchies, republics, democracies, and various combinations of these forms of government. History has shown, however, that problems inevitably arise when a constitutional government is ruled by one person or a small group of people. If all power is given to a select few, it is difficult to ensure that they will obey the limitations placed on them by a constitution. The rulers in such nations would control the armed forces and law enforcement agencies. How could citizens force the rulers to obey their constitution?

Monarchy—rule by a king or queen—was by far the most common form of government in the eighteenth century. The Founders preferred a form of government more broadly representative of the interests of the whole nation.

What Alternative Models of Government Could the Founders Choose From?

The most obvious alternative to monarchy was a **republic,** a model of government with which the Founders were familiar through their knowledge of ancient history. The Founders admired the republics of ancient Greece and Rome. They also had studied more recent examples of republican governments, such as the Italian city-states of the Renaissance and the **cantons** of Switzerland.

How did the Founders' knowledge of ancient Rome shape their views about government?

Courtesy of Bettmann/Corbis Images.

Key Note Terms

republic—a form of government in which the supreme political power resides in electorate, and administration is exercised by representatives who are responsible to the people

cantons—a small territorial district; esp. one of the twenty-two independent states which form the Swiss federal republic

The Founders differed among themselves about exactly what a republican government was. In general it meant a form of government:

- **Devoted to promoting the public good, the respublicae, which is Latin for "thing of the people"**
- **In which political authority was shared by all or most of the citizens rather than held by a hereditary monarch**
- **Whose political authority was exercised through the community's chosen representatives in government**

Today we view republican and democratic government as almost the same thing. The United States, we believe, is both a republic and a **democracy.** The Founders, however, drew a sharp distinction between the two forms of government. Democracy had traditionally meant a form of government in which ultimate authority was based on the will of the majority.

This majority usually consisted of those classes in the community that had the greatest number of people—it came from the Greek demos, meaning people. These classes tended to be the poorer people.

In its purest form, democracy also meant a government in which members participated directly in their own governance instead of through representatives. The Founders were familiar with democratic institutions. For generations, local government in many of the colonies tended to be democratic in nature. The New England "town meeting" is one example. Based on their reading of history and their own experience, however, the Founders were concerned about democracy as a model for state or national government. Their preference for the republican as opposed to the democratic model of government influenced the framing of the Constitution.

> ### Key Note Term
>
> **democracy**—a form of government in which political control is exercised by all the people, either directly or through their elected representatives

Conclusion

This lesson introduced you to some basic ideas of the natural rights philosophy and theories of government that were of great importance in the development of our government. This lesson also introduced you to some basic ideas the Framers used in creating the kind of government they thought would best protect the natural rights of each individual and promote the good of all.

In the following lesson, you will examine the developing republican government.

Lesson Review

1. Explain what is meant by each of the following ideas from the Declaration of Independence:

   - All men are created equal

   - People have certain rights that are unalienable

   - Unalienable rights include rights to life, liberty, and the pursuit of happiness

   - Governments are created to secure these rights

   - Governments derive their just powers from the consent of the governed

   - People have the right to alter or abolish their government if it becomes destructive of the purposes for which it was created

2. What is meant by "the law of nature" or "natural law"? How did Locke try to establish or figure out what limitations it imposed on human conduct?

3. How would you explain the difference between a limited government and an unlimited government? Do you think the difference is important? Why or why not?

4. What is a constitution? What is the difference between a constitution that establishes a constitutional government, and a constitution that does not?

Lesson 2

Developing Republican Government

Key Terms

Age of Enlightenment	Middle Ages
capitalism	mixed government
Christendom	nation-state
civic virtue	papacy
classical republicanism	providence
common good	public and private morality
established religion	Reformation
factions	Renaissance
hierarchical	representative democracy
Judeo-Christian	secular governments

What You Will Learn to Do

- Trace how the American ideas of individual rights developed

Linked Core Objectives

- Communicate using verbal, non-verbal, visual, and written techniques
- Apply critical thinking techniques

Skills and Knowledge You Will Gain Along the Way

- Examine how the ideas of classical republicanism influenced the Founders' ideas of what kind of government they wanted

- Distinguish between classical republicanism and the natural rights philosophy

- Recognize how the ideas of Judeo-Christian tradition, the Middle Ages, the Renaissance, the Reformation and the rise of nation-state and capitalism supported the founders' thinking about natural rights and classical republicanism

- Explore how James Madison refined the ideas of classical republicanism to meet the needs of the new Americans

- Define key words contained in this lesson

Chapter 2

Introduction

The Founders were influenced by many ancient thoughts and ideas. From the Roman perspectives of classical government to the Judeo-Christian traditions of moral obligation, our government began to shape into what Americans' experience and enjoy as privilege today. In this lesson you explore how the ancient world influenced republican government and how modern ideas of individual rights developed.

What the Founders Found in Classical Republicanism

Figure 2.2.1: The architectural style of some government buildings symbolize the influence of ancient Greece and Rome on the founders.

Courtesy of Lester Lefkowitz/Corbis Images.

Most of the public buildings and monuments in Washington, D.C., and state capitols across the nation are built in the "classical" style (see Figure 2.2.1). This architectural tradition symbolizes our nation's indebtedness to the world of ancient Greece and Rome, especially to their ideas about government.

The Founders had studied the history of the classical periods of ancient Greece and Rome. The society that had the greatest influence on their ideas was that of the Roman Republic, which lasted for almost 500 years—509 B.C. to 27 B.C. Many philosophers and historians believed the Roman Republic had provided Roman citizens with the most liberty under government that the world had ever known. It also was believed widely that the Roman Republic promoted the **common good,** that is, what was best for the entire society. The theory based on this form of society became known as **classical republicanism.**

In a classical republic, citizens and their government are supposed to work cooperatively to achieve the common good rather than their own personal or selfish interests. The Roman Republic was thought to be one of the best examples of this type of society. Americans in the eighteenth century shared the view that citizens should work to promote the common good. They also believed that the type of government and society most likely to promote the common good was only possible if the society and its citizens shared the following characteristics:

- **Civic virtue**
- **Moral education**
- **Small, uniform communities**

Civic Virtue

The classical republics demanded that their citizens have a high degree of **civic virtue** (see Figure 2.2.2). A person with civic virtue was one who set aside personal interests to promote the common good. Today we might describe this as "public spiritedness."

Citizens were expected to participate fully in their government to promote the common good. They were not to be left free to devote themselves only to their personal interests. They were discouraged from spending much time doing such things as making money or caring for their families. They also were discouraged from traveling or reading and thinking about things that had nothing to do with their government. If citizens had the freedom to do such things, it was feared, they might stop being reliable and fully dedicated to the common good.

Figure 2.2.2: President Jimmy Carter joins volunteers to construct low income housing.

Courtesy of Mark Peterson/Corbis Images.

Key Note Term

civic virtue—the dedication of citizens to the common good, even at the cost of their individual interests

To make sure citizens participated in their government, the classical republics often drastically limited individual rights. There was little concern with protecting an individual's privacy, freedom of conscience or religion, or nonpolitical speech or expression. Certain rights, however, were necessary for citizens to participate in governing themselves. These were political rights, such as the right to vote, to express ideas and opinions about government, and to serve in public office.

Moral Education

People who believed in classical republicanism were convinced that civic virtue is not something that comes automatically to people. Citizens must be taught to be virtuous by moral education based on a civic religion consisting of gods, goddesses, and their rituals.

Classical republicans believed that young citizens must be raised in a manner that develops the right habits. They should learn to admire the people with civic virtue described in literature, poetry, and music. The Founders themselves admired such heroes of antiquity as the Roman patriot and orator Cato and the citizen soldier Cincinnatus. The Founders believed they were examples of civic virtue whom Americans should emulate. George Washington was admired by his fellow Americans as a modern-day Cincinnatus because he sacrificed his private pursuits to lead the nation in war and peace. George Washington was often called "our Cincinnatus" because his fellow citizens believed he was an example of the civic virtue that all citizens should possess.

According to classical republicans, children, as well as adults, should be encouraged—partly by the belief in a watchful god or gods—to practice virtues, such as generosity, courage, self-control, and fairness. They should learn the importance of taking part in political debate and military service. The whole community must closely supervise the upbringing of the next generation of citizens and be attentive to how individuals behave in their daily lives.

Small, Uniform Communities

Classical republicans believed that a republican government would only work in a small community. A small community is necessary if people are to know and care for each other and their common good. In addition, the people must be very much alike. A great degree of diversity should not be tolerated. They did not believe, for example, that people should be very different in their wealth, religious or moral beliefs, or ways of life.

Classical republicans believed that if people differed greatly, they would divide into factions or interest groups, rather than work together for the common good. To prevent this, citizens should be encouraged, by education and example, to avoid the development of great differences in their ownership of property, religion, and way of life. To prevent diversity in religious beliefs and lifestyles, they believed the community should have one official, **established religion** and one set of family and moral standards to which all must conform.

Great inequalities of wealth led inevitably to corruption as well as to **factions** or interest groups. Individuals would be more concerned with their own interest rather than the interest of the community. Their fear of great economic inequality and the corrupting effect of luxury led the classical republicans to be wary of money-making and economic growth. Such economic growth, they thought, gave rise to the great economic inequality which was inconsistent with the goals of republicanism.

Key Note Term

established religion—an official, state-sponsored religion

Key Note Term

factions—a group that seeks to promote its own special interests at the expense of the common good

Why did classical republicans believe that republican government could only work in small, uniform communities?

Classical Republicanism

Give the following questions some thought and come up with your answers.

1. Identify someone living today who you think shows civic virtue. Explain the reason for your choice.

2. What did classical republicans think should be the goal of education? Do you agree? Why or why not?

3. What civic virtues are important for young people to have today and why?

4. What similarities and differences are there between your ideas about rights and those of the classical world?

Develop responses to the following questions. Be prepared to share your answers with the class.

1. The classical republican idea of civic virtue conflicted with the Founders' belief in natural rights and their understanding of human nature as defined by John Locke. Create a chart that illustrates the differences between natural rights and classical republicanism. In completing your chart, you may need to review some of the ideas presented in Lesson 1.

2. Suppose you were among the Founders chosen to participate in drafting a constitution. How might you reconcile these differences between natural rights and classical republicanism? Which ideas would you choose to emphasize? Why?

3. What problems might you encounter in transferring some of the ideas of classical republicanism to American society? How might you solve these problems?

How the Founders Thought a Government Should Be Organized to Promote the Common Good

In addition to the example of the ancient Roman Republic, the Founders also learned about republican government from writers of their own time. One of the most important of these was the Baron de Montesquieu (shown in Figure 2.2.3), a French writer who was widely admired by Americans. Montesquieu advocated a system that divided and balanced the power of government among the classes. This, he believed, was the best way to ensure that the government would not be dominated by a single social class and would be able to enhance the common good.

MONTESQUIEU

He admired the Roman Republic as a representative government that combined elements of three basic types of government: monarchy, aristocracy, and democracy. Because all classes shared power, this type of government seemed best for serving the common good.

Even though Britain was a monarchy, Montesquieu admired the British constitution. He believed it embodied the idea of a **mixed government,** in which power was divided among different classes in British society.

In some respects, the Founders were uncritical admirers of the ancient world, most especially the Roman Republic. They were inclined to exaggerate the degree to which these states represented the interests of the whole community rather than just the interests of the upper classes. They also overlooked the fact that the ancient republics depended upon the institution of slavery. Their admiration for classical republicanism was based on a somewhat idealized version of antiquity.

The Founders were aware of the difficulty in transplanting ideals of classical republicanism to the newly independent American states. They differed concerning the degree to which these ideals could be adopted. The classical republicanism of the ancient world only flourished in small, uniform communities.

The following expectations of classical republicanism posed several problems for the founders of the new American nation:

- **Caring for each other and the common good in small communities**
- **Believing that people must be very much alike**
- **Supervising citizens to avoid the development of great differences among them in their ownership of property, religion, and way of life**
- **Believing that great economic inequality is destructive of the common good**
- **Having one official "established" religion and one set of family and moral standards which everyone would follow**

Were the Founders more representative of the ideas of the natural rights philosophy or classical republicanism? Why?

Penns Treaty with the Indians *by Benjamin West, courtesy of the Pennsylvania Academy of the Fine Arts.*

The classical republican idea of civic virtue conflicted with the Founders' belief in natural rights and with their understanding of human nature as defined by Locke and the other natural rights philosophers. The natural rights philosophy considered the rights of the individual to be primary in importance. The state existed to serve the interests of the individual, instead of the other way around. In classical republicanism, the rights of the community as a whole came first.

Americans of the founding era seemed more representative of human nature as described by the natural rights philosophers than the ideal expected by the civic virtue of the classical republicanism. They and their ancestors had come to the new land to take advantage of the opportunities it offered. Such restless, diverse, and ambitious people were ill-suited for the ideals of self-sacrifice and conformity of classical republicanism.

James Madison and the Ideas of Classical Republicanism

James Madison was one of the most important Founders responsible for creating the U.S. Constitution. He has been called "the Father of the Constitution." He was very influential in translating the ideas of classical republicanism in such a way as to make them practical in the new American republic.

Madison defined the difference between democracies and republics in the following way:

- **In a democracy, the people administer the government themselves. These "direct democracies" must be confined to small communities like the ancient city-states of Greece.**

- **In a republic, the people's representatives administer the government, allowing it to be extended over a much larger area.**

Madison believed, therefore, that America could and should have a republican form of government. Laws would be made and administered by representatives elected by the people. Madison also accepted certain principles of democracy. He insisted that members of government should be elected by a large number of the people, rather than by a small number or a specially favored group.

Such a form of government was a democracy in the sense that it derived its authority—its right to govern—from the people as a whole. Madison's new definition of a republican government, therefore, also could be defined as a **representative democracy.** In this way the two classical ideas of republic and democracy were adapted to the new form of government created by the Founders.

Similar to the other Founders, Madison understood the importance of informed and public-spirited citizens to this new government. He had to modify the classic definition of civic virtue to make it practical in the very different conditions of America. He accepted the natural rights philosophers' view of human nature, that people were motivated primarily by self-interest. He believed that the pursuit of self-interest could in its own way further the common good. For example, a statesman's desire for fame and admiration from others would lead him to practice civic virtue. The common good could be served by each individual pursuing his or her economic self-interest. Each would contribute to the general prosperity.

Why did James Madison favor a constitution that limited the power of government?

Courtesy of the Colonial Williamsburg Foundation.

Madison also realized that as people pursued their own interests they sometimes act against the interests of others and against the common good. Any sound government had to make allowances for this. As Madison said, if all people were angels, there would be no need for government. He argued for a government that would encourage people to act as good republican citizens possessing the quality of civic virtue. At the same time, this government would guard against the consequences if they did not. This is why Madison favored a constitution that limited government by the following methods:

- **Separation of powers**
- **A system of checks and balances**

The American adaptation of the principles of classical republicanism was, then, a sort of compromise. The Founders created a form of government they called republican, even though it was different from the models of republicanism in the ancient world.

They believed that it was important for citizens to possess civic virtue. Civic virtue could not be relied upon, however. Therefore, the proper structure provided by a system of representation with separation of powers and checks and balances also was necessary to protect the common good.

Judeo-Christian Heritage Contributes to the Founders' Understanding of Human Rights

The Founders were heirs to another legacy of antiquity, as important in its own way as that of the Greeks and Romans. They belonged to a religious tradition thousands of years old: Judeo-Christianity. Because there are many different faiths within this tradition, most of the Founders had grown up in a religious environment. From early childhood, they were familiar with the teachings of the Bible.

The **Judeo-Christian** world view holds that the world was created and is governed by one God. Humanity occupies a special place in that creation. Each human being is created in God's image and each possesses an immortal soul. For many, the striving for salvation through obedience to God's divine law is of prime importance.

Some Founders were critical of organized religion and skeptical of certain religious doctrines. Most believed in a Supreme Being and in that Supreme Being's interest in humanity and affairs of the world. Above all, they were convinced of the importance of each person obeying the moral code that they believed was given by that Supreme Being.

As you know, the Declaration of Independence acknowledges the "Creator" who "endowed men with certain unalienable rights." The Founders often spoke of **Providence** to suggest their

belief in God's interest and involvement in the affairs of the world. During the writing of the Constitution in the summer of 1787, Benjamin Franklin encouraged his fellow delegates by declaring his conviction that "God governs in the affairs of men." Whatever their particular religious backgrounds, the Founders believed strongly in the importance of the moral principles of Judeo-Christianity to benefit the common good. Judeo-Christian morality was different from the Greek and Roman ideals of civic virtue. Instead of **public morality,** these principles emphasized **private morality** as expressed in biblical teachings such as the Ten Commandments and the Sermon on the Mount. To classical republican virtues—courage, moderation, and wisdom—Judeo-Christianity added other moral qualities, such as love and benevolence toward others.

To achieve what was best for society as a whole, the Founders thought that each person's moral principles and behavior should be based on both classical and Judeo-Christian virtues. They felt that the practice of religion would help people live according to such moral standards. Their religious faith also strengthened the Founders' belief in the ideals of justice and liberty. The Bible stories of the struggle of the Hebrews against oppression and tyranny helped to inspire the American Revolution. These words from the Book of Leviticus are inscribed on the Liberty Bell in Philadelphia: "Proclaim liberty throughout all the land unto all the inhabitants thereof."

Finally, the teachings of Judeo-Christianity also helped to develop the Founders' appreciation of individual rights. Classical republicanism put the good of the state and community above that of the separate interests of the individuals who belonged to it.

Key Note Term

Judeo-Christian—beliefs and practices which have their historical roots in Judaism and Christianity

Key Note Term

Providence—the care, guardianship, and control exercised by a deity

Key Note Term

private and public morality—the principles of civic virtues as expressed in Judeo-Christian teachings, as well as fundamental ideas about right and wrong that come from religion, ethics, and individual conscience

How were a person's rights and responsibilities determined in the Middle Ages?

Courtesy of F.P.G. International.

The Judeo-Christian view of the individual and his or her place in the world was different. Its teachings stressed the dignity and worth of each human being. It was believed that each person possessed an individual soul. Therefore, the individual assumed a new importance in people's thinking about society and government. Much in the Founders' commitment to liberty and individual rights sprang from their belief in the rightness of such ideals.

Concepts of the Individual and Society during the Middle Ages

Christianity spread rapidly in the centuries following the death of Jesus and eventually became the predominant faith within the Roman Empire. The Roman Empire collapsed in the fifth century A.D., but Christianity survived to shape European society in the centuries that followed. This period, from the fifth century to the fourteenth, we call the **Middle Ages.**

Medieval society was based on the ideas of unity, social harmony, and other-worldliness. The European people of the Middle Ages saw themselves united in a single society called **Christendom.** Their spiritual leader was the Pope in Rome. The Popes enjoyed great authority and respect throughout Europe. There were no nations at this time to compete for people's loyalty. Most people thought of themselves in terms of only two allegiances: to their own local community and to the great unity of Christendom with one "universal" or "catholic" church presiding over it.

Medieval ideas about society also reflected the harmony that was thought to exist between each individual and the whole of society. Society was sometimes compared to a body, in which some parts were more important than others but all parts were necessary for the good of the whole. The parts were dependent upon each other.

- **Society was divided into different classes and groups such as royalty, nobility, clergy, tradesmen, craftsmen, and peasants. Each class or group had certain rights and responsibilities.**

- Society was **hierarchical**, that is, groups and classes were ranked from the most important at the top to the least important at the bottom. There was no equality between groups and classes.

- Each individual's role in society was defined by his or her role in one of these groups. A person had little chance of leaving the group into which he or she had been born.

- Any rights and duties a person had were usually spoken of in terms of the group to which that person belonged. There was no concept of "natural" or "universal" rights belonging to all people.

Rights were seen as privileges or "liberties" belonging to particular groups in society. Members of the group enjoyed its "rights." There were few individual rights. Medieval society was also other-worldly in its interests and activities. Christianity taught that the primary purpose of this life was to achieve salvation after death in another spiritual eternal life. The most important institutions of the Middle Ages, including churches and monasteries, were devoted to this end. Whatever else people achieved in their lives was secondary.

Economic life in the Middle Ages was based on subsistence agriculture. Most people lived on small farms or manors, producing enough food for the inhabitants to live on. There were few towns or cities. Travel was limited. Most people spent their entire lives within a few miles of the place where they were born. The few economic markets were tightly regulated by the nobility.

Why did the Popes and the church attain such important status in the Middle Ages?

How was people's understanding of rights shaped by the economic and social structure of the Middle Ages?

Courtesy of UPI/Bettmann News Photo.

hierarchical—organized or classified according to rank, capacity or authority

Lesson 2 Developing Republican Government

More to Ponder

Take a moment and mull over the following questions. Be prepared to share your answers with the rest of the class.

1. What is meant by the rights of groups as opposed to the rights of individuals?

2. What are the advantages and disadvantages of viewing rights as being possessed by individuals rather than groups?

3. Give some contemporary examples of claims for group rights. What arguments can you make for and against these claims?

4. Should certain individuals in our society be given special rights and privileges because they are members of a particular social group?

The Renaissance

Key Note Term

nation-state—the modern nation as the representative unit of political organization

Key Note Term

Renaissance—the great revival of art, literature, and learning in Europe during the fourteenth, fifteenth, and sixteenth centuries, based on classical sources

During the medieval period, people did not strive to make "progress." That is, they did not believe that they could make things better for themselves and their children through hard work or individual initiative. Despite these attitudes, medieval cities did develop and prosper. Commerce began to flourish, cities grew, people started to travel more. **Nation-states** began to form. The invention of modern printing methods increased communication and knowledge.

The most important outcome of these changes was the **Renaissance.** The term Renaissance means "re-birth." It describes a rebirth or revival of intellectual life that began in Italy around the fourteenth century and spread throughout Europe. This new interest was inspired by the rediscovery of ancient Greek and Roman history, literature, and art, with a view of the world and humanity that was very different from that of medieval Christianity.

Instead of focusing only on other-worldly matters and the quest for salvation, people took an interest in the world around them. They directed their energy toward the possibilities of human achievement in this life rather than the life to come. They expanded their knowledge and began to develop new ideas about the world. Their art and architecture glorified the beauty of the human body; their literature and philosophy explored all aspects of human nature and human creativity.

During the Renaissance people began to accept the idea of progress and historical change. In many areas of life, greater importance was placed on the individual than on the class or group into which that individual had been born. People believed they could work to improve their positions in society. The new emphasis on individual opportunity led to an increased interest in the rights of individuals. This interest contributed to a reexamination of the individual's relationship to religious institutions and governments.

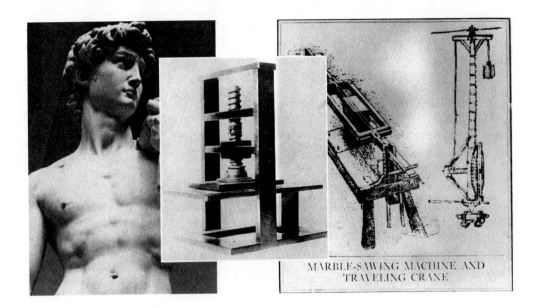

MARBLE-SAWING MACHINE AND
TRAVELING CRANE

How did Michelangelo's statue of David and changes in technology reflect changes in thinking that occurred in the Renaissance?

Courtesy of F.P.G. International.

The Protestant Reformation Advances the Cause of Individual Rights

The Protestant Reformation was a powerful stimulus to modern individualism. The **Reformation** was a religious reform movement that began in the early sixteenth century in Western Europe. It resulted in new ideas about religion, individual rights, and government. Like the Renaissance, the Reformation was a rebirth and rediscovery of certain things. Supporters of the Reformation believed they were returning to the original principles of Christianity.

Medieval society in Western Europe had been dominated by the Church of Rome. Religious reformers, studying the Bible and other ancient religious texts, began to challenge the doctrines, traditions, and practices of the Church of Rome. They believed that the medieval church had become corrupt and had lost sight of the original truths of Christianity. Some critics attempted to reform the church from within, but many Protestant reformers, like Martin Luther and John Calvin, established their own churches with the help of **secular governments.**

The Reformation was aided by the invention of the printing press. Books that formerly were scarce now became more available. The Bible was the most important of these books. For centuries the Bible had been printed only in Latin, which few people other than priests could read. Medieval Christians relied on the Church to interpret the word of God for them. During the Reformation, however, Bibles were printed in English, German, French, Italian, and Spanish. Individuals were encouraged to read the Bible in their native language to determine for themselves what it meant. Being able to read the Bible for oneself encouraged greater freedom of conscience.

Key Note Term

Reformation—sixteenth-century religious movement aimed at reforming the Roman Catholic church and resulting in the establishment of Protestant churches

Key Note Term

secular governments—a system of political power not exercised by ecclesiastical bodies or the clergy

Protestant religious doctrine emphasized the direct relationship between each individual believer and God. The result was to reduce the importance of the church and to increase the importance of the individual. All individuals were seen as equal in the eyes of God. Each person is to be respected and held accountable by God as an individual.

The spirit of free inquiry and individual conscience inspired by the Reformation contributed to the development of modern individualism. It also ultimately posed a threat to all established institutions and authority. Some religious reformers soon began to question the authority of the Protestant churches and the governments that supported them. In England, for example, reformers attacked the Church of England for not being Protestant enough. They were called Puritans because they wanted to "purify" the church. Some reformers sought to reform the established church. Others decided to separate from it. Many American colonies were originally settled by people seeking freedom to worship in their own way and new forms of government that would allow this.

The Rise of Modern Nation-States

The modern nation-state's development was speeded by the forces of change created by the Renaissance and Reformation. There were no nations, as we understand that word today, during the Middle Ages. The power of kings and princes did not reach very far. Power was exercised locally by authorities who usually inherited their power. In theory, at least, all secular governments were subservient to the Church of Rome. They had little authority over church officials and institutions in their territories.

Toward the end of the Middle Ages many of these secular governments were expanding and consolidating their power into independent states. The Reformation helped this development by challenging the Church of Rome. Some states, like England, broke free from the Church of Rome and created their own national churches. Others remained loyal to the **papacy** but reduced the authority of the Church of Rome within their territory.

Key Note Term

papacy—the office or authority of the Pope, the spiritual leader of the Roman Catholic church

How did the Renaissance, the Reformation, and the emergence of the modern nation-state make the rise of capitalism possible?

Courtesy of the Fishmongers Society of London.

Chapter 2 Foundations of the American Political System

The rise of the modern nation-state was very important to the development of modern ideas about government and rights. People began to think of themselves as citizens of a particular state or country, with public rights and duties. Political thought began to focus on the question of what kind of government would be best for these states. The modern nation-state also brought with it national legal systems and representative institutions of government.

The New Economic System of Capitalism

Among the forces that helped to break up medieval society and pave the way for the Renaissance was the increase in commercial trade and its expansion over greater distances. Eventually, this growth produced a new economic system called **capitalism.** Capitalism is an economic system in which

- **The means of producing and distributing goods are privately owned and operated for profit in competitive markets**
- **Production and distribution are not controlled by the government**

Under capitalism people gained more freedom to choose their occupations, start their own businesses, and own property. People had more control over their lives than had been possible in the Middle Ages.

People were able to pay more attention to their private interests than to the common good. They were encouraged to work to gain property and improve their positions in society. As a result, political and economic power shifted to a newly developed middle class of successful citizens.

How the Renaissance and Reformation Contributed to the Growth of Individual Rights

The Renaissance and Reformation produced a greater emphasis on the importance of the individual than had existed in the Middle Ages or in classical Greece and Rome. The ideas and opinions of individuals were valued. As the Renaissance emphasized individual activity and creativity, the followers of the Protestant Reformation emphasized the relationship between the individual believer and God. The rise of nation-states stimulated new thought about government and rights.

Capitalism translated this new spirit into economic opportunity. More individuals could compete on an equal footing and hope to improve their place in society.

How did increased interest in scientific study relate to the development of the natural rights philosophy?

The Age of Enlightenment

Key Note Term

Age of Enlightenment— an intellectual movement of the late seventeenth and eighteenth centuries that celebrated human reason and sought to realize its potential in all areas of human endeavor

The natural rights philosophy was a product of what is sometimes called the **Age of Enlightenment.** The Enlightenment was an intellectual movement of the late seventeenth and eighteenth centuries that celebrated human reason and sought to realize its potential in all areas of human endeavor. The Age of Enlightenment is also called the Age of Reason.

The worldly interests inspired by the Renaissance stimulated natural science—the study of the natural world and the laws that govern it. This new interest also was encouraged by commercial expansion and voyages of discovery beyond Europe. These voyages brought new knowledge about the natural world and about other cultures.

One advocate of scientific discovery, the English philosopher Francis Bacon, believed in the power of human reason and observation not only to understand nature, but also to control it for humanity's own purposes. "The end of scientific study," he said, "is the enlarging of the bounds of human empire, to the effecting of all things possible." The discoveries of scientists like Copernicus, Galileo, and Newton seemed to confirm Bacon's faith.

Eventually this spirit of scientific discovery was applied to human nature and society as well. During the Enlightenment people began to apply the method of scientific thinking to the study of society and politics.

The American Founders belonged to the Age of Enlightenment. They believed in the powers of reason and observation to understand the workings of governmental and societal institutions. They thought these powers also would be a guide in ways to improve institutions. With such faith and self-confidence, the Framers of our Constitution thought they could create a new order of government during one summer's deliberations in Philadelphia.

Conclusion

In this lesson you learned how the Founders were influenced by the ideas of classical republicanism: the importance of the Roman Republic and the moral ideal of civic virtue. You examined how these ideas shaped their thinking about what kind of government they wanted to create for the United States.

You learned about the principles of classical republicanism as well as the difficulties the Founders encountered in attempting to apply those principles to the new American nation. You also should understand how classical republicanism differed from the natural rights philosophy in its account of human nature and individual rights. You should be able to explain how James Madison was able to adapt the ideas of classical republicanism, democracy, and civic virtue to American circumstances.

You also examined the influence of the Renaissance, the Reformation, and the Enlightenment on the thinking of the Founders. You compared the difference between classical republican and Judeo-Christian ideas about the importance of the individual. You should understand how the Judeo-Christian tradition shaped people's outlook during the Middle Ages, providing one of the bases for modern constitutionalism. You also should be able to explain how the Renaissance, Reformation, rise of capitalism, rise of nationalism, and the Enlightenment led to the development of modern ideas about individual rights.

In the following lesson, you will learn about the British origins of American Constitutionalism.

Lesson Review

1. What is meant by the term "civic virtue"? Give an example of a situation in which someone is expected to show civic virtue.

2. How would you describe the differences between the natural rights philosophy and classical republicanism?

3. How would you describe the difference between the classical republican idea of civic virtue and Judeo-Christian ideas of morality?

4. What was the "Age of Enlightenment" and why is it sometimes called the "Age of Reason"?

Lesson 3

British Origins of American Constitutionalism

Key Terms

American Constitutionalism
burgesses
charters
common law
contracts
due process of law
Magna Carta
manorialism

monarch
parliamentary government
realm
rights of Englishmen
rule of law
tenets
vassal

What You Will Learn to Do

- Show how the Founders built on the principles of British representative government

Linked Core Objectives

- Communicate using verbal, non-verbal, visual, and written techniques
- Apply critical thinking techniques

Skills and Knowledge You Will Gain Along the Way

- Examine how the nature of the British constitution emerged from struggles between royalty, nobility and the church

- Identify how parliamentary government changed and began to represent the interests of all people

- Identify how the constitutional principles from the English Bill of Rights impacted the U.S. Bill of Rights

- Defend a position on the importance of specific rights such as habeas corpus and trial by jury and on what limitations, if any, should be placed on them

- Define key words contained in this lesson

Introduction

The American colonial period lasted for 150 years. The Founders were loyal subjects of the British crown and were proud to enjoy the rights of Englishmen as protected by the English constitution. The Founders were greatly impacted by the English form of government, which ultimately influenced the creation of the United States Constitution. In this lesson you explore how the establishment of representative government in British history influenced the Founders and helped establish some of our most important constitutional rights today.

How English Government Began

For several centuries after the fall of the Roman Empire, England was divided among a number of tribes, each ruled by its own leader or "king." These early kings were selected by councils of advisers because they were the strongest and most powerful members of their tribes. For many years these tribes were at war with each other. Eventually all the tribes of England became united under one king. Christianity increased the authority of kingship by teaching that kings were "anointed by God" and that all the people governed by the king were subject to his rule—which is why they were called "subjects."

England was too large for one person to rule because quick and efficient means of communication and travel did not exist. Most kings had to let people in local areas tend to their own affairs according to customs that had developed over the years.

Feudalism

A major change in the way England was ruled took place on October 14, 1066, when William the Conqueror, the leader of the Normans (from Normandy in France), invaded England and defeated King Harold at the Battle of Hastings (see Figure 2.3.1). William introduced the new system of feudalism to control the conquered land.

Figure 2.3.1: Feudalism, introduced after the Normans invaded England, changed the way people were governed.

Courtesy of Nik Wheeler/ Corbis Images.

How did feudalism change the way people were governed?

Key Note Terms

vassal—in feudal times, a person granted the use of land by a feudal lord in return for military or other service

contracts—binding agreements between two or more persons

manoralism—the form of economic life of the Middle Ages, when most people were involved in agriculture and land was divided up into self-contained farms or manors

Feudalism is not easy to define because it varied greatly in different times and different places. Generally, feudalism was a form of political organization in which a lord gave land to other men in return for their personal allegiance and for military and other service. The men who received land from the lord were known as **vassals** as they served their lord and were entitled to be protected by him.

Feudalism is important to the development of constitutional government because of its ideas about **contracts.** Feudal government depended upon a series of agreements or contracts between lords and vassals. Each contract included mutual rights and responsibilities. Thus, feudalism introduced the idea of government based on a contract— those in power pledged to respect the rights of the people who gave them allegiance.

The basis of this feudal system was land use. Parcels of land were divided into self-contained farms or manors. Peasants were legally required to remain on the land and in that sense were part of the property enjoyed by the owner or "lord" of the land. Even peasants, however, enjoyed certain customary rights on the manor. For this reason, the system of **manorialism** as well as feudalism helped to develop ideas about the fundamental rights of Englishmen.

Understanding the Rights of Englishmen

Key Note Term

rights of Englishmen—basic rights, established over time, that all subjects of the English monarch were understood to have

The **rights of Englishmen** had been established slowly over centuries of British history. They were certain basic rights that all subjects of the English monarch, king or queen, were believed to have. They were fundamental in the sense that they could not be changed or violated.

The Founders began their lives as loyal subjects of the British Crown, proud to enjoy the rights of Englishmen. This privilege, they believed, set them apart from the other peoples of the world. Centuries of respect gave these rights a special status which included:

- **The right to a trial by jury**
- **Security in one's home from unlawful entry**
- **No taxation without consent**

The historical sources of these rights are custom and law. They were confirmed by royal **charters** and became part of English common law. The **common law** consists of the accumulated legal opinions of judges explaining their decisions in specific court cases. These decisions provide guidelines or precedents for later judgments. The English common law provides the historical foundation of our American legal system.

The British Constitution

Unlike the U.S. Constitution, the British constitution did not exist before the creation of a government. The constitution of Great Britain is not a single written document. Instead it is made up of the common law, acts of Parliament, and political customs and traditions.

Three great historical documents are important in the development of the British constitution and the rights of the British people. These are the **Magna Carta** (1215), the Petition of Right (1628), and the English Bill of Rights (1689).

These documents were written during times of great conflict. Much of English history is the story of a bloody struggle for power between the most important groups in society. These groups were the royalty, nobility, and the clergy. By the thirteenth century, the struggle was mainly between royalty and the Parliament. Parliament was originally a council of nobles created to advise the **monarch.** It soon became the branch of government that represented the most powerful groups in the kingdom.

For hundreds of years, Parliament and the monarch struggled for power. During these conflicts, English subjects were jailed, tortured, and executed. Kings and queens defeated in battle were imprisoned and beheaded. Because of these conflicts, several important legal documents were written that limited the power of the monarch in order to protect the rights of other groups. These documents were important not only in English history, but also had a great influence on the Founders. One of the most important of these documents is described next.

Understanding the Magna Carta

The first great landmark of British constitutionalism and one of the great charters of human liberty originated as a quarrel between a feudal lord and his vassals. One of William the Conqueror's successors, King John, tried to take back some rights and powers of his barons. This was the title of nobility given to principal vassals. The result was a war between the barons and their king, a war that the barons won.

With the support of the church and others, the barons, in June 1215, forced John to sign the Magna Carta, meaning *Great Charter,* confirming certain traditional rights and, by implication, promising not to violate them again. Most of the rights in question were feudal privileges, enjoyed only by the feudal nobility. The **tenets** of the Magna Carta were very important in the later development of constitutional government:

How did the Magna Carta reduce the power of the English monarch?

Courtesy of Bettmann/Corbis Images.

Government should be based on the rule of law. The Magna Carta was perhaps the most important early example of a written statement of law limiting the power of a ruler. It expresses the idea of limited government by requiring the king to govern according to established rules of law. The Magna Carta, for example, states that no free man could be imprisoned or punished "except by the lawful judgment of his peers and by the law of the land." "Judgment of his peers" did not originally mean trial by jury as we understand it. This statement, however, did explain the principle of **due process of law,** whereby no government could take action against those it governed except by settled and generally agreed on procedures and rules.

Certain basic rights may not be denied by government. In limiting the power of the king, the Magna Carta also expressed the idea that established rights of the governed could not be violated. Most of the rights guaranteed in the Magna Carta belonged only to the feudal nobility. The Magna Carta did, however, secure some rights for others in English society. The king, for example, promised to respect the "ancient liberties and free customs" of London and other towns.

Government should be based on an agreement or contract between the ruler and the people to be ruled. The agreement in the Magna Carta was between the king and a very limited number of his subjects. It did not include the majority of the English people. It did, however, express the feudal principle of drawing up an agreement between parties as a basis for legitimate government.

Government by contract meant that if either side broke the agreement, that agreement would no longer be valid. Later generations also would discover in the Magna Carta the seeds of other important constitutional principles. For example, the American colonists found in King John's promise not to levy certain feudal taxes without the consent of "our common counsel of the kingdom" the principle of no taxation without representation and consent.

Analyzing and Evaluating Specific Rights

People have fought and died to establish such rights as those described in this lesson. It is often difficult, however, to understand their importance from merely reading about them. By examining specific rights more closely and discussing your opinions about them, you may be able to gain a greater appreciation of their meaning and importance. Let's examine more closely some of the provisions of the Magna Carta.

Two parts of the Magna Carta, Articles 39 and 40, contain some of the most important principles of modern constitutionalism. Read and discuss these provisions; then develop responses to the questions that follow. Be prepared to explain your answers to the class.

Article 39: No freeman shall be taken or imprisoned or disseised [dispossessed] or banished or in any way destroyed, nor will we proceed against or prosecute him, except by the lawful judgment of his peers and by the law of the land.

Article 40: To no one will we sell, to none will we refuse or delay, . . . justice.

1. What rights are listed in Articles 39 and 40? In what ways might the rights in Articles 39 and 40 be relevant to you today?

2. How do these rights limit the power of the king?

3. Why would the English nobles want to place such limits on the power of the king?

4. What values and interests are protected by these statements?

5. What events in the United States or other nations can you identify in which one or more of the above rights have been upheld or violated?

6. Do you think the declaration of these rights alone is enough to protect individuals from unfair and unreasonable treatment by their government? Why or why not?

7. At Runnymede in England, where King John signed the Magna Carta, there are three monuments. One is a tribute to U.S. President John Kennedy. Another is the Magna Carta national memorial erected by the American Bar Association. In addition there is one honoring the Commonwealth airmen who died in World War II. Why do you think the Magna Carta might be especially important to Americans?

Did the Magna Carta protect the rights of all Englishmen? Why?

Parliamentary Government in England

The Magna Carta brought the law to bear against a law-breaking king. It did not, however, solve the problem of how to make sure the king would continue to comply with the law. The Magna Carta gave King John's barons the right to go to war with him if he broke their agreement. Going to war, however, was not a satisfactory basis for assuring responsible government. A better way began to develop in the century following the Magna Carta.

In the feudal system English kings relied on councils to advise them in the task of governing. The councils came to be called parliaments, from the French word parler, to speak. At first these councils of advisers included only the leading nobles and clergy of the **realm.** Gradually, the number of members and the role of these councils expanded to more effectively represent the interests of the different parts of the realm.

In the fourteenth century these parliaments divided into two parts or houses: the House of Lords representing the interests of the feudal nobility and major churchmen; the House of Commons representing not the common people as we understand that term, but rather people who were not nobility but who still possessed wealth and stature in the kingdom. The Commons included knights, who represented the shires or counties of the kingdom, and **burgesses,** wealthy merchants and craftsmen, who represented the cities and towns of England.

Parliament and **parliamentary government** developed as a representative institution of government because the kings of England found it an effective way to raise money from their subjects. They also found it an efficient way to make important laws. Henry VIII (see Figure 2.3.2), for example, used the authority of Parliament to break away from the Church of Rome and to establish the Church of England. English subjects found Parliament to be an effective way to voice their grievances to their monarch and also to limit or check his or her power.

Eventually, Parliament became so important to English government that it was capable of challenging the king's ability to act without its support. The struggle for ultimate power in England's government came to a head in the seventeenth century, when the Stuart kings and their Parliaments quarreled over a variety of issues, including money, religion, and foreign policy. At the heart of these struggles was a key constitutional issue:

Key Note Terms

realm—a community or territory over which a sovereign rules; a kingdom

burgesses—wealthy merchants and craftsmen who represented the cities and towns of England

parliamentary government—a way of dividing legislative power to better represent the people

How did the English Parliament come to represent the interests of more people?

Courtesy of the Library of Congress.

Chapter 2   Foundations of the American Political System

- **Did the king have the authority or prerogative to act independently of established law and parliamentary consent?**

OR

- **Must the king govern through Parliament and accept the ultimate supremacy of Parliamentary law?**

The future of British and American constitutional government depended on the outcome of this struggle, which included a bloody civil war, the execution of one king, Charles I, and the overthrow of another, James II.

The Petition of Right

The constitutional struggles of seventeenth-century England included several important events. One of these events produced a constitutional document almost as important as the Magna Carta: the Petition of Right of 1628. Pressed for money, King Charles I sought to raise funds without the consent of Parliament. He also tried to force this money from his subjects through illegal pressures. For example, he required subjects to "quarter" or house soldiers in their homes.

In 1628 Parliament forced Charles to consent to the Petition of Right, which confirmed that taxes could only be raised with the consent of Parliament. It also guaranteed English subjects other rights, including a prohibition against requiring people to quarter soldiers in their homes. The Petition of Right thus strengthened the idea that English subjects enjoyed certain fundamental rights that no government could violate.

The Connection between the Petition of Right and the Magna Carta

One parliamentary leader in favor of the Petition of Right was the famous jurist Sir Edward Coke, who was greatly admired by the Founders. Coke championed the rights of Englishmen. He believed that the Magna Carta was not only a victory for feudal privilege but also a confirmation of the fundamental rights belonging to all Englishmen, rights that had existed since time immemorial. The Petition of Right, he believed, was, like the Magna Carta, a confirmation of these ancient rights.

Habeas Corpus

Another important milestone in this constitutional struggle was the Habeas Corpus Act of 1678, in which Parliament gained from English monarchs the right of their subjects to a legal document called a writ of habeas corpus. The Latin phrase habeas corpus means to "have the body." A writ of habeas corpus orders the government to deliver a person it has arrested to a court of law and explain why that person has been arrested and held. If the government cannot produce evidence to show that the arrested person may have broken the law, the person must be set free.

The English subject's right to a writ of habeas corpus may have existed in English law even before the Magna Carta. Its guarantee was also one of the provisions of the Petition of Right. English monarchs, however, had for centuries ignored this guarantee by using unlawful arrest and prolonged imprisonment without trial as weapons against their subjects.

Evaluating the Importance of the Rights to Habeas Corpus and Trial by Jury

Take a few minutes and examine the rights of habeas corpus and trial by jury. Your class should be divided into two groups; one group will read selection 1 and the other selection 2. Each group will then answer the questions that accompany their selection. Discuss your reading with the entire class.

Group 1: Habeas corpus. The writ of habeas corpus has been called the "Great Writ of Liberty." One constitutional scholar called it "the greatest guarantee of human freedom ever devised by man."

Now examine why this right was thought to be so fundamental.

Suppose you were arrested and imprisoned by the Queen of England. Although you have the right to be tried by the law of the land, the queen's jailers keep you in prison. They refuse to bring you before a court to be charged with a crime and tried.

How could the right to a writ of habeas corpus protect you from such treatment? How could the jailers be forced to bring you into a court of law for a fair hearing?

Suppose you had a family member, a friend, or a lawyer who knew you had been arrested and were being kept in prison. That person could go to court and ask the judge to issue a writ of habeas corpus. This writ would be an order by the judge to your jailer to bring you, that is your "body," to court and present evidence that you have broken the law. If there is evidence, you would be held for trial. If there is no evidence, you would be set free.

1. What limits does the right to a writ of habeas corpus place on the power of the monarch?

2. Why would the English Parliament want to place such limits on the power of the monarch?

3. What arguments can you make for this right today?

4. What examples of situations in the United States or other nations can you identify that uphold or violate this right?

5. Under what conditions, if any, do you think this right should be limited?

Why is the right to a writ of habeas corpus so important in protecting the rights of a person accused of crimes?

Group 2: Trial by jury. The right to a trial by a jury of one's peers is one of the oldest and most important of the fundamental rights of Englishmen. It has become an essential right in a free society.

Suppose you were arrested and imprisoned by the English king. A judge, appointed and paid by the king, has examined the evidence against you and decided you should be tried for breaking the law.

The English constitution guarantees you the right to be tried by a jury of your peers. This means that a group of people from your community will listen to the evidence the king's prosecutor has against you. They also will hear your side of the story. The jury has the authority to decide if you are guilty or innocent of breaking the law. Its verdict must be unanimous to find you guilty. Jurors also have the power to find you not guilty even if you have broken the law if they think the law in question is unfair.

1. What limits does the right to a trial by jury place upon the power of the monarch?

2. Why would the English Parliament want to place such limits on the power of the monarch?

3. What relation does the right to a trial by jury have to the separation of powers and checks and balances?

4. What arguments can you make for this right?

5. Under what conditions if any, do you think this right should be limited?

The English Bill of Rights of 1689

The struggle between the monarch and Parliament came to a head in a bloodless revolution known as the Glorious Revolution of 1688. King James II was overthrown and forced to flee the country. The king's son-in-law, Prince William of Orange, and his followers had suspected James II of trying to make Roman Catholicism the established religion in England and of resorting to various illegal acts to accomplish this.

In the Revolution Settlement that followed the Glorious Revolution, Prince William and his wife, Mary, succeeded to the throne. A condition of their succession, however, was that they agree to a Declaration of Rights. The Declaration was then enacted into law by Parliament as the English Bill of Rights. It became the cornerstone of the Revolution Settlement and of England's constitution.

What Protections Did the English Bill of Rights Include?

The English Bill of Rights was a practical and specific document rather than a statement of general constitutional principles. Its primary objective was to make sure that what James II had tried to do would never happen again. It limited the power of the monarch by placing the dominant power of government in Parliament and providing for the security of the Church of England against any attempts at counterrevolution by James or his descendants on behalf of Roman Catholicism.

The English Bill of Rights includes many ideas about rights and government that were later included in our Declaration of Independence, Constitution, and Bill of Rights. In addition to limiting the monarch's power to act without the consent of Parliament, it provides for such traditional rights of Englishmen as trial by jury, prohibition of cruel and unusual punishments, the right to petition the government, and the right to bear arms for personal defense—a right, however, granted only to Protestants.

The English Bill of Rights does not provide for freedom of religion. Nor does it guarantee freedom of the press or freedom of speech outside Parliament. An Act of Toleration, however, passed shortly after the Glorious Revolution, which gave freedom of worship to Protestant dissenters. Though not included in the act, Roman Catholics were thereafter generally left alone to practice their faith. The government also expanded freedom of the press by repealing the act that allowed censorship of printed material.

How Does the English Bill of Rights Differ from the U.S. Bill of Rights?

The English Bill of Rights differs from the U.S. Bill of Rights in several important respects. The former was ratified by Parliament and could be changed by Parliament. The U.S. Bill of Rights was ratified by the people and could only be changed with their consent through the amending process of the Constitution.

The English Bill of Rights was intended primarily to limit the power of the monarch and increase the power of Parliament. The U.S. Bill of Rights was intended to prohibit the federal government from violating the individual rights of all people and to protect the rights of minorities.

The Glorious Revolution and the English Bill of Rights, however, express several important constitutional principles that influenced our Constitution and Bill of Rights. These were

- **Rule of law**. The English Bill of Rights restated the old idea that legitimate government must be according to the rule of law. Both government and the governed must obey the laws of the land.

- *Parliamentary supremacy.* The Glorious Revolution finally settled the question of supremacy in the English government. While retaining important executive powers, the monarch must govern through Parliament. Parliamentary law was the highest law in the land.

- *Government by contract and consent.* By over-throwing a monarch who broke the law and by declaring respect for the English Bill of Rights as a condition for his successors, the Glorious Revolution confirmed the idea that government is based on a contract between the rulers and those who are ruled.

> ### Key Note Term
>
> **rule of law**—implies that government authority may only be exercise in accordance with written laws, which are adopted through an established procedure

British History and the Magna Carta

Think about the following questions. Be prepared to share your thoughts with the rest of your class.

1. In what ways did the British documents about rights reinforce the major ideas found in the Magna Carta? In what ways did they expand upon these ideas?

2. How are the ideas in the Magna Carta, the Petition of Right, and the English Bill of Rights related to the natural rights philosophy?

3. Why might an understanding of British history have led the Founders to want to protect the right of religious freedom and dissent?

Montesquieu and the British Constitution

Many Europeans admired the British constitution in the eighteenth century. They were impressed by the degree of liberty enjoyed by British subjects and by the growing power and wealth of the British Empire. One admirer of the British constitution was the French philosopher Montesquieu. His interpretation of the British constitution had a great influence on the Founders.

Montesquieu admired what he believed to be the "mixed" nature of the British constitution, which included the best of monarchy (the king or queen), aristocracy (the House of Lords), and democracy (the House of Commons). This constitution was, he believed, a modern example of the classical republican model of government. Montesquieu also saw in the British constitution the principle of separation of powers in government, whereby the executive, legislative, and judicial powers are independent of each other.

To some extent, however, Montesquieu misinterpreted how the British constitution worked. It was not as "mixed" in its composition as he believed. Both the House of Lords and House of Commons in the eighteenth century were predominantly aristocratic. Moreover, the three branches of government were not fully separated. The monarch through his or her ministers took an active part in the affairs of Parliament. English judges also were considered part of the executive branch.

The British constitution as secured by the Glorious Revolution did, however, create a balance of power between the monarch and the two houses of Parliament. Judges were granted independence from both the monarch and Parliament to interpret the law fairly. This balance of power was a first step toward the idea of separation of powers and checks and balances in our Constitution.

Conclusion

This lesson described how some basic rights of Englishmen were established and why they were important to the American colonists. You examined English government in its early stages from the ninth through the thirteenth centuries, known as the feudal period. You also examined the initial development of the English constitution, the Magna Carta, and its importance to the Founders.

This lesson described the evolution of constitutional government in England after the Magna Carta. You examined some early documents that protected rights in England and the origins of England's representative governmental institutions. You learned how these ideas and institutions influenced **American constitutionalism.** You also learned about some important differences between British and American constitutionalism.

The following lesson covers colonial government. In this lesson, you examine basic rights and constitutional government.

Key Note Term

American Constitutionalism— government in which power is distributed and limited by a system of laws that must be obeyed by the rulers

Chapter 2

Lesson Review

Lesson Review

1. What is meant by the "rights of Englishmen"? How were these rights established?

2. What was feudalism and how did it contribute to the development of constitutional government?

3. What is the Magna Carta? How was it created? How did it contribute to the development of constitutional government?

4. What is the common law? How does it develop?

Lesson 4

Colonial Government– Basic Rights and Constitutional Government

Key Terms

Boston Massacre
Boston Tea Party
committees of correspondence
constituents
covenant
Declaration of Independence
established religion
First Continental Congress
Fundamental Orders
of Connecticut
governor
indentured servant
Intolerable Acts
legislatures
magistrate

Massachusetts Body
of Liberties
Mayflower Compact
minutemen
primogeniture
Quartering Act
Seven Years War
Sons of Liberty
sovereignty
Stamp Act Congress
suffrage
Tea Act
The Laws and Liberties
writ of assistance

What You Will Learn to Do

- Form an opinion about how the Declaration of Independence reflects your ideas about the purpose of government and protection of individual rights

Linked Core Objectives

- Communicate using verbal, non-verbal, visual, and written techniques
- Apply critical thinking techniques

Chapter 2

Skills and Knowledge You Will Gain Along the Way

- Explain how differences between colonial America and Europe affected the Founders' beliefs about government and individual rights
- Consider how you, as a citizen today, would view the limitation of many rights to white, male, property owners
- Show how the Declaration of Independence justified the arguments for separation of the colonies from Great Britain
- Examine what the Declaration of Independence says about the purpose of government and protection of individual rights
- Define key words contained in this lesson

Introduction

In this lesson you will consider why the American colonists who founded your country decided to seek independence from England. You will examine how the Founders carefully crafted the Declaration of Independence to summarize their reasons for seeking independence and to lay the groundwork that would give us a government that would better protect our rights. Finally, you will have an opportunity to judge if the rights the American colonists worked to protect measure up to today's equal rights expectations.

Key Note Terms

Mayflower Compact—an agreement signed in 1620 by all adult males aboard the ship Mayflower, before landing in Plymouth, to form a body of politic governed by majority rule

covenant—a binding agreement made by two or more persons or parties

Colonial Settlement of America Inspired New Experiments in Constitutional Government

Almost half of our history as a people—over 150 years—took place before we gained our independence in 1776. This history had a great influence on the Founders. The many thousands of immigrants in the seventeenth and early eighteenth centuries came to America for various reasons. The most common were economic and religious. The English colonists brought with them English customs, laws, and ideas about good government. They were separated from England, however, by 3,000 miles of ocean. Consequently, the colonists soon discovered that they would have to improvise, adapt old ideas, and develop new ones if they were to survive.

In some respects, the settlement of America meant a return to a state of nature as later described by the natural rights philosophers. This new experience required new political solutions. One of our country's oldest and most famous charters, the **Mayflower Compact,** was a **covenant** or social contract, to which the Pilgrims agreed prior to landing in Plymouth, Massachusetts, in 1620 (see Figure 2.4.1). The Compact established a civil body authorized to make laws and appoint officers.

How does the Mayflower Compact reflect the principle of government by consent or social contract?

Courtesy of the Library of Congress.

Figure 2.4.1: The Mayflower Compact that established a civil body to make laws and appoint officers was in place before the Pilgrims landed at Plymouth Rock.

Courtesy of Bettmann/ Corbis Images.

Understanding the Uniqueness of the American Experience

The special conditions of an undeveloped land profoundly affected economic, social, and political life in colonial America. Land was cheap and readily available. People available to till this land or perform other jobs in colonial society were always in short supply.

Cheap land and the great demand for workers meant that most American colonists had far greater opportunities to get ahead and achieve prosperity than most people in Europe. While some became very wealthy, others failed, creating a class of American poor. But the great majority realized at least a moderate prosperity that was beyond their reach in Europe. Almost any white man with ambition could gain the 50 acres of land required as a qualification to vote in most colonies.

There was no nobility whose social and economic status was protected by law. In Great Britain laws prohibited the sale and distribution of property attached to a noble title; it had to be handed down to eldest sons—the right of **primogeniture.** Because economic and political power was based on this property, generations of noble families had a privileged status in English government and society.

It is true that those people who came from educated British families or those with great personal wealth had an advantage over those who arrived in the colonies almost penniless and unknown. But wealth and family name did not mean automatic success in a land without a rigid class system; and the lack of these advantages rarely held back for long those with ambition. The carpenter and brick mason, for example, enjoyed modest social status in England. The constant demand for new buildings in America, however, allowed such craftsmen to earn a living equal to many of their social "superiors." A well-born gentleman from Europe who considered hard work or manual labor beneath him might have a difficult time surviving in the colonies.

How did life in the American colonies break down the social and economic barriers so common in Europe?

Courtesy of the National Archives, Library of Congress.

Thus, there was greater equality among Americans than among Europeans in their economic, social, and political life. While some upper class Americans might not have liked this situation, equality of opportunity and the chance to better one's position in life became fundamental ideals in the American experience. In this land of almost unlimited opportunity, one of a candle maker's 17 children, Benjamin Franklin, could rise to become a great inventor, statesman, and diplomat. An English corset-maker's son, Thomas Paine, could become a famous writer on behalf of the American Revolution. Alexander Hamilton, the illegitimate son of poor parents, could become the first Secretary of the Treasury of the newly formed United States.

Examining an Original Document about Colonial Life

In the mid-eighteenth century a colonial farmer, Philip Taylor, wrote about his life on the border of what today is the state of Vermont. Read what he wrote and then be prepared to discuss your answers to the questions that follow.

We now have a comfortable dwelling and two acres of ground planted with potatoes, Indian corn, melon, etc. I have 2 hogs, 1 ewe and a lamb; cows in the spring were as high as 33 dollars, but no doubt I shall have 1 by fall. I am living in God's noble and free soil, neither am I slave to others . . . I have now been on American soil for two and a half years and I have not been compelled to pay for the privilege of living. Neither is my cap worn out from lifting it in the presence of gentlemen.

1. What was it that Philip Taylor liked about life in America?

2. What rights did he enjoy? How are they related to the ideas of the natural rights philosophers? Do you enjoy these rights today?

3. Given what you know of Philip Taylor's experiences, explain why he would be more or less likely to favor laws that

- Guarantee each individual the right to be secure in his property

- Limit an individual's right to buy and sell goods to anyone he or she chooses

- Give people certain rights because they are wealthy or from a certain family background or group

Basic Ideas of Constitutional Government Used by Colonial Governments

The colonies were originally founded by charters or grants given to private groups or individuals. These charters and grants said little about what form of local government the colonies should have. As a result, the colonies developed their own forms of government and America became a fertile ground for constitution making. The colonies depended more on written constitutional arrangements than was the case in England, whose own unwritten constitution represented centuries of evolution.

Key Note Term

established religion— an official, state-sponsored religion

In creating such limited government, the colonists tried to protect themselves not only from abuse of power by the English government in London, but also from abuses by colonial governments themselves. The first governments of many of the colonies lacked constitutional restraints that were later seen as essential. Some of the early colonial governments persecuted those who refused to conform to the **established religion.** Resistance to religious persecution in the colonies became an important stimulus to the advancement of constitutional ideas and institutions.

There are many stories of religious dissenters who were persecuted in these early years. Anne Hutchinson, a brilliant and talented woman, arrived in Massachusetts in 1634 with her husband and seven children. She gained great respect as a midwife, healer, and spiritual counselor. Before long she began preaching a theory of salvation that was contrary to the official Puritan beliefs. Not only was she a dissenter but as a woman she was particularly offensive to the male leaders of the community. Brought to trial, she was cast out of the colony as "a heathen and a leper."

Hutchinson fled Massachusetts to Rhode Island where religious dissenters were tolerated. It was the first colony to grant freedom of conscience to everyone. The Charter of 1663, provided that "noe [sic] person . . . shall bee [sic] any wise molested, punished, disquieted, or called in question, for any differences of opinione [sic] in matters of religion." Jews, Quakers, Catholics, and others not welcomed elsewhere found a haven in Rhode Island.

Key Note Term

Fundamental Orders of Connecticut— adopted in 1639, this series of laws is the first written constitution in North America

Others were inspired by constitutional values early on. The first colonial constitution was the **Fundamental Orders of Connecticut,** created in 1639, by three town settlements along the Connecticut River. Deriving its authority from all free men living in these towns, this constitution established a central legislative body for making laws. The other colonies would adopt constitutional arrangements of their own in the years that followed.

Chapter 2   Foundations of the American Political System

Some of these experiments were successful; others failed or had to be revised many times before they became practical. The forms of colonial government varied somewhat from colony to colony. They all, however, shared certain basic constitutional principles. These principles generally reflected the influence of England but in some ways they differed. The ideas of British constitutionalism embodied in the governments of the British colonies follow.

Fundamental Rights

The colonists were concerned foremost with protecting those fundamental rights they believed they had brought with them from England. At first these basic rights were seen as the ancient and fundamental rights of Englishmen. These basic rights were later described as the rights of all men. They were defined by the natural rights philosophers as the natural rights to life, liberty, and property.

Rule of Law

To protect their fundamental rights, the colonists insisted on the creation of a government of laws, in which those responsible for making and enforcing the laws could not exercise arbitrary power as had been the case in some of the first colonial governments. The colonial constitutions also included the idea that the English law was higher law and was superior to any laws the colonial governments might make.

Separation of Powers

To a greater extent than in the British government, colonial governments provided for a separation of powers among the three branches of government. In colonial governments the three branches tended to be more independent of each other. Separation of powers was evident in the following ways:

- *An executive branch.* **Governors** were responsible for carrying out and enforcing law. In most of the colonies by the time of the American Revolution, the governors were chosen either by the monarch or the proprietors. Only in Connecticut and Rhode Island were the governors elected by those men in the colonies who were allowed to vote.

Key Note Term

governor—the manager or administrative head of an organization, business, or institution

legislatures—an officially elected or otherwise selected body of people vested with the responsibility and power to make laws for a political unit, such as a state or nation

magistrate—a lower-level judicial officer, usually elected in urban areas, who handles traffic violations, minor criminal offenses, and civil suits involving small amounts of money

- *A legislative branch.* All the colonies had **legislatures** that were responsible for making laws. All but Pennsylvania were similar to the Parliament in Britain with an "upper house" such as the House of Lords and a "lower house" such as the House of Commons. Members of the upper house were either appointed by the governor or elected by the most wealthy property owners of the colony. The lower house was elected by all the men in the colony who owned a certain amount of property. Pennsylvania was an exception; it had only one house. More independent of the executive branch than the British Parliament, the colonial legislatures would eventually become the strongest of the three branches of government.

- *A judicial branch.* This branch was made up of judges called **magistrates** who were usually appointed by the governor. Their responsibility was to handle conflicts over the laws and to preside at trials of those accused of breaking the law. They also were responsible for making sure the colonies were being governed in a way that was consistent with English law and tradition.

Checks and Balances

Power was separated and in some cases shared among these branches, so that the use of power by one branch could be checked by that of another. That is, the power of one branch could be opposed and therefore limited by the power of another branch. The powers of the governors were checked because they could not

- **Collect taxes without the consent of the legislature**

- **Imprison people without a trial by a magistrate**

- **Set their own salaries**

The legislatures' powers were checked by

- **Reliance on the governor to enforce the laws that they passed**

- **The power of the judges to make sure they did not make laws that violated those of England**

- **The veto power held in some colonies by the governor**

The powers of the judges were checked by

- **Their being appointed by the governor**

- **The governor or legislature having the power to remove them if their decisions seemed inappropriate**

- **Their reliance on the governor to enforce their decisions**

- **The basic right of every Englishman to a trial by a jury of his peers from the community**

How did early colonial governments reflect the ideas of English constitutionalism?

Courtesy of the Library of Congress.

Representative Government and the Right to Vote

One of the most important constitutional developments during the colonial period was the growth of representative institutions in government. Representative government began soon after the first colonies were established. The first representative assembly was held in Virginia as early as 1619. The right of colonists to elect representatives was seen as a way to

- **Reduce the possibility that members of government would violate the people's rights**

- **Make sure that at least a part of the government could be counted on to respond to the needs and interests of the people, or at least of those people who had the right to vote. It also established firmly the principle that those governed could not be taxed without their consent or that of their representatives.**

Why Colonial Governments Became More Representative than Britain's

Similar to their English counterparts, the American colonists believed that the security of life and liberty depended upon the security of property. Thus, property had to be protected. This explains why in the colonies as well as England there was a property requirement for the enjoyment of political rights like voting. If one of the purposes of government was to protect property, it seemed reasonable to limit **suffrage** to those who possessed at least a small amount of property.

Fifty acres was the usual requirement for voting in the colonies. Because land was easily acquired in America, the body of eligible voters was proportionally larger than in England and the colonial legislatures were accordingly more representative. The economic opportunities in America meant that a larger proportion of colonial society enjoyed political rights than was the case in England.

There were other important differences between elections to the colonial legislatures and those to Parliament. More colonial elections offered the voters a choice of candidates. The colonial legislators were elected more frequently than members of Parliament, who usually faced reelection only once in seven years.

Unlike their British counterparts, colonial legislators usually came from the districts they represented and were considered to be the agents of their **constituents**' interests. By the time of the Revolution, members of the British Parliament, on the other hand, were said to be representative of the interests of the nation as a whole. The colonists were considered part of the British nation; therefore, the British argued, the colonies were represented in Parliament (see Figure 2.4.2).

Figure 2.4.2: Why did more people in America enjoy the right to vote than in England?

Courtesy of the Center for Civic Education.

The Basic Rights Most Americans Enjoyed

The royal charter that established the Jamestown colony in Virginia in 1607 declared that

[T]he persons that shall dwell within the colony shall have all Liberties as if they had been abiding and born within this our realm of England or any other of our said dominions.

Similar guarantees were included in the royal charters establishing Massachusetts, Maryland, and other colonies. Such guarantees echoed the ideals of the Magna Carta—that all Englishmen, wherever they went, enjoyed certain fundamental rights, which needed to be confirmed from time to time in official documents.

This tradition became a fundamental part of American constitutionalism and led eventually to the U.S. Bill of Rights. The first of the colonial charters of rights was the **Massachusetts Body of Liberties,** adopted in 1641. This charter secured the rule of law and protection of basic rights of persons living in that colony against any abuse of power by the colony's magistrates. In some respects this document was America's first bill of rights.

Why did the American colonists believe they enjoyed the same rights they had in England?

Courtesy of the Library of Congress.

No man shall be arrested, restrayned, banished nor anywayes punished . . . unless by vertue of some express laws of the country warranting the same.

The Body of Liberties guaranteed trial by jury, free elections, and the right of free men to own property. It also made it illegal for government to take property away without fair compensation. It prohibited forced self-incrimination as well as cruel and unusual punishment, rights that later were incorporated into the U.S. Bill of Rights. Although it limited suffrage in Massachusetts, the Body of Liberties granted nonvoters certain political rights, including the right of petition, which was to become part of the First Amendment.

Similar chartered guarantees of basic rights were later passed in other colonies. In addition to such guarantees as freedom from illegal arrest, trial by jury, and no taxation without consent, Pennsylvania's first constitution provided for freedom of conscience. By the eighteenth century all of America's colonies had come to acknowledge this basic right, though in some colonies full enjoyment of political rights remained restricted to those belonging to the established religion in the colony.

Most of these charters guaranteed rights that were familiar to English law. Sometimes they went even further than English law. The Massachusetts Body of Liberties, for example, was followed seven years later by an even more comprehensive code of laws, called **The Laws and Liberties** (1648). This code abolished the laws of primogeniture. It also provided more humane treatment of convicted criminals and debtors and simplified the judicial process.

Points to Ponder

1. Did the colonists enjoy a greater degree of representation in their local governments than British citizens had in Parliament? Why or why not?

2. Why were voting rights limited to men of property in the colonies and England despite the belief in representative government?

3. In what ways did the colonists' experience with limited self-rule for over 150 years affect their ideas about government?

> **Key Note Term**
>
> **The Laws and Liberties**—code that abolished the laws of primogeniture and provided a more humane treatment of criminals

Did All Americans Enjoy These Rights?

Not all Americans, however, enjoyed the rights that had been secured in the colonial constitutions. In some colonies the right to vote or hold office remained restricted to male Protestants, in others it was restricted to those who belonged to the established state religion.

Women were denied political rights. Colonial laws limited their ability to own property and manage their own legal and personal affairs. Although laws varied in different colonies, women usually had the legal status of underage children. When they married, they lost most of their legal identity to their husbands. According to English law,

> *The husband and wife, are one person . . . the very being or legal existence of the woman is suspended during the marriage.*

There were also in the colonies a large number of **indentured servants,** most of them white, who were little better than slaves while they completed their period of service. The most glaring example of the violation of rights was the permanent enslavement of Africans, which had become well established in the American colonies by the eighteenth century. Slaves, who made up 20 percent of the population at the time of the Revolution, were treated as property and thus denied their basic human rights. Much of the prosperity enjoyed by colonial Americans came from slave labor.

The contradiction between the colonists' demands for liberty and their continued tolerance of slavery was often noted by the British at the time of the American Revolution. As one English observer asked, *"How is it that we hear the loudest yelps for liberty among the drivers of negroes?"*

The Reverend Samuel Hopkins criticized his fellow Americans for *"making a vain parade of being advocates for the liberties of mankind, while . . . you at the same time are continuing this lawless, cruel, inhuman, and abominable practice of enslaving your fellow creatures."*

> **Key Note Term**
>
> **indentured servant**— voluntary servants who sold their labor for a period of four to seven years in exchange for passage to America

Evaluating the Institution of Slavery by Using the Natural Rights Philosophy

Twenty percent (700,000) of the 3,500,000 people living in the colonies in 1776 were enslaved Africans. Slavery flourished in the plantation economy of the southern colonies, but existed elsewhere and was legally recognized throughout the colonies. New York City had a significant slave population, as did New England.

There was some opposition to slavery among the population of free citizens as well as among the slaves themselves. Some opponents sought its peaceful abolition; others were willing to use violent or illegal means.

How does this diagram of a typical slave transport vessel show the inhumanity of the slave trade?

1. How might the natural rights philosophy be used to oppose slavery in the colonies?

2. How might the supporters of slavery also have appealed to the natural rights philosophy to justify their cause?

3. Is slavery compatible with the natural rights philosophy? Explain.

DESCRIPTION OF A SLAVE SHIP.

How does this diagram of a typical slave transport vessel show the inhumanity of the slave trade?

Courtesy of the Peabody Museum of Salem.

How the Colonial Experience Prepared Americans for Independence

By the time Americans became independent, they had acquired more than 150 years of experience in self-government at the local level. Such self-government had become necessary because of the colonies' distance from the government in England. This long experience in self-government would become invaluable in building a new nation.

The colonists had adapted the governmental institutions and constitutional principles inherited from England to meet their own special needs. They had created colonial constitutions that embodied such important principles as the rule of law and a separation of powers between the executive, legislative, and judicial functions of government, thus limiting the power of government through checks and balances.

Perhaps most important to America's future were the legacies of strong representative government and written guarantees of basic rights. As they developed, colonial legislatures became more representative and independent than the British Parliament. Colonial charters guaranteeing fundamental rights became treasured reminders of the colonists' constitutional inheritance.

Together, these two traditions of representative government and written guarantees of rights would provide a basis for the American Revolution.

Ask Yourself . . .

1. In what ways were eighteenth-century American and British societies similar or dissimilar in terms of the rights of individual liberty, equality of opportunity, and property?

2. What effect did colonial experiences have on the Founders' views about rights and government?

3. In what ways were liberty and opportunity for women and minorities restricted because of limited property rights in eighteenth-century America?

4. Do you think the same degree of social and economic opportunity exists for immigrants to America today? What has remained the same? What has changed?

Britain's New Policy toward the Colonies

After 1763, several factors caused the British to exert more control over the American colonies than in the previous 150 years. Britain had incurred large debts in its great victory over the French in the **Seven Years War** of 1756–1763. In North America this war was known as the French and Indian War. The British government was under heavy pressure to reduce taxes at home. To the British ministers this meant the American colonists paying a fair share of the war debt. Between the end of the war in 1763 and the Declaration of Independence in 1776, Britain tried to increase control of the colonies. To reduce tensions with the Native Americans, the British government passed a law forbidding the colonists from settling in the western territories. To raise revenue, the government increased control of trade and customs duties. The Stamp Act of 1765, introduced a new kind of tax on the colonists by

Key Note Term

Seven Years War—a series of dynastic and colonial wars between England and France; the American phase, fought between 1754 and 1764, is known as the French and Indian War

Why were the colonists angered by the Stamp Act of 1765?

Courtesy of the Metropolitan Museum of Art, New York.

imposing duties on stamps needed for official documents. To the British these measures seemed reasonable and moderate, but they had a common flaw. They lacked a fundamental principle of the natural rights philosophy—the consent of the governed.

The Colonists Resist British Control

Generations of colonists had grown used to very little interference from the British government in their affairs. The new policies meant a change in these conditions. Although some colonists accepted the new measures, many others resisted. New trade restrictions and taxes meant some colonists would lose money. Perhaps more important, the new regulations challenged their belief in representative government. Locke had said,

. . . the supreme power cannot take from any man any part of his property without his own consent . . . ,

Key Note Terms

Sons of Liberty—an organization of radicals created in 1765 in the American colonies to express colonial opposition to the Stamp Act

Stamp Act Congress—a meeting in New York in 1765, of twenty-seven delegates from nine colonies, the congress was the first example of united colonial action in the developing struggle against Great Britain

Quartering Act—also known as the Mutiny Act, the law passed by Parliament that authorized colonial governors to requisition certain buildings for the use, or "quartering" of British troops

that is, the consent of the majority, given it either by themselves or their representatives chosen by them.

The colonists believed that each man had a natural right to life, liberty, and property. Consequently, they thought that tax laws should only be passed in their own colonial legislatures, in which they were represented. "No taxation without representation" had become an established belief of settlers in the American colonies.

Colonists calling themselves the **Sons of Liberty** rioted against the Stamp Act. Representatives from the colonies met in the **Stamp Act Congress** to organize resistance—the first such gathering in American history. The British government's response created new grievances. For example, the **Quartering Act** of 1765, forced the colonists to shelter British soldiers in their homes. To the colonists this violated a basic guarantee of the Petition of Right.

Colonists charged with various crimes were transported to England for trials that were frequently delayed. The **Boston Massacre** of 1770, helped convince many Americans that the British government was prepared to use military and arbitrary rule to force the colonists into obedience. The **Tea Act** of 1773, reasserted the right of Parliament to tax the colonists and led to the **Boston Tea Party** (see Figure 2.4.3). The British government responded angrily with what were called the **Intolerable Acts,** closing Boston harbor to all trade. These measures attacked representative government in Massachusetts by giving more power to the royal governor, limiting town meetings, weakening the court system, and authorizing a massive occupation of the colony by British troops.

What basic rights are violated when the government orders private citizens to "quarter" soldiers?

Figure 2.4.3: Do you think Locke would have supported the colonists' actions in the Boston Tea Party? Why? Why not?

Courtesy of Bill Jacklin/Bridgeman Art Library.

Identifying Violations of Rights

Each of the following situations is based on the experiences of colonists in America. Each has at least one British violation of a right that Americans thought they should have. If you had been an American colonist at the time, what rights would you claim on the basis of such experiences?

1. Your name is Mary Strong. You have lived in Charlestown most of your life and have strong feelings about how Massachusetts is being governed. Whenever you speak your mind freely, you find yourself arrested and put in an iron device that fits over your head like a mask to prevent you from talking.

2. Your name is Elsbeth Merrill. While you were baking bread this afternoon and awaiting the return of your husband, an agent of the king arrived to inform you that you must shelter four British soldiers in your home.

3. Your name is Lemuel Adams and you have a warehouse full of goods near Boston Harbor. The king's magistrate gives British officials a **writ of assistance** that enables them to search all homes, stores, and warehouses by the harbor to look for evidence of smuggling.

4. Your name is James Otis. You represent colonists who have been imprisoned and are being denied their right to a trial by a jury from their own communities. You argue that to deny their traditional rights as British subjects is illegal because it violates the principles of the British constitution. The royal magistrate denies your request and sends the prisoners to England for trial.

5. Your name is William Bradford. You have been arrested and your printing press in Philadelphia destroyed for printing an article criticizing the deputy governor. In the article you said the governor was like "a large cocker spaniel about five-foot five."

Should publishers be prohibited from printing criticisms of government leaders? Why? Why not?

Colonists Organize to Resist British Control

Committees of Correspondence were formed to publicize colonial opposition and coordinate resistance throughout the colonies. In the fall of 1774, 12 of the 13 colonies sent representatives to a meeting in Philadelphia to decide on the best response to the actions of the British government. The meeting was the **First Continental Congress.** Its members agreed to impose their own ban on trade with Great Britain in an attempt to force the British government to change its policies toward the colonies. British officials, however, considered that decision an act of irresponsible defiance of authority and ordered the arrest of some leading colonists in Massachusetts.

By this time many of the more radical colonists, especially in New England, were beginning to prepare for war against Great Britain. They believed it was the right of the people to overthrow any government that no longer protected their rights. The colonists formed civilian militia of **Minutemen,** supposedly ready at a minute's notice to respond to the British attack that everyone expected.

On April 19, 1775, British troops tried to march to Concord, Massachusetts, where they had heard that the Minutemen had hidden arms and ammunition. The colonists were alerted by Paul Revere and William Dawes who rode through the countryside warning people that the British were about to attack. On that day, at the towns of Lexington and Concord, war broke out between the colonies and Great Britain—the "shot heard around the world" had been fired.

What ideas were used to justify the Revolutionary War?

Courtesy of the National Archives.

Understanding the Purpose of the Declaration of Independence

With Americans fighting the British, Richard Henry Lee of Virginia introduced a resolution in the Continental Congress on June 7, 1776, that called for a declaration of independence. The **Declaration of Independence** was accordingly drafted by Thomas Jefferson. The Declaration announced the final, momentous step in the colonies' resistance to the British government. It challenged the **sovereignty** of the crown.

Every state, no matter what its form of government or constitution, must have an authority beyond which there is no appeal. Sovereignty means that supreme authority in a state.

Sovereignty in Britain rests in the British Parliament. Parliament can, as some have said, "do anything but make a man a woman." It could, if it wished, repeal the English Bill of Rights or the remaining guarantees of Magna Carta or in other ways change Britain's unwritten constitution. Parliament would not likely use its sovereign power in such ways because of respect for the unwritten constitution by its members and by the British people as a whole.

Rebellion against the sovereignty of a government to which the colonists and generations of their forbears had sworn allegiance was a serious matter. Members of the Continental Congress believed it important to justify this action to other nations, to win both sympathy and active support.

Why did colonial leaders believe a formal declaration of independence was needed?

Courtesy of the National Archives.

The Main Ideas and Arguments of the Declaration

The Declaration of Independence is the best summary available of the colonists' ideas about government and their complaints about British rule. It does not make an appeal on behalf of the king's loyal subjects to the fundamental "rights of Englishmen." The Declaration renounces the monarchy itself and appeals to those natural rights common to all men and women everywhere. It identifies sovereignty with the people.

1. **The rights of the people are based on natural law that is a higher law than laws made by men. Its existence is "self-evident." It is given by God and is "unalienable." Neither constitutions nor governments can violate this higher law. If a government violates the law and deprives the people of their rights, they have the right to change that government or abolish it and form a new government.**

2. **A compact or agreement existed between the colonists and the king. By the terms of this compact, the colonists consented to be governed by the king—deriving his "just powers from the consent of the Governed"—so long as he protected their rights to "life, liberty, and the pursuit of happiness."**

3. **"Whenever any form of government becomes destructive of those Ends" for which government is created, it is the right of the people to "alter or abolish it" and to create a new government that will serve those ends.**

4. **The king had violated the compact by repeatedly acting with Parliament to deprive the colonists of those rights he was supposed to protect. These violations and other abuses of power, the Declaration argued, suggest the creation of an "absolute Tyranny" over the colonies by a "Tyrant" who is "unfit to be the Ruler of a free People." He is accused of:**

   - **Seeking to destroy the authority of the colonial legislatures by dissolving some and refusing to approve the laws passed by others**

   - **Obstructing the administration of justice by refusing to approve laws for support of the colonial judiciary and making judges dependent on his will alone**

   - **Keeping standing armies among the people in time of peace without the approval of the colonial legislatures**

   - **Quartering soldiers among the civilian population**

   - **Imposing taxes without consent**

   - **Depriving colonists of the right to trial by jury**

   - **Attacking the colonial charters, abolishing laws, and changing fundamentally the constitutions of colonial governments.**

5. **The colonists therefore had the right to withdraw their consent to be governed by the king of Great Britain and to establish their own government as "Free and Independent States . . . absolved from all allegiance to the British Crown."**

What problems did the newly independent states face?

Courtesy of the National Archives.

The American Revolution Impacts American Constitutionalism

During the first years of independence, the grievances that had persuaded the American colonists to seek independence had an effect on how Americans shaped their state and national governments. The abuses of power by the British government made them distrustful of strong central government and strong executive power. The violation of such fundamental rights such as the following convinced them to secure these rights by formal declarations in the new state constitutions and eventually in the U.S. Constitution.

- **Freedom of speech and assembly**
- **Trial by jury**
- **Security from illegal search and seizure of property, and**
- **Protection from military rule**

What Do You Think?

1. The Declaration of Independence states that people have a right to abolish their government. Under what circumstances, if any, do you think such an action is justified? Would the Founders agree?

2. Would the Declaration of Independence justify a state leaving the union if a majority of its citizens wished to do so? Why or why not?

3. What was the intended audience for the Declaration of Independence? Does this focus explain the Declaration of Independence's appeal to "natural rights" instead of to "rights of Englishmen"?

Conclusion

This lesson described how the basic ideas of constitutional government were developed and used in the American colonies before they gained their independence from Britain. You learned about social and economic conditions that were special to America. These conditions sometimes required old ideas to be adapted or discarded. Sometimes the creation of entirely new solutions was necessary.

You learned about the early development of America's own traditions of constitutional government. You should be able to explain how the differences between colonial America and Europe affected the Founders' political views. You also should have a better understanding of why the American colonists attached special importance to such constitutional principles as written guarantees of basic rights and representative government.

You also learned that the growth of the American colonies raised issues that were difficult to resolve peaceably. You considered the circumstances that produced the Declaration of Independence, as well as the major ideas about government and natural rights included in that document.

You should be able to describe British policies toward the colonies that the American colonists believed violated basic principles of constitutional government. You also should be able to explain the reasons why Americans resisted these policies and how this resistance led to the Declaration of Independence. Finally, you should be able to describe the arguments justifying the separation of the colonies from Great Britain that are found in the Declaration of Independence.

Next, you will learn about state constitutionalism. You will learn about the similarities and differences between state and national constitutionalism.

Lesson Review

1. What was the Mayflower Compact? Why was it drafted? How does it reflect the idea that government should be based on consent?

2. How would you describe the economic, social, and political conditions of life in colonial America? How were these conditions important in the development of American ideas about government?

3. What examples can you identify of written guarantees of basic rights in colonial America? How were these written guarantees important in the development of Americans' ideas about government?

4. How would you explain the term "sovereignty"? What was the conflict between Great Britain and the colonies over sovereignty? How was this conflict resolved?

5. What are the basic ideas and arguments set forth in the Declaration of Independence? Why was it written?

Lesson 5

State Constitutions

Key Terms

absolute veto
higher law
legislative supremacy
override
political guarantees
popular sovereignty
procedural guarantees of due process
representation
social contract
state declarations of rights
veto
Virginia Declaration of Rights

What You Will Learn to Do

- Examine how state constitutions support protection of individual rights

Linked Core Abilities

- Communicate using verbal, non-verbal, visual, and written techniques
- Apply critical thinking techniques

Skills and Knowledge You Will Gain Along the Way

- Explain the purpose of the state declarations of rights
- Explain the value of checks and balances
- Compare the early state constitutions and current state constitutions
- Define key words contained in this lesson

Did the Revolution return the colonists to a state of nature? Why?

Courtesy of the National Archives.

Introduction

The American Revolution returned the colonists to a state of nature. Colonial governments under British authority ceased to exist. New governments would have to be created, a task the newly independent states initiated soon after the war commenced. In this lesson you examine the main features of the written constitutions the thirteen new states created using the basic ideas of the natural rights philosophy, republicanism, and constitutional government.

Why the Colonies Returned to a "State of Nature"

In terms of the natural rights philosophy, the American Revolution returned the colonists to a state of nature. The old colonial governments under the authority of the British ceased to exist. New governments would have to be created. Soon after the Revolutionary War started in 1775, the 13 states began to develop their own written constitutions. Never before had so many new governments been created using the basic ideas of the natural rights philosophy, republicanism, and constitutional government.

Six Basic Ideas Included in the State Constitutions

The experiments of the new American states in constitution-making provided the Framers with valuable experience that later greatly influenced their writing of the

Key Note Terms

representation—the state or condition of serving as an official delegate, agent, or spokesperson

higher law—as used in describing a legal system, refers to the superiority of one set of laws over another

social contract—the agreement among all the people in a society to give up part of their freedom to a government in return for the protection of their natural rights by that government

popular sovereignty—the natural rights concept that ultimate political authority rests with the people

Constitution of the United States. The following basic ideas were included in these state constitutions:

- **Higher law and natural rights**
- **Social contract**
- **Popular sovereignty**
- **Representation** and the right to vote
- **Legislative supremacy**
- **Checks and balances**

Higher Law and Natural Rights

Every state constitution was considered a **higher law** and was based on the idea that the purpose of government was to preserve and protect citizens' natural rights to life, liberty, and property.

Social Contract

Each state constitution also made it clear that its government was formed as a result of a **social contract**—an agreement among its people to create a government to protect their natural rights.

Popular Sovereignty

In all the new state constitutions sovereign authority existed in the people. The authority to govern was delegated to the government by the sovereign people. This is considered **popular sovereignty.**

Representation and the Right to Vote

One of the most significant characteristics about each state constitution was the importance it placed on representation of the people in their government. All the state constitutions created legislatures that were composed of elected representatives of the people. Most of these constitutions required annual elections to their legislatures.

Some state constitutions gave the right to vote for representatives to all white male taxpayers. In most states, this right was limited to people who owned a specified amount of property, as it had been when the states were colonies. Since property was relatively easy to acquire in America, about 70 percent of adult white males could vote.

In seven states, free African Americans and Native Americans could vote if they met the property requirements. In New Jersey, the vote was given to "all inhabitants . . . of full age, who were worth fifty pounds" and who met a twelve-month residency requirement. Under these rules, both women and free African Americans were able to vote until 1807, when the law in New Jersey was rewritten to exclude women. Twelve states specifically denied women the right to vote by inserting the word "male" in their constitutions.

Legislative Supremacy

Legislative supremacy means "a government in which most of the power is given to the legislature." Most state constitutions relied on a strong legislature and majority rule to protect the rights of citizens. This reliance continued a development that had begun in the colonial period when the legislatures had become strong.

All the state constitutions included some separation of powers. This reflected the former colonists' distrust of executive power which they believed had been abused under British rule. The belief in legislative supremacy was based on the following:

- **The legislative branch of government, composed of representatives who are elected by the voters and vulnerable to removal by the voters, is the most democratic branch of government. Therefore, in a government based on popular sovereignty it is considered the safest branch in which to place the most power and the most likely to protect the rights of citizens and promote their welfare.**

- **The executive branch should not be trusted with much power because it is not easily controlled by the people. You may remember that the colonists' greatest problems with the British government had been with its executive branch—the king's ministers and the royal governors in the colonies.**

- **The colonists also distrusted the judicial branch—in this case, the king's magistrates—who tried them for breaking British law. The following examples of a preference for legislative supremacy can be found in the state constitutions:**

  - **The constitutions of most of the new states provided for executive branches but made them dependent on the legislatures. Pennsylvania's new constitution eliminated the office of governor altogether and replaced it with a twelve-man council. In other states, legislatures were given the power to select the governor or to control his salary.**

  - **Governors were allowed to stay in office for only one year. This limit was an attempt to make sure that the governor would not have time to gain much power while in office.**

  - **Appointments made by a governor had to be approved by the legislature.**

  - **Governors in most of the state constitutions were almost totally excluded from the process of lawmaking, which the legislatures kept to themselves. In all the states, the governor no longer had an absolute veto over legislation. He could still refuse to approve a proposed law in some states, but the legislatures in those states could override his veto by passing the proposed law again.**

  - **State legislatures exercised influence over the judiciary through control of salaries and length of tenure.**

Checks and Balances

Although the powers in the state governments were unbalanced in favor of strong legislatures, there were some checks provided by their state constitutions. Most of these checks existed within the legislatures themselves. For example, in every state except Pennsylvania and Georgia, the legislature was divided into two houses, just as was the case in the British Parliament. Since most important decisions had to be made by both houses, each had a way to check the power of the other house. Unlike Parliament and the colonial governments, however, both houses of the new state legislatures were made up of representatives elected by the people.

The voters could check the legislators' power by electing new representatives to both houses if they did not like the way the government worked.

Key Note Term

legislative supremacy— a system of government in which the legislative branch has the most power

Key Note Terms

absolute veto—the inviolable power to cancel or nullify a legislative act

override—to declare null and void; set aside

veto—the constitutional power of the President to refuse to sign a bill passed by Congress, thereby preventing it from becoming law

How Was the Massachusetts Constitution Different?

In 1780, Massachusetts became the last state to ratify a new constitution. Written principally by John Adams, the Massachusetts constitution was different from those of the other states. In addition to relying on popular representation as a means of preventing the abuse of power, it used a system of separation of powers and checks and balances. It gave government more effective checks on the powers of the state's legislature.

Because the Massachusetts constitution is more similar to the present Constitution of the United States than the other state constitutions, it is worth looking at in some detail. The following are some important characteristics of the Massachusetts constitution.

A Strong Executive Branch

Under the Massachusetts constitution, the governor was elected by the people. The writers of this constitution believed that because the governor would be elected by the people, it would be safe to trust him with greater power so that he would be able to protect their rights and welfare.

To enable the governor to be more independent of the legislature and to allow him to check the legislature's use of power, the Massachusetts constitution contained the following provisions:

- **The governor's salary was fixed and could not be changed by the legislature**

- **The governor had the power to veto laws made by the legislature, and his veto could only be overridden by a two-thirds vote of the legislature**

- **The governor could appoint officials to the executive branch and judges to the judicial branch**

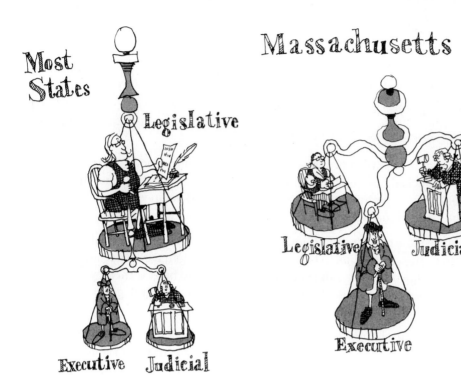

How did the Massachusetts constitution differ from those of the other states? Why did the Massachusetts constitution provide for a strong executive branch?

Representation of Different Groups in Society

Several other parts of the Massachusetts constitution show how that government was organized more like the British model of government than were those of the other states. This state constitution separated powers among the different classes in society to prevent one group from dominating the others. The Massachusetts constitution divided the people of the state into groups based on their wealth since there was no royalty or nobility.

- **Only people with a large amount of property could elect the governor**
- **People with slightly less property could vote to elect members of the upper house of the state legislature**
- **People with the minimum amount of property that qualified them to vote could vote for members of the lower house**

Thus, the Massachusetts state constitution expressed the classical republican ideal of mixed government. Consequently, it provided for more balance among the powers of the different branches of government. It did not make the legislature the most powerful branch as did the other state constitutions. This approach reveals different beliefs about the best ways to prevent the abuse of power by members of government.

The constitutions of the other states were based primarily on the idea that representation of the people in a strong state legislature was the best way to protect their rights. They reflected a basic trust in political power held directly by a majority of the people.

The Massachusetts constitution reflected a more skeptical view of human nature and of unchecked power held by any group in society. It was based on the idea that representation, separation of powers, and checks and balances were all essential for the protection of the rights of the people.

None of the state constitutions, however, relied entirely on the form of their governments to protect individual liberties. Most of them began with a declaration of rights. By doing this, they indicated that the citizens to be governed by these new constitutions possessed certain basic rights that existed prior to government and that no constitution or government could take away.

Americans in the colonial era attached great importance to guarantees of basic rights. Although the lists of rights differed somewhat from state to state, they were all based on the idea that people have certain inherent rights that must be protected. It was only after safeguarding these rights at the very start that the authors of these constitutions believed it proper to form state governments.

Taken together, the rights protected in the state declarations included all the fundamental rights guaranteed today in our Bill of Rights. By looking at these declarations and how they were developed, we can learn a great deal about how we came to have the rights we enjoy today under both our state and federal constitutions.

Important Ideas in the Virginia Declaration of Rights

On June 12, 1776, Virginia became the first state to adopt a declaration of rights, almost a month before the colonies declared their independence from Great Britain. The **Virginia Declaration of Rights** helped convince other colonies to vote for independence and influenced Thomas Jefferson's writing of the Declaration of Independence itself.

The Virginia Declaration was written primarily by George Mason (see Figure 2.5.1), who later opposed the ratification of the U.S. Constitution because it did not include a bill of rights. In writing Virginia's own bill of rights, Mason relied heavily on the writings of John Locke. He also was influenced by the ideas of classical republicanism and by the American colonial experience.

The Virginia Declaration of Rights stated:

- **That all power is derived from and kept by the people.**

- **That all men are by nature equally free and independent, and have certain inherent rights, of which, when they enter into a state of society, they cannot, by any compact, deprive or divest their posterity; namely, the enjoyment of life and**

liberty, with the means of acquiring and possessing property, and pursuing and obtaining happiness and safety.

- **The government is, or ought to be, instituted for the common benefit, protection, and security of the people. If a government does not serve these purposes, the people have an unalienable right to alter or abolish it.**

The Virginia Declaration also included many of the rights we enjoy today under both our state and federal bills of rights, such as the right to trial by jury, protection against forced self-incrimination and cruel and unusual punishments, freedom of the press, and the free exercise of religious beliefs. Concerning the right to religious freedom it stated:

That religion, or the duty we owe to our Creator, and the manner of discharging it, can be directed only by reason and conviction, not by force or violence; and therefore, all men are equally entitled to the free exercise of religion, according to the dictates of conscience.

The Virginia Declaration ended with a statement based on the ideas of classical republicanism about civic virtue and religious values:

No free government, or the blessings of liberty, can be preserved to any people but by a firm adherence to justice, moderation, temperance, frugality, and virtue. . . . it is the mutual duty of all to practice Christian forbearance, love, and charity, towards each other.

Lesson 5   State Constitutions   **121**

The framers of the Virginia Declaration believed that listing rights and establishing a constitutional government were not enough to guarantee people their freedom. They argued that each individual must accept the responsibility to live according to certain moral principles and ideals.

It is important to note that the Virginia Declaration omitted some important rights found in other state declarations and later made part of the U.S. Constitution.

Examining Historical Documents

Work with a study partner to complete the following exercise.

1. Refer to the Virginia Declaration of Rights in the Reference Section to this text. Identify specific examples of the following basic ideas:

   - Natural rights
     - Social contract
     - Individual rights
     - Limited government
   - Classical republicanism
     - Civic virtue
     - Common welfare
     - Political rights

2. Which historical experiences of the colonists seemed to have the greatest influences on the authors of the state declarations?

3. Why do you think that, generally, state constitutions protected rights first and then created governments with limited powers?

Rights Protected by the Other States

Key Note Term

political guarantees—
guarantee of varied rights

Most states adopted declarations or bills of rights that resembled Virginia's. The few that did not have such declarations included guarantees of certain rights in the main body of their constitutions. Similar to Virginia's the other states' declarations began with statements about natural rights, popular sovereignty, and the purposes of government. Some declarations also included the idea that civic virtue and a commitment to certain moral and religious principles were essential to preserving freedom.

Other states' declarations varied in the rights they chose to include or leave out. Most included such **political guarantees** as

- **The right to vote**
- **Free and frequent elections**
- **Freedom of speech and of the press**
- **The right to petition the government**
- **No taxation without representation**

They all included important **procedural guarantees of due process** such as

- **The rights to counsel and trial by jury**
- **Protection from illegal search and seizure**
- **Protection from forced self-incrimination, excessive bail and fines, and cruel and unusual punishment**

Most of the state declarations, including Virginia's, expressed a fear of military tyranny by condemning professional standing armies in time of peace and the quartering of troops in civilian homes. Many endorsed the idea of "well regulated" civilian militia and the right to bear arms.

Vermont took its commitment to natural rights literally by becoming the first state to outlaw the institution of slavery.

Ways the State Declarations Differ from the U.S. Bill of Rights

The **state declarations of rights** would have a great influence on the later drafting and adoption of the U.S. Bill of Rights. Many states drew from their own declarations to propose the rights that should be included in the federal version. The principal writer of the U.S. Bill of Rights, James Madison of Virginia, was strongly influenced by his own state's Declaration of Rights.

The state declarations, however, differed from the U.S. Bill of Rights in many ways. They resemble more the Declaration of Independence. They were written as preambles to the state constitutions to establish the moral and philosophical foundations of the state governments. They describe the purpose of government and set forth the principles of the natural rights philosophy and classical republicanism.

The circumstances at the time prompted the authors to make these pronouncements. The state declarations were written while Americans were in the midst of fighting a revolution. The authors of these documents were principled, law-abiding citizens who wanted to explain to their fellow citizens and the rest of the world why the violation of their rights had forced them into armed rebellion.

The U.S. Bill of Rights, on the other hand, was written after independence had been won and the Constitution had created a new government for the nation. The principles of government were already established. The Framers of the Bill of Rights did not believe there was a need to list those principles again. What was needed was a list of specific rights that should be protected from this new and stronger national government. The Bill of Rights is such a list.

The Bill of Rights was to go much further than the state declarations in its guarantee of freedom of religion. Several states, as well as Virginia, provided for the free exercise of religion, but at the same time permitted state religious establishments. They allowed tax money in their states to be spent to support a particular religion or denomination. In most states there continued to be religious requirements for holding public office that excluded Roman Catholics and Jews. The Bill of Rights not

Key Note Term

procedural guarantees of due process—refers to those clauses in the U.S. Constitution that protect individuals from unreasonable and unfair governmental procedures

Key Note Term

state declaration of rights—the citizens to be governed by these new constitutions possessed certain basic rights that existed prior to government and that no constitution or government could take away

only provides for freedom of religious practice, it also prohibits the federal government from passing any law for the establishment of a particular national religion. The Bill of Rights, therefore, protects equality as well as freedom of religion.

Conclusion

After declaring their independence from Great Britain, the colonists had to decide how they would govern themselves. The Articles of Confederation, which were the first attempt at establishing a government, were thought to be inadequate by leaders such as Madison, Washington, and Hamilton. Fifty-five men met in Philadelphia in 1787, and wrote and adopted the United States Constitution. These men became known as the Framers. The Constitution was not universally acclaimed, and its adoption and ratification gave rise to discussions of the most basic questions about political life and governmental institutions. In this lesson, you learned why the Articles of Confederation were replaced by the Constitution. You also learn the reasons the Framers created the United States government as they did. Different opinions held by Americans about the merits of the new Constitution also are presented.

Lesson Review

1. What basic ideas about government were contained in the new state constitutions?

2. Define the term "popular sovereignty."

3. What were the important differences between the Massachusetts constitution and the other state constitutions?

4. What important ideas did the Virginia Declaration of Rights contain? How was this document influential throughout the colonies?

Chapter 3

Creating the Constitution

Lesson 1

Articles of Confederation 1781

Key Terms

factions
loyalists
majority rule
national government

Chapter 3

What You Will Learn to Do

- Determine why the Founders created the Articles of Confederation and the concerns that resulted

Linked Core Abilities

- Communicate using verbal, non-verbal, visual, and written techniques
- Apply critical thinking techniques

Skills and Knowledge You Will Gain Along the Way

- Explain why Americans needed a national government after the colonies declared independence from Great Britain
- Explain how the Founders designed the first constitution, the Articles of Confederation
- Compare the advantages and disadvantages of the Articles of Confederation
- Define key words contained in this lesson

Introduction

The first government created by the Founders did not work well. Knowing the shortcomings of that government is important in understanding that unless a government is organized properly, it may not work very well. It also helps in understanding why our government is organized the way it is. In this lesson you find out why the Founders created the Articles of Confederation, the way they did it, and the problems that resulted from a weak national government.

How the Articles of Confederation Were Created

In 1776, each of the newly independent states created its own government. In addition to these state governments, Americans also considered creating a national government to manage relationships among the states and to unite the states in their relations with the rest of the world.

A **national government** was necessary to control trade among the states, and between the states and foreign nations, and to manage conflicts among the states about such issues as borders. Some leaders had seen the need for a national government for some time to deal with foreign relations and economic and commercial problems. Benjamin Franklin, who had proposed a colonial government in 1754, submitted a draft for articles of confederation to the Second Continental Congress in July 1775. Several other proposals were made that summer and fall, but the question of independence from Great Britain for the moment was more important than forming a national government.

On June 7, 1776, Richard Henry Lee introduced a set of resolutions to the Second Continental Congress; one was for independence, the other was to form a national government. From these resolutions came both the Declaration of Independence and the Articles of Confederation.

Problems Addressed in the Articles of Confederation

Two major problems made it difficult for the Continental Congress and the states to accept the Articles of Confederation:

- **The fear of creating a national government that was too strong**
- **The fear that some states would have more power than others in a national government**

Fear of a Strong National Government

After the war against Great Britain had started, each state was like a separate nation with its own constitution and government. To the people, their state was their "country" and all eligible voters could have a voice in government. They could elect

How did independence create a need for a national government?

members of their communities to represent their interests in their state legislatures. The government was close enough to most citizens so they could even participate in some of its activities.

The Founders agreed they needed a central government, but they were afraid of making one that was too strong. Americans believed that the British government had deprived people of their rights, including their right to be represented in government. They thought this was likely to happen with any central government that was both powerful and far away. Consequently, they were convinced that government should be close to the people so they could control it and make certain that it did not violate their rights. Finally, their study of history and political philosophy lead them to believe that republican government could only succeed in small communities where people shared common ideas and beliefs.

The Founders finally arrived at a solution to this problem—they created a weak national government. The government created by the Articles of Confederation was just a central legislature, the Confederation Congress. There were no executive or judicial branches. While Congress could establish courts for certain

Why did the Founders create a weak national government?

New York State Currency

What problems might result from each state issuing its own currency?

Courtesy of the Center for Civic Education.

limited purposes, most legal disputes were handled in state courts. Moreover, Article II states:

Each state retains its sovereignty, freedoms, and independence, and every Power, jurisdiction, and right, which is not by this confederation expressly delegated to the United States, in Congress assembled.

The Articles of Confederation left most of the powers of government with the states; the national government had little power over the states and their citizens. For example:

- **The Confederation Congress did not have any authority over any person in any state; only the state governments had authority over their citizens**

- **Congress did not have the power to collect taxes from the states or from the people directly; it could only request money from the state governments, which were supposed to raise the money from their citizens**

- **Congress did not have the power to regulate trade among the various states**

Fear That Some States Would Dominate Others in the National Government

The leaders in each state wanted to make sure that the new national government would be organized in a way that would not threaten their state's interests. As a result, the most important disagreement was about how states would vote in Congress. Would each state have one vote, or would states with greater population or wealth be given more votes than others? Decisions in the Congress would be made by majority vote. Some leaders were afraid that the majority would use its power for its own interest at the expense of those who were in the minority.

The solution to this problem was to give each state one vote in the Confederation Congress regardless of its population. The Articles also provided, however, that on important matters; for example, whether to declare war, nine states would have to agree. This way the seven smaller states could not outvote the six larger states.

Examining the Advantages and Disadvantages of the Articles of Confederation

Work with a study partner, or in small groups, to complete the following exercise.

Read the following excerpts from the Articles of Confederation. For each excerpt create a list of advantages to the states and/or to the national government resulting from the Article. Create a second list of the disadvantages to the states and/or to the national government resulting from the Article. When you finish, compare your lists and be prepared to share your ideas with the class.

Articles of Confederation

Article II. Each State retains it sovereignty, freedom and independence, and every power . . . which is not by the confederation expressly delegated to the United States, in Congress assembled.

Article V. No State shall be represented in Congress by less than two, nor more than seven members . . . In determining questions in the United States, in Congress assembled, each State shall have one vote.

Article VIII. All charges of war and all other expenses that shall be incurred for the common defense or general welfare . . . shall be defrayed out of a common treasury, which shall be supplied by the several States, in proportion to the value of all land within each State. . . . The taxes for paying that proportion shall be laid and levied by the authority and direction of the Legislatures of the several States. . . .

Article IX. The United States in Congress assembled shall also be the last resort on appeal in all disputes and differences . . . between two or more States. . . .

Article IX. The United States in Congress assembled shall also have the sole and exclusive right and power of regulating the alloy and value of coin struck by their own authority, or by that of the respective States. . . .

Article XIII. . . . nor shall any alteration at any time hereafter be made in any of [these articles]; unless such alteration be agreed to in a Congress of the United States, and be afterwards confirmed by the Legislatures of every state.

Weaknesses in the Articles of Confederation

On March 1, 1781, Maryland became the last state to ratify the Articles. Maryland had wanted western lands to be under the control of Congress, not of individual states. Not until New York, Connecticut, and Virginia surrendered their western claims did Maryland ratify the Articles.

You have seen how the people of the states attempted to deal with their fear of a strong national government by creating a national government that had very limited power. This reflected their belief that power that is not given is power that cannot be misused.

How was Congress's ability to govern hurt by not being able to collect taxes from the states?

The limitations of the Articles of Confederation and the difficulties that arose under them led to the decision to develop our present Constitution. These limitations include:

- *No money and no power to get it.* Congress had no power to tax. All it could do was request that state governments pay certain amounts to support the costs of the national government. This system did not work. Congress had borrowed most of the money it needed to pay for the Revolutionary War from Americans and foreigners, but had no way to pay its debts. The state governments and many of the people living in the states were also deeply in debt after the war. Therefore, when Congress requested $10 million from the states to pay for the costs of fighting the war, the states paid only $1.5 million.

- *No power over the state governments and their citizens.* Congress did not have the power to make laws regulating the behavior of citizens or the states or to force state governments or their citizens to do anything. The citizens could be governed only by their own state governments. This meant that if members of a state government or citizens within a state disobeyed a resolution, recommendation, or request made by the national government, there was no way the national government could make them obey. The Articles clearly stated that each state kept its "sovereignty, freedom, and independence." The national government's inability to make state governments and their citizens live up to treaties it had made led to a serious situation. Not all of the colonists had been in favor of the Revolutionary War; some had remained loyal to Great Britain. Thousands of these people, called **loyalists**, still lived in the United States. When the war was over, the national government signed a peace treaty with Great Britain called the Treaty of Paris. It was intended in part to protect loyalists' rights and ensure that they were treated fairly. Some of these loyalists owned property in the states and some had loaned money to other citizens.

Some state governments refused to respect this treaty. They often made it difficult for loyalists to collect the money owed to them by other citizens. In some cases the states had confiscated the loyalists' property during the war. The national government had no power to force the state governments to respect the property rights of the loyalists or to force individual citizens to pay back money owed to the loyalists. Thus, the national government was powerless to live up to its promise to the British government to protect the rights of these citizens.

- *Unenforceable trade agreements.* Although Congress had the power to make agreements with foreign nations, it did not have the power to make state governments live up to these agreements. This raised another difficulty. Some citizens imported goods from other nations and then refused to pay for them. Not surprisingly, people in foreign countries became reluctant to trade with people in the United States. In addition, when Great Britain recognized how weak Congress was in controlling foreign trade, it closed the West Indies to American commerce. As a result, many Americans lost money because they were unable to sell their goods to people in other nations. Others were not able to buy goods from abroad.

- *Unfair competition among the states.* Congress had no power to make laws regulating trade among the states. As a result, some states levied taxes on goods passing through them to other states. For example, both New York and Pennsylvania taxed goods going to New Jersey which was compared to "a keg tapped at both ends." Such activities prevented efficient and productive trade across state lines. It also worsened the economy, which was still recovering from the devastation of the war.

- *Threats to citizens' right to property.* Many people believed that one of the most serious problems in the United States during the 1780s was the failure of the state governments to protect their citizens' property rights. In most states the government was controlled by the legislative branch, composed of representatives elected by a majority of the people.

People with common interests formed **factions**. These factions sometimes formed majorities in the state legislatures. James Madison defined a faction as a group of people that seeks to promote its own interests above the interests of other individuals or groups. These groups were accused of making laws that benefited themselves at the expense of the minority and of the common good. For example, they passed laws that canceled debts and that confiscated the property of loyalists. They created paper money causing inflation that benefited debtors at the expense of their creditors. People hurt by such laws argued that their property was not being protected by their state governments. They claimed that the state governments were being used by one class of people to deny the rights of others.

Key Note Term

factions—groups that seek to promote their own special interests at the expense of the common good

Some people argued that these problems were the result of too much democracy in the state governments. They claimed that representative government with **majority rule** did not adequately protect the natural rights of individual citizens or the common good. They argued that majority rule, when the majority pursued its own selfish interests at the expense of the rights of others, was just another form of tyranny, every bit as dangerous as that of an uncontrolled king.

Key Note Term

majority rule—a principle of democracy which asserts that the greater number of citizens in any political unit should select officials and determine policies

Points to Ponder

1. The Articles of Confederation demonstrated a distrust of a strong national government. What were the historical and philosophical reasons for this distrust?

2. What were the positive and negative consequences of a weak national government?

3. Why do you think the smaller states were satisfied with government under the Articles of Confederation?

4. Many people today continue to distrust the federal government. In your opinion, is such distrust justified? Explain your position.

Shays' Rebellion Sows the Seeds of Change

Many people realized that the Articles of Confederation were weak, but it took a dramatic event to convince them of the need for a stronger national government. In 1786, a group of several hundred angry farmers in Massachusetts gathered under the leadership of Daniel Shays. Their intent was to attack the state government.

The farmers had serious economic problems. Those who could not pay their debts lost their homes and their farms. Some were sent to prison. Discontent arose among the people and mobs prevented the courts from selling the property of those who could not pay their debts.

Shays and his men needed weapons for their rebellion. They tried to capture the arsenal at Springfield, Massachusetts, where arms were kept for the state militia (see Figure 3.1.1). Although Shays' men were defeated, their rebellion frightened many property owners who feared similar problems might arise in their states.

The fears raised by such conflicts as Shays' Rebellion, combined with difficulties of raising revenues and regulating foreign trade, convinced a growing number of people to strengthen the national government. George Washington was one of these people. He wrote to James Madison saying, *"We are either a united people or we are not. If the former, let us act as a nation. If we are not, let us no longer act a farce by pretending to it."*

Figure 3.1.1: Shays' Rebellion forced people to examine the weaknesses of the national government.

Courtesy of Bettmann/ Corbis Images.

Achievements of the First National Government

Although the national government under the Articles of Confederation left much to be desired, it did accomplish a number of important things. The Revolutionary War (see Figure 3.1.2) was conducted under this government and, through the efforts of its diplomats it secured recognition of American independence by European governments.

Perhaps the most lasting achievement of the Confederation government was the Northwest Ordinance of 1787, which defined the Northwest Territory and created a plan for its government. The ordinance provided for the transition from territory to statehood for what would become five states north of the Ohio River and east of the Mississippi. The ordinance saw to it that the states provided for education by setting aside land for that purpose, and also stated that slavery would be forever prohibited from those lands.

The Confederation Congress could make these regulations for the Northwest Territory because it had complete control over it. Yet Congress had not the slightest control over enforcing its own treaties in the 13 states. By 1787, many people had agreed that the power of Congress needed to be adjusted, because such a situation could not last. The first steps then were taken to create a stronger national government.

Figure 3.1.2: Molly Pitcher carried water to the troops during the Battle of Monmouth in 1778. When her husband fell from heat stroke, she took his place.

Courtesy of Bettmann/ Corbis Images.

How did problems that arose in the Northwest Territory demonstrate the weaknesses of the new national government?

Conclusion

In this lesson you examined the national government formed by the Articles of Confederation. It was the first of two constitutions for a national government written between 1776 and 1787. In 1776, the Second Continental Congress voted to declare the colonies independent of the British government. The new states needed to cooperate to fight the war against the powerful British army and navy. One of the first tasks of the Congress was to organize a national government to fight the war.

The first government created by the Founders did not work well despite all their knowledge of political philosophy, history, and government. Knowing the shortcomings of that government is important in understanding that unless a government is organized properly, it may not work very well. It also helps in understanding why our government is organized as it is.

You should be able to explain why the newly independent Americans created their first constitution, the Articles of Confederation, as they did. You also should be able to explain why some people thought the government under the Articles of Confederation was not strong enough.

In the following lesson, you will take a look at what it took to create our Constitution.

Lesson Review

1. Why did the Articles of Confederation fail to provide for an executive and a judicial branch of government? How did the Articles of Confederation deal with fears that some states would dominate others in the national government?

2. What were some of the weaknesses of the Articles of Confederation? What were some of the achievements of the national government under the Articles of Confederation?

3 What was Shays' Rebellion? Why did it occur? What was its historical importance?

4. What is a "faction"? Why did some Founders consider factions to be a threat to natural rights?

Lesson 2

Creating Our Constitution

Key Terms

delegates
equal representation
executive
federal system
framers
House of Representatives
judicial

legislative
Philadelphia Convention
proportional representation
ratification
senate
Virginia Plan

What You Will Learn to Do

- Explain how the Philadelphia Convention and the Virginia Plan helped create the Constitution

Linked Core Objectives

- Communicate using verbal, non-verbal, visual, and written techniques
- Apply critical thinking techniques

Skills and Knowledge You Will Gain Along the Way

- Describe the steps leading to the calling of the Philadelphia Convention and the initial purpose of the Convention

- Describe the characteristics of the Framers who attended the Convention

- Describe the Framers' agreement on how to conduct the business of the Convention

- Defend positions on how the constitution should be developed—by Congress or by a special national convention

- Describe the basic elements of the Virginia Plan and the New Jersey Plan and the differences between them

- Relate the elements of the Virginia and New Jersey Plans to the basic ideas of government such as natural rights, republican government, and constitutional government

- Explain the reasons for the disagreements among the delegates regarding representation

Chapter 3

- **Evaluate the advantages and disadvantages of the Virginia and New Jersey Plans for a national government**
- **Explain why the Virginia Plan was used as the basis for the new Constitution rather than the New Jersey Plan**
- **Define key words contained in this lesson**

Introduction

The second U.S. Constitution was written at a convention held in Philadelphia in 1787. Both the New Jersey and the Virginia delegates to the convention submitted plans to organize the new national government. In this lesson you will learn how the Philadelphia Convention came to be, the major issues that were discussed and debated, and the role that the New Jersey and Virginia plans played in creating the Constitution.

Solving the Problems of the Articles of Confederation

Many political leaders, including Alexander Hamilton (see Figure 3.2.1) and James Madison, were dissatisfied with the government under the Articles of Confederation. They claimed the government was inadequate for meeting the problems of the United States.

A number of prominent leaders suggested holding a meeting of representatives of all the states. This idea of holding a special meeting or convention to discuss constitutional changes, instead of using the legislature, was an American invention. Most of the early state constitutions had been written by state legislatures. In 1780, Massachusetts became the first state to hold a constitutional convention. By 1786, Madison

Figure 3.2.1: Alexander Hamilton—1757–1804.

Courtesy of Archivo Iconografico, S.A./ Corbis Images.

and other leaders decided that if a convention could be used successfully in a state, it was worth trying at the national level.

In 1786, a meeting to discuss commercial problems was held in Annapolis, Maryland. Only five states sent representatives. Disappointed at the low turnout, Hamilton, Madison, and others wrote a report asking Congress to call a meeting in Philadelphia to suggest ways to change the Articles of Confederation to strengthen the national government. Congress did so after a delay of several months. Delegates to the **Philadelphia Convention** were authorized only to propose amendments to the Articles, not to develop an entirely new constitution which is exactly what they did.

Evaluating Alternative Political Strategies

Suppose you wanted to develop a plan to change the Constitution of the United States. Your class should be divided into two groups. Each group should adopt one of the positions. Be prepared to present and defend your assigned position.

Group 1. Position: The plan to change the Constitution should be developed by Congress and then submitted to state governments for approval.

Group 2. Position: The plan to change the Constitution should be developed at a special national convention of delegates from the states selected by their legislatures and then submitted to the people of their state for approval.

The Philadelphia Convention

Fifty-five delegates attended the meeting at Independence Hall (see Figure 3.2.2) that later became known as the Philadelphia or Constitutional Convention. This group of men is now often called the **Framers** of the Constitution. Most of the delegates were fairly young; the average age was 42. About three-fourths of them had served in Congress. Most were prominent in their states, and some had played important parts in the Revolution. Some were wealthy, but most were not. A French diplomat in America at the time said that the Framers *"without being rich are all in easy circumstances."*

Contemporary observers were impressed by the quality of the delegates to the Philadelphia Convention. Another French diplomat stationed in America observed that never before, *"even in Europe,"* had there been *"an assembly more respectable for talents, knowledge, disinterestedness, and patriotism."* From Paris, Thomas Jefferson wrote to John Adams in London that the convention *"is an assembly of demigods."*

We should remember, however, that some of the Framers were men of modest abilities or questionable motives. Probably the most balanced view of the men at Philadelphia has been given by Max Farrand, a historian, who wrote: *"Great men there were, it is true, but the convention as a whole was composed of men such as would be appointed to a similar gathering at the present time: professional men, business men, and gentlemen of leisure; patriotic statesmen and clever, scheming politicians; some trained by experience and study for the task before them; and others utterly unfit. It was essentially a representative body."*

Most of the Framers' stories are worth telling in detail, but here we are limited to introducing you to those who were the most important. We also will mention some leaders who did not attend the convention but who played a part in the establishment of our constitutional government.

George Washington

George Washington was probably the most respected and honored man in the country. During the Revolutionary War, he had left Mount Vernon, his Virginia plantation, to lead the American army to victory over the British. When the war was over, Washington returned to private life. Although convinced of the necessity for a strong national government, he was not interested in holding public office.

At first Washington refused the invitation to attend the convention. He later agreed to be a **delegate** from Virginia, fearing that if he did not attend, people might think he had lost his faith in republican government. Washington was unanimously elected president of the convention, though he was not active in the debates. His presence and support of the Constitution, together with the widespread assumption that he would be the nation's first president, were essential to the Constitution's **ratification** by the states.

Key Note Terms

delegate—a person chosen to act for or represent others, as at a convention

ratification—formal approval of the U.S. Constitution by the states

James Madison

Of all the Framers, James Madison probably had the greatest influence on the organization of the national government. Born in 1751, Madison was one of the youngest of the revolutionary leaders, but by 1787, his talents had long been recognized and admired. In 1776, at the age of 25, Madison had been elected to the Virginia convention, where he was named to a committee to frame the state constitution. There, he first displayed his lifelong commitment to freedom of religion. Madison was instrumental in persuading George Mason, author of the Virginia Bill of Rights, to change the clause that guaranteed "toleration" of religion to one that secured its "free exercise."

As a leader in Virginia politics and a member of the Confederation Congress, Madison was active in the 1780s, in support of a stronger national government. His influence at the convention was great, in part because he brought with him a plan he had already developed for creating a new national government—the **Virginia Plan.** After much debate over alternatives, this plan was used as the basis for discussion on improving the government. Had it not been for Madison, we probably would not know much about what happened during the convention. The Framers had decided to keep the discussions a secret, although delegates were free to take notes. Madison attended nearly every session and kept careful notes. Much of what we know today about what happened in the convention is based on his records.

Figure 3.2.3: Benjamin Franklin.

Courtesy of Bettmann/ Corbis Images.

After the convention, Madison collaborated with Alexander Hamilton and John Jay to write a defense of the new Constitution. This defense was a series of 85 articles written for newspapers in New York. In 1788, the articles were collected in a book called The Federalist. The articles urged citizens of New York to vote for delegates to the state ratifying convention who were favorable to the Constitution. The Federalist is probably the most important work written on the basic principles and ideas underlying our constitutional government.

Other Delegates

In addition to Washington and Madison, the delegates included many other prominent men. Benjamin Franklin (see Figure 3.2.3) was 81 and in poor health, but because he was internationally respected, his mere presence lent an aura of wisdom to the convention. Alexander Hamilton, although one of the strongest supporters of a strong national government, was outvoted within his own state delegation and left in frustration before the convention was half over. He returned for a few days and he signed the completed document in September. Hamilton played a major role in the struggle over ratification, as a principal author of The Federalist and as the leader of pro-Constitution forces in New York. James Wilson, although not as well known as Madison or Hamilton, was also a major influence in shaping the theory of the Constitution. Later, Wilson would lead the Federalist forces in Pennsylvania, and in 1789, President Washington appointed him a justice of the Supreme Court.

George Washington
(1732–1799)

James Madison
(1751–1836)

James Wilson
(1742–1798)

Courtesy of the National Portrait Gallery.

Elbridge Gerry
(1744–1814)

Roger Sherman
(1721–1793)

Edmund Randolph
(1753–1813)

Courtesy of the Center for Civic Education.

Lesson 2   Creating Our Constitution

Besides Madison and Wilson, the delegate who spoke most frequently at the convention was Gouverneur Morris of Pennsylvania. Edmund Randolph, who as Governor of Virginia was officially the head of the Virginia delegation, introduced the Virginia Plan into the convention.

Randolph, however, refused to sign the completed document. Roger Sherman of Connecticut was instrumental in forging the "Connecticut Compromise" on representation in Congress. George Mason, author of the Virginia Bill of Rights, believed that the national constitution also should contain explicit guarantees of fundamental rights. Like Randolph, he did not sign the Constitution. Elbridge Gerry, who also refused to sign the Constitution, later led the forces against ratification in Massachusetts. Later still, he served as vice president under President James Madison.

Founders Who Did Not Attend the Convention

There also were some important political leaders who did not attend the Constitutional Convention. Thomas Jefferson was in Paris as U.S. ambassador to France. John Adams, who was serving as U.S. ambassador to Great Britain, was recognized as a leading American political thinker. Adams had been a principal architect of the Massachusetts constitution of 1780. The first volume of his *Defense of the Constitutions of Government of the United States of America* had also appeared in early 1787.

Patrick Henry, the revolutionary leader, refused to attend the convention. He was against the development of a strong national government and was suspicious of what might happen at the convention. He supposedly said later that he had *"smelt a rat."*

Other leaders not present at Philadelphia included John Hancock, Samuel Adams, and Richard Henry Lee. Besides these prominent individuals, one state, Rhode Island, refused to be represented at the convention.

Points to Ponder

1. In what ways were the Framers representative of the American people in 1787? In what ways were they not?

   a. What criteria would you use to select a group of people to draft a constitution today?

   b. Explain any advantages and disadvantages that might result from using your criteria to select people to write a constitution compared with the group of Framers who actually wrote our Constitution.

   c. Are there any groups whose interests you feel do not need to be represented? Why or why not?

2. Would you agree with Thomas Jefferson's characterization of the Philadelphia Convention as an "assembly of demigods"? Explain your answer.

The Convention Began

By Friday, May 25, 1787, eleven days after the convention was scheduled to begin, delegations from a majority of the states were present in Philadelphia. George Washington was unanimously elected president of the convention, and a committee was appointed to draw up the rules for the meeting.

Chapter 3   Creating the Constitution

After the rules were agreed on, the convention got to work. Almost immediately, the Framers decided to ignore their instructions from Congress to limit their work to amending the Articles of Confederation. Instead, they voted to work on the development of an entirely new constitution.

The Framers decided that what was said in the convention should be kept secret. There were two reasons for this.

Why did the delegates to the Constitutional Convention decide to keep their deliberations secret?

- **The Framers wanted to develop the best constitution they could. This required a free exchange of ideas. They were afraid that if their debates were made public, many of the delegates would not feel free to express their real opinions.**

- **The Framers thought the new constitution would have a greater chance of being accepted if people did not know about the arguments that went on while it was being created.**

The Framers agreed that each state would have one vote at the convention, even though their delegations varied in size. They also agreed that a member could not be absent from the convention without permission if it would deprive a state of its vote. In addition, they adopted a rule making it possible to reconsider issues freely. This way no decision had to be made permanent until the entire plan was completed.

More Points to Ponder

1. Were the members of the convention right to ignore their original instructions? Why?
2. Should the debates at the Constitutional Convention have been open to the public? Why?

The Virginia Plan

Many delegates came to Philadelphia convinced that the defects of the Articles were so serious it would be better not to use them as a starting point. One of these was James Madison. Before the convention, he already had drafted a plan for a new national government, which came to be called the Virginia Plan. While they waited for the other state delegations to arrive, the Virginia delegates had agreed to put Madison's plan forward as a basis for the convention's discussions.

The most important thing to know about the Virginia Plan is that it proposed a strong national government. Under the Articles of Confederation, the national

federal system—a form of political organization in which governmental power is divided between a central government and territorial subdivisions

legislative—branch given the powers of taxes, trade, and control over the states

executive—composed of several persons appointed by Congress; this branch has the power to administer national laws, appoint other executive officials, and direct all military operations.

judicial—branch with the power to decide over cases involving treaties, trade among the states or with other nations, and the collection of taxes

House of Representatives—elected directly by the people of each state

Senate—the upper house of the U.S. Congress, to which two members are elected from each state by popular vote for a six-year term

proportional representation—the electoral system in which the number of representatives of a state in the House of Representatives is based on the number of people who live in that state

government could act only on the states, not on the people directly. For example, the national government could request money, but only the states had the authority to raise that money through taxes.

Under the Virginia Plan, the national government would have the power to make and enforce its own laws, and to collect its own taxes. Each citizen would be governed under the authority of two governments, the national government and a state government. Both governments would get their authority from the people. The existence of two governments, national and state, each given a certain amount of authority, is what we now call a **federal system.** In addition, the Virginia Plan recommended the following:

- Three branches—**legislative, executive,** and **judicial**—would compose the national government. The legislative branch would be more powerful than the other branches because, among other things, it would have the power to select people to serve in the executive and judicial branches.

- The national legislature, Congress, was to have two houses. A **House of Representatives** would be elected directly by the people of each state. A **Senate** would be elected by the members of the House of Representatives from lists of persons nominated by the legislature of each state.

- The number of representatives from each state in both the House and the Senate would be based on the size of its population or the amount of its contribution to the federal treasury. This system of **proportional representation** meant that states with larger populations would have more representatives in the legislature than states with smaller populations.

The Virginia Plan gave the legislative branch of the national government the following powers:

- Make all laws that individual states were not able to make, such as laws regulating trade between two or more states

- Strike down state laws that it considered to be in violation of the national constitution or the national interest

- Call forth the armed forces of the nation against a state, if necessary, to enforce the laws passed by Congress

- Elect people to serve in the executive and judicial branches of government

What Do You Think?

1. What are the advantages and disadvantages of having two houses of Congress? Explain what position you would take on this question.

2. Why do you suppose the Virginia Plan gave Congress the power to strike down laws made by state legislatures? What arguments could you make for or against giving Congress this power?

3. In what ways does the Virginia Plan correct what the Framers perceived to be weaknesses in the Articles of Confederation?

Why were delegates from small states suspicious of the Virginia Plan?

The Framers' Reaction to the Virginia Plan

There was considerable debate among the Framers over the Virginia Plan. In the early weeks of the convention, as specific features of the plan were discussed, a major disagreement over representation became apparent.

- **The larger states wanted both houses of the national legislature to be based on proportional representation. They argued that a government that both acted on and represented the people should give equal voting power to equal numbers of people.**

- **The smaller states wanted equal representation—equal voting power for each state. Their position was based on their fear that unless they had an equal voice, as they did under the Articles of Confederation, the larger states would dominate them.**

By mid-June this disagreement had created a crisis for the convention. The delegates from the small states, led by William Paterson of New Jersey, asked for time to come up with an alternative to the Virginia Plan.

The New Jersey Plan

On June 15, Paterson presented the small states' plan, which has become known as the New Jersey Plan. The small states did not wish to create a national government in which they had little power. They argued that the best and safest thing to do would be to keep the framework of the Articles of Confederation, as they had been asked to do. The following are some of the main parts of the plan.

> **Key Note Term**
>
> **equal representation—** equal voting power for each state

Legislative Branch

Congress would have only one house, as in the Confederation, and it would be given the following increased powers:

- *Taxes.* **The national government would be given the power to levy import duties and a stamp tax to raise money for its operations, together with the power to collect money from the states if they refused to pay.**

- *Trade.* **Congress would be given the power to regulate trade among the states and with other nations.**

- *Control over the states.* **The laws and treaties made by Congress would be considered the supreme law of the land. No state could make laws that were contrary to them.**

Executive Branch

This branch would be made up of several persons appointed by Congress. They would have the power to administer national laws, appoint other executive officials, and direct all military operations.

Judicial Branch

A supreme court would be appointed by the officials of the executive branch. It would have the power to decide cases involving treaties, trade among the states or with other nations, and the collection of taxes.

Developing and Defending Positions

The Virginia and New Jersey Plans each had certain benefits and costs. Understanding these is helpful in making an intelligent decision about which was the better plan. Work in small groups to identify and describe the benefits and costs of each plan and list them on a chart similar to the following one. Select the plan that your group thinks would make a better government. Be prepared to explain and defend the reasons for your decision.

Why the Virginia Plan Was Used

The New Jersey Plan continued the system of government existing under the Articles of Confederation. In this system, the national government represented and acted upon the states rather than directly representing and acting upon the people. The New Jersey Plan did contain useful suggestions to solve some weaknesses of the Articles of Confederation. By the time the New Jersey Plan was presented, after two weeks of debate on the Virginia Plan, many delegates had become convinced that the national government needed new powers and a new organization for exercising those powers.

When the vote was taken on June 19, the New Jersey Plan was supported by the delegations from New Jersey and Delaware, by a majority of the New York delegation since Hamilton was always outvoted by his two colleagues, and by half the Maryland delegation. So, the Virginia Plan continued to be the basis for the convention's discussion.

A number of major issues had not been resolved, however. Among them were two potentially explosive ones.

- **How should the number of representatives from each state be determined? According to population? Many delegates still argued that each state should have an equal vote, no matter how large or small its population.**
- **What powers should the national government have?**

There were serious disagreements among the delegates. These disagreements were so intense that the convention nearly failed.

Conclusion

The second U.S. Constitution was written at a convention held in Philadelphia in 1787. This lesson described the idea of a constitutional convention, how the Philadelphia Convention come to be, some of the most important people who attended it, and some of the first steps they took to create our present Constitution.

You should be able to describe the steps leading to the calling of the Philadelphia Convention and some of the leading Framers who attended it.

Both the Virginia and the New Jersey delegates to the Philadelphia Convention submitted plans to organize the new national government for the Framers' consideration. After considerable debate, the Virginia Plan was used as the basis for the new Constitution. Not all the recommendations in the plan were accepted. An understanding of both plans and the debates over them should increase your understanding of the Constitution and the continuing debates over how our government is organized.

You should be able to explain the differences between the Virginia and the New Jersey Plans. You also should be able to explain why the Virginia Plan was used as the basis of our Constitution.

The balance of power is covered in the following lesson.

Lesson Review

1. Why did Congress call for a constitutional convention? What did Congress authorize the delegates to the Philadelphia Convention to do?

2. How would you describe the delegates to the Philadelphia Convention? What prominent political leaders attended?

3. Why did the delegates to the Philadelphia Convention decide to conduct their deliberations in secret?

4. Why is it said the delegates to the Philadelphia Convention ignored their instructions?

5. What was the conflict between larger and smaller states over representation in Congress? Which states favored equal representation, and which favored proportional representation? What is the difference between equal and proportional representation?

Lesson 3

Balancing Power

Chapter 3

Key Terms

appellate jurisdiction
apportioned
balance of power
bills of attainder
electoral college
electors
enumerated powers
equal representation
executive power
executive departments
ex post facto laws
fugitive slave clause

The Great Compromise
impeach
judicial review
legislative power
necessary and proper clause
original jurisdiction
proportional representation
separated powers
supremacy clause
treason
veto

What You Will Learn to Do

- Categorize the powers granted to the legislative, judicial and executive branches of government

Linked Core Abilities

- Communicate using verbal, non-verbal, visual, and written techniques
- Apply critical thinking techniques

Skills and Knowledge You Will Gain Along the Way

- Explain how and why the Framers developed the present system of representation in Congress and the advantages and disadvantages of this system

- Describe how Article 1 of the Constitution delegates explicit powers to the Congress and limits the powers of both the national and state governments

- Describe the "three-fifths clause" and the "fugitive slave clause" and explain what issues they were intended to resolve

- Defend positions on disagreements at the Philadelphia Convention over representation and slavery

- Explain the basic organization of the executive and judicial branches set forth in Articles II and III of the Constitution
- Describe the limitations on the powers of the executive and judicial branches
- Explain why the Framers developed the Electoral College as the method for selecting the President
- Defend positions on the influence of the presidency over legislation
- Define key words contained in this lesson

Introduction

Key Note Term

balance of power—the division of governmental powers in such a way that no one individual or group can dominate or control the exercise of power by others

The Framers of the Constitution addressed a variety of concerns, issues and problems as they worked to establish the national government. Specific powers were granted and denied to each of the three branches of government: the legislative branch, the executive branch, and the judicial branch. This distribution of power resulted in a **balance of power** designed to keep any one branch from becoming too powerful. In this learning plan you will explore how the Framers addressed a variety of issues and concerns facing them as they established the national government and how they distributed power among the three branches of government.

Organizing the Legislative Branch

After agreeing to use James Madison's Virginia Plan as the starting point for discussion of a new constitution, the Framers still faced two major decisions: they had to decide what powers to give the new government and how to organize the new government.

The Framers believed that the most important role would be held by the legislative branch. That is why Article I of the Constitution deals with the legislative branch. The first debates, therefore, were about the duties and powers that should be given to Congress and how it should be organized. The Framers encountered problems in developing Article I that are still being debated today.

Disagreements about Representation

Continuing the British and colonial practice of two-house legislatures, every state except Pennsylvania had a legislative branch with two houses. There also was a widespread belief that a two-house legislature would be less likely to violate the people's rights. Each house could serve as a check on the other.

Key Note Term

proportional representation—the electoral system in which the number of representatives of a state in the House of Representatives is based on the number of people who live in that state

The Virginia Plan's proposal to create a two-house Congress was not controversial. What was controversial in the plan was the principle of **proportional representation.** James Madison, James Wilson, Rufus King, and others who represented states with large populations, thought that the number of members in both houses should be based on the number of people they would represent.

They argued that because the new government would operate directly on the people, it was only fair that a state with a larger number of people should have a greater voice, that is, more votes, in the national government.

The delegates from states with smaller populations were afraid that proportional representation would result in a national government dominated by the more populated states. They argued that each state should have the same number of representatives in Congress, equal representation. These delegates also were convinced that the people of their states would never approve the Constitution if it did not preserve equality among the states.

On July 2, the Framers voted on whether there should be **equal representation** in the upper house of Congress. The result was a tie, five states to five, with Georgia divided. Neither side seemed willing to compromise, and delegates began to fear that the convention would end in disagreement and failure. As a result, a special committee, composed of one delegate from each state, was formed. This committee was responsible for developing a plan to save the situation. Some supporters of the Virginia Plan, including James Madison and James Wilson, were against giving this responsibility to a committee. Most of the Framers disagreed with them, however, and the committee went to work.

Developing and Defending Plans for Representation

Your class should be divided into committees of about five students each. Each committee should have some students who represent small states and some who represent large states. The task of each committee is as follows:

1. Develop a plan for how many representatives each state should be allowed to send to the Senate and to the House of Representatives. Your committee may decide, of course, that there is no need for a two-house Congress and that a single house will represent the people most effectively.

2. Select a spokesperson to present your committee's plan to the entire class. Then all members of the committee may help to defend its plan against criticisms by members of other committees.

3. Following the presentation of all the plans, each committee may revise its original plan if it wishes.

The entire class should then examine the plans made by all the committees and try to reach agreement on a plan. Compare the plans of the committees and the final class plan with the plan of the Framers described in the next section.

The Great Compromise

The result of the special committee's work is known as the Connecticut Compromise or **The Great Compromise.** The committee adopted a proposal previously suggested by Connecticut delegates Roger Sherman and Oliver Ellsworth. The Great Compromise contained the following ideas:

- **The House of Representatives would be elected by the people on the basis of proportional representation.**

- **There would be equal representation of each state in the Senate. The legislature of each state would select two senators.**

How did the Connecticut Compromise resolve differences in the Virginia and New Jersey Plans?

Key Note Term

apportioned—the allocation of legislative seats

- **The House of Representatives would be given the power to develop all bills for taxing and government spending. "Direct" taxes would be assigned and divided— apportioned—among the states by population. The Senate was limited to either accepting or rejecting these bills, but it could not change them. This provision was later changed to permit the Senate to amend tax bills developed in the House and to develop appropriation bills itself.**

As in most compromises, each side gained a little and lost a little. The small states received the equal representation in the Senate that their delegates wanted to protect their interests. Many delegates also believed that a constitution without equal representation of states in at least one house of Congress would not be approved by the smaller states. The large states gave up control of the Senate but kept their control of the House of Representatives. The House was also given important powers regarding taxation and government spending.

The result was that the more populous states would have more influence over laws to tax the people and over how the money would be spent. The larger states also would pay the larger share of any direct taxes imposed by Congress. The decisions of the House of Representatives, however, always would be subject to the check of the Senate, in which the small states had equal representation.

When the committee presented this compromise to the convention, it was bitterly fought by some members from the larger states, including Madison, Wilson, and Gouverneur Morris. They viewed the idea of state equality in the Senate as a step away from a national government, back toward the system under the Articles of Confederation. Delegates from the small states remained suspicious as well. Two delegates from New York, who had consistently voted with the smaller states, left the convention and did not return. The crisis was over when the compromise passed by one vote.

Points to Ponder

1. Are there good arguments today in support of continuing to divide Congress into two bodies, a Senate and a House of Representatives? If so, what are they?

2. What contemporary issues do you know about that involve conflict over the fairness of representation in Congress?

3. Why should senators be selected for six years and members of the House of Representatives for only two years? Do you think members of the House of Representatives would more effectively represent their constituents if they could serve longer terms?

What Powers Did the Constitution Give to Congress?

The Framers intended the new government to be a government of enumerated-specifically listed powers. They thought it was important to list the powers of each branch of government so that there would not be any confusion about what they could and could not do.

Most of the powers of Congress are listed in Article I, Section 8 of the Constitution. It includes such important matters as the power:

- **To lay and collect taxes**
- **To pay the debts and provide for the common defense and general welfare of the United States**
- **To regulate commerce with foreign nations, and among the several states**
- **To declare war**
- **To raise an army and navy**
- **To coin money**

The Framers also intended the new system to be a government of **separated powers,** or, as political scientist Richard Neustadt has called it, "a government of separated institutions sharing powers."

Each branch of the government is given powers that enable it to check the use of power by the others. In Article I, Congress was given the power to **impeach** the President, other executive branch officials, or members of the federal judiciary and remove them from office.

The executive and judicial branches also have checks, or controls, on Congress. The Framers specifically gave Congress the power to make all other laws that are "necessary and proper" for carrying out the enumerated powers. This is called the **necessary and proper clause.**

Key Note Terms

separated powers—the division of powers among different branches of government

impeach—charging a public official with a crime in office for which they can be removed from power

necessary and proper clause—the clause in Article I of the U.S. Constitution that gives Congress the power to make all laws that are "necessary and proper" to carry out the powers expressly delegated to it by the Constitution

What Power Did the National Government Have over State Governments and the People?

One reason the Framers agreed to meet in Philadelphia was their concern about some things that state governments were doing. They believed that some states were undermining Congress's efforts to conduct foreign relations, and they feared that, in others, individual rights might be threatened by the state governments. They also knew that the national government had no power to enforce its decisions. The Framers all agreed they had to create a national government with more power than the government had under the Articles of Confederation. They did not agree, however, about how much power the new national government should have over citizens and the state governments.

The Framers resolved their disagreements by establishing a national government with authority to act directly on the people in certain specific areas. The national government no longer would be dependent on the states for income or for law enforcement. The state governments, however, would keep many of the more important powers over people's daily lives. The states would keep their powers over education, family law, property regulations, and most aspects of everyday life. The people would not feel they had surrendered too much power to a distant government.

The Framers included a number of phrases in the Constitution that set forth the powers of the national government. They also included phrases that limited the power of both the national government and state governments. Some of the more important of these are listed in the following sections.

Some Powers of the National Government

The **supremacy clause** says that the Constitution and all laws and treaties approved by Congress in exercising its **enumerated powers** are the supreme law of the land. It also says that judges in state courts must follow the Constitution, or federal laws and treaties, if there is a conflict with state law.

Key Note Terms

supremacy clause— Article VI, Section 2 of the U.S. Constitution, which states that the Constitution, laws passed by Congress, and treaties of the United States "shall be the supreme law of the land" binding on the states

enumerated powers— those rights and responsibilities of the U.S. government specifically provided for and listed in the Constitution

- Article I, Section 8 gives Congress power to organize the militia of the states and to set a procedure for calling the militia into national service when needed
- Article IV, Section 3 gives Congress the power to create new states
- Article IV, Section 4 gives the national government the authority to guarantee to each state a republican form of government
- Article IV, Section 4 also requires the national government to protect the states from invasion or domestic violence

Limits on Power of the National Government

The Constitution includes several limitations on the power of the national government. Article I, Section 9 prohibits the national government from:

- Banning the slave trade before 1808
- Suspending the privilege of the writ of habeas corpus except in emergencies
- Passing any **ex post facto laws**, laws that make an act a crime even though it was legal at the time it was committed
- Passing any **bills of attainder**, laws that declare a person guilty of a crime and decrees a punishment without a judicial trial
- Taxing anything exported from a state
- Taking money from the treasury without an appropriation law
- Granting titles of nobility

Article III defines the crime of **treason** and prohibits Congress from punishing the descendants of a person convicted of treason. Article VI prohibits the national government from requiring public officials to hold any particular religious beliefs.

Key Note Terms

ex post facto laws—a criminal law that makes an act a crime that was not a crime when committed, that increases the penalty for a crime after it was committed, or that changes the rules of evidence to make conviction easier

bills of attainder—an act of legislature that inflicts punishment on an individual or group without a judicial trial

treason—in the U.S. constitution, treason is "giving aid and comfort" to the enemy during wartime

Why was it important to have only one monetary system for the nation?

Courtesy of the U.S. Bureau of Engraving.

Limits on Powers of State Governments

Article I prohibits state governments from:

- **Creating their own money**
- **Passing laws that enable people to violate contracts, such as those between creditors and debtors**
- **Making ex post facto laws or bills of attainder**
- **Entering into treaties with foreign nations or declaring war**
- **Granting titles of nobility**

Article IV prohibits states from:

- **Unfairly discriminating against citizens of other states**
- **Refusing to return fugitives from justice to the states from which they have fled**

Issues That Separated the Northern and Southern States

The Great Compromise had settled the disagreement between large and small states over how they would be represented in Congress. Many other issues still had to be resolved. Two of the most critical disagreements were those between the southern and northern states on the issues of slavery and regulation of commerce.

Slavery had been practiced for almost as long as there had been colonies in America. Many Framers were opposed to slavery, and some northern states had begun to take steps toward abolishing it. Still, in the south, slave labor was widely used in producing crops. Slaveholders considered their slaves to be personal property, and wanted to continue using them (see Figure 3.3.1).

Figure 3.3.1: While the north was working towards abolishing slavery, the south still used slave labor.

Courtesy of Bettmann/ Corbis Images.

Delegates from the southern states told the convention that their states would not ratify a constitution that denied citizens the right to import and keep slaves. If the Constitution interfered with slavery, North Carolina, South Carolina, and Georgia made it clear that they would not become part of the new nation. Some delegates from the New England states, whose shipping interests profited from the slave trade, were sympathetic to the southern position.

Compromises Persuade the Southern States to Sign the Constitution

After considerable debate, the Framers agreed on a way to satisfy both northern and southern delegates. This agreement gave Congress the power to regulate commerce between the states, which the northern states wanted. The delegates defeated a southern attempt to require a two-thirds vote of both houses to pass laws regulating commerce. To satisfy the southern states, the Constitution provided that the national government would not interfere with the slave trade earlier than 1808.

The Framers also agreed that each slave would be counted as three-fifths of a person when determining how many representatives a state could send to the House of Representatives. Each slave also would be counted as three-fifths of a person when computing direct taxes. The **fugitive slave clause** of Article IV was another concession to the southern states. It provided that slaves who escaped to other states must be returned to their owners.

Key Note Term

fugitive slave clause— provided that slaves who escaped to other states must be returned to their owners

$100 REWARD!

RANAWAY

From the undersigned, living on Current River, about twelve miles above Doniphan, in Ripley County, Mo., on 3d of March, 1860, A NE GRO MAN, about 30 years old, weighs about 160 pounds; high forehead, with a scar on it; had on brown pants and coat very much worn, and an old black wool hat; shoes size No. 11.

The above reward will be given to any person who may apprehend this said negro out of the State; and fifty dollars if apprehended in this State outside of Ripley county, or $25 if taken in Ripley county.

APOS TUCKER.

Examining Northern and Southern Positions on Slavery

The words "slave" and "slavery" are never used in the Constitution. Although the delegates voted to give constitutional protection to slavery, many of them were not proud of having done so. They considered it to be a necessary evil, at best, and many hoped it would go away by itself, if left alone. As we now know, this protection of slavery almost destroyed the United States. Work in small groups to develop positions on the following questions from both a northern and southern perspective. Then develop a position on the final question.

1. What arguments could have been made for or against the Framers' decision to include the value of property, including enslaved Africans, in calculating the number of representatives a state should have? Should property in the form of enslaved Africans have been treated differently from other forms of property?

2. Should the settling of fundamental issues, such as whether to allow slavery, have been left up to each state?

3. What problems, if any, arise from trying to make judgments about positions that were taken 200 years ago?

Why the Framers Wanted to Limit Executive Power

The Articles of Confederation did not provide for an executive branch, but the Confederation Congress had found it necessary to create executive officials for specific purposes. The Framers wanted to give the executive branch of the new government enough power and independence to fulfill its responsibilities. They did not, however, want to give the executive any power or independence that could be abused. Americans and Englishmen believed that the king, through the use of bribes and special favors, had been able to control elections and exercise too much influence over Parliament. The British constitution permitted members of Parliament to hold other offices at the same time, and even today members of the executive branch, such as the prime minister, are also members of Parliament. In the eighteenth century, the Crown used its exclusive power to appoint people to office to reward friendly members of Parliament.

The Framers thought these actions upset the proper balance of power between the monarch and Parliament. It was the destruction of this balance that Americans referred to when they spoke of the corruption of Parliament by the Crown. They also believed that royal governors had tried to corrupt colonial legislatures in the same way.

This destruction of the proper balance of power among different branches of government, many Americans thought, led to tyranny. Consequently, it is not surprising that, after their experience with the king and his royal governors, the Americans provided for very weak executive branches in most of the state constitutions. This, however, created other difficulties. The weak executives were unable to check the powers of the state legislatures. These legislatures passed laws that, in the opinion of many, violated basic rights, such as the right to property.

The problem that faced the Framers, then, was how to create a system of government with balanced powers. They wanted to strengthen the executive branch without making it so strong that it could destroy the balance of power among the branches and thus endanger the rights of the people.

Organizing the Executive Branch

The Framers had to resolve a number of basic questions in organizing the executive branch. Each question concerned the best way to establish an executive branch strong enough to balance the power of the legislature, but not so powerful it would endanger democratic government.

Single or Plural Executive

Should there be more than one chief executive? The Framers agreed that there should be a single executive to avoid the possible problem of conflict between two or more leaders of equal power. Some delegates also argued that it would be easier for Congress to keep a watchful eye on a single executive. On the other hand, those who argued for a plural executive claimed that such an executive would be less likely to become tyrannical.

Term of Office

How long should the chief executive remain in his position? The convention considered a seven-year term for the President, but many delegates thought seven years too long. The final decision was to set the term of office at four years.

Re-election

Should the executive be eligible for re-election? Under the original proposal for a seven-year term of office, the President would not have been eligible for re-election. When the term was reduced to four years, the Framers decided to allow the President to run again. The Constitution originally set no limit on the number of times a President could be re-elected. The Twenty-second Amendment, passed in 1951 after President Franklin D. Roosevelt (see Figure 3.3.2) held four terms of office, however, sets the limit at two terms.

The nation celebrates the swearing in of the first president, George Washington.

Courtesy of the National Archives, Library of Congress.

Figure 3.3.2: After Franklin D. Roosevelt was elected to the office of president four times, a two-term limit was set by Congress.

Courtesy of Oscar White/Corbis Images.

Deciding on the President's Powers

The most important question the Framers faced was what the powers of the executive branch would be. The executive powers include the responsibilities for:

- **Carrying out and enforcing laws made by Congress**
- **Nominating people for federal offices**
- **Negotiating treaties with other nations**
- **Conducting wars**

In addition, the President is given the power to:

- **Pardon people convicted of crimes**
- **Send and receive ambassadors to and from other countries**

Although the Framers thought the executive branch should have enough power to fulfill its responsibilities, they also wanted to be sure it did not have too much power. They limited the powers of both the executive branch and the legislative branch by making them share many of their powers. This was intended to keep the powers balanced and to provide each branch with a way to check the use of power by the other branch. This sharing of powers was accomplished in the following ways.

Veto

The President shares in the **legislative power** through the **veto.** Although the President can veto a bill passed by Congress, the bill can still become a law if two-thirds of both houses of Congress vote to override the veto.

Appointments

The power to appoint executive branch officials and federal judges is shared with Congress. The President has the power to nominate persons to fill those positions, but the Senate has the right to approve or disapprove of the persons nominated. To prevent corruption of Congress, members of Congress are not allowed to hold another federal office.

Treaties

The power to make treaties also is shared. The President has the power to negotiate a treaty with another nation, but the treaty must be approved by a two-thirds vote of the Senate.

War

Although the President is Commander in Chief, only Congress has the power to declare war. Congress also controls the money necessary to wage a war; therefore, the power to declare and wage war also is shared.

Key Note Terms

legislative power—the power to write and enact laws

veto—the constitutional power of the president to refuse to sign a bill passed by congress, thereby preventing it from becoming a law

Articles I and II

Although it includes several important powers, Article II seems short and vague when compared with Article I. It speaks of "**executive power**" but does not define it. **Executive departments** are mentioned, but there are no provisions for creating them, deciding how many there should be, or how they should operate. By comparison, Article I included a specific list of "legislative powers" granted by the Constitution.

The veto power appears in Article I, Section 7, although the term is not used. Article II, Section 3 states that the President has the duty to suggest legislation. These are examples of the executive sharing the legislative power.

The Constitution also gives Congress the power to impeach the President, members of the executive branch, and federal judges. Only the House of Representatives can bring the charges. The Senate holds a trial to determine the official's guilt or innocence. If found guilty by two-thirds of the Senate, the official will be removed from office.

The Framers had some experience with elected executives in the states, yet they could not be sure exactly what the Presidency of the United States should be like. Many decisions were left to Congress. The Framers also trusted George Washington, who was almost universally expected to become the first President. They thought that he could be counted on to fill in the Constitution's gaps and set wise examples that would be followed by later Presidents.

Identifying the Powers of the President to Influence Legislation

The President has the power to veto bills passed by Congress and the power to recommend to Congress legislation that he considers "necessary and expedient." Answer the following questions. It may be helpful to consider some things that have changed since the Constitution was written.

1. In what other ways can a President have an influence on legislation being considered in Congress?

2. Does the party system give a President more influence in Congress when he is a member of the majority party?

3. Has the presence of television increased the power of the Presidency and weakened that of Congress?

How Presidents Would Be Selected

The main alternatives debated by the Framers were to have the President selected indirectly or directly by a majority vote of the people. Among the indirect methods they considered were selection by

- **Congress**
- **State legislatures**
- **State governors**
- **A temporary group elected for that purpose**

The Framers knew that the group with the power to select the President would have great power over the person who held the office. They were concerned that this power might be used to benefit some people at the expense of others. It might also make it difficult for the President to function properly.

If Congress were given the power to choose the President, then limiting the term of office to a single, long term would be a way to protect the President from being manipulated by Congress to get reelected. This is why the Framers also decided that Congress could neither increase nor decrease the President's salary once in office.

If a President were not chosen by Congress, then providing for a shorter term of office would make the President more accountable to the people. Reelection then would be the will of the people and the President could run for reelection many times.

The problem was given to a committee to develop a plan that a majority of the Framers would support. The committee's plan was a clever compromise. It did not give any existing group the power to select the President. The plan shows that the Framers did not trust any group—the people, the state legislatures, or Congress—to make the selection. In such a large country, the people could not be personally familiar with the candidates and their qualifications, in the Framers' judgment.

The state legislatures and Congress, they thought, might use their power to upset the balance of power between the national and state governments, or between the executive and legislative branches.

Instead, the committee proposed what we now call the Electoral College, which would have the responsibility of electing the President. The main parts of this plan are described below.

- The **Electoral College** would be organized once every four years to select a President. After the election, the college would be dissolved.
- Each state would select members of the Electoral College, called **electors**.
- Each state would have the same number of electors as it had senators and representatives in Congress. The method for choosing electors would be decided on by the state legislature.
- Each elector would vote for two people, one of whom had to be a resident of another state. This forced the elector to vote for at least one person who might not represent his particular state's interests.
- The person who received the highest number of votes, if it was a majority of the electors, would become President. The person who received the next largest number of votes would become Vice President.
- If two people received a majority vote, or if no one received a majority vote, then the House of Representatives would select the President by a majority vote, with each state having only one vote. In case of a vice-presidential tie, the Senate would select the Vice President.

> ### Key Note Terms
>
> **electoral college**—the group of presidential electors that casts the official votes for president after a presidential election
>
> **electors**—a group of persons selected by each state party to vote for that party's candidates for president and vice president if the party's candidates win the popular vote in the general election in that state

The compromise was eventually approved by the Framers, but only after much debate and revision. Although quite complicated and unusual, it seemed to be the best solution to their problem. There was little doubt in the Framers' minds that George Washington would easily be elected the first President. There was great doubt among the Framers, however, that anyone after Washington could ever get a majority

*How did the Framers'
expectation that George
Washington would be the
first president affect their
writing of Article II of the
Constitution?*

*Courtesy of the Library of
Congress.*

vote in the Electoral College. They believed that in almost all future elections the final selection of the President would be made by the House of Representatives.

More Points to Ponder

1. What arguments can you give to support the use of the Electoral College to select the President? Explain why you agree or disagree with these arguments.

2. What qualifications do you think a person should have, beyond those already in the Constitution, in order to be President? Do you think these qualifications should be required by law? Why or why not?

3. Is it still reasonable to have one person serve as the head of the executive branch? Might it be more reasonable to have two people—one for domestic and one for foreign policy?

What Questions Did Organizing the Judicial Branch Raise?

A national government, with power to act directly on citizens, needed a system for deciding cases involving its laws. This function could be left to state courts, but then the federal laws might be enforced differently from state to state. The Framers realized that some kind of national courts would be needed, at least to resolve disputes involving federal laws.

A judicial branch also would complete the system of separation of powers. They had fewer problems agreeing on how to organize the judiciary than they had with the other two branches.

Many of the Framers were lawyers, and so most of them already agreed about how courts should be organized and what responsibilities and powers they should be given. They also agreed that all criminal trials should be trials by jury. This was a very important check, in their minds, on the power of the government.

Why did the Framers think it was important to protect the independence of the judicial branch?

Courtesy of the National Archives, Supreme Court Historical Society, Ralph C. Jones.

The Framers created the Supreme Court as the head of the federal judiciary, and gave Congress the power to create lower federal courts. They also reached several other important agreements:

- **Judges should be independent of politics so that they can use their best judgment to decide cases and not be influenced by political pressures.**
- **The best way to make sure that judges would not be influenced by politics was to have them nominated by the President. The President's nomination would need to be ratified by the Senate.**

The Framers thought that appointing the judges by this method rather than electing them would remove them from the pressures of political influence. In addition, the judges would keep their positions "during good behavior." This meant that they could not be removed from their positions unless they were impeached and convicted of "treason, bribery, or other high crimes and misdemeanors."

There was also a good deal of agreement about the kinds of powers that the judicial branch should have. The judiciary was given the power to

- **Decide conflicts between state governments**
- **Decide conflicts that involved the national government**

And finally, they gave the Supreme Court the authority to handle two types of cases. These are

Key Note Terms

original jurisdiction—
the legal authority of a
court to be the first to
hear a case

appellate jurisdiction—
the legal authority of a
court to hear appeals
from a lower court

- Cases in which the Supreme Court has **original jurisdiction**. These are cases which the Constitution says are not to be tried first in a lower court, but which are to go directly to the Supreme Court. Such cases involve a state government, a dispute between state governments, and cases involving ambassadors.

- Cases that have first been heard in lower courts and that are appealed to the Supreme Court. These are cases over which the Supreme Court has **appellate jurisdiction**.

What Do You Think?

1. What are the advantages and disadvantages of having federal judges appointed, not elected, to serve "during good behavior"?

2. Should the composition of the Supreme Court be reflective of the political, economic, racial, ethnic, and gender diversity of our citizenry? Why or why not?

3. What role, if any, should public opinion play in the Supreme Court deciding a controversial case?

4. It has been argued that the Supreme Court is the least democratic branch of our federal government. What arguments can you give for and against this position?

The Question of Judicial Review Left Unanswered

Key Note Term

judicial review—the
power of the courts to
declare laws and
actions of the local,
state, or national gov-
ernment invalid if the
courts decide they are
unconstitutional

One important matter not decided by the Framers was whether the Supreme Court should be given the power of **judicial review** over the acts of the executive and legislative branches. To do so would give the judiciary the authority to declare acts of these branches of the national government unconstitutional. This would mean giving one branch the power to ensure that the other branches did not exceed the limitations placed on them by the Constitution. The power to declare that legislative acts had violated their state constitution already had been exercised by the courts in several states.

Some Framers simply assumed that the judiciary would have the power to rule on the constitutionality of laws made by Congress. Nothing specific was decided on this subject at the convention. This assumption, however, is one reason why the delegates rejected a proposal to let the Supreme Court and President act as a committee to review bills passed by Congress and decide if they should become law. The only reference in the Constitution to the general powers of the judiciary is at the beginning of Article III: The "judicial power of the United States, shall be vested in one supreme court. . . . "

The power of the Supreme Court to declare acts of Congress unconstitutional was clearly established by the Supreme Court itself in 1803.

Conclusion

This lesson explained why the Framers thought that the executive and judicial branches were needed in the new government and how they organized those branches. It also described the difficulties the delegates had in deciding how best to control the power of the executive, and how and why they created an unusual way of selecting the President. In addition, it described the responsibilities given to the judicial branch and considered some of the powers of both branches that were not directly given in the Constitution, such as the power of judicial review.

This lesson also described the basic organization of Congress. It explained why Congress was organized into two houses, why representation in the House of Representatives is based on population, and why each state selects two senators. The lesson also described some powers of Congress as well as some limitations on its powers. It concluded with a discussion of the issues that caused disagreement between the southern and northern delegates.

In the following lesson, you will learn about debates over the Constitution.

Lesson Review

1. What is meant by "enumerated powers"? Why did the Framers decide to specifically enumerate the powers granted to Congress?

2. How did the Framers deal with the issue of slavery? Why did they choose to take the approach they did?

3. What issues did the Framers have to decide regarding the organization of the executive branch of government and how did they resolve these issues?

4. How did the Framers make sure the executive branch would have enough power to fulfill its responsibilities, but not so much power that it could dominate the other branches of government?

Lesson 4

The Debate over the Constitution

Key Terms

agrarian
Anti-Federalist
Federalist
ratify

What You Will Learn to Do

- Analyze the conflicting positions relating to the ratification of the Constitution

Linked Core Abilities

- Communicate using verbal, non-verbal, visual, and written techniques
- Apply critical thinking techniques

Skills and Knowledge You Will Gain Along the Way

- Explain the comments made by Benjamin Franklin and James Madison who favored the adoption of the Constitution

- Explain the position of George Mason and give arguments in support of and in opposition to his criticisms of the Constitution

- Explain the arguments of the Anti-Federalists and how those arguments were based upon traditional ideas of republican government

- Explain the responses of the Federalists to the criticisms of the Anti-Federalists

- Explain how the debate between the Federalists and Anti-Federalists led to the development and adoption of the Bill of Rights

- Explain why the Federalists wanted the Constitution to be ratified in state conventions, and the arguments they used to justify this procedure which is included in Article VII of the Constitution

Chapter 3

- **Explain the arguments made by the Federalists in support of the Constitution, including how the Federalists' arguments differed from classical arguments about republican government**
- **Define key words contained in this lesson**

Introduction

Not all of the delegates to the Constitutional Convention supported the adoption of the Constitution. Many delegates had reservations about all or parts of the document. Those opposed to ratification were called **Anti-Federalists** while those in support of ratification were called **Federalists.** In this lesson you will explore the arguments presented by both sides, and discover how some of the differences were ultimately settled.

What the Framers Thought When the Philadelphia Convention Ended

The Constitution has been described as "a bundle of compromises." As you have seen, such prominent features of the Constitution such as the different plans for representation in the House and the Senate and the method of selecting the president, were settled by compromise. Compromise means, however, that everyone gets less than they want. There were enough compromises in the completed Constitution that nearly every delegate could find something he did not like. During the four months the delegates spent putting the Constitution together, there were some strong disagreements. Some had walked out of the convention, and three refused to sign the finished document.

Figure 3.4.1: Howard Chandler Christy's "The Signing of the Constitution of the United States."

Courtesy of the Commission on the Bicentenary of the U.S. House of Representatives.

Benjamin Franklin argued in support of the Constitution. George Mason argued against it. Mason was one of the three delegates remaining until the end of the convention who refused to sign the document.

Franklin Defends the Work of the Convention

On the last day of the convention, September 17, 1787, Benjamin Franklin prepared a speech intended to persuade all the delegates to sign the completed Constitution. The following speech was read by James Wilson because Franklin's age and illness made him too weak to deliver it himself.

"I confess that there are several parts of this Constitution which I do not at present approve. . . . [But] the older I grow, the more apt I am to doubt my own judgment, and to pay more respect to the judgment of others . . . . In these sentiments . . . I agree with this Constitution with all its faults, if they are such; because I think a general Government necessary for us . . . [and] I doubt . . . whether any other Convention we can obtain, may be able to make a better Constitution. For when you assemble a number of men to have the advantage of their joint wisdom, you inevitably assemble with those men all their prejudices, their passions, their errors of opinion, their local interests, and their selfish views. From such an assembly can a perfect production be expected? It therefore astonishes me . . . to find this system approaching so near to perfection as it does . . . . Thus I consent . . . to this Constitution because I expect no better, and because I am not sure, that it is not the best. . . . If every one of us in returning to our Constituents were to report the objections he has had to it . . . we might prevent its being generally received, and thereby lose all the salutary effects and great advantages resulting naturally in our favor among foreign Nations as well as among ourselves, from a real or apparent unanimity. . . . On the whole . . . I cannot help expressing a wish that every member of the Convention who may still have objections to it, would with me on this occasion doubt a little of his own infallibility, and to make manifest our unanimity put his name to this instrument."

George Mason Objects to the Constitution

Less than a week before the convention ended, George Mason wrote a list of objections on his copy of the draft of the Constitution. The list was later printed as a pamphlet during the ratification debate. The following are some of his more important objections:

- **The Constitution does not contain a Bill of Rights.**

- **Because members of the Senate are selected by state legislatures, it means that they are not representatives of the people or answerable to them. They have great powers, such as the right to approve the appointment of ambassadors and treaties recommended by the president. They also have the power to try the president and other members of the government in cases of impeachment. These powers place the senators in such close connection with the president that together they will destroy any balance in the government, and do whatever they please with the rights and liberties of the people.**

- **The national courts have been given so much power that they can destroy the judicial branches of the state governments by overruling them. If this were to happen, and the only courts available were federal courts, most people would not be able to afford to have their cases heard in these courts, because they would need to travel a**

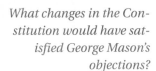

great distance. Rich people would have an advantage that would enable them to oppress and ruin the poor.

- The Constitution does not provide for a council to serve as advisers to the president. Any safe and regular government has always included such a council. Such a council would take the place of the Senate in advising the president on appointments and treaties, and the head of the council would take the place of the vice president. Without it, the president will not get proper advice, and will usually be advised by flattering and obedient favorites; or he will become a tool of the Senate.

- The President of the United States has the unlimited power to grant pardons for crimes, including treason. He may sometimes use this power to protect people whom he has secretly encouraged to commit crimes, and keep them from being punished. In this way he can prevent the discovery of his own guilt.

- The Constitution says that all treaties are the supreme law of the land. Since they can be made by the president with the approval of the Senate, together they have an exclusive legislative power in this area. This means they can act without the approval of the House of Representatives, the only branch of the legislature that is directly answerable to the people.

- The Constitution only requires a majority vote in Congress, instead of a two-thirds vote, to make all commercial and navigation laws. The economic interests of the five southern states, however, are totally different from those of the eight northern states, which will have a majority in both houses of Congress. Requiring only a majority vote means that Congress may make laws favoring the merchants of the northern and eastern states, at the expense of the agricultural interests of the southern states. This could ruin the southern states' economies.

- Because the Constitution gives Congress the power to make any laws it thinks are "necessary and proper" to carry out its responsibilities, there is no adequate limitation on its powers. Congress could grant monopolies in trade and commerce, create new crimes, inflict severe or unusual punishments, and extend its powers as far as it wants. As a result, the powers of the state legislatures and the liberties of the people could be taken from them.

Mason also had made other criticisms of the Constitution during the convention. Some were accepted by the Convention; others were incorporated in the Bill of Rights, which was added in 1791.

Franklin Describes the Significance of the Convention

The final entry that Benjamin Franklin made in his notes on the convention describes the scene as the delegates were signing the document they hoped would become the Constitution of the United States.

During convention sessions, why might Franklin have had trouble telling if the "sun behind the president" was "rising or setting"?

Courtesy of the Center for Civic Education.

"Whilst the last members were signing it, Doctor Franklin looking toward the President's Chair, at the back of which a rising sun happened to be painted, observed to a few members near him that Painters had found it difficult to distinguish in their art a rising from a setting sun. I have, said he, often in the course of the Session . . . looked at that [sun] behind the President without being able to tell whether it was rising or setting: But now at length I have the happiness to know that it is a rising and not a setting Sun."

Analyzing the Positions of Gerry and Hamilton

The following remarks were made by two of the Framers on the last day of the convention. One of these Framers signed the Constitution; the other did not. What do the following comments tell you about the differences of opinion among the Framers concerning the Constitution they had developed? What were some problems they thought might arise in getting it approved?

". . . every member [of the convention] should sign. A few characters of consequence, by opposing or even refusing to sign the Constitution, might do infinite mischief. . . . No man's ideas were more remote from the plan than [mine are] known to be; but is it possible to deliberate between anarchy . . . on one side, and the chance of good to be expected from the plan on the other?"

Alexander Hamilton

". . . a Civil war may result from the present crisis. . . . In Massachusetts . . . there are two parties, one devoted to Democracy, the worst . . . of all political evils, the other as violent in the opposite extreme . . . for this and other reasons . . . the plan should have been proposed in a more mediating shape."

Elbridge Gerry

Anti-Federalists View the Importance of Representative Government and Civic Virtue

Most Americans were suspicious of government, but the Anti-Federalists were especially mistrustful of government in general and strong national government in particular. This mistrust was the basis of their opposition to the Constitution. They feared it had created a government the people could not control.

In general, the Anti-Federalists were older Americans who had grown up believing in the basic ideas of republicanism. These included the idea that in a republic, the greatest power should be placed in a legislature composed of representatives elected by the people of the community. It had always been thought that this kind of representative government would only work in a small community of citizens with similar interests and beliefs, because in such a community it would be easier for people to agree on what was in their common interest.

In addition, it was widely believed that people living in small **agrarian** communities would be more likely to possess the civic virtue required of republican citizens. Living closely together they would be more willing to set aside their own interests when necessary and work for the common good.

The Anti-Federalists understood that the Federalists were proposing a government that was the opposite of this type of republican government. It was large and powerful, it included numerous diverse communities, and its capital would be far away from most of the people it represented. The Anti-Federalists believed such a system would inevitably pose a threat to the rights of the people.

Many distinguished Americans were Anti-Federalists. Leaders included George Mason and Elbridge Gerry. Both had attended the Philadelphia Convention but had refused to sign the Constitution. Richard Henry Lee was a leading revolutionary and signer of the Declaration of Independence, but fought against the ratification of the Constitution. Patrick Henry had always opposed the idea of a strong national government; he became a leading Anti-Federalist.

Mercy Otis Warren, a playwright, also opposed ratification. She, like the others, wrote pamphlets explaining why she did not support the Constitution. Other prominent Anti-Federalists included Luther Martin, Robert Yeates, and George Clinton.

Many arguments were made both for and against the Constitution. Most of them had to do with three basic questions:

- **Would the new Constitution maintain a republican form of government?**

Figure 3.4.2: Patrick Henry (1736–1799)

Courtesy of the Museum of Fine Arts Boston.

- **Would the federal government have too much power?**

- **Was a bill of rights needed in the Constitution?**

Anti-Federalists Arguments

Mercy Otis Warren was a playwright as well as an Anti-Federalist writer. She is noteworthy because of her unusual ability to enter the man's world of early American politics. Her main criticisms of the Constitution are a good example of the Anti-Federalist position. The Anti-Federalists argued that the Constitution had the following flaws:

- **It should have been developed in meetings whose proceedings were open to the public**

- **It would undermine a republican form of government**

- **It gave too much power to the national government at the expense of the powers of the state governments**

- **It gave too much power to the executive branch of the national government at the expense of the other branches**

- **It gave Congress too much power because of the "necessary and proper clause"**

- **It did not adequately separate the powers of the executive and legislative branches**

- **It allowed the national government to keep an army during peacetime**

- **It did not include a bill of rights**

Anti-Federalists' Fear of a Strong National Government

Warren and the other Anti-Federalists feared that, because of these flaws in the Constitution, the new national government would be a threat to their natural rights. They also thought that the Constitution had been developed by an elite and privileged group to create a national government for the purpose of serving its own selfish interests. Warren and most of the Anti-Federalists thought that the only safe government was one that was local and closely linked with the will of the people, and controlled by the people, by such means as yearly elections and thus replacing people in key positions often.

Debate over a Bill of Rights

The lack of a bill of rights proved to be the strongest and most powerful weapon of the Anti- Federalists in their struggle to defeat the Constitution. The most frequent arguments they used were the following:

- **The way the government is organized does not adequately protect rights. Only the House of Representatives is chosen directly by the people. The federal government** is too far removed from average citizens to care about their concerns. The federal government's power could be used to violate citizens' rights.

- The federal government's powers are so general and vague that they can be used to give the government almost unlimited power. It can make all laws that are "necessary and proper" to promote the "general welfare." The Constitution allows the federal government to act directly on citizens. Therefore, its powers over citizens are almost unlimited.

- There is nothing in the Constitution to stop the federal government from violating all the rights that are not mentioned in it. Some rights are included and some are not. There is no mention, for example, of freedom of religion, speech, press, or assembly. Because they are omitted from the Constitution, the government is free to violate them.

- A bill of rights would quiet the fears of many people that a strong central government could violate their rights. After all, Americans recently fought a revolutionary war to secure their fundamental rights. They do not want a constitution that places those rights in jeopardy.

- A bill of rights is necessary to remind the people of the principles of our political system. As one Anti- Federalist put it, there is a necessity of "constantly keeping in view . . . the particular principles on which our freedom must always depend."

Demand for a Bill of Rights Unites the Anti-Federalists

The Anti-Federalists often disagreed with each other about why they opposed the Constitution, and they were not a well-organized group. They were united, however, in their opposition to the new federal government described in the Constitution. They soon realized that the best way to defeat the Constitution was to use the issue of a bill of rights.

There was a widespread fear of a strong and powerful federal government, combined with the belief that a bill of rights was necessary to protect people from government. If people needed to be protected from their relatively weak state governments, they certainly needed protection from the vastly more powerful federal government. In addition, it was easier for the Anti-Federalists to dramatize the lack of a bill of rights than the issues of taxes or the powers of the state governments.

What do you think are the most compelling arguments for and against ratification of the Constitution?

The lack of a bill of rights became the focus of the Anti-Federalist campaign. It was a highly emotional issue for the men and women who had just fought a revolution to secure their rights. In several states, the question of a bill of rights was used effectively to organize opposition to the ratification of the Constitution.

Many Anti-Federalist leaders, such as George Mason, hoped to defeat the Constitution so that a second constitutional convention would be held. There, the Anti-Federalists hoped, they would have more influence in creating a new government.

Federalists Ask Voters to Approve the Constitution

The Federalists knew that many members of Congress and the state governments were against the new Constitution, largely because it reduced their powers. So the Federalists decided not to ask the Congress or state governments to approve the Constitution, even though they were expected to do so.

James Madison developed the plan presented by the Federalists. The plan was to go directly to the voters to get them to approve the Constitution. The Constitution would be presented to special ratifying conventions to be held in each state. The delegates would be elected by popular vote of the people for the sole purpose of approving the Constitution. Madison's plan was consistent with the idea in the Preamble to the Constitution that says, "We the People . . . do ordain and establish this Constitution. . . ."

The Federalists' plan was another example of the social contract idea. The people who were to be governed by the new national government were asked to consent to its creation and obey its decisions. You may recognize this as the method for establishing a government set forth in the natural rights philosophy of John Locke and in the Declaration of Independence. In Jefferson's words, just governments "derive their . . . powers from the consent of the governed." Some people had argued, for example, that the Articles of Confederation were not valid or legitimate because they had never been presented to the people for their consent.

The Framers at the convention approved this plan for ratifying the Constitution. They included a provision that would put it into effect after being ratified by just nine of the thirteen state conventions.

After they had agreed on their strategy, the Federalists encouraged their associates in the states to organize the state conventions and elect delegates to them as quickly as possible. They knew the Anti-Federalists had not had enough time to organize their opposition. The Federalists had worked on the Constitution for almost four months. They knew the arguments for and against it and had gathered support. They thought that if the conventions acted quickly, the Anti-Federalists would have little time to organize their opposition to the Constitution's ratification.

Struggling for Ratification

Despite the advantages of the Federalists' position, the Anti-Federalists were able to put up a strong fight. The debates in the states over ratification lasted ten months. It was an intense and sometimes bitter political struggle. One of the most difficult fights for ratification was in New York. To help the Federalist cause, three men—Alexander Hamilton (see Figure 3.4.4), James Madison, and John Jay—wrote a series of essays published in three New York newspapers. They also were used in the Virginia ratification debates and are an important source of information about the conflict over the convention. The articles were not intended to present all sides. Their purpose was to convince people to support the ratification of the Constitution. These essays are now called *The Federalist*. They are considered to be the most important work written in defense of the new Constitution.

In defending the new Constitution, the writers of *The Federalist* were very skilled at using basic ideas about government that most Americans understood and accepted.

They presented the Constitution as a well-organized, agreed-on plan for national government. The conflicts and compromises that had taken place during its development were not stressed in an attempt to present the Constitution as favorably as possible.

How the Federalists Responded to Anti-Federalists

The Anti-Federalists had some traditional arguments about what made a good government on their side as well. The Federalists were better organized, however. The Federalists' arguments in support of the Constitution claimed that it provided a solution for the problem of creating a republican government in a large and diverse nation. They were able to convince a significant number of people to support their position by the following arguments:

- **The civic virtue of the people cannot be relied on alone to protect basic rights**

- **The way the government is organized will protect basic rights**

- **The representation of different interests in the government will protect basic rights**

The civic virtue of the people could no longer be relied on as the sole support of a government that would protect the people's rights and promote their welfare. Throughout history, the Federalists argued, the greatest dangers in republics to the common good and the natural rights of citizens had been from the selfish pursuit of their interests by groups of citizens who ignored the common good.

Therefore, for almost 2,000 years, political philosophers had insisted

Figure 3.4.4: Alexander Hamilton (1757–1804).

Courtesy of the Art Commission of New York.

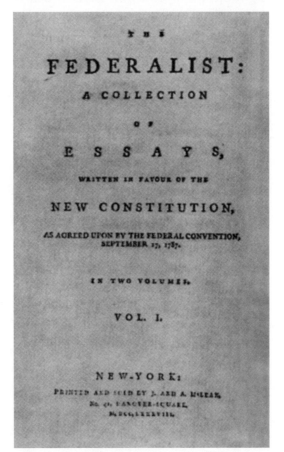

What role did The Federalist *play in ratification of the Constitution?*

Courtesy of the National Archives.

that republican government was only safe if the citizens possessed civic virtue. By civic virtue they meant that citizens had to be willing to set aside their interests if it was necessary to do so for the common good.

Recent experiences with their state governments had led a number of people to doubt that they could rely on the virtue of citizens to promote the common good and protect the rights of individuals. Many of the state legislatures had passed laws that helped people in debt at the expense of those to whom they owed money. These laws were seen by many as an infringement on property rights that were, after all, one of the basic natural rights for which the Revolution had been fought in the first place.

If the proper working of a republican form of government could not rely on the virtue of its citizens, what could it rely on? How could a government be organized so it would not be dominated by self-interested individuals or factions at the expense of others?

The way in which the Constitution organized the government, including the separation of powers and checks and balances, was the best way to promote the goals of republicanism. A major idea in *The Federalist* is that the national government set forth in the Constitution did not have to rely solely on the civic virtue of the people to protect citizens' rights and promote their welfare. The writers believed that it was unrealistic to expect people in a large and diverse nation, living hundreds of miles apart, to be willing to give up their own interests for the benefit of others. The Federalists argued that the rights and welfare of all would be protected by the complicated system of representation, separation of powers, and checks and balances provided by the Constitution. They also believed that the method of electing senators and presidents would increase the possibility that they would have the qualities required of good governing officials.

The Federalists took the position that the Constitution's strength was that it provided for different branches of government that would represent the different interests of the people. They also claimed that this complicated system would make it impossible for any individual or faction—or even a majority—to take complete control of the government to serve its own interests at the expense of the common good or the rights of individuals.

The large size of the nation, they argued, would make it particularly difficult for any one faction to attain a majority. Because so many interests and factions would be represented in the national government, it would be less likely that any one of them would dominate.

Some would argue that the system was so complicated that it would be difficult to get anything done, especially if one or more interested and powerful groups objected to something that was being planned. Madison, in *The Federalist,* clearly did not see this as a disadvantage. One of his criticisms of the state legislatures had been that they passed too many laws in the first place. Most of the Framers believed that the best way to prevent a bad law from being passed was to prevent a law from being passed at all.

The representation of different interests in the government would protect basic rights. The branches of the national government, the power each had distributed to it by the Constitution, and the interests each was supposed to represent are as follows:

- *Legislative branch.* **The House of Representatives would protect the people's local interests, since representatives would be chosen from small congressional districts. The Senate would protect the people's state interests, since it would be elected by state legislatures.**

- *Executive branch.* The president would protect the people's national interests, since he would be elected by a method that required electors to select him from among leaders who had achieved national prominence.

- *Judicial branch.* The Supreme Court would protect the people's fundamental interests, since it was independent of political manipulation and therefore responsible only to the Constitution.

Did the National Government Have Too Much Power?

The Federalists admitted that the new national government had much more power than the old national government. It had more control over the states, but it was a government limited to enumerated powers. The federal system and checks and balances ensured that those limits would not be violated. As a result, they claimed, the increased powers given to the government under the Constitution could only be used to protect, not violate, the rights of the people. Critics feared that giving so much power to a national government might be a serious threat to their rights and welfare.

The Federalists used a number of arguments to counter those demanding a bill of rights. The most important of these arguments included:

- **The complexity of the government and the diversity of the nation to protect rights.** A large republic makes it nearly impossible for a "majority faction" to have its way.

- **The Constitution does protect a number of specific rights.** These include right to habeas corpus; prohibition of ex-post facto laws and bills of attainder; protection against violations of contracts; guarantee in criminal cases of trial by jury in the state where the crime was committed; and protection against accusations of treason by its careful definition.

- **A bill of rights is unnecessary in a nation with popular sovereignty.** Previous bills of rights, such as the English Bill of Rights, protected people from a powerful monarch over whom they had no control. Under the Constitution, the people have the power to remove elected officials from office. The protections of such bills of rights are therefore unnecessary under the Constitution.

- **The Constitution does not give the federal government the power to deprive people of their rights.** It gives government only limited powers to do specific things-enumerated powers. There is no need to list rights that the government has no power to violate.

- **Declarations of rights are ineffective and dangerous.** Most state constitutions are prefaced with bills of rights, but these bills did not stop state governments from violating citizens' rights. No state had a comprehensive list of rights, that is, a bill that listed all the rights that were protected.

Apparently as a result, some state governments felt free to violate important rights unlisted in their bills. Since it is impossible to list all rights, it is better to have no list at all. Government officials might feel free to violate unlisted rights.

Despite these arguments, the Federalists found it necessary to agree to the Anti-Federalists' demands for a bill of rights.

The Federalists Give in to the Demand for a Bill of Rights

The Federalists worked hard to overcome the objections of the Anti-Federalists. By June of 1788, nine states had voted to **ratify** the Constitution. New Hampshire was

Key Note Term

ratify—to approve and sanction formally

the ninth and last state needed to make the Constitution the highest law of the land. The important states, New York and Virginia, had not yet approved the Constitution. The debates were very close in these states because of the fear of creating such a large and powerful national government.

Finally, a compromise was reached. To get some Anti-Federalists to support the Constitution, the Federalists agreed that when the first Congress was held, it would draft a bill of rights to be added to the Constitution. The bill was to list the rights of citizens that were not to be violated by the federal government. The Federalists insisted that the bill of rights include a statement saying that the list of rights should not be interpreted to mean that they were the only rights the people had.

Because the Federalists' agreed to sponsor a bill of rights, much of the Anti-Federalists' support toward not ratifying the Constitution was reduced. It deprived the Anti-Federalists of their most powerful weapon. In some states, Massachusetts for example, the agreement was enough to win a close ratification vote, 187 to 168. Then, at last, New York and Virginia also voted for ratification. The Anti-Federalists had lost their battle to reject or revise the Constitution but they had won an agreement to add a bill of rights.

The Federalists deserve the credit for writing the Constitution, which created our present form of government; however, the Anti-Federalists' objections to the Constitution resulted in the addition of the Bill of Rights. The Bill of Rights has proved to be vitally important to the protection of basic rights of the American people and an inspiration to many beyond America's shores.

Conclusion

This lesson covered the Constitution's ratification arguments between the Federalists and Anti-Federalists. You learned why some were opposed to confirming this document, and why others were in agreement. You also learned how some of the differences were ultimately settled.

This ends Chapter 3, "Creating the Constitution." In the following chapter, "Shaping American Institutions and Practices," you will learn how the new United States government was organized, how political parties formed, and about the division of power in the newly formed government.

Lesson Review

1. Why is the Constitution described as "a bundle of compromises"?

2. What arguments did the Anti-Federalists make with regard to the need for a bill of rights?

3. What tactics did the Federalists employ to win the struggle for ratification of the Constitution?

4. What arguments did the Federalists make to resist the demand for a bill of rights? Why did they eventually give in to this demand?

Shaping American Institutions and Practices

Chapter 4

Lesson 1

Constitution Used to Organize New Government

Key Terms

bureaucracy
federal district court
Judiciary Act of 1789
president's cabinet

What You Will Learn to Do

- Identify how the Constitution was used to organize the new government

Linked Core Objectives

- Communicate using verbal, non-verbal, visual, and written techniques
- Apply critical thinking techniques

Skills and Knowledge You Will Gain Along the Way

- Explain that the Constitution provides a general framework outlining how the government should be organized and should operate, and that details are added by the government as the need arises

- Explain how Congress used Article II of the Constitution to name the new president and vice president

- Explain the importance and the methods of raising revenue to fund the new government

- Describe how Congress organized the executive branch and the unforeseen growth of this branch and the federal bureaucracy

- **Describe the federal court system that was established by Congress in the Judiciary Act of 1789**
- **Define key words contained in this lesson**

Introduction

This lesson explains the steps taken by the First Congress to name a president and vice president, to provide funding for the new government, to draft a bill of rights, and to organize the executive and judicial branches.

When you complete this lesson, you should be able to explain how the Constitution provides an outline of the federal government's organization and that details are added by the government itself. You also should be able to explain how the First Congress used the Constitution to name a president and vice president and to raise revenue to fund the new government. You should be able to describe how Congress organized the executive branch and how it has expanded. In addition, you should be able to describe how the federal court system was established in the **Judiciary Act of 1789.** Finally, you should be able to explain how the Bill of Rights was added to the Constitution.

Key Note Term

Judiciary Act of 1789— an act to establish the Judicial Courts of the United States

Tasks of the First Congress

The newly elected senators and representatives of the First Congress met in New York in April 1789 to begin their work. Five of their tasks were:

- **Naming the new president and vice president**
- **Providing money for the government**
- **Organizing the executive branch of government**
- **Organizing the judicial branch of government**
- **Drafting a bill of rights**

The following sections describe how Congress accomplished these tasks within constitutional guidelines.

Naming the New President and Vice President

Article II of the Constitution deals with the executive branch of the federal government. Section 1 of that article sets forth the way the president and vice president are selected. Electors are appointed by state legislators; these electors vote for the candidates. After the ballots are collected, the president of the Senate is to supervise the counting of the ballots. In 1789 the votes showed, as expected, that George Washington had been elected President. John Adams, with the second highest number of votes, became Vice President.

Providing Money for the Government

The First Congress was faced with a serious problem —the federal government had no income. Finding a source of income was a matter of high priority. In addition to deciding what taxes to collect, besides those on imports, Congress had to design a method for collecting them. Many members of the First Congress thought that raising revenue would be one of their most important accomplishments. They were reluctant to put off discussing the issue, and believed it should be addressed even before something as important as a bill of rights.

Organizing the Executive Branch

The Constitution gives Congress the power to organize the executive branch. When the First Congress met, its members were concerned about controlling the executive branch and preventing the president from gaining too much power. This concern was made clear in the debate over how the president should be addressed. It was first proposed that he be referred to or introduced as "His Highness, the President of the United States of America." They decided that this would not be proper because the nation was a republic, not a monarchy. Instead, Congress agreed on the simpler, more democratic title of "The President of the United States."

The First Congress created three departments to carry on the business of the executive branch. The persons in charge of these departments were to be appointed by the president and called "secretaries." These officials were very important under President Washington because he used the secretaries as his advisers. It was not until President Jackson's time, in the 1830s, that they became known as the **president's cabinet.** The first departments and their secretaries were:

- *State Department*—**Thomas Jefferson was the first Secretary of State. This department was responsible for dealing with other nations, as well as for many domestic matters, such as registering patents and copyrights.**

- *War Department*—**Henry Knox was the first Secretary of War. This department was responsible for handling the nation's defense.**

- *Treasury Department*—**Alexander Hamilton was the first Secretary of the Treasury. This department was responsible for taking care of the financial affairs of the federal government. In addition to these three, Edmund Randolph was selected to be**

Key Note Term

president's cabinet— the President's hand picked advisors, each in charge of a different government office or department

the Attorney General. It was his responsibility to handle all Supreme Court cases involving the federal government, and to give legal advice to the President and other members of the executive branch.

Today the organization of the executive branch of the federal government is far more complex than it was during the early years of the nation. When Thomas Jefferson was president, 1801-1809, there were 2,210 people working in the branch and its three departments. By the mid-1990s, more than three million people were working in the 14 departments and numerous other federal agencies of the executive branch.

The Constitution does not mention a federal **bureaucracy.** The Founders probably did not expect the executive branch to grow so large or to have so many responsibilities. Still, the framework for government set up in the Constitution has been able to deal with these developments. To get a better understanding of the organization of the executive branch today, see the simplified organizational chart in Figure 4.1.1.

Organizing the Judicial Branch

Article III of the Constitution says that the "the judicial power of the United States, shall be vested in one supreme court, and in such inferior courts as the Congress may from time to time . . . establish." The Framers wrote only this very general guideline and gave the First Congress the task of organizing a system of federal courts. Congress complied by passing a law known as the Judiciary Act of 1789. It established two kinds of federal courts below the Supreme Court.

- **Congress established a federal district court in each state. These federal courts were responsible for the first hearing or trial of many cases involving the Constitution, federal laws, and disputes between citizens of different states.**

- **Congress also established a system of circuit courts, in which serious crimes could be tried. These courts would also hear appeals from the district courts and review their cases for errors of law. Until 1891, when the Circuit Courts of Appeals were established, a circuit court was composed of a district judge and a justice of the Supreme Court.**

> ## Key Note Term
>
> **bureaucracy—**
> government characterized by specialization of functions, adherence to fixed rules, and a hierarchy of authority

> ## Key Note Term
>
> **federal district court—**
> a district court of law and equity that hears cases under federal jurisdiction

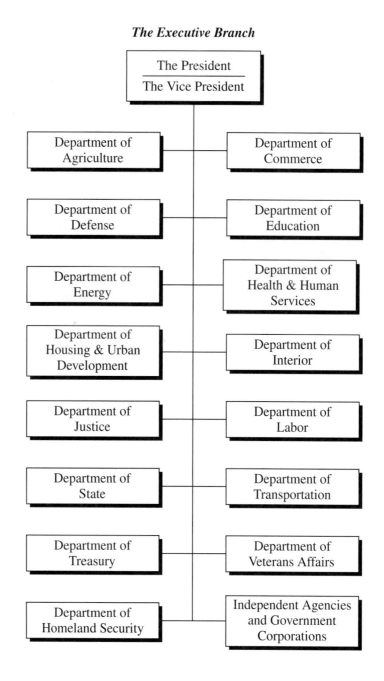

The Executive Branch

In addition to the system of federal courts established by the Constitution and Congress to rule on federal cases, each state had its own courts established by its legislature to rule on cases of state law. This system of federal and state courts is organized today in much the same way it was in 1789.

Today the United States Supreme Court plays an important role in our federal government. In the beginning, however, the Supreme Court's role was much less significant. One of the first justices, John Rutledge, did not attend a single session of the Supreme Court during the first two years. The first chief justice, John Jay, spent little time on the job; he spent a year in England on a diplomatic mission and ran for gov-

The United States Court System

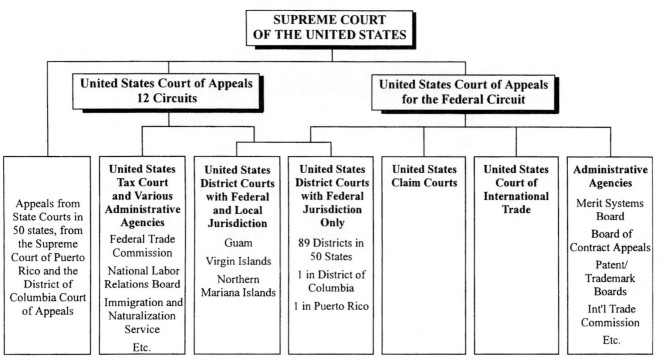

Why has the U.S. court system grown so much more complex than originally outlined by the Framers?

Courtesy of the Center for Civic Education.

ernor of New York twice. Oliver Ellsworth, the next chief justice, resigned his position in 1800. No one considered the Supreme Court an important part of the federal government.

Drafting a Bill of Rights

During the struggle to get the states to ratify the Constitution, the document had been criticized for not having a bill of rights. To answer this objection, the Federalists agreed to the addition of a bill of rights as soon as the new government was established.

In his inaugural address on April 30, 1789, George Washington urged Congress to respond to the widespread demand to add a bill of rights to the Constitution. When the First Congress met, James Madison wanted to fulfill the promise made by the Federalists during the ratification debates. Madison was aware that many people were still very suspicious of the new government. They would be watching closely to see if the Federalists would keep their promises.

Madison began his task by sorting through the more than 200 amendments recommended by states during the ratification debates. Most fell into two groups:

- **They placed additional limitations on the powers of the federal government**
- **They protected individual rights**

When he introduced a bill of rights, Madison was careful not to include any proposals that would limit the power of the federal government and increase that of the states. This led some Anti- Federalists, such as Patrick Henry, to reject Madison's bill. Others, such as George Mason for example, approved of the amendments. Madison's draft did include many of the suggestions from the states that protected individual rights such as freedom of religion, speech, press, and assembly, and the rights of petition and trial by jury. Introduction of the Bill of Rights convinced enough Anti-Federalists to support the government so that the movement for a second constitutional convention quickly died. Now the new government could get on to other important tasks.

Conclusion

This lesson covered how the Constitution provides a general framework outlining how the government should be organized and should operate. This included how revenue is raised for government, how the executive branch is organized, how the new president and vice president will be named, how the judiciary structure is organized, and the initial drafting of a Bill of Rights for individual freedoms.

The following lesson examines the Bill of Rights, an important part of our U. S. Constitution that guarantees all citizens specific rights and freedoms.

Lesson Review

1. What were some of the important tasks the First Congress had to address in 1789?

2. What departments did Congress create to do the work of the executive branch of the national government? What responsibilities did each of these departments have?

3. Define the term "bureaucracy." How has the federal government's bureaucracy changed since Jefferson was President?

4. How did the Judiciary Act of 1789 organize the system of federal courts?

Lesson 2

Bill of Rights

Key Terms

bills of attainder
enumeration
ex post facto laws
habeas corpus
impeachment
provision

What You Will Learn to Do

- Examine the reasons behind the development of the Bill of Rights

Linked Core Objectives

- Communicate using verbal, non-verbal, visual, and written techniques
- Apply critical thinking techniques

Skills and Knowledge You Will Gain Along the Way

- Explain the importance of the rights the Framers included in the body of the Constitution to limit the powers of the federal government and protect the rights of the people

- Explain why the Anti-Federalists wanted a Bill of Rights added to the Constitution

- Explain why Madison proposed adding a Bill of Rights to the beginning of the Constitution and why the Bill or Rights was added as a series of amendments instead

- Describe the amendments Madison proposed to protect individual rights from abuse by state governments

- Defend positions on the importance of the Second Amendment—the right of the people to keep and bear arms

- Define key words contained in this lesson

Introduction

The Federalists argued that separation of powers, checks and balances, the federal system, and the size and diversity of the nation provided the best protection for the rights of individuals. In particular, they pointed to provisions in the new Constitution that prohibited both the federal and state governments from violating important rights.

In this lesson you will examine the rights the Framers included in the Constitution and discuss their importance. In addition, you will learn of the struggle to add a Bill of Rights to the Constitution, reactions to the Bill of Rights, and the reasons it provided only limited protection of rights. After completing this lesson, you should be able to list the rights the Framers included in the Constitution. You should be able to describe these rights, explain why they were chosen, and explain their importance. You also should be able to explain the conflict over adding a bill of rights to the Constitution, the result of the conflict, and why the Bill of Rights had such a limited effect on the lives of Americans at the time.

Specific Rights Protected in the Constitution

The Framers included a number of provisions in the Constitution to protect specific rights. These **provisions** protected rights of individual citizens and persons holding public office in the federal government. Each provision was designed to prevent the type of abuse the Framers had seen in British history, their own colonial and state governments, or the national government under the Articles of Confederation.

These rights are divided into three groups to make it easier to understand their functions and importance. The Constitution provides protection of:

- **Political independence and other rights of public officials**
- **Individual rights against violation by state governments**
- **Individual rights against violation by the federal government**

Protection of Political Independence and Other Rights of Public Officials

The Framers saw the need to protect the political rights of public officials. These rights include:

- **Freedom of speech for members of Congress is protected so they cannot be arrested for anything they say on the floor of Congress.**

Daniel Webster Addressing Congress

Should members of Congress have immunity for statements made in Congress?

Courtesy of the National Archives

- Members of Congress cannot be arrested for minor crimes they commit while Congress is in session.

- Congress also is prohibited from imposing a religious test on people who hold federal office. This means that people cannot be required to express certain religious beliefs as a qualification for holding office.

- If members of the executive or judicial branches are accused of misconduct in office, the **impeachment** clauses protect their right to a fair hearing.

Protection of Individual Rights against Violation by State Governments

Many individual rights are protected against violation by state governments. These rights include:

- No state can pass any law "impairing the obligation of contracts." This means, among other things, that a state legislature cannot pass a law releasing people from the responsibility to pay their debts.

- The Constitution protected the property rights of citizens who held slaves. Enslaved Africans were considered the personal property of the slaveholder. This provision required state governments to return any slave who had fled from another state, a provision later overturned by the Thirteenth Amendment.

- Both federal and state governments were prohibited from passing **ex post facto laws** and **bills of attainder**.

Why did the Framers believe it was necessary to protect the obligation of contracts?

Protection of Individual Rights against Violation by the Federal Government

Not only are individual rights protected from violations of the state, but they are also protected by violations by the federal government. These rights include:

- **Habeas corpus and trial by jury in criminal cases.**
- **Protection from the accusation of treason by defining this crime very specifically and narrowly. This definition cannot be modified by Congress; it can only be changed by a constitutional amendment.**

Madison's Proposed Amendments to the Constitution

When the First Congress met on June 8, 1789, James Madison introduced his amendments on the floor of the House of Representatives. In his speech, he tried to assure the Federalists that his amendments would not radically change the Constitution they had supported. He also tried to convince the Anti-Federalists that his amendments would protect individual liberties.

Madison suggested that an introductory statement be added to the Constitution. This introduction would contain the basic ideas about government stated in the Declaration of Independence:

- **The purpose of government is to protect the rights of the people**
- **The people are the ultimate source of its authority**

Why were members of the House of Representatives not interested in Madison's speeches in support of a bill of rights?

Such statements frequently appeared at the beginning of state constitutions to reaffirm the principle of popular sovereignty.

Madison was convinced that the greatest danger to individual rights came from groups who might use the government to serve their own interests at the expense of others. He thought that state governments were more easily used by factions than the national government. Consequently, he feared that state governments were a greater threat to individual rights than the federal government.

He proposed what he considered "the most valuable amendment in the whole list." This proposed amendment stated, "No state shall violate the equal rights of conscience, or the freedom of the press, or the trial by jury in criminal cases."

Madison also included in his proposal an amendment to deal with the criticism that a list of rights would endanger those rights not listed. When adopted it became the Ninth Amendment. The Ninth Amendment clearly states that the Bill of Rights is only a partial list of the people's rights. It says, "The **enumeration** in the Constitution of certain rights shall not be construed to deny or disparage others retained by the people." This means that the specific enumeration (listing) of people's rights should not be interpreted to deny or lessen the importance of other rights held by the people.

Finally, Madison argued that the amendments he had drafted should be included in the Constitution itself. He did not think they should be added as a separate list at the end of the Constitution.

Key Note Term

enumeration—an act of enumerating

Congress' Response to Madison's Proposals

Although Madison's speech was eloquent, members of the House of Representatives appeared completely unmoved by his suggestions. Every speaker who followed him either opposed a Bill of Rights or argued that the House had far more important business. Six weeks later Madison again asked the House to vote on his amendments, but the House sent them to a committee instead of debating them.

Finally, in August, the House agreed to consider Madison's amendments. The House made some changes and sent Madison's draft to the Senate. At the insistence of Roger Sherman, the amendments were to be added at the end of the Constitution rather than placed in the body of the document as Madison had suggested. Sherman argued that it was too early to begin rewriting the Constitution itself. If amendments were listed separately, it would be clear which parts were original, and which ones had been added later. He also feared that if they were added to the body of the Constitution, the entire document would need to be ratified again.

Because Senate debate was not open to the public, little is known about what happened there. We do know that the Senate made significant changes in the House version. The senators also eliminated the amendment that would have prohibited state governments from violating the right to freedom of conscience, speech, press, and trial by jury in criminal cases.

With ratification by Virginia, the ninth state to give its approval, the Bill of Rights became a part of the Constitution on December 15, 1791.

The People's Response to the Bill of Rights in 1791

The reaction of most Americans to the Bill of Rights was lukewarm, at best. Its passage had little effect on the average person. The Supreme Court ruled in 1833 that the Bill of Rights applied only to the federal government. As a result, it was not until adoption of the Fourteenth Amendment—almost 150 years after approval of the Bill of Rights—that citizens would be protected by the Constitution from violations of these rights by their state governments as well.

The Anti-Federalists, who had based much of their opposition to the Constitution on the lack of a Bill of Rights, were unhappy with its passage. They thought it spoiled their chances to rewrite the Constitution. They said the amendments were "good for nothing." "I believe," said Senator William Grayson of Virginia, "as many others do, they will do more harm than good."

At the same time, many Federalists were angry with Madison for pushing the Bill of Rights through Congress. At best, they considered it of little importance. Even Madison, tired of all the disagreement and dissent, had come to think of the whole experience as a "nauseous project."

Critical Thinking Exercise

Developing and Defending Positions on the Second Amendment

The Second Amendment reads, "A well regulated Militia, being necessary to the security of a free State, the right of the people to keep and bear Arms, shall not be infringed."

One basic belief of classical republicanism was that a standing professional army was the enemy of freedom. Only a citizen militia, in which each member of the community had the duty to serve, could provide security without threatening the liberties of the people.

This fear of standing armies and the belief in a citizen militia was supported by political philosophers as well as by historical experience. For example, when the American colonists began to oppose British policies, Parliament passed a law banning the shipment of arms to the colonies.

The first colonial armed rebellion was a patriot raid on the British Fort William and Mary. It was there that arms and ammunition were seized and secretly distributed throughout the colonies—arms that were later used to fire the "shot heard 'round the world" at Lexington and Concord.

James Madison argued during the ratification debates that one reason Americans need not fear the power of the new federal government was that the citizens had "the advantage of being armed, which you possess over the people of almost every other nation. . . . In the several Kingdoms of Europe . . . the governments are afraid to trust the people with arms."

The Anti-Federalists strongly supported the right of citizens to bear arms. Patrick Henry declared, "The great principle is that every man be armed. Everyone who is able may have a gun." Richard Henry Lee argued that "to preserve liberty, it is essential that the whole body of people always possess arms, and be taught alike, especially when young, how to use them."

It was with this understanding that the Second Amendment was written. It was passed on a voice vote, without objection, and was approved by the Senate. It was ratified by the people with little debate.

Do you think the Second Amendment is as important today as it was in the eighteenth century?

What argument would you make for the right of the citizens to bear arms today? How might that argument differ from the arguments Americans made in the 1790s?

What limitations, if any, do you think should be placed on the right to bear arms? How would you justify those limits?

Weapons seizure in New York, 1991

Why is the question of a person's right to bear arms more controversial today than when the Constitution was written?

Courtesy of AP/Wide World Photos.

The Framers' Awareness of Other Threats to Rights

Some people argue that the Framers were not sufficiently aware of important threats to rights from sources other than government. They did not foresee threats arising from economic power, for example, or religious and racial prejudice. Therefore, some people argue that the Framers did not understand that the power of government can be used to protect the rights of some individuals against threats from other individuals, groups, or organizations.

In the Twentieth century, the Bill of Rights has become something it never was in the Eighteenth century. It is, perhaps, the most important single document protecting individual rights. The struggle to extend its protections to all Americans has taken more than 200 years, however, and the struggle continues.

Conclusion

This lesson covered the Bill of Rights, what it contains, and how it came to be. You learned about James Madison and his efforts to have the Bill of Rights included in the Constitution, and the opposition this document evoked.

In the next lesson, you learn about the rise of political parties in the newly formed United States. You will examine how these parties evolved and the importance they played in American history in the past as well as their place in the present.

Lesson Review

1. What rights did the Framers include in the body of the Constitution? Why did they choose to protect these rights? Why are these rights important?

2. How would you explain the meaning of the Ninth Amendment?

3. Why was Madison concerned about the possible violation of individual rights by state governments? What amendment did he propose to address this concern?

4. Why did the Bill of Rights have little effect on the average person when it was first adopted?

Lesson 3

Rise of Political Parties

Key Terms

Alien and Sedition Acts
faction
Federalist Party
general welfare clause
necessary and proper clause
political parties
Republican Party
revolution of 1800

What You Will Learn to Do

- Compare the role of political parties in early America to the role they play today

Linked Core Objectives

- Communicate using verbal, non-verbal, visual, and written techniques
- Apply critical thinking techniques

Skills and Knowledge You Will Gain Along the Way

- Explain why the framers opposed the development of political parties
- Explain the basis of the disagreement between the Federalists and the Republicans over the interpretation of the Constitution, and the relationship of this disagreement to the emergence of political parties
- Explain the arguments between Jefferson and Hamilton over the establishment of the Bank of the United States, foreign relations, and the Alien and Sedition acts
- Explain the significance of the presidential election of 1800 and the reasons for the demise of the Federalist Party after the War of 1812
- Explain the role of political parties today
- Define key words contained in this lesson

Chapter 4

Key Note Terms

Federalist Party—the party who supported the radification of the Constitution, advocated a strong central government, believed in or supported a federal system or government

faction—a party, in political society, combined or acting in union, in opposition to the government, or state: usually applied to a minority, but it may be applied to a majority; a combination or clique of partisans of any kind, acting for their own interest; especially if greedy, clamorous, and reckless of the common good

Introduction

Soon after the government was established, there was an unforeseen development to which the Framers were very much opposed. This was the formation of political parties. This lesson describes how political parties came to be formed and describes the importance of political parties to our present system of government.

When you complete the lesson, you should be able to explain why the Framers were opposed to the idea of political parties. You should also be able to explain the conflicting points of view that led to the development of political parties, the reasons for the demise of the **Federalist Party,** and the role that political parties play in American politics today.

Madison's View of Factions

James Madison argued in The Federalist that one of the Constitution's major advantages was that it organized the government in such a way that "factions" would be controlled. He defined a **faction** as a group of citizens, either a majority or a minority, that pursues its own interests at the expense of the common good. Many Framers agreed that factions were dangerous to republican government for this very reason.

George Caleb Bingham's "The County Election"

What has been the role of political parties in elections?

Courtesy of Bettman/Corbis Images.

Madison argued that people would always join with others of similar interests and opinions to advocate policies favorable to themselves. There would be, however, many interests and opinions in a large commercial society. This diversity, he said, would keep any one interest group or faction from gaining control of the government. He argued that the influence of factions would be limited by the complicated system of government planned by the Constitution.

The size and diversity of the nation, as well as the complexity of the government, would limit the ability of any single faction to form a majority. That way, no single group could control the government solely for its own interests. Instead, the different groups would have to work together through bargaining and compromise to create coalitions that would promote the interests of a majority as well as protect minority interests.

In spite of Madison's intent and these safeguards, factions in the form of **political parties** did develop and are now an accepted part of the American political system.

The Development of Political Parties

When George Washington was president, he sought advice from people whose opinions he most valued. He appointed two such persons as his secretaries—Secretary of State Thomas Jefferson and Secretary of the Treasury Alexander Hamilton. Each had very different ideas about what the government's policies should be, and the two were often in conflict.

Why is there no mention of political parties in the Constitution?

Courtesy of Catherine Karnow/Corbis Images.

In time, after Washington began to accept Hamilton's opinions in foreign as well as domestic affairs, Jefferson resigned from his position. During this period, Hamilton and his followers became known as Federalists. Jefferson and his followers became known as Republicans. Jefferson's Republicans eventually became today's Democratic Party, not the **Republican Party.** The differences of opinion between the Federalists and the Republicans played a large part in the development of political parties in the United States.

The basic disagreement between Hamilton and Jefferson concerned the way the powers of the new federal government were to be used.

Hamilton and the Federalists argued that the Constitution had created a government designed to take on national problems. As long as a problem was national, they said, the federal government could and should deal with it, whether or not it was specifically mentioned in the Constitution.

Jefferson and the Republicans argued that the Constitution's description of the powers of the federal government was so vague that, using the Federalists' approach, the government would be able to do whatever it wanted. Republicans believed that if the government were free to define its own powers, the liberty of the people would be threatened. They argued that the government should be strictly limited to its enumerated powers.

Article I, Section 8—The Powers of Congress

No part of the Constitution did more to raise the fears of Jefferson and his followers than Article I, Section 8, which sets forth the powers of Congress. Although it does seem to limit Congress by clearly listing a number of its responsibilities and powers, it also contains two clauses which are very general. These are the **general welfare clause** and the **necessary and proper clause**. These clauses state that Congress shall have the following powers:

- **To lay and collect taxes . . . to pay the debts and provide for the common defense and general welfare of the United States**
- **To make all laws which shall be necessary and proper for carrying into execution the foregoing powers, [the powers given to Congress under Section 8]**

The Federalists thought that the Constitution gave the federal government certain broad responsibilities and its powers should be equal to those responsibilities. This "energetic" use of the federal government's power was exactly what Jefferson and some Republicans feared.

The Federalists believed that because the people had delegated these powers to the federal government, the people could reduce or eliminate the powers by amending the Constitution, if they chose. The enumeration of powers in the Constitution clearly gave the federal and state governments independent spheres of responsibility and this was a sufficient limitation on the powers of both.

Conflicts between the Federalists and the Republicans

The differences in political philosophy between Hamilton and Jefferson led them to disagree greatly on a number of specific issues regarding how the new government should be run. One of the issues on which they took opposing sides was the establishment of the Bank of the United States. As Secretary of the Treasury, Hamilton wanted to demonstrate the power of the federal government and strengthen the new nation's weak economy. To achieve these goals he made a number of recommendations to the Congress. One was that it passed a law establishing the Bank of the United States. Congress passed the law and, thus, aroused much controversy.

Hamilton said that the creation of the Bank was a "necessary and proper" method of carrying out the responsibilities given to Congress by the Constitution, such as collecting taxes and regulating trade.

Jefferson replied that the "necessary and proper" clause should be interpreted as if it read "absolutely and indispensably necessary." Clearly, this interpretation would have severely limited the power of Congress. Certainly, the creation of the Bank would not have passed this restrictive test. Jefferson understood this, as this was exactly what he intended.

President Washington accepted Hamilton's position. He signed the legislation establishing the Bank of the United States. Thus, a large step was taken toward increasing the power of the federal government.

Federalist and Republican Views on the War between Great Britain and France

In 1793, war broke out between France and Great Britain. The Federalists and Republicans disagreed on what the United States should do. Federalists wanted the United States to help the British since Americans had more trade with the British than with the French. They also opposed the radicalism of the French Revolution of 1789. The Republicans wanted the United States to help the French, who had helped the Americans fight the British during the Revolutionary War. They also supported the revolution against the French monarchy.

President Washington tried to prevent people from dividing into opposing camps over this issue. He declared that the United States was neutral and would not take sides in the war. When he left office after his second term, he warned the country against entering into permanent alliances with foreign governments. He also warned the American people to avoid what he called the "spirit of party."

By the time Washington retired, however, party conflict was becoming a fixture in American politics. Washington's great personal prestige had shielded him from attacks. No one could take the place of Washington though, and his successors have all been subject to attacks from the opposition.

The Alien and Sedition Acts

In the election of 1796, John Adams, a Federalist, became president. But Thomas Jefferson, a Republican, was elected vice president. This increased the conflict between the Federalists and the Republicans. Jefferson and his followers criticized the way

Why did the Federalists try to silence criticism of the government in the press?

Adams and the Federalist majority in Congress were running the government. Adams and the Federalists were able to get laws passed called the **Alien and Sedition Acts.** These laws gave the president the power to force foreigners to leave the country if he considered them dangerous. They also made it a crime for editors, writers, or speakers to attack the government.

Jefferson and the other Republicans were outraged at the laws and at their enforcement by Federalist judges. They knew the laws were intended to keep them from criticizing the government. They hoped that federal judges would declare the acts unconstitutional. But several Republican newspaper editors and a member of Congress were fined and put in jail for writing and speaking against the government.

Finally, Madison joined with Jefferson to write the "Kentucky and Virginia Resolutions." They claimed that the states had a right to decide if the federal government had exceeded its powers. These resolutions claimed the state legislatures had the power to declare laws made by Congress, such as the Alien and Sedition Acts, null and void. The resolutions were not accepted by the other states. If they had been, they would have given the states a large amount of power over the federal government.

Key Note Term

Alien and Sedition Acts—gave the President the power to imprison or deport aliens suspect of activities posing a threat to the national government

The "Revolution of 1800"

The Presidential election of 1800 was the first to feature candidates for president and vice President who were openly supported by political parties. Federalists supported John Adams for President. Republicans supported Thomas Jefferson. Although the candidates themselves did not campaign, the election created bitter party disagreements. The Alien and Sedition Acts were often cited by Republicans as proof that Federalists were not fit to govern.

The election of 1800 was of great importance to the new government. Both the Federalists and the Republicans accused each other of wishing to destroy the Constitution, yet they both accepted the results of the election. On March 4, 1801, the Federalists turned over control of the federal government to the Republicans. For the first time in modern history, control of a government was given to new leaders as the result of a "democratic revolution" rather than by hereditary succession or violent overthrow. Jefferson later called it the **Revolution of 1800** and said that it was more important than the Revolution of 1776.

The Federalists tended to be suspicious of democracy. The mood of the country, however, was becoming increasingly democratic. In the face of this growing spirit of equality, Federalists could not compete with Republicans, who represented the beliefs and opinions of the common people.

After the War of 1812, the Federalist Party was no longer significant in American politics.

Key Note Term

Revolution of 1800—the election of 1800 where the Republicans took control of both houses and Thomas Jefferson became President and Aaron Burr became Vice President

George Bush, Ross Perot, and Bill Clinton in a 1992 presidential debate

Have political parties advanced or inhibited representative democracy?

Courtesy of AP/Wide World Photos.

Political Parties in Today's Political System

Political parties are now an accepted part of the American political system. Many people argue that as the nation became more democratic, political parties were inevitable. Political parties serve several important purposes:

- **They provide people with a way to organize support for candidates for public office**
- **They are a means of persuading more people to vote**
- **By joining a political party, people indicate their support for the policies of that party**
- **Political parties serve as an outlet for popular passions and provide forums for deliberating about public policies**
- **In times of rapid political change, parties can provide a way of making sure that people demand a change of government, not a change of constitutions**

Many historians and political science professionals question whether political parties have advanced or inhibited representative democracy. Some of the questions over which they debate include:

- **What were the Federalists' objections to political parties? What relevance, if any, do these objections have today?**
- **What are the functions of political parties today? In what ways, if any, do they serve the common good?**
- **Is it possible to have a democracy without political parties?**

Conclusion

The rise of political parties in the United States was a natural evolution as our country grew and developed. The opposing views between Hamilton, Jefferson, and the groups they represented brought about the two-party system we use today.

In the next lesson, you will examine the process of judicial review, and how the Supreme Court gained this power. You will also learn the continuing controversies resulting from the Supreme Court having the power of judicial review.

Lesson Review

1. Define the term "faction." What factors did Madison rely on to prevent factions from gaining control of the national government?

2. What are the "general welfare" and "necessary and proper" clauses of the Constitution? Why were Jefferson and other Founders concerned about these clauses?

3. What were the Alien and Sedition Acts? How did Jefferson and Madison respond to these laws?

4. Why did Jefferson refer to the presidential election of 1800, as the "Revolution of 1800?" What was significant about this election?

Lesson 4

Judicial Review

Chapter 4

KEY TERMS

commission
judicial review
legal remedy
original jurisdiction
precedents
unconstitutional
writ of mandamus

What You Will Learn to Do

- Contrast various positions on Judicial Review

Linked Core Objectives

- Communicate using verbal, non-verbal, visual, and written techniques
- Apply critical thinking techniques

Skills and Knowledge You Will Gain Along the Way

- Explain the differing arguments on whether the Supreme Court should have the power of judicial review
- Explain the relationship of judicial review to representative democracy and constitutional government
- Describe how Chief Justice Marshall claimed the power of judicial review for the Supreme Court in the case of Marbury v. Madison and explain his argument
- Explain the various methods of constitutional interpretation that influence the way the Supreme Court arrives at a decision and the arguments for and against each of them
- Explain a variety of factors that may influence the justices' opinions
- Define key words contained in this lesson

Introduction

Throughout our history, there have been strong differences of opinion about whether the judicial branch should have the power of judicial review and how that power should be used. The controversy raises basic questions about representative government and majority rule on the one hand, and constitutional government, its constitutional powers, and the protection of basic rights and of minorities on the other.

This lesson defines the practice of judicial review and explains how the Supreme Court gained this power. It also helps you understand the continuing controversies resulting from the Supreme Court having the power of judicial review.

When you finish this lesson, you should be able to explain different positions regarding judicial review and its role in a constitutional democracy. You should also be able to describe the issues raised in the Supreme Court case Marbury v. Madison (1803) and how Chief Justice Marshall claimed the power of judicial review for the Supreme Court.

Defining Judicial Review

Judicial review is the power of the judicial branch of a government to decide if acts of the legislative or executive branches violate a nation's constitution. If a court reaches the decision that the action of the other branch violates the Constitution, it then declares the action to be null and void. That means that the law or act is not to be obeyed or enforced. In the United States, the federal judiciary, headed by the United States Supreme Court, now has this power, even though it is not specifically mentioned in the Constitution. State courts have this power over the other branches of state governments.

How does judicial review strengthen the judicial branch of government?

Judicial Review Strengthens the Judicial Branch of Government

One new idea about government that developed in this nation was the idea that the judicial branch should have the power to interpret the Constitution and decide what it means. The Supreme Court can decide that a law passed by Congress or a state legislature violates the Constitution and therefore is not to be obeyed or enforced.

The Founders were familiar with the idea that a part of government could be given the power to decide whether activities of other parts of government violated the "higher law" of a nation. Under British rule, the Privy Council, a group that advised the monarch, had the power to veto laws passed by colonial legislatures if they violated British laws. After the American Revolution, some state courts had declared laws made by their own legislatures **unconstitutional.**

If you read the Constitution, you will not find any mention of the power of judicial review. As you will see, however, soon after the beginning of the new government, the Constitution was interpreted to give the Supreme Court this power.

Key Note Term

unconstitutional—not in keeping with the basic principles or laws set forth in the Constitution of a state or county, especially the Constitution of the United States

The Supreme Court Establishes Its Power of Judicial Review

The question of whether the Supreme Court should have the power of judicial review over the legislative and executive branches of the federal government was discussed during the Philadelphia Convention and ratification debates. Although nothing in the Constitution clearly gives the Court this power, many historians believe that most of the Framers assumed that the federal courts would have this power. Alexander Hamilton, for example, made this assumption in The Federalist #78:

> [T]he courts were designed to be an intermediate body between the people and the legislature, in order, among other things, to keep the latter within the limits assigned to their authority. . . . [W]hen the will of the legislature, declared in its statutes, stands in opposition to that of the people, declared in the Constitution, the judges ought to be governed by the latter rather than the former.

One of the arguments in favor of a bill of rights made by James Madison in 1789 was that it would give the judiciary a "check" on congressional violations of rights. This argument also had been made by Thomas Jefferson when he wrote to Madison encouraging him to support a bill of rights.

The first use of the power of judicial review, however, did not have to do with fundamental rights but with taxes. In 1794, Congress put a federal tax on carriages. The Supreme Court agreed to hear a case challenging the tax as unconstitutional. The Court decided that the tax was constitutional. Because the Court upheld the law, the case was not controversial. When the Court first decided that an act of Congress was not constitutional, the idea of judicial review became very controversial. The case was Marbury v. Madison, decided in 1803.

Events Leading to the Supreme Court Case Marbury v. Madison

In the election of 1800, Republican candidate Thomas Jefferson defeated the incumbent Federalist president, John Adams. Although the election was decided on February 17, Jefferson did not take office until March 4, 1801. Until then, John Adams and the Federalists were still in power. The Federalists passed a new judiciary act creating a number of new federal courts. Adams appointed Federalists to these courts. Some were not appointed until March 2 and 3, 1801. He also appointed his secretary of state, John Marshall, to be the chief justice of the United States.

When Thomas Jefferson became president, the commissions, which officially gave several of these Federalists their new jobs as judges, had not been delivered to them. They were supposed to have been delivered by the outgoing secretary of state, John Marshall. Jefferson did not want more Federalists serving as judges, so he forbade the new secretary of state, James Madison, to deliver the commissions.

One **commission** not delivered was that of William Marbury. He had been appointed by President Adams to serve as a justice of the peace for the District of Columbia. Marbury tried to find a way to get what he believed was rightfully his. He discovered that the Judiciary Act of 1789 gave the Supreme Court the power to issue a **writ of mandamus.** In this case, Marbury argued that it was Madison's duty to give him the commission. He asked the Supreme Court to issue a writ of mandamus ordering Madison to deliver it.

This put Chief Justice Marshall in a difficult position. He was worried about what might happen if the Supreme Court ordered Madison to deliver Marbury's document and President Jefferson ordered him not to, as he had threatened. Courts must rely on the executive branch for enforcement of laws. If Jefferson were to refuse to obey the order of the Supreme Court, it would make the Court appear weak and powerless. If the Supreme Court did not order the president to deliver the document, however, the Court would look weak.

Major Issues in Marbury v. Madison

Chief Justice Marshall was faced with a difficult problem. He solved the problem in an unusual and ingenious way. In arriving at his solution, Marshall asked three key questions:

1. **Does Marbury have a right to the appointment?**

2. **If Marbury has a right to the appointment and his right has been violated, do the laws of the country give him a way to set things right?**

Chief Justice John Marshall (1755–1835)

Courtesy of the Library of Congress.

Key Note Terms

commission—an authority, or request, given to another to carry out some act or duty. In particular, a formal written authority given to one party to act in place of another

writ of mandamus—it is a command issuing in the name of the sovereign authority from a superior court having jurisdiction, and is directed to some person, corporation, or interior court, within the jurisdiction of such superior court, requiring them to do some particular thing therein specified, which appertains to their office and duty, and which the superior court has previously determined, or at least supposes to be consonant to right and justice

3. **If the laws of the country give Marbury a way to deal with this problem, is that a writ of mandamus from the Supreme Court?**

Marshall's Decision

Marshall answered "yes" to the first two questions, and "no" to the third.

- *Does Marbury have a right to the appointment?*—Marshall reasoned that the appointment had been signed by the president and sealed by the secretary of state; therefore, Marbury had the right to hold the office for five years as provided by law.

- *Do the laws of the country give Marbury a way to have things set right?*—Marshall reasoned that the secretary of state is an officer of the government directed by the Constitution and laws made by Congress to perform certain duties, such as delivering commissions. When the secretary of state refused to do so, he broke the law and violated Marbury's rights. Marshall also determined that Marbury should have a **legal remedy**.

- *Is asking the Supreme Court for a writ of mandamus the right legal remedy?*—On this point, Marshall said "no." He argued that the part of the Judiciary Act that gave Marbury the right to ask the Supreme Court to issue a writ of mandamus was unconstitutional. The Constitution clearly limits the Supreme Court's **original jurisdiction** to "cases affecting ambassadors, other public ministers and consuls, and those in which a state shall be a party." Marbury was not an ambassador, minister, consul, or a state, so the Supreme Court did not have the power to hear his case unless it was first heard in a lower court and then appealed to the Supreme Court.

Marshall reasoned that the part of the Judiciary Act that gave Marbury the right to have his case heard before the Supreme Court changed the Constitution. Because Congress did not have the authority to change the Constitution, that part of the Judiciary Act was unconstitutional.

Chief Justice Marshall did not order Secretary Madison to deliver the documents. Thus, the Court avoided the almost certain embarrassment of having the President, Thomas Jefferson, refuse to obey the Court's order. In the process, Marshall established a much more important power for the Supreme Court. By declaring a part of the Judiciary Act unconstitutional, the Supreme Court gained the power of judicial review simply by exercising it.

Significance of the Supreme Court's Decision in *Marbury v. Madison*

Although a direct confrontation over the Marbury appointment was avoided, Jefferson was opposed to the idea of judicial review. He argued that each branch should judge for itself whether a law was constitutional. No one branch, Jefferson believed, should have the power to determine constitutionality for the others. If Congress decided that an act was constitutional, and the president agreed and signed the bill, the Court should respect those judgments.

Marshall justified the Court's use of the power of judicial review with the following argument: When the people adopted the Constitution, they agreed that it would be the

Key Note Terms

legal remedy—correcting a dispute or problem by a legal means

original jurisdiction—the legal authority of a court to be the first to hear a case

supreme law of the land. Therefore, they had consented to be governed by its rules, which included certain limitations on the powers of Congress. When Congress violates those limitations, it has violated the will of the people as expressed in the Constitution. If the Supreme Court did not have the power of judicial review, there would be no effective way to enforce the limitations placed on the powers of Congress in the Constitution. Its powers would be unlimited, and we would no longer have a constitutional government. The judiciary, therefore, is the guardian of the Constitution.

Why Has Judicial Review Remained Controversial?

Most Americans recognize judicial review as a necessary power in our constitutional framework. They do not always agree, however, on how the courts should use this power. The Supreme Court often hears controversial cases about which there are strong feelings. Many of these cases involve disagreements about the proper role of government and the meaning of the Constitution. It is inevitable that some people will support the Court's decisions and some will criticize them. These disagreements are often over the methods used to interpret the Constitution.

Four Methods Used to Interpret the Constitution

It is important to remember that judicial review is not an active power. That is, the Supreme Court cannot simply declare a law unconstitutional. The Court only hears "cases and controversies." That means that the parties to the case, such as Marbury and Madison, must have a valid dispute that the Court can settle. Most cases must go through the proper steps in lower courts before they are heard by the Supreme Court.

After the Supreme Court agrees to hear a case on a constitutional issue, the justices face the difficult question of deciding whether the federal government or a state government has violated the Constitution. Understanding the meaning of some parts of the Constitution is fairly easy because they are quite specific. For example, there is little disagreement about what is meant in Article II by, "neither shall any person be eligible to that office [of president] who shall not have attained to the age of 35 years," or in Article I, "No tax or duty shall be laid on articles exported from any state."

Not all parts of the Constitution are so clear. For example, the Constitution is open to interpretation when it makes the following statements:

- **Congress shall have the power to make laws that are "necessary and proper" to carry out its responsibilities**
- **Citizens are protected against "unreasonable searches and seizures"**
- **No state shall "deprive any person of life, liberty, or property without due process of law"**

Controversies over how the Constitution should be interpreted often focus on methods of interpretation. The following sections examine four of those methods.

Using the Literal Meaning of the Words in the Constitution

With this method of interpretation, the justices should consider the literal or plain meaning of the words in the Constitution, or study what the words meant at the time they were written, and base their decisions upon them.

The Court's decisions should be based, as closely as possible, on how the Framers meant the Constitution to be interpreted. If the meaning of the words is clear, then this is the best way to find out what they meant. Also, by relying on the plain meaning, the law becomes certain and predictable.

What problems might arise in trying to discover the intentions of the Framers?

The problem with this method, its critics say, is that Congress must still interpret the Constitution. Not only are phrases like "general welfare" vague, but some questions are not answered at all. For example, the Constitution gives Congress the power to establish an army and a navy. Does Congress not then have the power to establish an air force?

Using the Intentions of Those Who Wrote the Constitution

This method of interpretation is related to the "plain meaning" method. Unlike the plain meaning method, however, the "intention" method concedes that the Constitution, by itself, does not reveal its own meaning. Instead, we should look at the intentions of those who framed it. Judges should make decisions that are consistent with those intentions. They should not decide on the basis of their own understanding of what the Constitution's words mean.

Critics argue that this method also asks judges to do something impossible. There were 39 signers of the Constitution, and each may have had different views of what its various provisions meant. Madison and Hamilton disagreed on the meaning of the "necessary and proper" clause in their dispute about setting up a national bank. Both were Framers. Which Framer was correct?

Using Basic Principles and Values in the Perspective of History

Besides its specific listing of powers, the Constitution is built upon some basic ideas about government. These include ideas of the natural rights philosophy, the principles of constitutionalism, and republican government. These ideas have a life of their own, and as the nation matures so does our understanding of these basic principles. People who hold this view believe that the justices should frame their decisions within the context of these principles and values without ignoring the realities of contemporary society.

Judges have a responsibility not to hold back social progress by sticking to out-moded interpretations.

Using Contemporary Social Values in Terms of Today's Policy Needs

This method argues that the justices should use contemporary social values in interpreting the Constitution to fit today's policy needs.

Critics say the perspective of history and today's policy needs methods give judges too much power. The proper way to change interpretations of the Constitution is through the amending process. Controversial decisions are much better left in the hands of the elected branches, who represent the will of the majority.

Judicial Review In Practice

In practice, justices tend to use all four previously discussed methods of interpretation. They also are influenced by other considerations. These include the **precedents** courts have established in previous cases; current social policies; political and economic concerns; and, to greater or lesser degrees, their personal political, economic, and moral beliefs.

Despite these influences, the justices are conscious of their responsibility to take an objective view of the constitutional issues involved and not decide on the basis of their own personal feelings. This may mean that the Supreme Court will rule that a law is constitutional even if the justices feel that it is unwise.

Although it would be unrealistic to pretend that the personal preferences of justices never affect the decisions of the Court, it is reasonable to claim that the continued authority of the Court depends on its being faithful to both the language and spirit of the Constitution.

Key Note Term

precedents—legal principle, created by a court decision, which provides an example of authority for judges deciding similar issues later

Conclusion

This lesson examined the process of judicial review. It covered how Chief Justice Marshall claimed the power of judicial review for the Supreme Court in the case of Marbury v. Madison, as well as the various methods of constitutional interpretation that influence the way the Supreme Court arrives at a decision. You learned that there are a variety of factors that may influence the justices' opinions.

Next, you will increase your understanding of the federal system created by the Constitution. You will examine important Supreme Court opinions that deal with the division of power between the federal and state governments and learn about continuing problems in the relationship between the nation and the states.

Lesson Review

1. How would you explain the power of "judicial review"? How did the Supreme Court acquire this power?

2. What were the circumstances that led to the Supreme Court's decision in the case of Marbury v. Madison? What were the important issues in this case? How did the Supreme Court's decision resolve these issues? Why is Marbury v. Madison an historically important decision?

3. What are some different approaches to interpreting the Constitution? What objections can be made to these approaches?

4. Explain the idea that courts should be guided by "precedents" in deciding cases.

Division of Power

KEY TERMS

confederation
federal system
sovereignty
supremacy clause
unitary government

What You Will Learn to Do

- Differentiate between the powers of federal and state governments

Linked Core Objectives

- Communicate using verbal, non-verbal, visual, and written techniques
- Apply critical thinking techniques

Skills and Knowledge You Will Gain Along the Way

- Describe the source of federal and state power
- Explain the differences between federal, unitary and confederate forms of government
- Explain the importance of McCulloch v. Maryland and its main arguments
- Explain how the commerce clause in Article I has been used to expand the regulatory powers of Congress
- Explain the importance of Gibbons v. Ogden and its main arguments
- Describe a number of factors which have contributed to the expansion of the power of the federal government
- Define key words contained in this lesson

Introduction

The purpose of this lesson is to increase your understanding of the federal system created by the Constitution. It also discusses important Supreme Court opinions that deal with the division of power between the federal and state governments. Finally, it introduces you to continuing problems in the relationship between the nation and the states as well as the expanded role of the federal government.

When you complete the lesson, you should be able to describe the basic characteristics of a federal system and give a brief explanation of the Supreme Court's opinion in McCulloch v. Maryland and its importance. You also should be able to describe some of the events which have led to the expanded power of the federal government.

The Uniqueness of the Federal System

Our system of government is quite complicated. It differs in two important ways from other national systems in existence when the Constitution was written. **Sovereignty** is held by the people. In other nations, the ultimate authority was thought to be the government, even if its authority was received from the people. For example, in some nations the king was sovereign. In Great Britain, "king in Parliament" was sovereign. This meant that the king and Parliament, acting together, held the ultimate authority.

In the Preamble to the Constitution, the Framers set forth this new idea of sovereignty when they wrote, "We the People of the United States . . . do ordain and establish this Constitution for the United States of America." Under this new system, sovereignty remains in "the people," who delegate certain powers to the government. The government has the powers that the people give it, but the people retain the supreme authority.

Our government is a **federal system.** This means that the people have not delegated all the powers of governing to one national government. Instead, the people have delegated certain powers to their state governments, in their state constitutions. As citizens of the nation, they have delegated, in the United States Constitution, certain powers to the national government. Finally, certain powers have been kept by the people and not delegated to any government.

Previous Types of Government

Before our government was established under the Constitution, most nations had been organized in one of two ways—**unitary** systems of **government,** such as Great Britain, or confederal systems of government known as **confederations,** such as Switzerland.

The Constitution established a system that is a combination of both unitary and confederate sys-

How do the people grant authority to government at all levels?

tems. It is like a unitary government because the members of the House of Representatives are elected by the people from electoral districts of equal population. More importantly, it acts directly on the people in fulfilling the responsibilities it has been given by the Constitution.

At the same time, it is like a confederation because it was ratified by state conventions, amendments are ratified by states, senators were originally chosen by state legislatures, and each state is represented by the same number of senators. In addition, the national government's power is limited to certain responsibilities.

The result of this complicated system is that both the federal and the state governments have certain powers over individual citizens, while sovereignty remains with the citizens. This system has many possibilities for disputes, most of which come down to the simple question, "Which powers have been delegated to which government?" This question was raised during the ratification debates and has remained one of the central issues in American politics ever states.

The Supreme Court and the Power of Judicial Review over State Governments

There were many disagreements at the Philadelphia Convention over what powers the federal government should have. There was no doubt, however, that whatever those powers were, they were superior to those of the state governments. Article VI states:

> *This constitution, and the laws of the United States which shall be made in pursuance thereof; and all treaties made . . . under the authority of the United States, shall be the supreme law of the land; and the judges in every state shall be bound thereby, anything in the constitution or laws of any state to the contrary notwithstanding.*

This section of the Constitution is known as the **supremacy clause.** It has been interpreted to mean that the United States Supreme Court can declare that state laws in violation of the Constitution or of federal laws "made in direct pursuance" of the Constitution should not be enforced. The First Congress also made this power clear in the Judiciary Act of 1789.

The Supreme Court first used its power of judicial review over state governments in 1796. After the Revolutionary War, the United States signed a peace treaty with the British that said all debts owed by Americans to British subjects would be paid. The state of Virginia had passed a law canceling all debts owed by Virginians to British subjects. Since this law clearly violated the peace treaty, the Supreme Court ruled that the law could not be enforced because the laws and treaties made by the federal government are the supreme law of the land. As a result, citizens of Virginia were responsible for paying their debts.

The Case of McCulloch v. Maryland (1819)

The Supreme Court's decision that the national government had the power to make and enforce treaties did not provoke much controversy. After all, the national government had been created to take care of foreign affairs. Its domestic powers

Key Note Term

supremacy clause—Article VI, Section 2 of the U.S. Constitution, which states that the Constitution, laws passed by Congress, and treaties of the United States "shall be the supreme law of the land" binding on the states

How did issues related to the creation of the Second Bank of the United States help define the authority of the federal government?

Courtesy of the Center for Civic Education.

were more controversial. How far did the powers of Congress extend? What powers were reserved for the states? Were there areas where both governments had power?

A dispute over the powers of the state and federal governments came to the Supreme Court in 1819 in the case McCulloch v. Maryland. This case involved a bank created by the federal government, the Second Bank of the United States. The Bank was extremely unpopular in the southern and western states. People there argued that the Bank favored the interests of wealthy shippers and merchants, and that it gave the federal government too much power. Some states attempted to prevent its operation.

In 1818, the Maryland legislature placed a heavy tax on all banks not chartered by the state. There was only one bank that fit the description: the Maryland branch of the Bank of the United States. James McCulloch, the cashier of the branch, refused to pay the tax and was sued by the state of Maryland.

The state courts upheld the right of Maryland to tax the federal bank. McCulloch appealed to the Supreme Court.

McCulloch v. Maryland was one of the most important cases to be decided in the early days of the Supreme Court. Two key issues were involved. First, did Congress have the power to create a bank? Second, could the state of Maryland tax a branch of the federal bank? The Supreme Court ruled that Congress did have the authority to create the bank. Chief Justice John Marshall said that this power was given to Congress by the "necessary and proper" clause of the Constitution. He used much the same reasoning Hamilton had used earlier to persuade President Washington to sign legislation creating the First Bank of the United States.

Turning to the second issue, Marshall insisted that the authority of the federal government comes from the people rather than from the state governments. The Constitution had not been adopted by state governments, but by people gathered in state conventions. Therefore, the Constitution gained its authority directly from the people. For this reason, the federal government, in fulfilling the responsibilities given it by the Constitution and ultimately by the people, is superior to the state governments. This is why the Framers included the supremacy clause, he argued.

Basing his argument on the supremacy clause, Marshall held that when a state law conflicts with a constitutional federal law, the federal law must be obeyed. Maryland's attempt to tax the federal bank, therefore, was illegal, because "the power to tax involves the power to destroy." Marshall argued that if federal agencies could be taxed by the states, their existence would be dependent on the will of the states. The American people, Marshall claimed, did not design their federal government to be dependent on the states.

Marshall's ruling in McCulloch v. Maryland clearly established the supremacy of the federal government within its sphere of authority and increased the powers of Congress.

Commerce Power

The Constitution gives Congress the power to "regulate Commerce . . . among the several states." So, what is "commerce?" In 1824, the Supreme Court gave a very wide definition of commerce in the case of Gibbons v. Ogden. The dispute was about whether a federal license to operate steamboats between New York and New Jersey took precedence over a state license issued by New York. The Court ruled that "navigation" was part of commerce, so the federal license took precedence.

In the late nineteenth century, the Supreme Court took a much more limited view of commerce. It also took a very limited view of "interstate." As a result, the Court denied Congress the power to regulate such things as child labor in factories. The Court ruled that manufacturing was not part of commerce. It was also something that was done entirely within a single state.

In a dramatic switch by the Court in National Labor Relations Board v. Jones and Laughlin Steel Corp. (1937), the previous reading limiting the commerce definition was abandoned. As a result, Congress has been able to regulate such things as minimum wages and job safety. It also has been able to enact laws regulating things that seem far removed from "commerce." For example, the Civil Rights Act of 1964 is partly based on the commerce power. The prohibitions against discrimination in employment and public accommodations are limited to employers and establishments affecting interstate commerce.

Today's Federal Government Authority

Citizens demand more from the federal government today than they did in the past. In addition, the United States' political and military role in the world has greatly increased. As a result, the federal government now has far more power than anything the Framers could have imagined.

In some ways it can be argued that what the Anti-Federalists feared has indeed occurred—the federal government now has power over areas of people's lives that used to be controlled by the states or by the people themselves. There are two important points to remember about federalism today:

- **Most of the decisions about how much power is left to the states are made by Congress, not by the Supreme Court. The Supreme Court has interpreted the Constitution to give federal government more power than it had in the past. Congress decides, on the basis of practical and political considerations, whether the federal or state governments should fulfill certain responsibilities.**

- **In spite of the federal government's increased power, most of the laws that affect us directly are state laws. These include most property laws, contract laws, family laws, and criminal laws.**

The power of the federal government is not limited, of course, to making laws. Indeed, it is increasingly common for the federal government to attempt to influence state law by the use of federal funds. For example, in the past the federal government used highway funds to encourage the states to set uniform speed limits. If a state did not agree to do this, it did not receive federal highway funds.

Two hundred years ago, the Framers could not have predicted the relationship today between the power of the states and the power of the federal government. The complexities of the new system of political organization they created, as well as the realities governments confront, make it equally unlikely that we can predict with a high degree of accuracy the nature of the relationship in the future.

Conclusion

During this lesson, you learned about the division of power in the United States between the federal and state governments. You examined some of the problems in the relationship between the nation and the states as well as the expanded role of the federal government. You also learned about some of the events that have led to the expanded power of the federal government.

This lesson concludes the chapter on American institutions and practices. In the following chapter, you will learn more about the Bill of Rights and how it has developed and expanded as our country grows.

Lesson Review

1. Define the term "sovereignty." In our system of government, who or what has sovereign authority?

2. How would you explain the difference between a "unitary" system of government and a "confederation"? In what ways does the government of the United States combine features of both unitary and confederate systems?

3. What is the "supremacy clause"? What does it mean? Why is it important?

4. What are some examples of the federal government's assumption of power over areas of people's lives that used to be controlled by the states or by the people themselves? How has this occurred?

Bill of Rights Developed and Expanded

Chapter 5

Lesson 1 —————

Constitutional Issues and Civil War

Key Terms

emancipation
perpetual union
secession
sectionalism

What You Will Learn to Do

- Illustrate the causes and effects of the Civil War

Linked Core Objectives

- Communicate using verbal, non-verbal, visual, and written techniques
- Apply critical thinking techniques

Skills and Knowledge You Will Gain Along the Way

- Explain how sectional differences and territorial expansion during pre-Civil War America encouraged different interpretations of the Constitution

- Explain how the institution of slavery forced Americans to examine and debate the nation's most fundamental principles

- Explain how the Dred Scott case intensified the conflict between the ideas of personal liberty and property rights

- Explain how the Civil War challenged the Framer's belief that they had created a perpetual union expressing the sovereign authority of the American people as a whole

- Explain the significance of the Emancipation Proclamation

- Explain the purpose and substance of the Thirteenth, Fourteenth, and Fifteenth Amendments to the Constitution

- Explain why the Civil War Amendments and subsequent civil rights legislation were ineffective in protecting the rights of African Americans

- Define key words contained in this lesson

Introduction

In this lesson you will examine how sectional interests in the young nation created different interpretations of the Constitution. The issue of slavery widened those differences to a point that resulted in the Civil War which has been the greatest failure in America's history of constitutional government. By examining the great pre-Civil War debate over the meaning of the Constitution and the Union, you will have a better understanding of the nature of America's founding principles.

Also in this lesson you will examine the laws passed and the amendments added to the Constitution after the Civil War. These were intended to free enslaved Africans and give them the same rights other Americans had. These amendments, however, were not enough to guarantee the new citizens their rights. You learn how some states passed their own laws to deny African Americans their rights and prevent them from developing political power.

When you complete the lesson, you should be able to explain the major arguments that were made about the proper relationship between the nation and the states. You also learn how the institution of slavery forced a debate over the nation's most fundamental principles. You should be able to explain the significance of the Civil War and the Emancipation Proclamation for the development of the American political system.

You should be able to explain how the federal government attempted to use the Civil War Amendments to the Constitution to protect the rights of African Americans. You should be able to describe how the government used civil rights legislation to achieve the same end. You should also be able to explain how these attempts to end political discrimination against African Americans were limited at the state level.

Understanding the Problems Created by the Growth of the United States

From 1789 to 1861, the population of the United States increased from 4 million to 30 million. Twenty-one new states joined the Union. By the 1850s, when California and Oregon were admitted to the Union, the United States had become a truly continental nation.

Moreover, the growth in the size of the country was matched by economic development. The Northeast became a booming manufacturing center and the South became the world's largest producer of cotton. The vast prairies of the Midwest were a new source of wheat, cattle, and corn. This dramatic growth, however, also created problems.

Various sections of the country were divided by different economies and different ways of life. This gave rise to serious differences of opinion about the proper role of the national government and the relationship between the nation and the states. These disagreements were intensified by the issue of slavery.

Disagreements about the relationship between the nation and the states already existed during the writing, adoption, and ratification of the Constitution. These

How did the issue of the extension of slavery into the territories help bring about the Civil War?

Courtesy of the Center for Civic Education.

SLAVE AND FREE TERRITORIES

FREE
SLAVE
DECISION LEFT TO TERRITORY

disagreements developed further with the rise of political parties in the early years of the nation. Jeffersonian Republicans emphasized state and local power in a strictly interpreted Constitution that granted the national government only specifically listed powers. Federalists such as Alexander Hamilton and John Marshall argued for a broad interpretation of the Constitution that allowed for a strong national government possessing implied, as well as enumerated powers.

In time, **sectionalism,** economic, and other conflicts among various sections of the country intensified disagreements about the power of the national government and the relationship of the nation to the states. The Northern and Southern states were especially adamant about the question of tariffs, which the North favored and the South opposed.

Compromise was part of the American political tradition. It had been the key to the successful deliberations of the Constitutional Convention. The sectional interests of early nineteenth-century America might have been settled through political compromise, if it were not for the reemergence of an issue about which there could be no accommodation—slavery. The institution of slavery also had challenged the Framers. A majority of the Framers may have assumed that slavery would eventually disappear of its own accord because they had provided an opportunity for Congress to act after 1808 to abolish the slave trade. This did not happen, however. Slavery was regarded as primarily a local matter for each state to decide.

Though slavery eventually disappeared in all the Northern states and was banned by law from the Northwest Territory, it survived in the South. In the South, growth in cotton production was used as a rationale for slavery's continued existence. Slavery became a symbol of the sectional rivalries between North and South. Americans on both sides were forced to examine and debate the nation's most fundamental principles and identity.

- **Do we believe in the principles of the Declaration of Independence or not?**
- **Are we one nation or a confederacy made up of the various states?**

These were the constitutional issues that were at stake at the outbreak of the Civil War.

Dred Scott (c. 1795–1858)

Why was the decision in the Dred Scott case a major defeat for antislavery forces?

Courtesy of Corbis Images.

The Dred Scott Decision

One of the most important and controversial Supreme Court decisions in American history was the Dred Scott decision of 1857. Dred Scott was an enslaved African who had been taken to the free state of Illinois and the free Wisconsin Territory and, later, back to Missouri, a slave state. In 1846, Scott sued the man who held him in servitude on the grounds that he had achieved his freedom by residing in free territory. When the Missouri Supreme Court ruled against him, Scott sued in the federal Circuit Court in Missouri. When that court also ruled against him, Scott's attorney appealed the case to the U.S. Supreme Court.

Chief Justice Roger Taney wrote the Court's opinion, which reached several conclusions. Two were explosive in their significance:

- **Blacks, whether slave or free, could not be citizens of the United States. Individual states might grant them state citizenship, but they could not enjoy the rights and protections of national citizenship under the Constitution. Taney reached this conclusion on the ground that blacks were not recognized as U.S. citizens when the Constitution was ratified.**

- **The federal government did not have the right to exclude slavery from the territories. Enslaved Africans, Taney argued, were property and property rights were protected under the due process clause of the Fifth Amendment to the Constitution. The right to own slaves, in other words, was protected by the Constitution. A slaveholder, therefore, had the right to take enslaved Africans into the territories.**

What was President Lincoln's view of the principle of secession?

Courtesy of the Library of Congress.

Taney hoped that by invoking the authority and prestige of the Supreme Court in so definitive a ruling, he could peacefully resolve the conflict over slavery and avoid a civil war. His opinion, however, had exactly the opposite effect. Some believe that the Dred Scott decision was one of the principal causes of the Civil War.

The South Secedes

In 1860 Abraham Lincoln was elected president in one of the nation's most significant elections. The election was marked by the controversy about slavery. Faced with the prospect of a national administration committed to the restriction and eventual abolition of slavery, the Southern states responded with **secession.** One by one, they voted to leave—secede from the Union and form a new union called the Confederate States of America. The Southern secessionists believed they had a constitutional right to do this, based on their view of the Union as a compact of sovereign states. If the Union was only a federation of sovereign states, they could leave the Union to protect their basic rights.

President Lincoln and most Northerners, however, denied the constitutional right of any state to secede from the Union. Secession was not sanctioned by the Constitution and was, therefore, an act of rebellion or revolution. They believed that the Framers had created a **perpetual Union.**

The Struggle to Preserve the Union Becomes a Crusade for Freedom

At the outset of the Civil War, President Lincoln and most Northerners believed the war's objective was to preserve the Union. Though personally opposed to slavery, Lincoln believed his public duty as president was the defense of the existing Constitution, even if that meant the continued existence of slavery. Refusing to recognize the right of secession, he viewed the war as a "domestic insurrection." He hoped it would be concluded quickly and the Union would be preserved.

From its onset in April 1861, the war became a long and bloody conflict that hardened views on both sides. Eventually, supporters of the Union recognized that victory would require the conquest and destruction of much of the South. The

Key Note Terms

secession—the act of seceding

perpetual union—lasting for eternity

prolonged and bitter struggle opened the way for an expansion of the war's objectives. As the war dragged on, there was increased support in the North for demands that victory should mean the end of slavery. Only in this way, many believed, could the war find a purpose worthy enough to justify its terrible cost. As one long-time opponent of slavery declared:

> [T]his is not a war of geographic sections, nor political factions, but of principles and systems. [It is] a war for social equality, for rights, for justice, for freedom. Its outcome should not be the preservation of the old Union, but rather the creation of a new nation freed of slavery.

Lincoln Issues the Emancipation Proclamation

For over a year President Lincoln resisted pressures to expand the war's aims to include the abolition of slavery. As he told the newspaper editor, Horace Greeley:

> My paramount object . . . is to save the Union. . . . If I could save the Union without freeing any slave, I would do it; and if I could save it by freeing all the slaves, I would do it; and if I could do it by freeing some and leaving others alone, I would also do that.

Lincoln hoped to persuade the Southern states to cease their rebellion and he was worried about alienating those slave-holding states, such as Kentucky, that had remained loyal to the Union. At most, Lincoln was prepared to support a gradual and voluntary ending of slavery.

By the summer of 1862, Lincoln had become convinced that winning the war required him to adopt the last of the three alternatives he had stated in his letter to Greeley—to free those enslaved Africans in the rebellious states. For Lincoln, this partial **emancipation** was a military necessity, and he was prepared to use his wartime powers as commander in chief to carry it out. He believed that the abolition of slavery would destroy the South's ability to make war.

Five days after the North's victory at Antietam (Sharpsburg) in September 1862, Lincoln issued his preliminary announcement of the Emancipation Proclamation. He announced that all enslaved Africans in states or parts of states still in rebellion on January 1, 1863, "shall be then, henceforward, and forever free." The president's action was a small step, justified only as a "fit and necessary war measure."

Critics denounced it as an empty gesture. It left alone slavery in areas under federal control and abolished it only where the government then lacked the power to make emancipation a reality. Moreover, had all the Southern states ceased their rebellion before the January deadline, the war would have ended with slavery intact.

Effects of the Emancipation Proclamation

For all its limitations, the Emancipation Proclamation had a very important political and symbolic significance. The fight for the Union was now committed in principle to a partial ending of slavery by force of arms. Lincoln had taken the first step in making the war not only a struggle for the preservation of the Union but for its founding principles as well. In his annual message to Congress, issued a month

before the Emancipation Proclamation was to take effect, Lincoln outlined a plan for the total abolition of slavery and declared:

> *Fellow-citizens, we cannot escape history. . . . The fiery trial through which we pass, will light us down, in honor or dishonor, to the latest generation. . . . In giving freedom to the slave, we assure freedom to the free-honoring alike in what we give, and what we preserve. We shall nobly save, or meanly lose, the last best hope of earth.*

The Roles of Free Blacks and Slaves in the Civil War

The Civil War finally resolved this great constitutional issue. The victory of the North also ended forever the idea of secession as a constitutional right and with it, the vision of the Union as a mere federation of states. Though states would continue to enjoy a significant amount of power and independence in the system of federalism created by the Constitution, the Civil War marked the beginning of a development that has continued to the present day. This is the supremacy of the national government, with powers sufficient to promote the "general welfare" of the people as a whole.

The nature of the Union was not the only issue to be resolved in the war's outcome. The issue of slavery had been settled as well. As Lincoln declared at Gettysburg, the war had made possible "a new birth of freedom."

The Reconstruction Period

The period after the Civil War is called Reconstruction. States that had seceded were being brought back into the Union. The Republican Party, which got most of its support from the Northern states, continued to dominate the federal government. The Democratic Party was strongly supported in the South. Many Confederate leaders were members of the Democratic Party.

Because most slaveholders also had been members of the Democratic Party, it was expected that the freed blacks would vote for the Republican Party. As you shall see, this expectation strongly influenced some political battles fought over the rights of African Americans during Reconstruction.

Constitutional Amendment after the Civil War

The Civil War ended more than 200 years of slavery in America. Shortly after the war, three amendments, commonly called the Civil War Amendments, were added to the Constitution. These amendments are:

- **The Thirteenth Amendment (1865) abolished slavery "within the United States, or in any place subject to their jurisdiction."**
- **The Fourteenth Amendment (1868), among other things, made all persons born or naturalized within the United States citizens. It also prohibited any state from making or enforcing any law that abridged the privileges or immunities of citizens.**
- **The Fifteenth Amendment (1870) prohibited the national and state governments from denying citizens the right to vote because of their race, color, or status as former slaves.**

The first session of Congress held after the Civil War was in December 1865. Congress and many state governments immediately passed laws designed to protect the rights of African Americans. When Congress tried vigorously to implement these laws, its efforts were strongly resisted by whites, especially in the South, who opposed racial equality. Eventually public support for protecting the rights of the newly freed people grew weaker and, by the late 1870s, the Fourteenth and Fifteenth Amendments had become useless as a tool for protecting their rights.

Understanding the Effect of the Thirteenth Amendment

The Thirteenth Amendment, ratified in 1865, was intended to end slavery and the unfair treatment of African Americans throughout the nation. Several states did pass laws to expand the rights of African Americans. In 1865, both Illinois and California passed laws allowing blacks to testify against whites in trials. Massachusetts passed a law prohibiting racial discrimination in public accommodations. In 1868, both Minnesota and Iowa passed laws giving African American males the right to vote.

Some states refused to ratify the Thirteenth Amendment. Others demanded that the federal government pay their slaveholders for the loss of their laborers. Although some Southerners were in favor of freeing the enslaved Africans, many were not. Slavery had accustomed Southerners to seeing blacks as inferior. Plantation and farm owners had grown accustomed to using enslaved Africans as a cheap form of labor.

Many Northerners also were interested in cheap labor. White workers had been organizing into labor unions and were demanding better pay and working conditions. Owners of factories and other businesses saw the newly freed African Americans as a source of cheap labor. Some workers in the North feared that black workers might compete for jobs by accepting lower wages. These Northerners wanted African Americans to stay in the South and West where they would not pose a threat to job availability or the power to organize for better working conditions.

The Black Codes

After the Civil War, the federal government kept Union troops in the South to protect African Americans. Southern legislatures passed laws called the Black Codes in an attempt to convince the federal government that they would treat African Americans fairly. Supposedly, these laws protected the rights of African Americans. The Black Codes were actually intended to prevent the former slaves from developing the political power they might have gained with education and the right to vote.

For example, the Black Codes protected the rights of African Americans to marry, own property, travel, work for pay, and sue in court. In fact, they severely limited these rights. African Americans could only marry other African Americans. They could own property, but few white people would sell it to them. They could travel, but only after dark and in the baggage cars of trains. They could work for pay, but few employers would pay them fair wages. They could sue for damages in court, but their right to sue white people was meaningless because cases were tried by white judges and juries who were hostile to black people.

In the Southern states, the educational opportunities for blacks were far fewer than those for whites. Schools for black students were usually inferior to those for white students. Black students could only go to school with other black children. People were discouraged from starting schools for African Americans and sometimes such schools were burned. White supremacists did not want African Americans to be educated and those found with books were sometimes whipped.

Why did some people want to prevent African Americans from getting an education?

Courtesy of the Cook Collection, Valentine Museum, Richmond, Virginia.

Vigilante groups such as the Ku Klux Klan intimidated, terrorized, and sometimes killed black people and the whites who helped them claim their rights. African Americans could rarely look to their local or state governments for protection from such treatment. Law enforcement agencies and the courts were biased against black people and the whites who sympathized with them. African Americans were tried by all-white juries who rarely decided a case in their favor, no matter what the facts were.

When the Union troops withdrew, a reign of terror began in the South. Black people trying to gain their rights were assaulted and lynched. A white state senator who was sympathetic to the cause of African Americans was found with his throat slit. Others were lynched with signs hung around their necks saying such things as "beware, ye guilty, both white and black." Black Codes clearly placed the political power of the Southern states in the hands of white men.

The Civil Rights Act of 1866

It became clear to members of Congress that the Thirteenth Amendment was not enough to protect the rights of African Americans. In an attempt to provide help, the Civil Rights Act of 1866 was passed over the veto of President Andrew Johnson.

Despite the passing of this legislation, little changed. The president refused to enforce the laws and the Supreme Court refused to listen to people who complained that their rights, supposedly protected by the Civil Rights Act, had been violated.

Many political leaders in the North and elsewhere were outraged by the treatment of African Americans in the South. Republicans also were concerned that their power in the federal government might soon be endangered by the new Democratic representatives elected to Congress by the Southern states.

As a result of these concerns, Republicans in Congress drafted the Fourteenth and later the Fifteenth Amendment to be added to the Constitution. These amendments were written for both moral and political reasons. Many Republican leaders strongly believed in protecting the rights of African Americans. For this reason, they argued that only if Southern black people had the right to vote would the officials of their state and local governments be responsive to them and protect their rights.

In addition to protecting the rights of African Americans, Republicans also were interested in increasing the political power of black citizens in the Southern states. This was intended to keep the Republican Party in power in the federal government and to limit the growing power of the Democratic Party.

The Fourteenth Amendment

The Republicans had gained their objective and they dominated Congress. Strong laws were passed by Congress to enforce the Fourteenth Amendment. During the late 1860s and 1870s, state legislatures and courts in both the North and South tried to expand the rights of African Americans and enforce laws against discrimination. These efforts were not always successful.

The Fifteenth Amendment

The failure of the Fourteenth Amendment to protect adequately the rights of black citizens led to the adoption of the Fifteenth Amendment in 1870. This amendment contains the following two sections:

Section 1. **The right of citizens of the United States to vote shall not be denied or abridged by the United States or by any state on account of race, color, or previous condition of servitude.**

Section 2. **The Congress shall have the power to enforce this article by appropriate legislation.**

This amendment was clearly intended to protect the right of African Americans to vote. People believed that black citizens should have the same rights as all other citizens. The immediate effect of this amendment and the legislation passed to support it was that, during the late 1860s through the 1880s, large numbers of African Americans voted. They gained considerable political power and they used it to protect their rights.

Eliminating the African American Power Base in the South

After the Reconstruction period, Southern states began passing laws to destroy the political power of blacks in the South. The following are the major types of laws that were used to eliminate the participation of African Americans in politics in the Southern states.

- *Poll taxes.* **Some states passed laws that required citizens to pay a tax before voting. Since most black people were desperately poor, these taxes greatly reduced the number who could vote.**

- *Literacy tests.* **Some states required citizens to take tests proving they could read or write before they were allowed to vote. Since most African Americans in the South had been prevented from learning how to read or write, these tests denied them the right to vote. Furthermore, these tests were administered by white people who prevented even literate African Americans from passing.**

- *Grandfather clauses.* **Laws were passed that allowed people in the South to vote, even if they could not read or write, if their grandfathers had voted. Since no African Americans had grandfathers who had voted, these laws denied African Americans the right to vote.**

In what ways did the laws in this illustration deny African Americans the right to vote?

In the years following the Civil War, there was less and less talk about the rights and living conditions of African Americans. Unfortunately, the federal Bill of Rights offered little relief against injustice.

The Fourteenth Amendment contains the clause, "No state shall make or enforce any law which shall abridge the privileges or immunities of citizens of the United States." The Supreme Court was asked in the Slaughterhouse Cases of 1873 to rule that this clause protected the rights listed in the Bill of Rights from violation by state governments. The Court refused. The states still had the power to pass laws that violated the Bill of Rights. As a result of the Court's opinion in these cases, the privileges and immunities clause of the Fourteenth Amendment has been of little use in protecting individual rights to this day.

Congress passed the Civil Rights Act of 1875 to give the federal government the power to enforce the protections of citizens' rights guaranteed under the Fourteenth Amendment. This act was not enforced by the executive branch. Later, the Supreme Court declared the Civil Rights Act of 1875 unconstitutional.

Rutherford B. Hayes of Ohio was the Republican candidate for president in 1876. Hayes won the election with a minority of the popular vote, but a majority of the electoral vote.

Hayes had campaigned under the promise that he would remove the remaining federal troops from the South. In 1877, soon after he was elected, he appointed a former Confederate leader to the cabinet. It was a symbolic gesture, but a clear signal. It was time to get on with expanding the economy and territory of the United States. Reconstruction was over.

Sojourner Truth
(c. 1797–1883)

How did Sojourner Truth and other community leaders struggle to win rights for African Americans?

Courtesy of the New York Historical Society.

Hayes and his supporters did not want to spend more time and money on the former slaves. They wanted to let Southern leaders handle their own problems. As the president told African Americans on a supposed "good will tour" of the South, "Your rights and interests would be safer if this great mass of intelligent white men were left alone by the federal government."

Hayes refused to enforce the Fourteenth and Fifteenth Amendments. One result of this failure was that African Americans learned to look to themselves and their own community institutions for help. Ministers, teachers, and community leaders such as Sojourner Truth became the backbone of the continuing struggle for the rights of African Americans. They formed the leadership of the black community for the next hundred years.

Nevertheless, despite their limited effectiveness, the Civil War Amendments had created a constitutional basis for expanding the rights of individuals and minorities.

Conclusion

This lesson covered a dark period in the history of the United States—the Civil War and the Reconstruction Period. You learned that the Civil War, in great part, came about due to the South desiring to keep slaves. You learned that the Dred Scott decision played a large part in the nation going to war over the issue of slavery.

You also learned how President Abraham Lincoln's Emancipation Proclamation helped bring about the end of the Civil War. The post-war Reconstruction Period brought three new Constitutional Amendments, as well as the Civil Rights Act of 1866 and The Black Codes that tried to limit any power base that might be developed by former slaves.

The next lesson covers the Fourteenth Amendment. You will learn what events brought about this amendment and how it has impacted American living then and now.

Lesson Review

1. What was the Dred Scott case about? Why was the Supreme Court's decision in that case important?

2. How did Southern states justify their decision to secede from the Union? How did President Lincoln and other Northerners justify treating secession as an act of rebellion? And how did the Black Codes further the suppression of slaves in the South?

3. What was the Emancipation Proclamation? Why did Lincoln issue it?

4. How would you describe the period after the Civil War known as Reconstruction? What Amendments were passed during this period?

Lesson 2

Fourteenth Amendment

Key Terms

double jeopardy
due process
incorporation
procedural due processs
selective incorporation
substantive due process

What You Will Learn to Do

- Explain how the Fourteenth Amendment expanded constitutional protection of rights

Linked Core Objectives

- Communicate using verbal, non-verbal, visual, and written techniques
- Apply critical thinking techniques

Skills and Knowledge You Will Gain Along the Way

- Explain the purpose and the three key provisions of the Fourteenth Amendment: privileges and immunities, due process of law, and equal protection of the laws

- Explain the differences between procedural and substantive due process

- Explain the difference between the ideas of equality of condition and equal protection of the laws

- Explain what is meant by "incorporation" and how the Supreme Court has used the Fourteenth Amendment to protect individual rights against the actions of state governments

- Describe the effect that incorporation has had on the federal system and the power of the states

- Define key words contained in this lesson

Introduction

Next to the preservation of the Union and the abolition of slavery, the most important constitutional development of the post Civil War era was the passage of the Fourteenth Amendment. Originally intended to protect the rights of newly freed African Americans, the "Great Amendment," as it is sometimes called, has become a principal guarantee of the rights of all Americans, as important as the Bill of Rights itself.

In this lesson you examine those provisions of the Fourteenth Amendment that have made it so important. They gave new meaning to our concepts of citizenship, due process of law, and equal protection of the laws. You also examine the process of incorporation, by which many protections included in the Bill of Rights have been expanded to protect the rights of individuals against actions by state governments.

When you finish the lesson you should be able to explain the purpose of the Fourteenth Amendment and its three key provisions—privileges and immunities, due process of law, and equal protection of the laws. You also should be able to explain the distinctions between procedural and substantive due process; and different interpretations of the word "equality" in the principle of equal protection of the laws. Finally, you should be able to define incorporation and describe its effect on the federal system and the power of the states.

The Fourteenth Amendment

The Fourteenth Amendment was initiated by Congress as part of its Reconstruction policy for the defeated South. Sections 1 and 5, the first and last sections of the amendment, remain among the most important words in our Constitution:

> *Section 1. All persons born or naturalized in the United States and subject to the jurisdiction thereof, are citizens of the United States and of the State wherein they reside. No State shall make or enforce any law which shall abridge the privileges or immunities of citizens of the United States; nor shall any State deprive any person of life, liberty, or property, without due process of law; nor deny to any person within its jurisdiction the equal protection of the laws.*

> *Section 5. The Congress shall have power to enforce, by appropriate legislation, the provisions of this article.*

The constitutional guarantees expressed in Section 1 and the power of Congress to enforce them, as provided for in Section 5, are what make the Fourteenth Amendment important to us today.

Defining Citizenship

The Fourteenth Amendment changed the definition of citizenship. Section 1 of the Amendment first declares that "all persons born or naturalized in the United States and subject to the jurisdiction thereof, are citizens of the United States and of the State wherein they reside." To protect the rights of African Americans, the authors of the Fourteenth Amendment first of all had to establish that African Americans were, in fact, citizens of the United States. The Dred Scott decision said that they were not.

Among its other goals, the Fourteenth Amendment was intended to nullify this decision that had helped to cause the Civil War.

The Amendment also cleared up some confusion left by the Framers. The Constitution mentions citizenship but does not define it. During the decades before the Civil War, the relationship between citizenship rights in various states and the relationship between state and national citizenship was unclear.

Section 1 clarifies that United States citizenship is paramount to state citizenship, and that U.S. citizens have certain rights that no state government can take away.

Extending the Meaning of Due Process of Law

Section 1, Fourteenth Amendment: [N]or shall any State deprive any person of life, liberty, or property, without due process of law.

Due process of law is one of the oldest constitutional principles. The concept appears in the Magna Carta, as well as in later landmarks of English and American constitutional history. The principle of due process of law is expressed in the Declaration of Independence and in the original Constitution.

Key Note Term

due process—the right to due process

The words "due process" were first added to the Constitution in 1791 when the Fifth Amendment was ratified, which provided that no government can be above the law. Both the lessons of history and the natural rights philosophy declare that each person possesses rights to life, liberty, and property. Government cannot interfere with these rights except according to established procedures of law.

The principle of due process of law is one of the most important protections against arbitrary rule. The Fifth Amendment prevents the federal government from depriving any person of life, liberty, or property without due process of law. Many state declarations of rights provide the same protection against the actions of state governments. The Fourteenth Amendment requires state governments to respect due process of law and gives the federal government the power to enforce this requirement.

Procedural and Substantive Due Process of Law

Due process originally meant that government must use fair procedures in fulfilling its responsibilities. This is known as procedural due process. It requires that the procedures used by government in making, applying, interpreting, and enforcing the law be reasonable and consistent.

Procedural due process limits the powers of government to protect individual rights. For example, police must use fair procedures in investigating crimes and in arresting and questioning suspects. Courts must use fair procedures in trying people suspected of crimes. The legislative and executive branches must treat people fairly, as well. Congress, for example, is required to follow due process when it conducts hearings.

Over the years this traditional definition of due process of law has been expanded to include **substantive due process** as well. This is the requirement that government cannot make laws that apply to situations in which the government has no business interfering. It requires that the "substance" or purpose of laws be constitutional. For example, the right to substantive due process prohibits government from making laws or taking actions that interfere with certain areas of your life. These are areas, such as personal privacy, that the government has no right to regulate. It is not the business of government to interfere with what you believe, what friends you choose to associate with, the kind of work you want to do, where you want to travel, or whom you want to marry.

Though not specifically mentioned in the Constitution or Bill of Rights, such basic freedoms are protected by substantive due process. Before the Civil War, the Supreme Court used the idea of substantive due process several times in decisions regarding laws made by Congress. Chief Justice Taney used it in the Dred Scott decision to declare that Congress could not prohibit a slaveholder from taking slaves into the territories. Such a prohibition, Taney argued, was a violation of due process under the Fifth Amendment.

It was only after the adoption of the Fourteenth Amendment, however, that the idea of substantive due process became widely used. This was because the due process clause of the Fourteenth Amendment applied to the states. At that time state legislatures were more active than Congress in passing laws that affected the lives of citizens.

Promoting Equal Protection of the Laws

Section 1 of the Fourteenth Amendment concludes by declaring that no state may "deny to any person within its jurisdiction the equal protection of the laws." By this provision the amendment gave a new importance to the principle of equality in the Constitution. As one of the Fourteenth Amendment's authors, Senator Jacob M. Howard of Michigan, declared,

"It establishes equality before the law, and it gives, to the humblest, the poorest, the most despised . . . the same rights and the same protection before the law as it gives to the most powerful, the most wealthy, or those most haughty. . . . Without this principle of equal justice to all men and equal protection under the shield of the law, there can be no republican government and none that is really worth maintaining."

> ### Key Note Terms
>
> **procedural due process**—a course of formal proceedings (as judicial proceedings) carried out regularly, fairly, and in accordance with established rules and principles
>
> **substantive due process**—requirement that laws and regulations must be related to a legitimate government interest (as crime prevention) and may not contain provisions that result in the unfair or arbitrary treatment of an individual

How are you protected by your right to due process?

The authors of the Fourteenth Amendment did not intend to protect a right to equality of condition. That would mean that government was responsible for guaranteeing that all its citizens were equal in the amount of property they possessed, their living standards, education, medical care, and working conditions. The authors of the Fourteenth Amendment wanted to create a society in which all people were treated equally before the law.

Equal protection of the laws meant that no individual or group was to neither receive special privileges nor be deprived of certain rights under the law. The Fourteenth Amendment does not, however, prevent legislatures from passing laws that treat some people differently when there is a reasonable basis for doing so. For example, it does not prevent a legislature from passing a law granting the privilege of a driver's license only to those 16 or older, or denying the right to purchase alcoholic beverages to persons younger than 21. The equal protection clause was intended to prevent legislatures from passing laws that unreasonably and unfairly favor some groups over others.

Making the Bill of Rights Applicable to State Governments

The Bill of Rights was originally intended to limit the powers of the federal government to protect the rights of the people and the states. The Bill of Rights did not protect the rights of individuals from state or local governments.

Does equal protection of the law mean that all people have a right to equality of condition? Why? Why not?

Courtesy of the Center for Civic Education.

The Fourteenth Amendment provided a basis for removing this limitation by specifically prohibiting the states from violating a person's right to life, liberty, and property without due process of law. It also gave the federal government the authority to enforce this prohibition.

In a sense, **incorporation** turned the original intent of the Bill of Rights upside down. In addition to limiting the powers of the federal government in order to protect state and local rights, the incorporation of most of the Bill of Rights in the Fourteenth Amendment became a means by which the federal government prevented state and local governments from violating individual rights.

Incorporating the Fourteenth Amendment into the Bill of Rights

During the first decades after the ratification of the Fourteenth Amendment the courts interpreted the amendment in a way that relied on the states to be the principal protectors of individual rights. Most judges at that time did not want to change the balance of power in the federal system. To do so would dramatically expand federal control over the criminal justice systems of the states, as well as over other areas that had been under local control since colonial times.

In Gitlow v. New York (1925), the Supreme Court began to identify certain fundamental rights protected by the due process clause of the Fourteenth Amendment. In that case the Court recognized the rights of free speech and free press as among the

personal rights to liberty protected by the due process clause of the Fourteenth Amendment. In a series of cases during the next two decades, the Court ruled that all the rights in the First Amendment—assembly, petition, and religion as well as speech and press—were protected from state action by the due process clause.

The Supreme Court was reluctant, however, to apply to the states those provisions in the Fourth through the Eighth Amendments that concerned criminal procedures. This was an area where state governments had been more active than the federal government and where procedural rights varied greatly from state to state. The justices did not find it reasonable, therefore, for the federal government to apply the specific procedural guarantees of the Bill of Rights as a "strait jacket" on the states.

Moreover, a majority of justices at this time did not believe that such specific procedural guarantees were as fundamentally important as the rights guaranteed by the First Amendment. First Amendment rights were considered preferred freedoms, without which a free society could not exist.

During the 1930s the Supreme Court did recognize certain rights of criminal procedure as being essential to protecting liberty under the due process clause. For example, in Powell v. Alabama (1932) it ruled that the right to counsel in death penalty trials was required by the due process clause. But in Palko v. Connecticut (1937) the Court ruled that the Fifth Amendment's protection against **double jeopardy** was not essential to due process.

Key Note Term

double jeopardy—the act of putting a person through a second trial for an offense for which he or she has already been prosecuted or convicted

Speaking for the Court, Justice Benjamin Cardozo tried to sharpen the distinction between fundamental and non-fundamental rights. The former, he said, were "of the very essence of a scheme of ordered liberty."

Most, but not all, of the Supreme Court justices at that time agreed with this position. One who did not was Justice Hugo Black. He argued that choosing between essential and nonessential rights in the Bill of Rights allowed judges to write their own subjective views into the law and caused too much confusion. Black believed that all the specific rights in the Bill of Rights should be incorporated into the due process clause of the Fourteenth Amendment. By this he meant that they should be applied to the states with exactly the same meaning and in exactly the same way as the Bill of Rights applied them to the federal government.

For a time, a majority of justices on the Supreme Court rejected Black's arguments for complete incorporation. State courts were not held accountable to most of the judicial protections in the Bill of Rights. The Supreme Court applied instead what Justice Felix Frankfurter called a fair trial standard. Decisions were based on whether the state in a given case had abided by those "canons of decency and fairness" fundamental to traditional notions of justice, but not necessarily in accord with the specific provisions of the Bill of Rights.

Then, in the 1960s, the Supreme Court changed course. It rejected the fair trial standard for a **selective incorporation** of most of the criminal procedure guarantees in the Bill of Rights. A general right to counsel, protection against self-incrimination and double jeopardy, and other procedural guarantees were found to be essential to due process under the Fourteenth Amendment.

Nonetheless, the Court avoided total incorporation. Certain specific provisions in the Bill of Rights have not yet been incorporated. These include the right to bear arms, to be protected against the quartering of troops in private homes, the right to an indictment by a grand jury, and the right to a jury trial as guaranteed by the Sixth and Seventh Amendments.

The Supreme Court has prohibited states from violating additional rights that do not specifically appear in the Bill of Rights. For example, in 1965 the Court ruled in Griswold v. Connecticut that the due process clause includes a right to marital privacy that forbids states from outlawing the use of contraceptives. In recent years the scope of the due process clause has become important in the constitutional debate about abortion.

The Results of the Incorporation of Rights

When the Bill of Rights only limited the power of the federal government, it was of almost no importance in protecting the rights of individuals. The great change occurred when the Supreme Court applied the protections of the Bill of Rights to the states through the due process clause of the Fourteenth Amendment. Instead of limiting only the power of the federal government, the Bill of Rights now also limits the power of state governments in an effort to achieve the fundamental purpose of the Constitution—protecting the rights of American citizens.

> ### Key Note Term
>
> **selective incorporation**—a theory or doctrine of constitutional law that those rights guaranteed by the first eight amendments to the U.S. Constitution that are fundamental to and implicit in the concept of ordered liberty are incorporated into the Fourteenth Admendment's due process clause

Conclusion

In this lesson, you learned that the Fourteenth Amendment is called "The Great Amendment," and has become a principal guarantee of the rights of all Americans. You learned the process of incorporation, by which many protections included in the Bill of Rights have been expanded to protect the rights of individuals against actions by state governments.

This lesson covered the purpose of the Fourteenth Amendment and its three key provisions—privileges and immunities, due process of law, and equal protection of the laws. You learned the differences between procedural and substantive due process; and different interpretations of the word "equality" in the principle of equal protection of the laws.

In the next lesson, you learn about the start of the civil rights movement in the United States. You will examine its roots and the continuing efforts to ensure that all American citizens enjoy equal rights.

Lesson Review

1. How did the Fourteenth Amendment change the definition of citizenship?

2. Explain the concept of due process of law. How does the Fourteenth Amendment extend the guarantee of due process of law?

3. Explain the doctrine of incorporation. What positions have been taken by Supreme Court justices regarding this doctrine?

4. How has the Fourteenth Amendment enhanced the importance of the Bill of Rights?

Lesson 3

Civil Rights Movement

Key Terms

civil disobedience
Civil Rights Act of 1964
National Association for the Advancement
of Colored People (NAACP)
nonviolent direct action
separate but equal doctrine
token integration

What You Will Learn to Do

- Examine how the civil rights movement used the constitution to achieve its goals

Linked Core Objectives

- Communicate using verbal, non-verbal, visual, and written techniques
- Apply critical thinking techniques

Skills and Knowledge You Will Gain Along the Way

- Explain how the Supreme Court's application of the equal protection clause has changed from the late nineteenth century to the present
- Explain the "separate but equal doctrine" established by the Supreme Court decision in the case of Plessy v. Ferguson and describe the consequences of the Plessy decision
- Explain the role of the legislative, executive, and judicial branches of government in ending legal segregation
- Describe how the civil rights movement is a good example of citizens using rights protected by the Constitution to secure other constitutional rights
- Define key words contained in this lesson

Introduction

Key Note Term

nonviolent direct action—peaceful tactics used as a means of gaining one's civil or political ends

In this lesson you will consider how the Fourteenth Amendment and other parts of the Constitution made it possible to secure and expand the rights of American citizens. The focus of the lesson is the Civil Rights era, a century after the Civil War. You will examine Supreme Court decisions which interpreted the equal protection clause differently at different times in our history. You will study the effects of the "separate but equal doctrine" and how the civil rights movement of the 1960s used both the protections of the Constitution and **nonviolent direct action** to end legal segregation.

When you finish the lesson, you should be able to explain how the Supreme Court's application of the equal protection clause has changed from the late nineteenth century to the present. You should be able to explain the "separate but equal doctrine" and the significance of the Supreme Court decisions in Plessy v. Ferguson as well as Brown v. Board of Education. You also should be able to describe the roles of the legislative, executive, and judicial branches of government in ending legal segregation. You should be able to describe how members of the civil rights movement used nonviolent direct action and their constitutional rights to oppose legal segregation and secure additional rights.

Significance of the Plessy v. Ferguson Decision

Key Note Term

separate but equal doctrine—the argument, once upheld by the Supreme Court, that separate public facilities were constitutional if the facilities were of equal quality

The promised protection of rights under the Fourteenth Amendment did not last long. With the end of Reconstruction, Southern whites soon regained control of state governments and passed laws that once again reduced African Americans to second-class citizens.

Both state and federal courts upheld the right of states to pass such laws despite the equal protection clause. In the case of Plessy v. Ferguson (1896), the U.S. Supreme Court established the **separate but equal doctrine** that was to deny African Americans equal rights for more than half a century. It established the legal basis for racial segregation, which required African Americans to use separate schools and other

How did "separate but equal" facilities deny African Americans equal protection of the law?

Courtesy of the Center for Civic Education.

public facilities. Louisiana had passed a law requiring railroad companies to provide separate but equal cars for black passengers and white passengers. African American leaders claimed this law violated their rights under the equal protection clause of the Fourteenth Amendment. They decided to challenge the constitutionality of the law in court and chose Homer Plessy to make the test case.

Plessy bought a train ticket but insisted on riding in the "whites only" car. He was arrested and convicted. He then appealed his case to the Supreme Court.

The question before the Supreme Court was whether the Louisiana law violated the equal protection clause. Claiming that the authors of the Fourteenth Amendment had never intended to enforce a social intermingling of the races, the Court held that to separate blacks and whites did not in itself suggest one race was inferior to the other. Because the law required that blacks and whites be provided equal facilities, the Court concluded that no unfair discrimination had occurred. The Louisiana law was declared constitutional.

Plessy v. Ferguson departed from the interpretation of the Fourteenth Amendment established in the post Reconstruction years. Even though the Supreme Court had interpreted the equal protection clause very narrowly, it had consistently forbidden states from officially discriminating between the races. The Plessy decision now allowed open discrimination.

Not all members of the Court agreed with the majority. Justice John Marshall Harlan, a white southerner, wrote a strong dissenting opinion. He argued that in allowing state-enforced segregation of the races, the Louisiana law implied that blacks were an inferior group, or "caste," and thus violated the equal protection clause of the Fourteenth Amendment. Harlan declared:

> "Our Constitution is color-blind and neither knows nor tolerates classes among citizens. In respect of civil rights, all citizens are equal before the law. . . . [T]he judgment this day rendered will prove to be quite as pernicious as . . . the Dred Scott case."

Consequences of Plessy v. Ferguson

As a result of the majority decision in Plessy, segregation and discrimination against African Americans became even more widespread in the South. A web of state laws and local ordinances soon segregated almost every area of public life: schools, hotels, restaurants, hospitals, streetcars, toilets, and drinking fountains. Courtrooms even kept separate Bibles for administering the oath. The establishment of white supremacy required the destruction of African American political power. During the years following Plessy, a variety of devices were adopted to evade the intent of the Fifteenth Amendment and deny African American citizens the right to vote. Legislative devices such as literacy tests, poll taxes, and grandfather clauses, took advantage of the poverty and lack of education among African Americans.

When such discriminatory regulations failed to keep African Americans from the polls, physical intimidation and threats of economic reprisals were used. As a result, voting by blacks declined dramatically. By 1910 fewer than 20 percent of African American citizens voted in most of the South, in the Deep South fewer than 2 percent voted. The white supremacy created through these laws and regulations became known as Jim Crow.

How did segregated facilities undermine the intent of the Fourteenth Amendment?

Courtesy of the Library of Congress.

Origins of the Civil Rights Movement

Despite the return of white supremacy in the decades following Reconstruction, the struggle for racial equality did not disappear altogether. Even during the height of Jim Crow many courageous African Americans and their white allies were able to chip away at the wall of discrimination.

The National Association for the Advancement of Colored People

In 1909 the **National Association for the Advancement of Colored People** (NAACP) was founded. The NAACP's team of able lawyers began to challenge Jim Crow laws in the courts and legislatures. The NAACP set as its primary goals the removal of segregation laws and the restoration of voting rights for African Americans.

All aspects of life for African Americans living in the South were tainted by segregation. In Montgomery, Alabama, on December 1, 1955, Rosa Parks (see Figure 5.3.1), a black woman, was arrested when she refused to give up her bus seat to a white man. Local civil rights leaders convinced Ms. Parks to fight the charges, and they called for a boycott of the Montgomery bus system. Some community leaders pledged their support for the action. Rev. Martin Luther King, Jr., a new minister at the Dexter Avenue Baptist Church, assumed a major leadership role in the boycott which lasted 400 days. Finally, the boycott ended in December 1956 when the Supreme Court forced Montgomery city officials to end segregation on city buses.

Significance of Brown v. Board of Education

The NAACP set as its priority the end of segregation in education. They developed a strategy of demonstrating through test cases that southern education was not living up to the conditions of "separate but equal" laid down in the Plessy decision. This

Figure 5.3.1:
Rosa Parks (1913–)

Courtesy of Bettmann/
Corbis Images.

was done through the efforts of a team of talented African American lawyers, including Charles Houston and Thurgood Marshall. They produced evidence to show that southern schools, though separate, were not equal in the facilities and advantages they offered African Americans.

Brown v. Board of Education of Topeka (1954) involved the schools in Topeka, Kansas. An African American girl was denied enrollment at the school in her neighborhood. She was forced to attend a school that was much farther from her home. Her father sued the board of education to allow her to attend the nearer school.

In appealing this case to the Supreme Court, the lawyers of the NAACP adopted a somewhat different strategy. They produced evidence to show the damaging effects of segregated schools on the psychological development of black children. The Court accepted this argument and, under the leadership of Chief Justice Earl Warren, handed down a unanimous decision, which declared:

> *"To separate [children] from others of similar age and qualifications solely because of their race generates a feeling of inferiority as to their status in the community that may affect their hearts and minds in a way unlikely ever to be undone. . . . [Therefore] separate educational facilities are inherently unequal . . . [and deny] the equal protection of the laws guaranteed by the Fourteenth Amendment."*

Making a court decision was one thing; enforcing it was another. In 1955 the Court handed down a second Brown decision that concerned implementation of the Court's 1954 decision. It ordered an end to segregated schools "with all deliberate speed." Lower courts were authorized to approve desegregation plans and were allowed to take into account local conditions in approving such plans.

Lesson 3   Civil Rights Movement

In making this cautious and flexible decision, the Supreme Court acknowledged the serious impact the first Brown decision would have on American society.

As expected, reaction to the school desegregation decision among many white southerners was hostile. They viewed it as an attack on their "way of life," which had been accepted as legal under the Constitution for more than half a century. Southern leaders promised "massive resistance" and organized White Citizens Councils throughout the South. Resistance involved both legal and illegal tactics. They included delaying maneuvers in the courts and very limited or **token integration.**

Southern state legislatures passed new laws making it possible for white students to attend private schools with state financial support. They also passed student placement laws allowing local school officials to impede integration through the use of placement tests and other administrative procedures. Some school districts closed their schools altogether rather than integrate.

When legal tactics failed, some resistant southerners resorted to violence and other forms of intimidation. This was evident in the first important confrontation over integration in Little Rock, Arkansas. The Arkansas governor allowed the state national guard and a local mob to prevent the court-ordered integration of a city high school in 1957. President Dwight Eisenhower responded by sending in units of the 101st Airborne Division of the U.S. Army.

George E.C. Hayes, Thurgood Marshall, and James M. Nabrit

What was the significance of Thurgood Marshall's victory in the Brown v. Board of Education *case?*

Courtesy of AP/Wide World Photos.

The president had reservations about court-ordered integration. He feared quick implementation, "I don't believe," he said, "you can change the hearts of men with laws or decisions." President Eisenhower also realized, however, that the law of the land had to be upheld. His forceful response to the crisis in Little Rock was the first time since Reconstruction that federal troops had been used to defend the civil rights of American citizens.

Little Rock's high school was integrated under the protection of federal troops. Throughout the South, the pace of integration was slow. Neither the government nor organizations like the NAACP had the resources to challenge segregation everywhere. The task of implementing the Supreme Court's decision had to be fought school district by school district. In the 1960s, however, the federal government initiated a policy of withholding funding from schools that did not integrate and courts began to insist on positive results in school integration plans. Thereafter, the pace of school integration quickened. By the 1970s the South could rightly claim that it had the most integrated schools in the nation.

The Civil Rights Movement and Nonviolence

Though encouraged by the Supreme Court's ending of legal segregation, African Americans became frustrated with the slow pace of implementing court decisions. Leaders realized they could not rely entirely on the government to further the cause of civil rights.

Following the success of the Montgomery bus boycott, Rev. Martin Luther King, Jr. organized a meeting of 60 southern ministers in Atlanta, Georgia. Out of this meeting the Southern Christian Leadership Conference (SCLC) was formed. King and the other leaders organized and conducted workshops throughout the South where people taught the principles of nonviolent direct action.

Nonviolent direct action sometimes used the tactics of **civil disobedience.** This involved the open violation of what were believed to be unjust laws, together with a willingness to accept the consequences through passive or nonviolent resistance. Those engaged in direct action would not resist arrest and imprisonment, nor respond with violence to the physical or other abuse they might suffer. The effectiveness of these tactics had been proven by the great Indian leader, Mohandas Gandhi, who used them to win independence for India from Great Britain.

Key Note Term

civil disobedience—the refusal to obey a law, usually on the ground that is morally unjust, or to protest a government policy. Civil disobedience is a form of nonviolent resistance and is aimed at arousing public opinion against the law or policy

U.S. soldiers in front of Central High School, Little Rock, Arkansas, 1957.

Why was it necessary to use federal troops to integrate schools in the South?

Courtesy of the Library of Congress.

Figure 5.3.2: Sit-in demonstration at a lunch counter in Mississippi, 1963.

Courtesy of AP/Wide World Photos.

African American students throughout the South had taken up the protest movement. In April 1960, leaders of the SCLC invited 100 student leaders to attend a conference in Raleigh, North Carolina, to discuss ways to coordinate their efforts to make them more effective. Out of this meeting emerged a new organization, the Student Nonviolent Coordinating Committee (SNCC).

The energy and commitment of the members of SNCC led the organization to play an important role in helping achieve the goals of the civil rights movement. By September 1961, 70,000 black and white students were staging sit-ins for social change. They conducted sit-ins (see Figure 5.3.2), sleep-ins, pray-ins, and other actions to protest the segregation that existed in every type of facility open only to whites.

Origins of the Civil Rights Act of 1964

Although President John F. Kennedy supported the enforcement of existing laws and court decisions on civil rights, he was reluctant at first to enlarge the government's authority by proposing new legislation. Events resulting from nonviolent direct action in 1963 changed his mind.

In the spring of that year, Rev. Martin Luther King, Jr. and other civil rights leaders decided to protest segregation and job discrimination in Birmingham, Alabama, known for its tough enforcement of Jim Crow laws. Sit-ins and protest marches prompted a brutal response by local police. Scenes of civil rights protesters being attacked by fire hoses and police dogs were carried on television and in newspapers around the world. The events in Birmingham shocked the consciences of many people and became an embarrassment to the country. They also set off a wave of protests in almost 200 other cities in the South.

These events persuaded President Kennedy that the time had come for the government to increase its commitment to civil rights. In a nationally televised address in June 1963, he told his fellow citizens:

> *"We are confronted primarily with a moral issue. It is as old as the Scriptures and is as clear as the American Constitution. The heart of the question is whether all Americans are to be afforded equal rights and equal opportunities. . . . [T]he time has come for this nation to fulfill its promise."*

Then on August 28, 1963, more than 200,000 people, most of them African Americans, converged on Washington, D.C., to demonstrate for a full and speedy program of civil rights and equal job opportunities.

President Kennedy announced that he would be asking Congress to enact major new civil rights legislation. Because he was assassinated, Kennedy did not see his proposed civil rights legislation enacted. Most of what he proposed became law in the **Civil Rights Act of 1964.** It included the most far-reaching civil rights legislation in history. It outlawed discrimination in hotels, restaurants, theaters, and other places of public accommodation. The act also gave the government new authority to bring about school integration and prohibited job discrimination by businesses and labor unions. Constitutional authority for the act came from the commerce clause of Article I, Section 8, which gave Congress the right to regulate activities having to do with interstate commerce.

What limits, if any, should be placed on protests that use civil disobedience?

Courtesy of AP/Wide World Photos.

Key Note Term

Civil Rights Act of 1964—an act of Congress designed to protect the rights of individuals to fair treatment by private persons, groups, organizations, businesses, and government

Civil Disobedience in a Constitutional Democracy

While imprisoned during the protests in Birmingham, Alabama, in 1963, Rev. Martin Luther King, Jr. wrote the Letter from Birmingham City Jail. Nonviolent direct action, he said, forces a community to confront its unjust laws and customs. "It seeks so to dramatize the issue that it can no longer be ignored."

The letter defends civil disobedience by maintaining that "an individual who breaks a law that conscience tells him is unjust and who willingly accepts the possibility of imprisonment in order to arouse the conscience of the community . . . is in reality expressing the highest respect for law."

As Rev. King pointed out, civil disobedience is as old as the death of Socrates and the martyrdom of the early Christians. Its tactics were used by the American revolutionaries, by abolitionists, and by women's rights advocates. Civil disobedience was practiced by those opposed to the Vietnam War and even more recently by those opposed to abortion.

Even some early supporters of the civil rights movement, however, questioned the correctness of civil disobedience. Such tactics, they argued, might be justified in a dictatorship or totalitarian state, but should not be used in a constitutional democracy where there is a "government of laws not men."

How the Civil Rights Movement Used Constitutional Rights to Achieve Its Objectives

The civil rights movement is a good example of citizens using rights protected by the Constitution to secure other constitutional rights. Rev. Martin Luther King, Jr. reminded his followers in the Montgomery Bus Boycott that "One of the great glories of democracy is the right to protest for right."

The struggle to realize the ideals of the Fourteenth and Fifteenth Amendments would not have been possible without those rights of protest guaranteed in the First Amendment: freedom of speech, the press, assembly, and petitioning for the redress of grievances. As Rev. King said in 1965:

> "We march in the name of the Constitution, knowing that the Constitution is on our side. The right of people peaceably to assemble and to petition the government for the redress of grievances shall not be abridged. That's the First Amendment."

In seeking their rights as citizens, civil rights organizations also created civic education programs across the South for the training of black leaders in the struggle.

During the 1950s and 60s, when the Supreme Court was particularly active in securing the rights of equality for racial minorities, it also was using the due process clause of the Fourteenth Amendment to secure procedural rights in criminal proceedings.

How would you evaluate the contributions of Rev. Martin Luther King, Jr. to the civil rights movement?

Courtesy of AP/Wide World Photos.

In the 1960s the Court greatly expanded the protections available to individuals suspected or charged with a crime. Most of the judicial protections in the Bill of Rights were incorporated in the due process clause of the Fourteenth Amendment. The Court's decisions reflected a change of attitude about criminal justice in American society.

Conclusion

This lesson took a look at the civil rights movement from its inception through the 1960s. You learned how the Supreme Court's application of the equal protection clause changed from the late nineteenth century to the present. You learned about the "separate but equal doctrine," established by the Supreme Court decision in the case of Plessy v. Ferguson.

This lesson also covered the role of the legislative, executive, and judicial branches of government in ending legal segregation, and how the civil rights movement is a good example of citizens using rights protected by the Constitution to secure other constitutional rights.

Obtaining the right to vote is discussed in the following lesson. You will learn how minorities and women fought not only the states but the federal government to secure their right to vote.

Lesson Review

1. Explain the "separate but equal" doctrine established by the Supreme Court in the case of Plessy v. Ferguson. What important consequences of this doctrine can you identify?

2. What is meant by "Jim Crow" laws? How did they affect everyday life?

3. What was the case of Brown v. Board of Education about? What was the Supreme Court's decision in this case? Why is this case important?

4. What was the Civil Rights Act of 1964? How has it been an important source of protection of rights?

5. How were the rights of assembly and petition, and freedom of speech and of the press used to help achieve the goals of the civil rights movement?

Lesson 4

Right to Vote

Key Terms

Fifteenth Amendment
franchise
Nineteenth Amendment
referenda
suffrage
Twenty-fourth Amendment
Twenty-sixth Amendment

What You Will Learn to Do

- Chart the evolution of voting rights in the United States

Linked Core Objectives

- Communicate using verbal, non-verbal, visual, and written techniques
- Apply critical thinking techniques

Skills and Knowledge You Will Gain Along the Way

- Provide an account of the history of the expansion of suffrage in the United States
- Explain ways in which suffrage was denied to various groups in the past
- Describe general voting requirements today
- Describe how the extension of the right to vote is related to some of the fundamental ideals and principles of our constitutional government
- Define key words contained in this lesson

Introduction

Suffrage has been a subject of controversy throughout our history. During the colonial period and the early years of our nation, voting was generally restricted to white men who owned property. Although the majority of white males qualified for suffrage, other people, such as women, African Americans, Native Americans, and members of certain religious groups, were usually denied the right to vote. In this lesson, you will examine how the right to vote during the last 200 years has been extended to almost every citizen 18 years of age or older.

When you have completed this lesson, you should be able to describe the extension of voting rights as a result of changes in the voting laws in the various states, amendments to the Constitution, and decisions of the Supreme Court. You should also be able to describe how the extension of the right to vote is related to some fundamental ideas and principles about constitutional government that you have studied.

Key Note Term

suffrage—a vote cast in deciding a disputed question or in electing a person to office

Comparing Civil and Political Rights

A distinction is sometimes made between civil and political rights in a free society. Civil rights usually refer to those rights that we enjoy as private individuals and that protect us from the unwarranted interference of government. Most of the provisions in the Bill of Rights are civil rights, including those rights that grant us due process of law.

Political rights refer to those rights that allow us to influence the actions of our government and to participate in government ourselves. The Constitution provides us with the right to vote and to hold public office. Those rights in the First Amendment that protect liberty in our private lives also give us the power to influence our government through freedom of speech, the press, and the right to assemble and petition for the redress of grievances. These First Amendment freedoms, therefore, are both civil and political rights.

America is one of the world's oldest democracies, but that democracy has meant different things throughout our history. Our constitutional democracy is based on the sovereignty of the people, but the number of citizens entitled to exercise that sovereign power was once much smaller than it is today. The expansion of the right to vote to all citizens represents one of the great themes in our history, in some respects the most important theme. As the Supreme Court declared more than a century ago, the right to vote is "a fundamental right, because it is the preservative of all rights."

At the Philadelphia Convention, the Framers could not agree on who should be given the right to vote. As a result, the Constitution simply stated that members of the House of Representatives were to be elected by the people in each state who, under state law, were eligible to vote for the lower house of their state legislature. The Constitution, therefore, left to each state government the power to decide who could vote. As a result, many of the early battles about voting rights took place at the state level.

Extending the Right to Vote to All White Men

Since the founding of the country, white men have had the right to vote and take part in government, but usually they had to meet certain qualifications. In some states, the right to vote included the requirement that a person belong to a particular religious group. By the time the Civil War started, however, an increased number of white men had gained the right to vote.

During the Revolutionary War, six state governments eliminated all property requirements and gave the right to vote to all white males, rich or poor. At the same time, three other state governments increased the property requirements, limiting the right to vote.

Thomas Paine, in the following statement, clearly described the issue of linking the right to vote with the ownership of property.

> *"You require that a man shall have sixty dollars worth of property, or he shall not vote. Very well, take an illustration. Here is a man who today owns a jackass, and the jackass is worth sixty dollars. Today the man is a voter and he goes to the polls and deposits his vote. Tomorrow the jackass dies. The next day the man comes to vote without his jackass and he cannot vote at all. Now tell me, which was the voter, the man or the jackass?"*

Following the election of Thomas Jefferson as president in 1800, many states began eliminating the property requirement for voting. Between 1812 and 1821, six new western states became part of the nation and they granted the vote to all white males. During the same period, four of the older states that had property requirements abolished them.

Andrew Jackson ran for president in 1828. His support came from many men who had just won the right to vote. In this election, three times more Americans voted than ever before. Jackson's election represented a new era in American politics, in which the spirit of democracy and equality began to influence the nation's political institutions. Suffrage continued to be extended to more white males. As new states in the West entered the Union, they did so with nearly universal white male suffrage. One by one, most of the older states amended their election laws by removing property qualifications. In most cases these reforms were accomplished peacefully. In Rhode Island, one of the last states to extend the right to vote to all white males, the issue resulted in

Why was it important to extend voting rights to all Americans?

Courtesy of AP/Wide World Photos.

Chapter 5   Bill of Rights Developed and Expanded

a small civil war. In 1841 the leader of **franchise** reform in Rhode Island, Thomas Dorr, led his followers in an armed attack on the state capitol. By the time of the Civil War, nearly all white male suffrage had been realized in the United States.

Extending the Right to Vote to African American Males

The **Fifteenth Amendment** was added to the Constitution in 1870, just after the Civil War. Although the Fifteenth Amendment guaranteed the right to vote to African American males, many states in the South passed laws that made it almost impossible for these new voters to exercise their right.

As a result of the civil rights movement of the 1950s and 1960s, the federal government began using its power to protect the rights of African Americans against political discrimination. In 1964, the **Twenty-fourth Amendment** was added to the Constitution prohibiting the use of poll taxes as a means of denying the right to vote in federal elections. The following year, Congress passed the Voting Rights Act. This act gave additional protection by authorizing the federal government to oversee the registration of voters in areas where state officials had regularly prevented African Americans from registering to vote. The Supreme Court ruled in Harper v. Virginia Board of Elections (1966) that the use of poll taxes in state elections was a violation of the equal protection clause of the Fourteenth Amendment. Thus, by the mid-60s, great progress had been made in ensuring that African American men could enjoy the right to vote as it had been guaranteed by the Fifteenth Amendment almost a century earlier.

Extending the Right to Vote to Women

Closely linked with the struggle of African Americans for freedom and equality was the struggle for women's rights. It took even longer for women to win the actual right to vote than it did for African American men. For most of the history of the United States, women did not have the right to vote or take part in government. Women were the largest group of people ever denied the right to vote in our country. The struggle to gain this right was long and difficult because it challenged strongly held traditional beliefs about women's roles in society.

During the time Congress was considering the Civil War Amendments, leaders of the women's movement asked that the right to vote be expanded to include women. These leaders, including Susan B. Anthony, hoped their long support of the antislavery cause would be rewarded. Their appeal was denied. Male antislavery leaders refused to extend the vote to women. Instead, they specifically included the term "male citizen" for the first time in the Constitution. The Fourteenth Amendment prohibits any state from denying the right to vote to males.

The exclusion of women in the Fourteenth Amendment did not prevent states from granting women the right to vote. In 1874, people in favor of women's rights argued before the Supreme Court that the following clause gave women the right to vote:

> *"All persons born or naturalized in the United States, and subject to the jurisdiction thereof, are citizens of the United States and of the State wherein they reside."*

The Supreme Court denied this claim. They ruled in Minor v. Happersett (1875) that being a citizen does not automatically give a person the right to vote. It was not unconstitutional for states to deny the vote to women.

Key Note Terms

franchise—a privilege or right officially granted a person or a group by a government

Fifteenth Amendment—right of citizens to vote

Twenty-fourth Amendment—the right of citizens of the United States to vote in any primary or other election for President or Vice President, for electors for President or Vice President, or for Senator or Representative in Congress, shall not be denied or abridged by the United States or any State by reason of failure to pay any poll tax or other tax

Why were women denied the right to vote until 1920?

Figure 5.4.1: Susan B. Anthony (1820–1906).

Courtesy of the Center for Civic Education.

In 1876, Susan B. Anthony (see Figure 5.4.1), led a delegation of women to the Philadelphia Centennial Celebration of the Declaration of Independence. Although no women had been invited to participate in the program, Anthony's protest included reading the Women's Declaration of Rights:

> *"Yet we cannot forget, even in this glad hour, that while all men of every race . . . have been invested with the full rights of citizenship under our hospitable flag, all women still suffer the degradation of disfranchisement."*

Wyoming gave women the right to vote while it was still a territory. The story is told that when certain members of Congress argued against this "petticoat provision," the Wyoming legislature said it would rather stay out of the Union for 100 years than join it without allowing women to vote. Wyoming was admitted to the Union.

After Wyoming, other western states quickly extended the right of suffrage to women. By the end of World War I, more than half of the states had given women the right to vote.

In 1875, the Supreme Court had ruled that being a citizen did not automatically give a person the right to vote. States could deny this right to women if they chose. It was not until 1920, 50 years after African American men won the right to vote, that women were guaranteed the same right under the **Nineteenth Amendment.**

Pressure for a woman suffrage amendment mounted during World War I as women entered the work force in record numbers. The uncertainty and slowness of state-by-state victories encouraged women to push harder for an amendment to the Constitution giving them the right to vote. In 1918, President Woodrow Wilson announced his support for the proposed amendment. In 1920, even though there was still considerable opposition to granting suffrage to women, the Nineteenth Amendment was finally ratified. Women had the right to vote after being denied that right for more than 130 years. The Nineteenth Amendment states:

Key Note Term

Nineteenth Amendment—women's suffrage rights

- *Section 1.* The right of citizens of the United States to vote shall not be denied or abridged by the United States or by any State on account of sex.
- *Section 2.* Congress shall have the power to enforce this article by appropriate legislation.

Extending the Right to Vote to Native Americans

The Constitution, as originally adopted, mentioned Indians twice. Under Article I, "Indians not taxed" were excluded from state populations for purposes of apportioning taxes and representatives in Congress. Also under Article I, Congress is accorded the power to "regulate commerce with foreign nations, among the several States, and with the Indian Tribes."

The implications of these provisions as interpreted by the Supreme Court are twofold:

- **Native Americans were not citizens of the United States or the states in which they resided**
- **Native American tribes were distinct political societies whose foreign and domestic relations were to be managed by the federal government of the United States**

Their early relationship with the federal government affected the civil rights of Native Americans in profound ways. The most obvious is that Native American people, as citizens of distinct political communities, enjoyed none of the constitutional rights reserved to citizens.

Following the Snyder Act of 1924, all Native Americans were made United States citizens, although some had acquired citizenship earlier through other legislation. The assumption underlying this federal policy was that the tribes would eventually disappear and Native Americans would be citizens only of the federal and state governments. When that assumption proved false and the tribes did not disappear, what resulted was the dual citizenship that Native Americans have today.

Many states, however, continued to discriminate against Native Americans for purposes of voting, jury duty, and providing testimony in court. The Voting Rights Act of 1965 and its amendments were efforts to address the problem of discrimination against all minorities.

Extending the Right to Vote to Eighteen-Year-Olds

Before 1971, only Alaska, Georgia, Hawaii, and Kentucky had allowed persons younger than twenty-one to participate in elections. In 1970, Congress, in amending the Voting Rights Act, included a section that said no one should be denied the right to vote on the grounds of age if they were eighteen-years-old or older. This law was challenged in the case of Oregon v. Mitchell (1970) and the Supreme Court was divided. Four justices felt that Congress had the power to lower the voting age to eighteen; four other justices concluded that Congress had no such power. Justice Hugo Black cast the decisive vote. He ruled that Congress could regulate the voting age in national elections but not in state elections. He argued that the Constitution leaves to the states the power to regulate the elections of their own public officials. The Congress does have the authority, however, to lower the voting age in federal elections.

What can be done to increase the number of eligible Americans who participate in elections?

Courtesy of AP/Wide World Photos.

Within six months of the Court decision, the **Twenty-sixth Amendment** was ratified by the required number of states. The Amendment states:

Section 1. **The right of citizens of the United States, who are eighteen years of age or older, to vote shall not be denied or abridged by the United States or by any State on account of age.**

Section 2. **The Congress shall have the power to enforce this article by appropriate legislation.**

Key Note Term

Twenty-sixth Amendment—an amendment to the U.S. Constitution, ratified in 1971, lowering the voting age to 18

Key Note Term

referenda—the submission of a proposed public measure or actual statute to a direct popular vote

Current Level of Democracy in the U.S.

Over the course of two centuries we have used our Constitution to achieve nearly universal adult suffrage. From a fraction of the country's population in 1789, "We the People" has grown to include nearly every American of voting age. In most respects the United States is the most democratic nation on earth. Americans can use the power of the ballot box to choose more public officials at more levels of government than do voters in any other democracy. Through special **referenda** we can even use our votes to make laws.

As the nation's democratic opportunities have expanded, though, the willingness of American citizens to participate has decreased. There has been a steady decline in voter turnout in recent years. Only 57 percent of eligible citizens voted in the 1992 presidential election. Fewer than 50 percent now vote in non-presidential or "off-year" elections. A century ago more than 70 percent of eligible voters regularly went to the polls. The United States now ranks 11th among the world's democracies in the percentage of eligible voters who exercise that right.

One reason for this decline is the difficult and complicated registration procedures of many states. Citizens in most of the other democracies in the world find it easier to register to vote. Recent changes in registration laws have made it somewhat less difficult for potential voters in this country. The decline in voting also reflects the declining influence of political parties, especially at the local level. In the past, party organizations could be counted on to "get out the vote."

Whatever the causes, many people today worry about the unwillingness of so many Americans to use this most fundamental right of citizenship. They fear it may reflect a decline in civic-mindedness and a growing sense of alienation from government—the belief that "my vote doesn't count." By leaving the matter of governing entirely with bureaucrats and lobbyists, "We the People" may become less represented and less representative than we were 200 years ago. The future of democracy will be one of the great issues that America's younger citizens must face as the nation enters its third century.

Examining the Reasons Why Young Americans Do Not Vote

Voter turnout is strongly influenced by socioeconomic status and education. Generally, better off and better educated American citizens use their right to vote to a much greater extent than do poor or uneducated citizens.

Those who can understand and analyze public affairs are more likely to take an active interest in them. Completing the course of study in this book will probably increase the chance that you will participate in the democratic process in the years ahead.

Voting is also a function of age. Older Americans, those in middle age and retirement, have almost twice the voting percentage as young Americans aged 18–20. In 1992, although 80 percent of registered young people actually voted, this was only 40 percent of the young people eligible to vote. Some experts suggest that older citizens vote in greater percentages because they see more of a connection between government policies and the concerns of their individual lives.

Are some Americans still denied the opportunity to vote? Explain.

Conclusion

This lesson examined all American's right to vote. You learned that not everyone in this country had always enjoyed the simple act of voting, but that African Americans, Native Americans, and women all had to fight for this right. You learned about Constitutional Amendments that ensured the right of voting to all U.S. citizens. You also learned that not everyone chooses to participate in the election of local, state, and national elections for a variety of reasons.

Lesson Review

1. How would you explain the difference between civil and political rights?

2. How did the Constitution deal with the right to vote? How has this been changed by amendments to the Constitution?

3. Why was the struggle to secure the right to vote for women so difficult?

4. What are some factors that affect voter turnout in the United States?

Lesson 5

Using the Law to Correct Injustice

Key Terms

affirmative action
aggressive recruitment programs
Education Amendment of 1972
Equal Employment Opportunities
Equal Pay Act of 1963
preferential treatment programs
quotas and group entitlements
Regents of the University of California v. Bakke (1978)
remedial programs
reverse discrimination

What You Will Learn to Do

- Defend a position about the acceptability of an affirmative action program under the equal protection clause

Linked Core Objectives

- Communicate using verbal, non-verbal, visual, and written techniques
- Apply critical thinking techniques

Skills and Knowledge You Will Gain Along the Way

- Explain the purposes of affirmative action programs, their relationship to the purposes of the Fourteenth Amendment, and the issues raised by affirmative action
- Evaluate positions on issues of affirmative action and on the present guidelines used to determine the constitutionality of affirmative action programs
- Define key words contained in this lesson

Chapter 5

Introduction

This lesson focuses on to what extent the Constitution and other laws can be used to address injustice and other problems in modern-day America. This lesson discusses the history and rationale for affirmative action as well as some types of other programs available. As a result of this lesson, you will be able to defend a position on an issue involving affirmative action and on the guidelines used to determine the constitutionality of these programs.

Examining the Role of Law in Solving Problems

The nineteenth-century observer of American democracy, Alexis de Tocqueville, observed that most public issues in the United States eventually become legal questions. What he meant was that Americans try to address and resolve their problems in terms of law and constitutional principles.

Our commitment to constitutional government provides the foundation for most of our attempts to resolve the problems in our society. You have examined many examples of this American faith in constitutionalism. You have learned how we have used the Constitution to abolish slavery, restructure the Union, and expand equality in civil and political rights to minorities and women. With remarkably few changes in its content, the Constitution has proved itself capable of addressing these problems and adjusting to the vast changes in the nation during the last 200 years. To a large extent, Chief Justice Marshall's faith in a Constitution "intended to endure for ages to come . . . to be adapted to the various crises of human affairs" has been confirmed. Perhaps the most important legacy of the civil rights movement has been the sustained commitment to equality and protection of rights for all people in the United States. Both government policies and court decisions have continued the effort to eliminate discrimination, not only against African Americans, but against all "historically excluded groups."

Equal Protection Clause

In recent years, the equal protection clause of the Fourteenth Amendment has been expanded to prevent discrimination on the basis of age, gender, and ethnic background as well as race. Court decisions banning such discrimination have been reinforced by laws passed by Congress. The Civil Rights Act of 1964 outlawed job discrimination by private employers and labor unions. It also created an **Equal Employment Opportunities** Commission to monitor compliance. Subsequent legislation by Congress extended the protection to additional groups and applied the laws to small companies and unions as well.

Women represent the largest group to benefit from these anti-discrimination efforts. They were among the groups protected from employment discrimination by the 1964 Civil Rights Act. The **Equal Pay Act of 1963** prohibited discrimination on the basis of gender in job pay. The **Education Amendment of 1972** outlawed gender discrimination in any educational program that receives federal aid.

Key Note Terms

equal employment opportunities— prohibits employment discrimination based on race, color, religion, sex, or national origin

Equal Pay Act of 1963— to prohibit discrimination on account of sex in the payment of wages by employers engaged in commerce or in the production of goods for commerce

Education Amendment of 1972— no person in the United States shall, on the basis of sex, be excluded from participation in, be denied the benefits of, or be subjected to discrimination under any educational program or activity receiving Federal financial assistance

The nation's courts have wrestled with the problems of how to determine when discrimination exists. Should it be measured by the intent of the person or institution accused of discrimination or should it be determined by results, regardless of intent? Who should carry the burden of proving discrimination, those making the accusation or those being accused? Why do some people claim that equality of opportunity is not enough to remedy past injustice?

There has been remarkable progress in recent years in providing equal protection of the laws to persons deprived of this right in the past. Some people argue, however, that the American emphasis on "equality of rights" instead of "equality of condition" results in an unacceptable inequality in our society. They argue that an emphasis on equal rights does nothing to address wide differences in wealth, power, and education. Consider the three following examples of how these differences in condition can make equality of rights meaningless.

Political Influence

All persons have an equal right to participate in the political process by voting, expressing their views, and petitioning and lobbying government officials. Despite this equal right, however, not all Americans have the same ability to influence the government. Many people are not well educated and do not have the necessary understanding of how government works in order to influence its decisions. Many people without financial resources are more concerned with economic survival than with spending the time and energy required to influence their elected officials. On the other hand, people who are wealthy, well-educated, and have contact with powerful people often are able to use this knowledge and wealth to further their own political interests. As a result, despite equality of political rights, wealthy and more educated people generally have greater influence than under educated people or those without adequate financial resources.

Does the government have an obligation to provide a defendant with the best possible legal counsel?

Rights of the Accused

All persons accused of a crime have the right to be defended by a lawyer. If they cannot afford to hire a lawyer, the court will provide one. A wealthy person, however, can hire the best criminal lawyer available. In such a situation, the poorer person might have to depend on an overworked or less experienced lawyer to handle his or her defense.

Right to an Education

Although the Constitution does not guarantee the right to education, every state offers free public education. The quality of education, however, varies widely. Public education is largely supported by property taxes. Children who live in poor communities often attend schools that have larger classes, fewer educational materials, fewer enrichment classes, lower teachers' salaries, and ill-kept buildings and equipment.

Affirmative Action

Many people believe that eliminating the legal barriers to equal opportunity is not enough. The effects of past discrimination and continued prejudice against women, racial and ethnic minorities, and others, still exist. Established patterns of prejudice and discrimination, some argue, hinder people from taking advantage of opportunities provided by law. It is not enough, they say, to sit back and passively wait for the effects of past legal discrimination to disappear. They believe that something positive or "affirmative," must be done to further the goal of equality of opportunity.

In the 1960s, as a result of such concerns, President Lyndon Johnson and others urged Congress to create programs that would go beyond merely removing legal barriers to equal opportunity. Such programs would open up opportunities in education and employment, provide remedial help, and, in some cases, preferential treatment for members of groups discriminated against in the past. These programs were called **affirmative action.**

Key Note Term

affirmative action—a policy or a program that seeks to redress past discrimination through active measures to ensure equal opportunity, as in education and employment

Supporters of these programs claim that they are designed to make equality of opportunity a reality. They say affirmative action helps remedy the wrongs and reduce the handicaps caused by the unjust way women and minorities have been treated in the past. Affirmative action includes the following types of programs.

Aggressive Recruitment Programs

Aggressive recruitment programs are conducted by business, industry, and government to make sure that when opportunities in education and employment occur, women and members of minority groups are encouraged to apply for them. For example, it is common for many people to learn of jobs from friends. Such practices may perpetuate existing patterns that deny equal employment opportunities to members of other groups. In this type of situation, providing equal opportunity would mean widely advertising the availability of jobs to members of all groups that might be interested.

Remedial Programs

Remedial programs include education programs in pre-schools and in elementary and secondary schools. These programs are designed to help students with particular educational and economic needs gain the basic skills to succeed in school and in the job market. Some programs help students to learn useful occupations. Others give remedial tutoring and assistance to students in college as well as to adults who want to improve their knowledge and skills. There has been little controversy about providing remedial programs, although some complain that there are not enough programs available for all children and adults who need them.

> **Key Note Term**
>
> **aggressive recruitment programs**—to obtain replacements for or new supplies of something lost, wasted, or needed

> **Key Note Term**
>
> **remedial programs**—supplying a remedy

In what ways have preferential treatment programs helped some groups gain access to jobs and careers that were previously closed to them?

Preferential Treatment Programs

Preferential treatment programs are designed to compensate for the effects of past discrimination against women and minorities. These programs are designed to give members of these groups preferred treatment in gaining jobs and access to higher education. People argue that preferential treatment for such groups is required to:

- **Balance the advantages white men have received from hundreds of years of preferential treatment**

- **Promote diversity in colleges and universities in order to produce a less race-conscious and more racially fair society**

- **Include people of different racial, religious, and ethnic groups whose perspectives help to improve educational programs for all**

Affirmative Action Controversy

Affirmative action programs, particularly those calling for preferential treatment, are very controversial. Many events in the nation's constitutional history have produced tensions and conflicts between equally worthy ideals.

The debate about affirmative action programs involves such a conflict. Supporters of the programs point to America's historic commitment to equality of opportunity. Critics of affirmative action, on the other hand, appeal to another of this country's fundamental ideals—the rights of the individual. That is, each American should be rewarded according to his or her own merits, and not because of favoritism, privilege, or membership in a particular group.

Some opponents of affirmative action programs that involve preferential treatment believe that these programs violate the rights of the individual. In the interest of promoting equality the programs create new forms of inequality. To overcome past discrimination, some early preferential treatment programs called for setting aside a certain number of positions in colleges and businesses for qualified members of minority groups. Sometimes these programs established goals and timetables for filling positions to reflect the proportion of minorities and women in the community.

For example, if 25 percent of a community belonged to a particular minority, a college might have set a goal of recruiting students from that group so that the student body reflected that same percentage. Hiring or granting other benefits to individuals based on explicit racial quotas, however, is illegal except where justified to remedy the effects of demonstrated past discrimination. The use of **quotas and group entitlements** in education and employment has led to claims of unfairness from those who do not belong to groups receiving preferential treatment. Many people whose parents, grandparents, or in some cases themselves, had to overcome prejudice and hardship without the benefit of government programs resent what they see as government-supported favoritism of special groups.

Critics of affirmative action claim that such programs violate the ideals of the civil rights movement. Quotas and other forms of preferential treatment, they say, result in **reverse discrimination.** Just as it was wrong in the past to discriminate against people because of their gender, race, religion, or ethnic background, it is wrong now to discriminate in favor of people on the same basis. The equal protection clause of the Fourteenth Amendment was intended to remove racial and other discriminatory barriers, not create them.

Appealing to America's great traditions of individual rights and equality of opportunity, critics of affirmative action remind us of the long struggle to establish individual rights. This emphasis on individual rights distinguishes modern constitutionalism from the concept of rights in the ancient world and the Middle Ages.

Advocates of affirmative action respond by pointing out that the ideals of equality of opportunity and individual merit were never a reality in the past. For centuries a section of the population took advantage of privilege, social connections and the exclusion of women and non-whites. Some reverse discrimination is, therefore, necessary to remedy this past injustice by breaking down the legal and informal structures on which it was based.

Examining a Supreme Court Opinion on Affirmative Action

The following study provides you with an opportunity to discuss a Supreme Court case that illustrates the difficulty of designing reasonable and fair programs to promote the goals of affirmative action while not violating the right of the individual to equal protection of the law. Read the summary of the facts and opinions in this case. Be prepared to take a position and defend it.

Regents of the University of California v. Bakke (1978)

As part of its affirmative action program, the Medical School of the University of California at Davis set aside 16 places for minorities out of its entering class of 100. Alan Bakke (see Figure 5.5.2), a non-minority applicant, was denied admission even though his test scores were higher than those of most of the minority applicants who were accepted.

Figure 5.5.2: Allan Bakke, center, receiving his degree in medicine from the Medical School at the University of California at Davis.

Courtesy of AP/Wide World Photos.

Bakke sued in the California courts claiming that the admissions policy of the university violated the 1964 Civil Rights Act and denied him the right to equal protection of the laws guaranteed by the Fourteenth Amendment. The California Supreme Court agreed with Bakke's claim. The case was appealed to the U.S. Supreme Court which also ruled in Bakke's favor in a 5-4 decision. Bakke was accepted into the medical school.

The five-member majority of the Court, however, was not in agreement on why they voted in Bakke's favor. Four of the justices said the university quota system violated a prohibition of the 1964 Civil Rights Act; it is unlawful to exclude anyone on the basis of race from any program receiving federal funds. The university received federal funds.

The fifth justice, Lewis F. Powell, concluded that the racial quota was also a violation of the equal protection clause of the Fourteenth Amendment. Powell's opinion was based on the following points:

- **He stated that it was a violation of the Constitution to place the burden of remedying the effects of past discrimination on individuals who had nothing to do with such discrimination.**

- **He rejected quotas.**

- **He approved, however, the consideration of race as a factor in an admissions policy meant to promote diversity in the student body. Such diversity is an acceptable goal for universities.**

The four dissenting members of the Supreme Court claimed that the university quota system was a reasonable way to help remedy the effects of past discrimination against racial and ethnic minorities.

The sharply divided opinions among the justices in the Bakke decision indicate the problem the nation's courts have faced in reconciling certain types of affirmative action programs with the Constitution. Courts have had little difficulty in approving remedial education and minority recruitment programs. Preferential treatment of minorities, however, has presented a more difficult issue.

Since the Bakke decision, the Supreme Court has ruled on several cases involving preferential treatment. Its decisions have not always been consistent, but they have produced the following general guidelines:

- **Affirmative action programs should be temporary arrangements to remedy the consequences of past discrimination.**

- **Any particular program should be designed to remedy the consequences of past discrimination in a specific situation rather than the more general problems of injustice in society at large.**

- **In applying an affirmative action program, the chance of unfair consequences for non-minority individuals should be minimized. The Supreme Court, however, has ruled that even quotas may be used as a temporary remedy when the problems resulting from past discrimination are particularly serious.**

Conclusion

Affirmative action and other methods of using the law to correct injustices are never without controversy and debate. In this lesson, you learned that the Constitution and other laws can be interpreted to help those who have suffered discrimination. You also learned that although these interpretations can be helpful, they are not without opponents and never without heated discussion.

This ends Chapter 5, "Bill of Rights Developed and Expanded," of Unit 6, "Citizenship in American History and Government." Chapter 6 examines the Bill of Rights in detail.

Lesson Review

1. **How would you explain affirmative action programs? What purposes are they intended to serve? What constitutional issues do they raise?**

2. **What are some laws passed by Congress to end unfair discrimination?**

3. **What is meant by the term reverse discrimination? How is this idea used to argue against affirmative action programs?**

4. **What guidelines have been established in Supreme Court decisions with regard to affirmative action programs?**

Chapter 6

The Bill of Rights

Lesson 1

First Amendment and Freedom of Religion

Key Terms

established church
establishment clause
free exercise clause
Great Awakening
separation of church and state

What You Will Learn to Do

- Compare different interpretations of how the first amendment applies to the government's power over religion

Linked Core Objectives

- Communicate using verbal, non-verbal, visual, and written techniques
- Apply critical thinking techniques

Skills and Knowledge You Will Gain Along the Way

- Identify the history and importance of religious freedom
- Distinguish between the meanings of the establishment and free exercise clauses of the First Amendment
- Explain the different interpretations of the establishment clause
- Explain conflicts that may exist between the establishment and free exercise clauses
- Explain the issues and considerations involved in limiting the free exercise of religious beliefs
- Evaluate positions on issues regarding the establishment and free exercise clauses
- Define key words contained in this lesson

Introduction

Two clauses in the First Amendment protect freedom of religion. These are the "establishment" and "free exercise" clauses. In this lesson you will examine the Founders' belief that religion and government should be separate. Each clause deals with a different part of this separation. The "establishment" clause prohibits the federal government from establishing one or more official religions or churches for the nation. The "free exercise" clause prevents the government from putting unreasonable restrictions on particular religious practices.

When you complete this lesson, you should be able to explain the importance of freedom of religion, describe the differences between the establishment and free exercise clauses in the First Amendment. You also should be able to explain different interpretations of the establishment clause and the conflicts between the establishment and free exercise clauses. Finally you should be able to explain the issues and considerations involved in limiting the free exercise of religious beliefs.

Historical Background of Religious Freedom

At the time of the first settlements in America, Europe was suffering from religious wars that had torn the continent apart since the early sixteenth century. This religious revolt, known as the Reformation, led to more than a century of bloodshed as Catholics and Protestants struggled for political power. Once in power, each group often attempted to eliminate its opponents through banishment, jail, torture or death.

Almost every nation in Europe had a government-sponsored Christian church, sometimes called an **established church.** In each nation there was only one established church. The established church in England, for example, was the Church of England. In France and Spain, the Roman Catholic Church was established, while in some German states and in Sweden the Lutheran Church was the official church.

People who did not belong to the established church were denied certain rights. They were often excluded from universities and disqualified from civil and military offices. Sometimes they were persecuted or even killed for their beliefs. Most Europeans in the seventeenth century accepted the idea of an established religion. The idea that several different religions could coexist was not yet widely accepted. In most of the early colonies there was little tolerance for religious differences. Not only did most colonies have an established church, but in many cases there was intolerance for nonmembers.

By the time of the American Revolution, people had become more tolerant. The religious revival of the mid-eighteenth century, known as the **Great Awakening,** drew many away from established religions and into new religious groups. This gave rise to the idea that all Protestant groups were equal. Diverse religious groups often existed in the same community, and people became used to living and working with others who had different beliefs. The large number of religious groups made it unlikely that one particular church could dominate all others.

Key Note Term

established church—a church that is recognized by law, and sometimes financially supported, as the official church of a nation

Key Note Term

Great Awakening—swept the English-speaking world, as religious energy vibrated between England, Wales, Scotland, and the American colonies in the 1730s and 1740s

It became increasingly difficult for one church to claim special privileges. As a result, even those colonies that had an established religion did not support only one church. Government assistance was given to several churches in an effort to support religion in general rather than a particular state church. Support, however, usually was given only to the Protestant form of the Christian religion. Catholics, Jews, and other groups were not supported and were sometimes discriminated against.

How did the colonial experience shape the Founders' views on freedom of religion?

Courtesy of Culver Pictures.

Eighteenth-century Americans generally thought that religion was important in developing the character needed to maintain a free society. Yet by the time the Constitution was written, most Americans also thought that freedom of belief was an essential right that needed protection.

Americans considered freedom of religion to be something that strengthened both "church" and "state."

The Founders and the Separation of Church and State

There are two basic reasons why early Americans argued for the **separation of church and state:**

- **To protect religion from being corrupted by the state**
- **To protect good government from corruption caused by religious conflict**

People such as Roger Williams, the founder of Rhode Island, believed separation was essential so that religion would be safe from corruption by the state. He insisted that there should be a "wall of separation between the garden of the Church and the wilderness of the world." Thomas Jefferson thought that separation was important in keeping religious conflicts from corrupting government. James Madison combined these two views in his opposition to a religious establishment. He, of course, wrote the First Amendment.

Madison, like Jefferson, believed that individuals in a free society should have freedom of conscience—the right to decide for themselves what to believe. He worried that freedom of conscience would be threatened if government supported some religions but not others.

Key Note Term

separation of church and state—principle is part of our historical, legal and political social heritage and preserves and protects our religious liberties

Government should do only what is necessary to keep the peace and prevent one religious group from violating the rights of others. He concluded that to achieve this goal government should not interfere with religion in any way.

The Constitution Protects Religious Freedom

Before the Bill of Rights, the only mention of religion in the Constitution was the ban placed on religious tests for holding public office in the federal government stated in Article VI. This was a significant step in protecting religious freedom. In 1787, most states still had established religions or religious tests for office. Many Americans did not believe that non-Protestants could be trusted with public office. The Constitution opened the door to people of all religions.

Most but not all states followed the example of the federal government and abolished religious tests for holding state office. It was not until 1868, in North Carolina and 1946, in New Hampshire that such tests were abolished. A 1961, Supreme Court case held Maryland's religious test unconstitutional, and since then they have been prohibited entirely.

At the same time, a number of states still supported Protestant Christianity as an established religion. It was not until 1833, when Massachusetts changed its constitution to separate church and state that established religion in America was eliminated.

How the Bill of Rights Prohibits State Establishment of Religion

The First Amendment says "Congress shall make no law respecting an establishment of religion, . . ." It is clear that Madison wanted to end the practice of having the federal government declare an established church; a practice still prevalent in Europe at the time.

Some people supported the adoption of the First Amendment because they thought it would prevent Congress from interfering with their state religious establishments. After the Fourteenth Amendment incorporated the First Amendment, however, the **establishment clause** was understood to prevent state establishment of religion as well.

How Courts Interpret the Establishment Clause

There is general agreement that the establishment clause means that government may not sponsor an official church. There is considerable disagreement, however, about the meaning of the establishment clause of the First Amendment. The disagreement can be summarized as follows.

- ***The broad interpretation.*** **People holding this position argue that the First Amendment prevents the government from providing any aid to any religion whatsoever. They believe that no tax money can be used to support any religious activity, practice, or institution. The government, however, may give religious groups the same services everyone else receives, such as police and fire protection. The government may provide assistance that makes it easier for people to exercise their religion. For example, schools may excuse students from classes during religious holidays.**

Does prayer in public schools violate the establishment clause? Does a moment of silence violate the free exercise clause?

Courtesy of the Library of Congress.

- *The narrow interpretation.* **People holding this position argue that government is prohibited from giving one religious group preferential treatment. They believe the First Amendment does not prohibit government from supporting religion, as long as it does so impartially. This group supports placing the words "In God We Trust" on money and allowing nondenominational school prayer.**

- *The literal interpretation.* **People holding this position suggest that the First Amendment only prohibits the establishment of an official government religion. They would not prohibit the government's participation in particular religious practices. For example, the government may participate in Christmas celebrations as long as Christianity is not declared an official established religion.**

People using a broad interpretation of the First Amendment often oppose these kinds of actions. People who hold either the broad or narrow interpretation agree, however, that the First Amendment prohibits government acknowledgment of Christmas as a holiday if the holidays of other religious groups are not recognized.

In 1947 the Supreme Court made the establishment clause of the First Amendment applicable to the states through its incorporation into the Fourteenth Amendment. Since that time, the Court has heard many cases involving freedom of religion. These have involved such issues as prayer in schools, Christmas displays of Nativity scenes, and various kinds of support for religious education.

Although most people agree that church and state should be separate, we are no closer today to defining that separation than we were in 1791.

Taking and Defending a Position on the Establishment Clause

Each of the following situations is based on a case that reached the Supreme Court.

Under a Pennsylvania law, the state reimbursed private schools for teachers' salaries, textbooks, and instructional materials in math and science. Although the law generally applied to private schools, 96 percent of the money went to religious schools. Opponents argued that this kind of public support was unconstitutional. They felt it amounted to a subsidy for the schools' whole program, including religious instruction.

New York City arranged a voluntary program permitting its public schools to release students during school hours to receive off-campus religious instruction. Opponents complained that this violated the establishment clause.

The New York State Board of Regents required teachers to begin each school day by leading their class in a nondenominational prayer written by state officials. Students who did not wish to participate were permitted to remain silent or be excused from the classroom. The parents of ten students claimed the prayer was against their religious beliefs and violated the establishment clause.

The city of Pawtucket, Rhode Island, put up a Christmas display that included a Santa Claus house, reindeer pulling Santa's sleigh, a Christmas tree, and a large banner reading "Season's Greetings." It also contained a crèche with the figures of the infant Jesus, Mary, Joseph, angels, shepherds, kings, and animals. Opponents complained that this violated the establishment clause.

1. What position would people who hold the broad interpretation of the establishment clause take on this issue? The narrow interpretation? The literal interpretation? Explain your answers.

2. What arguments can you make for permitting the government to do what it did? What values and interests are involved?

3. What arguments can you make for prohibiting the government from doing what it did? What values and interests are involved?

Rights Protected by the Free Exercise Clause

The establishment clause prevents the government from requiring citizens to practice a particular religion. The **free exercise clause** is intended to make sure that people who want to practice their religion will be permitted to do so.

There are two parts to freedom of religion: the freedom to believe and the freedom to practice religious beliefs. The Supreme Court has said that individuals have an absolute right to freedom of belief or conscience. The government may not interfere with this right. Under certain conditions, however, the right to practice one's beliefs may be limited to protect other important values and interests. The problem is deciding which religious practices should be protected by the First Amendment and which practices government may limit.

Conflicts between the Free Exercise and Establishment Clauses

There are times when the free exercise clause and the establishment clause of the First Amendment come into conflict. For example, consider the following situations:

- If the government pays to provide for chaplains in the armed forces and in prisons, is it violating the establishment clause? If the government failed to provide chaplains, would it be limiting the free exercise of beliefs by persons in the armed forces or in prison?

- If public school officials excuse Jewish students from attending classes on Yom Kippur to attend religious services, are they creating a preference for a particular group that violates the establishment clause? If they deny students the right to be absent, are they prohibiting the free exercise of their religion?

- On August 11, 1984, President Reagan signed into law the Equal Access Act. It requires secondary schools to allow student religious groups to hold meetings in school buildings if other groups or social clubs are given the same opportunity. If schools do not provide meeting facilities for student religious groups, are they limiting their free exercise? If they do, are they violating the establishment clause?

Balancing the Rights of "Free Exercise" against Other Interests of Society

The justices of the Supreme Court often have held differing opinions on the issues you have been discussing. Sometimes they have overruled earlier decisions. The justices have continually attempted to refine the "tests" or considerations used to make a decision.

The Court has considered some issues several times. For example, when the health of the community must be balanced against the religious beliefs of an individual or group, public health is considered to be more important.

By contrast, when the life, health, or safety of individuals, rather than the community, is involved, the Court has upheld the right of mentally competent adults to make their own decisions based on their religious beliefs. For example, an adult may refuse to receive a blood transfusion even if his or her life is at risk. Parents, however, may not refuse a transfusion for their children, and the courts may step in to protect the rights of minors.

Should public school officials be allowed to require inoculations against communicable diseases for students whose parents argue against them on religious grounds?

Courtesy of AP/Wide World Photos.

Lesson 1 First Amendment and Freedom of Religion

The Court also has protected the right of students to refuse to salute the flag or attend high school if this is against their religious beliefs. In deciding such cases, the Court asked whether the government had a compelling state interest, one that was great enough to justify limiting the individual's free exercise of religion. For example, the justices considered the government's requiring a student to salute the flag to be an unreasonable attempt to force a student to accept a belief.

Conclusion

Freedom of religion is one of the best known rights in this country. In this lesson, you learned why it was important to the Founders that all Americans could pursue their rights to believe and worship as they choose, and why there needs to be a division between church and state.

In the following lesson, you will learn how the First Amendment encourages and protects the freedom of expression, and where it draws the line on free speech.

Lesson Review

1. How would you explain the principle of "separation of church and state"? What reasons can you identify to support this principle?

2. What are "religious tests" for public office? What does the Constitution say about them?

3. What is the "establishment clause"? What disagreements have arisen over how courts should interpret it?

4. What is the "free exercise clause"? How have courts tried to balance the individual's right to free exercise of religion with the interests of society?

Lesson 2

First Amendment and Freedom of Expression

Key Terms

clear and present danger
libel
neutrality
Sedition Act of 1798
seditious libel
time-place-and manner restrictions

What You Will Learn to Do

- Defend your position on an issue that involves the First Amendment's right to freedom of expression

Linked Core Objectives

- Communicate using verbal, non-verbal, visual, and written techniques
- Apply critical thinking techniques

Skills and Knowledge You Will Gain Along the Way

- Explain the importance of freedom of expression to both the individual and society
- Examine the historical significance of freedom of expression
- Explain considerations useful in deciding when to place limits on freedom of speech and press
- Evaluate proposed standards for determining the proper scope and limits of freedom of expression
- Evaluate positions on issues involving the right to freedom of expression
- Define key words contained in this lesson

Introduction

The First Amendment says that "Congress shall make no law . . . abridging the freedom of speech, or of the press, or the right of the people peaceably to assemble, and to petition the Government for a redress of grievances." Together these four rights may be considered as one—the right to freedom of expression.

In this lesson you will examine the benefits that freedom of speech and freedom of the press offer to the individual and society, why they were important to the Founders, and the circumstances under which the government should be able to limit them.

When you finish this lesson, you should be able to explain the importance of freedom of expression to both the individual and society and its historical significance. You should be able to explain considerations useful in deciding when to place limits on freedom of speech and press and be able to take, defend, and evaluate positions on issues involving the right to freedom of expression.

The Importance of Protecting the Right to Freedom of Expression

The First Amendment was written because the Founders believed that the freedom to express personal opinions is essential to a free government. The Founders knew from their own experience and knowledge of history that the freedom to write and publish must be protected from government interference.

It is not easy for anyone to tolerate the speech or writings of those with whom they strongly disagree. In a democracy, the danger to freedom of speech comes not only from government officials but also from majorities intolerant of minority opinions.

The pressures to suppress freedom of expression are widespread and powerful in any society. It is important, therefore, to remind ourselves constantly of the important benefits of freedom of expression to the individual and society. Among the arguments that favor free speech are the following:

- **Freedom of expression promotes individual growth and human dignity. The right to think about and arrive at your own conclusions concerning morality, politics, or anything else, is part of individual freedom. That right would be meaningless without the freedom to speak and write about your opinions, and without the freedom to test those opinions by comparing them with the views of others.**

- **Freedom of expression is important for the advancement of knowledge. New ideas are more likely to be developed in a community that allows free discussion. As the British philosopher John Stuart Mill (1806–1873) said, "Progress is possible only when all points of view can be expressed and considered." This way, scientific or other discoveries can form the basis for future discoveries and inventions.**

- **Freedom of expression is a necessary part of our representative government. In our system of government, the government responds to the will of the people. If the people are to instruct government properly, they must have access to information, ideas, and different points of view. Freedom of expression is crucial both in determining policy and in monitoring how well the government is carrying out its responsibilities.**

- **Freedom of expression is vital to bringing about peaceful social change. The right to express one's ideas freely provides a "safety valve" for strongly held opinions. Freedom of expression allows you to try to influence public opinion through persuasion rather than by resorting to violence.**

- **Freedom of expression is essential for the protection of all individual rights. The free expression of ideas and the right to speak against the violation of one's rights by others or by the government are essential for the protection of all the other rights of the individual.**

How Freedom of Expression Was Protected in Early America

Many ideas about the importance of freedom of speech and of the press were brought to America from England. In the seventeenth century, the English won the right to speak and publish without prior censorship. They could still be prosecuted afterward for what they said or wrote, however, under the common law of **seditious libel.** This law made it a crime to publish anything that might be injurious to the reputation of the government.

There is no indication that the Framers intended the Constitution or the Bill of Rights to prevent prosecution for seditious libel. The common view, in both America and Britain, was that no one should be able to make false or malicious accusations against the government.

The Constitution makes no mention of a free press, however, because the Framers believed, as Roger Sherman of Connecticut declared, "The power of Congress does not extend to the Press." The First Amendment was designed to quiet fears that Congress might interfere with the press in any way. These fears seemed to be confirmed by the passage of the **Sedition Act of 1798.** This act, passed by some of the same people who approved the Bill of Rights, indicates that some Americans still had a narrow view of free expression.

Many people, however, opposed such limitations. One reason the Republicans won the election of 1800 was that they were viewed as supporters of political freedom. By 1800, freedom of speech and press were beginning to be considered an essential part of free government.

The Trial of John Peter Zenger

What is "seditious libel"? The common law definition was vague. In general, it meant defaming or ridiculing officers of the government, or the constitution, laws, or government policies, in a way that might jeopardize "public peace." This included not only things that were false and malicious, but also things that were true.

In 1735, John Peter Zenger, a New York printer, was charged with seditious libel by the colonial authorities. Zenger's lawyer argued that what Zenger had published was true, and therefore could not be libelous.

The judge told the jury that the common law did not permit truth as a defense. It was the judge's prerogative to decide, as a matter of law, whether the articles met the definition of seditious libel. He instructed the jury that the only thing they could decide was the "fact" of whether Zenger was the publisher of the articles in question. If he was the publisher, which Zenger did not deny, then he was guilty, pure and simple.

The jury ignored the judge's instructions and found Zenger not guilty because the information he reported in the articles was true. Many Americans believed that this case not only established an important right of freedom of the press, but also proved the importance of the jury as a check on arbitrary government.

Suppression of Freedom of Expression

There has been pressure at many times throughout history to suppress unpopular ideas. Restrictions generally have been imposed during times of war or when the government has felt threatened. Before the Civil War, for example, Congress made it a federal offense to send abolitionist literature through the mail. The early years of the twentieth century were marked by fears of the growing labor movement, socialism, communism, and anarchy. From World War I through the McCarthy era of the 1950s, state and federal governments prosecuted many suspected anarchists, socialists, and communists for advocating draft resistance, mass strikes, or overthrow of the government.

These actions raised serious questions about the right of free speech and led to a number of Supreme Court cases. Since the 1960s, however, there have been fewer attempts to prosecute those who advocate their beliefs including belief in the benefits of a different form of government.

How might government persecution of dissidents, which occurred during the McCarthy era, endanger a free society?

Courtesy of AP/Wide World Photos.

Evaluating and Developing Positions on the Scope and Limits of Freedom of Expression

Judges, professors of constitutional law, and other students of the Constitution have tried to develop standards that will help us decide when freedom of expression may be limited. The following are two positions that judges and others have proposed.

People have argued that the rights of certain groups to express their ideas should not be protected by the First Amendment. Typically, these are groups that advocate overthrowing our representative government. They may also be groups that express malicious ideas that violate the dignity and feelings of other people in the community.

People often conclude this position by arguing that only people who agree to abide by the rules of our society, such as those in the Constitution and the Bill of Rights, should be allowed to participate in free and open discussion.

They also argue that to give government the power to suppress the expression of ideas that some people find unacceptable is too dangerous. It gives government the power to decide what beliefs and opinions are acceptable and unacceptable. A quotation attributed to Voltaire, the eighteenth century French author most noted for his criticism of tyranny and bigotry, summarizes this position, "I may disapprove of what you say, but will defend to the death your right to say it."

What rights, values, and interests of individuals and society might be promoted or endangered by the position that advocates limiting the freedom to express anti-democratic ideas?

What rights, values, and interests of individuals and society might be promoted or endangered by the position which advocates limiting freedom of expression rarely, if ever, no matter how dangerous or obnoxious these ideas may be?

Commonly Accepted Limitations on Freedom of Expression

Despite the statement in the First Amendment that "Congress shall make no law . . . abridging the freedom of speech," most people argue in favor of limiting freedom of expression in certain specific situations.

Suppose the First Amendment were interpreted to mean that there could be no laws at all limiting speech. If so, people would be able to say anything they wanted at any time they wanted. People could lie in court and deprive others of their right to a fair trial. People could scream in libraries, give political speeches in the middle of church sermons, or speak through loudspeakers in neighborhoods in the middle of the night.

Most judges and legal scholars believe the First Amendment should not be interpreted to protect freedom of expression in situations such as those above. In some situations, limiting freedom to speak may actually increase a person's ability to be heard. For example, there are rules governing when someone may talk at a meeting or debate. You may have the right to protest a government policy you do not like, but you do not have the right to do so with a loudspeaker in a residential area in the middle of the night.

How would you define speech that presents a clear and present danger to society?

These limitations on freedom of expression are referred to as **time-place-and manner restrictions.** They govern when, where, and how you may speak, not what you may say. Most people agree that these limitations do not violate the right to free expression so long as they do not make it difficult nor impossible for you to express your ideas to others. These regulations must not favor some opinions over others. For example, one group may not be given a permit to speak in a public park when other groups are forbidden to do so.

Considerations the Supreme Court Has Used to Limit Freedom of Expression

The difficult question for the Court to decide is when freedom of expression should be limited to protect other important social goals. The Supreme Court has upheld time, place, and manner restrictions, so long as they are neutral and applied fairly.

The idea of **neutrality** is important, for the Court has generally taken the position that no matter how dangerous or obnoxious the ideas, people should be allowed to express their views freely. Yet the Court will sometimes allow speech to be limited based on its content. Over the years, the courts have developed guidelines to use in balancing the right to free expression against other important rights and interests of society. For example, suppose your right to free expression could endanger the public safety or national security. If the danger is considered great enough, the courts will decide that your right to free speech must be limited. No one has the right to publish secret military information, or the names of U.S. intelligence agents overseas, for example.

> **Key Note Term**
>
> **time-place-and manner restrictions**—a statute of government action that restricts the time, place or manner of speech

> **Key Note Term**
>
> **neutrality**—the state or quality of being neutral; the condition of being unengaged in contests between others; state of taking no part on either side; indifference

Forms of Expression Protected by the First Amendment

The courts have upheld laws prohibiting speech or writings that present a **clear and present danger** to others or to society. Examples include giving away national security secrets, lying under oath, or **libel.** The courts also have said that you may not engage in speech that could directly lead to violence or cause a riot.

Some judges and scholars have argued that the authors of the First Amendment did not intend it to protect all kinds of speech and press. Their belief in the need to protect free expression was based on the idea that the free exchange of political ideas was essential to democracy. It was not their intention to protect speech that was blasphemous, obscene, or libelous.

To some degree the courts still maintain that the speech protections of the First Amendment only apply to certain kinds of speech. Obscenity, for example, is not protected. The Supreme Court, however, in a series of decisions, has made it increasingly difficult to determine what is "obscene." Consequently, although obscene speech is not protected there are fewer successful prosecutions of obscene speech because of changing community and legal standards.

Commercial speech, such as advertising, also receives less protection by the courts. Regulations that prevent consumer fraud and false advertising, for example, are permitted. In addition, commercial speech may be regulated for reasons of public health. This is why the government can ban cigarette advertising on television.

When the rights of free press come into conflict with the right to a fair trial, the courts have generally upheld the right of reporters to cover trials. Judges have been told to find other ways to protect the defendant's right to a fair trial.

Taking and Defending Positions on an Issue of Freedom of Expression

Colleges and universities are places where free inquiry, debate, and expression are highly valued. Professors and students are supposed to have great freedom to explore, express, debate, and discuss both popular and unpopular ideas. The university ideal is a place where all ideas are worthy of exploration.

In years past, most students at major colleges and universities were white. Today, student bodies of colleges and universities better reflect the diversity of our nation.

Despite the increased understanding of diversity in the United States, conflicts among students along racial, ethnic, and religious lines have occurred on college campuses. As a result, university administrators and student governments have attempted to promote civility and understanding on campus by various means.

What limitations, if any, should be placed on speakers on college campuses?

Recently, at more than 200 colleges and universities across the nation, student codes of conduct or "speech codes" were established. They are designed to prevent statements or comments about race, gender, religion, national origin, or sexual orientation that might offend some people. The goal of such codes is to discourage prejudice and create a more comfortable learning environment for all students.

Supporters of the codes explain that "freedom of expression is no more sacred than freedom from intolerance or bigotry." Critics charge that the result has been to violate students' and teachers' right to free expression. They refer to various instances in which students have been suspended or expelled for comments that were offensive to others.

Issue: On a typical college campus, a large number of students of relatively diverse backgrounds are thrown together in crowded living conditions.

1. Do you think these conditions distinguish the campus from the larger society? If so, do you think this would support the claim that different rules governing speech are needed on campus than those that apply to the society at large?

2. Should any limits be placed on the freedom of expression of professors whose courses are required of all students for graduation?

3. What issues of freedom of expression are involved in this situation?

4. What values and interests are involved?

5. What arguments might be presented by persons holding the position that the right to free expression by people expressing undemocratic ideas can be limited?

6. What arguments might be presented by persons holding the position that the right to free expression should not be limited, even for those expressing dangerous or obnoxious ideas?

Lesson 2 First Amendment and Freedom of Expression

Conclusion

Freedom of speech is one of the most important rights protected by the Constitution. This right protects not only spoken words, but also the written word such as allowing the press to present opposing views.

In the next lesson, you will examine freedom of assembly and the importance of being able to gather in public places.

Lesson Review

1. What rights, considered together, make up "freedom of expression"?

2. Why is it important to protect freedom of expression?

3. What is "seditious libel"? What examples can you give of circumstances in which laws against seditious libel were used to try to suppress criticism of the government?

4. How would you explain "time, place, and manner" restrictions on freedom of expression? What conditions must such restrictions meet in order to be valid?

5. Under what circumstances may limitations on expression be based upon its content?

6. What is meant by the term "libel"?

Lesson 3

First Amendment and Freedom of Assembly

Key Terms

gag rule
lobby
public forum
redress of grievances
right to assembly
right of association and right of petition

What You Will Learn to Do

- Classify different interpretations of how the first amendment protects freedom of assembly, petition and association

Linked Core Objectives

- Communicate using verbal, non-verbal, visual, and written techniques
- Apply critical thinking techniques

Skills and Knowledge You Will Gain Along the Way

- Explain the purpose and importance of the rights of assembly, petition and association
- Describe how rights of assembly and petition have been used and what limitations are placed on them
- Relate the right of association to the First Amendment
- Define key words contained in this lesson

Introduction

Key Note Term

redress of grievances—
a setting right, as of
wrong, injury, or oppres-
sion; as, the redress of
grievances; hence, relief;
remedy; reparation;
indemnification

The First Amendment says that "Congress shall make no law . . . abridging . . . the right of the people peaceably to assemble, and to petition the government for a **redress of grievances.**" In this lesson you will examine the importance and historical background of these rights. You will also discuss an important related right—freedom of association.

When you finish this lesson, you should be able to explain the importance of the rights to freedom of assembly, petition, and association. You should also be able to describe the history of these rights and in what types of situations they might be limited. Finally, you should be able to take and defend a position on an issue involving these rights.

The Importance of the Rights to Assembly, Petition, and Association

Key Note Term

right to assemble—the
right to meet to gather
in groups

As you have seen, the First Amendment protects your rights to form your own opinions, including those about politics and religion. It also protects your right to communicate those opinions to others. These rights would not mean very much, though, if the government had the power to prevent people from getting together to express their views. The people's **right to assemble** and petition the government—to ask the government to take action or change its policies—enhances the First Amendment's protection of our political rights.

A related right that has been recognized by courts is the right of association. We are free to associate with others who share our opinions. These associations include political groups, church groups, professional associations, social clubs, and community service organizations. All are protected by the right to associate freely.

Why the Rights of Assembly and Petition Were Important to the Founders

Key Note Term

right of association and
right of petition—to
associate with anyone
you desire and to deliver
a petition

The rights of assembly and petition were part of English common law for hundreds of years and were seen by Americans as fundamental to a constitutional democracy. Historically these two rights have been associated with each other. People thought that the purpose of the right to assemble was to petition the government. The **right of petition** was recognized in the Magna Carta; in fact, the Magna Carta itself was a petition addressed to the king demanding that he correct certain wrongs. A resolution of the House of Commons in 1669, along with the English Bill of Rights of 1689, guaranteed English subjects the right to petition both the House of Commons and the monarch.

The American colonists considered the right to petition a basic right of Englishmen and used it often. Because they could not send representatives to Parliament, they saw the right of petition as an important means of communication with the British government. One of the colonists' frustrations in the years before the Revolution was the feeling that Parliament was ignoring their petitions.

During and after the Revolution, most states protected the rights of assembly and petition, either within their state constitutions or in their state bills of rights. Today, the rights of assembly and petition have been included in all but two of the fifty state constitutions.

Using the Rights of Assembly and Petition

From the beginning, Americans have felt free to ask the government for action on issues that were important to them. In the 1790s, one task that faced the First Congress was acting on thousands of petitions for pensions or for back pay promised to the widows and orphans of soldiers in the Revolutionary War. Often, as with the Revolutionary War widows, people were asking the government to keep its promises.

In the 1830s, Congress received numerous petitions urging that slavery be abolished in the District of Columbia. The feeling against abolitionists was so strong that in 1836 Congress passed a **gag rule** to prevent debate on all petitions related to slavery. This rule not only prevented any discussion of ending slavery, it limited the ways nonvoters could express their views. The use of the right to petition was an important way for women, African Americans, and others who were denied the right to vote to communicate with public officials. The gag rule was finally repealed in 1844, thanks to the leadership of former president John Quincy Adams, a member of Congress at that time.

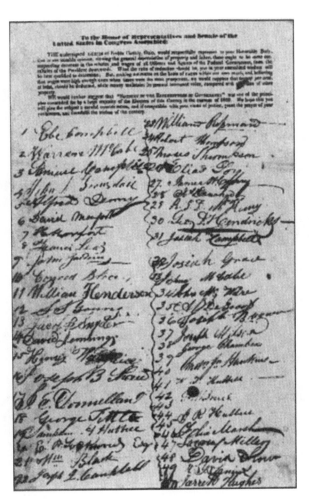

Figure 6.3.1: The right to petition has been used by Americans to influence their elected representatives.

Courtesy of the Library of Congress.

There are other instances when the United States government has tried to silence its critics. For example, during the Great Depression, a "Bonus Army" of World War I veterans converged on the nation's capital in the summer of 1932 to petition Congress for early payment of their military bonuses. Congress refused to support the bill and half the veterans returned home. Several thousand, however, remained in a camp outside the city. President Herbert Hoover ordered General Douglas MacArthur and the Army to drive the veterans out of the camp. General MacArthur did so with tanks, guns, and tear gas, killing two veterans and wounding several others.

The right to petition has been used by Americans to influence their elected representatives.

The importance of the right to assemble is nowhere better illustrated than in the civil rights movement of the 1950s and 1960s. Under the leadership of the Reverend Martin Luther King, Jr., thousands participated in the march for "Jobs and Freedom."

Today, the right to petition is widely used at the local, state, and federal levels. Groups that do not have the money to buy advertising often use the freedom to assemble and petition to make their views known by attracting the attention of the mass media.

The right to petition, however, includes much more than formal petitions. Faxes, email, phone calls, and letters to public officials are methods of petitioning the government. The right to petition is not limited to people wishing the government to

Why is the right to assemble fundamental to a democratic society?

correct wrongs. It is used by individuals, groups, and corporations to **lobby** government officials to try to persuade them to adopt policies that will benefit their interests or the interests of the country as a whole.

Placing Limitations on the Right of Assembly

The rights of free speech and assembly protect the rights of people to march and demonstrate. It is expected that these rights will result in activities where people express strongly held views on political, economic, and social issues. The government is responsible for making sure that demonstrations are "peaceable" and do not endanger community safety or unreasonably inconvenience the public.

Public property is owned by the people. It would appear, therefore, that people have a right to assemble on public property to speak and in other ways demonstrate their views on different issues. As with all other rights, in some situations it may be reasonable and fair to limit this right. Judges and other students of the Constitution have taken different positions on this question. Some argue that people should be able to assemble on any public property so long as it does not disrupt the normal use of that property. Others argue that the right to use public property should be limited to only those places, such as street corners and parks that are traditionally associated with free speech.

Key Note Term

lobby—communicating with political decision makers to try to influence them on a political matter

Developing Standards to Use in Limiting Freedom of Assembly

The following seven situations raise questions about when people should be able to assemble and demonstrate on public property.

1. Demonstrators are marching in front of a private home to protest the actions of the person who lives there.

2. People are assembling to march through a shopping mall.

3. People are marching through a public school while it is in session.

4. Pickets are blocking the entrance to a factory.

5. Pickets are blocking the entrance to an abortion clinic.

6. A group is demonstrating by sitting on the floors of the hallways of government buildings such as city hall, the university, and the courts.

7. A group is demonstrating during rush hour on a bridge over an expressway.

List the rights, values, and interests involved in each situation; then, develop one or more considerations that should be used in balancing these factors. For example, what considerations should be used in deciding when public safety should outweigh the right to demonstrate?

1. What arguments might be given in each situation by people supporting the right to assemble and to demonstrate?

2. What arguments might be given by those opposing the assembly and demonstration?

3. What competing values and interests are involved in each situation?

Supreme Court Limitations on Freedom of Assembly

In general, it has been assumed that the government has the power to impose time, place and manner restrictions on the right to assemble just as it does on the right of freedom of expression.

The courts have said that any regulation must

- **Be designed to protect a legitimate government interest and not be intended to suppress free speech or assembly**

- **It must be applied in a non-discriminatory manner. That is, it cannot put restrictions on assembly that only apply to certain groups or only because of theme or subject.**

The courts have ruled that the right of assembly extends to meetings held in **public forums** such as streets, parks, and sidewalks. Free access to public property has historically been especially important for people who cannot afford more costly ways to communicate, such as advertising in newspapers or on television.

Key Note Term

public forum—an open place for free speech

Protecting the Right of Association

Although the right of association is not mentioned in the Constitution, courts have said that it is implied by the other rights in the First Amendment; in particular, by the rights of free speech and assembly. The right to associate freely with one's fellow citizens is part of living in a free society.

The government should not interfere with your right to join with others, it is argued, whether it be in private clubs, college fraternities, political parties, professional organizations, or labor unions.

The first time the Supreme Court dealt with an issue regarding the freedom of association was in 1958. The state of Alabama had ordered the National Association for the Advancement of Colored People (NAACP) to disclose its membership lists. During this time, the NAACP was engaged in a bitter civil rights struggle. The Supreme Court thought that if the NAACP membership lists were made public, this might lead to hostile acts against its members. The Court ruled in NAACP v. Alabama (1958) that freedom of association is protected by the First Amendment and that Alabama's demand for the membership lists violated this right.

Soon after the Alabama ruling, however, the Court upheld laws that required disclosure of membership lists of the Communist party. In Barenblatt v. U.S. (1959) the Court justified their decision on the ground that the organization advocated the violent overthrow of the government.

One question that this raises is whether the right of association means you have the right not to associate with certain people. Should private organizations be able to prohibit some people from becoming members? For example, should the government be able to require private golf courses to admit African Americans or private men's clubs to admit women? This question involves the right of equal protection as well as that of association.

In cases involving this question, the Supreme Court has ruled that the government cannot interfere in a person's choices about whom to associate with in private life. On the other hand, the court has ruled that in some situations that go beyond close personal relationships and involve larger social purposes, the government may force private organizations not to discriminate on the basis of race, gender, or ethnic background.

These issues can be very difficult. The difficulties reflect the tension between two important ideals:

- **Eliminating unfair discrimination in American life**
- **The right of each individual to live his or her own life as free as possible from government interference**

One hundred fifty years ago, Alexis de Tocqueville (1805–1859) commented on the Americans' tendency to join together to solve common problems. The exercise of freedom of association was, Tocqueville thought, one of the outstanding characteristics of American citizenship. It is difficult to imagine the development of American labor unions and political parties, as well as a host of other organizations that play important roles in our civic life, without the exercise of this right.

Tocqueville believed that the freedom to associate was essential for preserving free government. Americans did not need to rely on the government to solve all their problems because private groups could organize themselves quickly to respond to common concerns or needs. Tocqueville thought that this helped to make Americans more public-spirited. Americans were aware that they were responsible for helping to achieve the common good, and that they could each do something to help achieve it.

Do people have a right to join in private associations which exclude others on the basis of gender, race, religion, or ethnicity?

Lesson 3 First Amendment and Freedom of Assembly

Taking and Defending a Position on a First Amendment Issue

Board of Education of the Westside Community Schools v. Mergens (1990) involves most of the First Amendment rights you have been studying—religion, speech, and association. Read the summary of the following case and then address the questions following the case summary.

In 1984, Congress passed the Equal Access Act, which prohibits any public secondary school that receives federal funds and provides facilities for extracurricular organizations from discriminating against student clubs because of their religious or philosophical orientation.

Westside High School is a public school in Omaha, Nebraska, with about 1,500 students. Students have the opportunity to participate in a number of groups and clubs, all of which meet after school on the school's premises. Among these groups are the Creative Writing Club, the Math Club, and the Future Medical Assistants. School board policy requires that each group have a faculty sponsor and none can be sponsored by any organization that denies membership based on race, color, creed, gender, or political belief.

In January, 1985, Bridget Mergens met with the Westside principal to request permission to form a Christian Club whose purpose would be "to permit students to read and discuss the Bible, to have fellowship, and to pray together." The club would be open to all students, regardless of religious beliefs. There would be no faculty sponsor.

Both the principal and the district superintendent denied the request. They said, first of all, the sponsor requirement was not met. More importantly, permitting the religious club to meet on school property would be unconstitutional. The school board upheld the denial.

Mergens and her parents sued the school for violating the Equal Access Act and the First Amendment protections of free speech, association, and free exercise of religion. The trial judge ruled in favor of the school saying that the Equal Access Act did not apply because all the other clubs at school were related to curriculum and linked to the school's educational function.

The U.S. Court of Appeals reversed the lower court ruling because it said there were other school clubs, such as the Chess Club and the Surfing Club, that were not directly related to the school's educational function. The school district appealed to the Supreme Court.

1. What First Amendment issues are raised in this case?

2. What values and interests are in conflict in this case?

3. What arguments can you make for allowing the group to meet?

4. What arguments can you make for prohibiting the group from meeting?

Conclusion

In this lesson, you learned that one of the rights the Constitution protects is the right to gather in public places. This is called the freedom of assembly. Individuals or groups can gather in public locations and discuss or protest any government policy, and may do so without fear of punishment.

The following lesson covers procedural due process. You will learn how due process protects individuals from possible abuses of power, the difference between procedural and substantive due process, and the history of due process.

Lesson Review

1. How would you explain the rights of assembly, petition, and association?

2. How would you describe the historical origins of the rights of assembly and petition?

3. How have the rights of assembly and petition been important in American history?

4. What restrictions have been imposed on the right of assembly, and how have these restrictions been justified?

Lesson 4

Procedural Due Process

Key Terms

adversary system
general warrants
inquisitorial system
procedural due process
reasonable doubt
substantive due process
writs of assistance

What You Will Learn to Do

- Evaluate the significance of Procedural Due Process

Linked Core Objectives

- Communicate using verbal, non-verbal, visual, and written techniques
- Apply critical thinking techniques

Skills and Knowledge You Will Gain Along the Way

- Describe the differences between procedural and substantive due process of law
- Explain the procedural due process rights included in the Constitution and the Bill of Rights
- Identify the differences between an adversary and an inquisitorial system
- Identify violations of due process
- Define key words contained in this lesson

Introduction

In this lesson you will further examine one of the key provisions of the Fourteenth Amendment raised in Chapter 5, Lesson 2—due process. You will discuss how it protects individuals from possible abuses of power, the difference between procedural and substantive due process, and the history of due process. Finally, you will examine some violations of due process in a contemporary situation.

When you finish this lesson, you should be able to explain why the Founders considered this right so important. You also should be able to explain the purpose and importance of procedural due process and to identify violations of due process in a specific situation.

Difference between Procedural and Substantive Due Process of Law

Substantive due process limits the degree to which government can interfere with a person's life, liberty, or property. **Procedural due process,** on the other hand, limits the procedures that may be used by government when interfering with life, liberty, or property. It requires the government to use fair procedures when investigating, trying, or punishing someone for a crime.

Procedural due process limits the powers of law enforcement agencies and courts. These limits protect both the innocent and the guilty against possible abuses of official power. Certain due process rights are protected in the body of the Constitution. For example, it guarantees the right to a writ of habeas corpus and trial by jury in criminal cases.

The Fourth through Eighth Amendments protect rights of people who are suspected of, charged with, or convicted of crimes. These Amendments also guide judges in conducting trials, appeals, and sentencing.

Key Note Terms

substantive due process—the fundamental constitutional legal theory upon which the Griswold/Roe/Casey privacy right is based; the doctrine of Substantive Due Process holds that the Due Process Clause not only requires "due process," that is, basic procedural rights, but that it also protects basic substantive rights

procedural due process—basic function is to provide "an opportunity to be heard . . . at a meaningful time and meaningful place," promoting fairness in dispute resolution

How does the right to a trial by jury provide a check on the power of the state?

Courtesy of Ron Chapple/Taxi/Getty Images.

The Historical Background of Procedural Due Process

In English law one of the first procedural due process rights to develop was that to a "speedy and public trial." The Magna Carta helped to establish this right in Article 40: "To no one will we sell, to none will we refuse or delay, right or justice." In the centuries that followed, trial by jury also became a right of procedural due process as the jury system spread throughout England with the expansion of royal courts and the common law. This right is guaranteed in our Bill of Rights by the Sixth Amendment.

Many other procedural rights valued by Americans were first asserted in England during the religious strife of the sixteenth and seventeenth centuries. In those days, following the "wrong" religion was usually a very serious crime-either treason or heresy, or both. The right against self-incrimination grew out of the practices of the infamous Court of High Commission and Court of the Star Chamber. People could be forced to appear before these courts, and required to take an oathcall on God to witness their truthfulness. Lying under oath meant not only committing the crime of perjury, but also committing a sin.

It was not uncommon for authorities to use torture to compel people to confess to crimes. Even after torture was banned, the government continued to punish people for refusing to answer questions at their trials. The practice of torture also led to the

In what ways did the Framers' knowledge of history and their experiences influence the writing of the Bill of Rights as it relates to due process?

Eighth Amendment provision that bans "cruel and unusual punishments." This provision, which was taken almost word for word from the English Bill of Rights, still did not prevent some punishments that we would not allow today.

The Fourth Amendment requirement that law enforcement officers obtain a warrant before searching someone's home stems from the common law principle that "a man's home is his castle." Common law prevented judges from giving law enforcement officials **general warrants.** A general warrant did not describe specifically the places to be searched, or the persons or things to be seized.

The American colonists experienced the injustice of both general warrants and **writs of assistance,** which were issued by British officials enforcing customs laws. The officials often used warrants and writs to harass and intimidate innocent people.

Importance of Procedural Rights in an Adversary Legal System

The legal system in England and the United States is known as an **adversary system.** This means that in most legal cases, civil or criminal, there are two opposing, or "adverse" parties, and each party does its best to prove its case before an impartial judge or jury.

An adversary system may be contrasted with an **inquisitorial system,** which is the system that prevails in France and other European countries. In these systems, the judge acts as a kind of combination judge and prosecutor. The accused is expected to answer the judge's questions truthfully and may not invoke a right against self-incrimination. The judge examines witnesses and evidence, and if the judge decides that there is enough proof of guilt, the case goes to a panel of presiding judges who review the evidence and make a final decision. There are no jury trials, fewer lawyers, and court proceedings are usually much shorter. In spite of the lack of procedural guarantees, it does not appear that there is a greater number of unfair convictions in countries that have an inquisitorial system.

The adversary system is characteristic of English law and the systems that developed from it. Because each side must do its best to prove its case, we consider it important that neither side has any unfair advantage. Over the years, due process rights have been expanded to try to equalize the power of the individual and the power of the government.

An important procedural right that does not appear in our Constitution is the requirement that in criminal cases the government must prove its case "beyond a **reasonable doubt.**" The government must prove that the defendant is guilty; the defendant is not required to prove his or her innocence.

The idea of "innocent until proven guilty" is the foundation of all other due process rights. Most of the time we do not think about what kind of legal system we have, or what alternative legal systems might be like. The adversary system is often defended because it seems to be more likely to get to the truth. If each side can develop its evidence, present its witnesses, and make its arguments, it gives the judge or jury a clear-cut decision to make. Critics, however, charge that an adversary system is wasteful and inefficient, and does more to increase the influence of lawyers than to uncover the truth.

Key Note Terms

general warrants—a precept issued by a magistrate authorizing an officer to make an arrest, a seizure, or a search, or do other acts incident to the administration of justice

writs of assistance—court orders that authorized customs officers to conduct general (nonspecific) searches of premises for contraband

adversary system—system of law, generally adopted in common law countries, that relies on the skill of the different advocates representing their party's positions and not on some neutral party, usually the judge, trying to ascertain the truth of the case

inquisitorial system—a legal system where the court or a part of the court is actively involved in determining the facts of the case

reasonable doubt—the level of certainty a juror must have to find a defendant guilty of a crime; a real doubt, based upon reasons and common sense after careful and impartial consideration of all the evidence, or lack of evidence, in a case

Whether or not the inquisitorial system produces results that are as fair as those in an adversary system, it is unlikely that there will be a movement away from the current system in the United States. The adversary system is consistent with Americans' long-standing suspicion of government power, and with our basic ideas of fairness.

How the Bill of Rights Guarantees Due Process

The important guarantees of due process appear in the Fourth through the Eighth Amendments. The Fourth and the Fifth Amendments protect rights that apply to people who are being investigated as criminal suspects, but have not necessarily been charged with a crime. Thus, they limit the government's power to search private homes and papers, conduct wire taps, seize evidence, and charge people with crimes.

The Fifth through Eighth Amendments protect rights of people who are on trial for crimes, those who want to appeal a sentence or verdict, or those who have received a sentence after conviction.

The Seventh Amendment also guarantees a right of trial by jury in civil cases. That means that in a federal lawsuit between two people, or between a person and a corporation, a jury trial can be requested.

The Importance of the Protection Provided by Procedural Due Process

The individual's right to procedural due process has been called the greatest protection in the Constitution from the abuse of power by government. The amendments guaranteeing procedural due process are the most important of all the amendments. These amendments were based on centuries of experience in which governments routinely violated due process rights.

Many people question why the Founders placed such importance on rights that are designed to protect individuals accused of breaking the law. Many Americans before and during the Revolution suffered from Great Britain's violation of their procedural rights , although these rights were a part of the British constitution. The colonists knew that just because a person was accused of a crime did not mean that the person was guilty.

The protection of procedural rights is just as important and difficult today as it was in colonial America. This is why an understanding of the principles of due process should be the responsibility of every citizen. Studies have shown that many Americans do not understand due process of law or do not even think it is important unless they have personally suffered a violation of their rights. As a result, the public often does not support due process rights, and public debate on issues of due process is often misinformed.

Why is it important for the courts to try to balance the rights of a person accused of a crime against the rights of the rest of the community?

Identifying Violations of Due Process

The following situation is an actual case. Fortunately, it is not typical of our criminal justice system. Yet for such a situation to occur, even infrequently, confirms that there is a constant need to ensure that all rights that constitute due process are respected.

In 1980 in a small town, a sixteen-year-old white girl disappeared while looking for a restroom at a high school. Two custodians later found her body hidden in the loft of the school auditorium. She had been raped and strangled. The community in which this crime occurred was one with a history of racial prejudice and conflict.

The custodians were Jones, a white man, and Smith, an African American. Both were questioned by the police and made to sign statements explaining where they had been and how they had found the body. They were taken to a hospital and were made to give samples of their saliva, blood, and hair. Then a police officer drove them back to the high school. As he dropped them off, he said, "One of you two is gonna hang for this." Then he turned to Smith and said, "Since you're the black, you're elected." One week later, Smith was arrested for raping and murdering the girl. He was tried and convicted by an all white jury from which qualified blacks had been excluded, and he was sentenced to death.

A writ of habeas corpus to the state supreme court was filed, and a hearing was held seven years later. The appeals court judge found that the arresting officer and district attorney suppressed evidence favorable to Smith. They had lied and created false testimony to have Smith charged and convicted.

At Smith's trial, the medical evidence that would have shown that Smith was innocent was "lost." The medical examiner "forgot" the results of the autopsy, "lost" his notes on his findings, and "lost" the samples he had taken from the victim's body.

A police officer threatened witnesses whose testimony supported Smith's innocence, then coached witnesses to lie in court. The officer also falsified the findings of the lie-detector test that supported Smith's innocence.

The sheriff defied the original trial court's order to release Smith on bail. The judge, rather than enforcing his order, changed it and denied bail. Smith's defense lawyer won two stays of execution, which saved his life while he waited for his case to be heard by the appeals court.

The judge who presided over the 1987 hearing stated in his findings that Smith "did not receive a fair trial, was denied the basic fundamental rights of due process of law, and did not commit the crime for which he now resides on death row." At the end of the hearing the judge stated, "In the thirty years this court has presided . . . no case has presented a more shocking scenario of the effects of racial prejudice, perjured testimony, [and] witness intimidation. . . . The continued incarceration of [Smith] under these circumstances is an affront to the basic notions of fairness and justice."

It took two more years for the state supreme court to uphold the order of the appeals court judge and to set Smith free. The court stated, "Due process of law is the cornerstone of a civilized system of justice. Our society wins not only when the guilty are convicted but when criminal trials are fair; our system of justice suffers when an accused is treated unfairly."

1. Why is procedural due process called the cornerstone of a civilized system of justice?

2. What limits, if any, would you put on the number of times a person could use the right to a writ of habeas corpus to appeal a case to a higher court? Explain your position.

3. Why is procedural due process as important and difficult today as in colonial times?

4. The statement by the British jurist Sir William Blackstone (1723–1780) is often quoted "Better that nine guilty men go free than one innocent man be convicted." Do you agree or disagree? Would you agree if the figures were "ninety-nine" and "one"?

How the Rule of Law Protects the Rights of Individuals

Due process includes the basic idea that government officials must obey the law. This idea is hundreds of years old. Today, no one who has the power to make laws, enforce them, or interpret them can be excused from obeying the law.

In our system, we believe it is fundamentally important that any decision about taking away someone's rights be made according to fair, established procedures. By insisting that procedures be followed carefully, we hope to reduce the risk that mistakes, prejudices, or the personal beliefs of government officials will lead to innocent people being accused or convicted of crimes. The government can best encourage the people to respect the law by obeying the law itself.

Many people believe that the Fourth, Fifth, Sixth, and Eighth Amendments are the very heart of the Bill of Rights and the whole theory behind rule of law. These amendments and the Supreme Court's extensions of them distinguish our society from many others. Even today Great Britain does not allow a citizen accused of a crime the full range of rights Americans enjoy.

Although we have not always lived up to the ideal of due process, as Frederick Douglass once said, "There is hope for a people when their laws are righteous, whether for the moment they conform to them or not."

Conclusion

In this lesson, you learned about procedural due process. You learned about the differences between an adversary system and an inquisitorial system of law. This lesson also showed you how due process protects the individual by requiring that government t officials obey the law.

In the following lesson, you will learn about protection against unreasonable law enforcement. You will learn that the government must respect the right that all persons are innocent until proven guilty.

Lesson Review

1. How would you explain the concept of "procedural due process"? Why is procedural due process important?

2. What are the historical origins of procedural due process? What guarantees of procedural due process are contained in the Bill of Rights?

3. What are the important differences between an "adversary system" of justice and an "inquisitorial system" of justice?

4. How is procedural due process related to the idea of "the rule of law"?

Lesson 5

Protection against Unreasonable Law Enforcement

Key Terms

exclusionary rule
immunity
Miranda Rights
misdemeanor
probable cause
right against self-incrimination
right to privacy
warrant

What You Will Learn to Do

- Interpret how the Fourth and Fifth Amendments protect citizens against unreasonable law enforcement

Linked Core Objectives

- Communicate using verbal, non-verbal, visual, and written techniques
- Apply critical thinking techniques

Skills and Knowledge You Will Gain Along the Way

- Explain the purpose and history of the Fourth Amendment
- Explain the issues raised in interpreting and applying Fourth Amendment protections against warrant less searches
- Identify the importance of the Fifth Amendment provisions for citizens
- Define the common limitations on the right against self-incrimination
- Define key words contained in this lesson

Introduction

Both the Fourth and Fifth Amendments put limits on the methods used by law enforcement officials investigating crimes. The idea behind both amendments is that the government must respect the principle that people are innocent until they are proven guilty.

The Fourth Amendment limits the powers of law enforcement officials to enter and search people's houses or to stop and search someone without reasonable cause. The Fifth Amendment contains several other important protections. This lesson focuses on protecting individuals from being forced to confess to a crime. You examine the history of these rights and their importance to the Framers of the Constitution.

When you finish this lesson, you should be able to explain the purpose and history of the Fourth Amendment, issues raised in its interpretation, and the importance of the Fifth Amendment provision against self-incrimination. Finally you should be able to take, defend, and evaluate positions on cases involving the right against self-incrimination.

The Purpose of the Fourth Amendment

Although the Fourth Amendment originally limited only the powers of the federal government, it has been applied to state and local governments by its incorporation into the Fourteenth Amendment. The intent of the amendment can be discovered fairly easily by reading it even though the authors used several legal terms, as well as phrases that are not defined ar d now require interpretation.

The right of the people to be secure in their persons, houses, papers, and effects, against unreasonable searches and seizures, shall not be violated, and no **warrants** shall be issue, but upon **probable cause,** supported by oath or affirmation, and particularly describing the place to be searched, and the persons or things to be seized.

The Fourth Amendment

Although the Fourth Amendment does not specifically state that it protects the **right to privacy,** it has been interpreted to protect this right, which is one of the most significant protections of human freedom and dignity found in the Bill of Rights.

The protection of privacy from invasion by government officials is highly valued for its own sake. It also is important to the right to freedom of conscience, thought, religion, expression, and property. Without the right to privacy, these other valued rights could be violated by government officials. Such a danger is particularly acute today with advanced surveillance technology and computers available to the government. If people were under constant or periodic observation by government, how free would they be to discuss differing opinions about our political system?

Key Note Terms

warrants—in law, written order by an official of a court directed to an officer

probable cause—reasonable grounds for belief that an accused person is guilty as charged or that a crime has been committed

right to privacy—to be secure in your own person and belongings

The importance to a free society of the protections against unreasonable searches and seizures was stressed by Justice Robert Jackson soon after he served as a judge at the Nuremberg trials of Nazi war criminals in 1949 when he said:

> *"Among the deprivations of rights, none is so effective in cowing a population, crushing the spirit of the individual and putting terror in every heart as uncontrolled search and seizure. It is one of the first and most effective weapons in the arsenal of every arbitrary government."*

The Fourth Amendment prohibits law enforcement officers from searching or seizing people or their property unless there is probable cause—a good reason for suspecting a person of breaking a law. Its authors, however, decided not to allow police officers themselves to decide what constitutes probable cause. The amendment requires police officers to present their reasons for a search or seizure to a judge or a magistrate. If the judge or magistrate agrees there is probable cause to suspect a violation of law, the law enforcement officer is given a warrant—a written document giving permission for a search or seizure, as shown in Figure 6.5.1.

The Fourth Amendment has, however, been interpreted to allow searches and arrests without a warrant under certain circumstances. The Fourth Amendment provides further protection for individuals by limiting the power of judges to issue warrants. Warrants must specifically describe "the place to be searched and the persons or things to be seized." A judge cannot give law enforcement officers a warrant that enables them to search anything they please.

In recent times the Fourth Amendment's protections have not been limited to physical intrusions by government on an individual's person or property. The Fourth

Figure 6.5.1: Search warrants protect every person's right to be secure.

Courtesy of the Center for Civic Education.

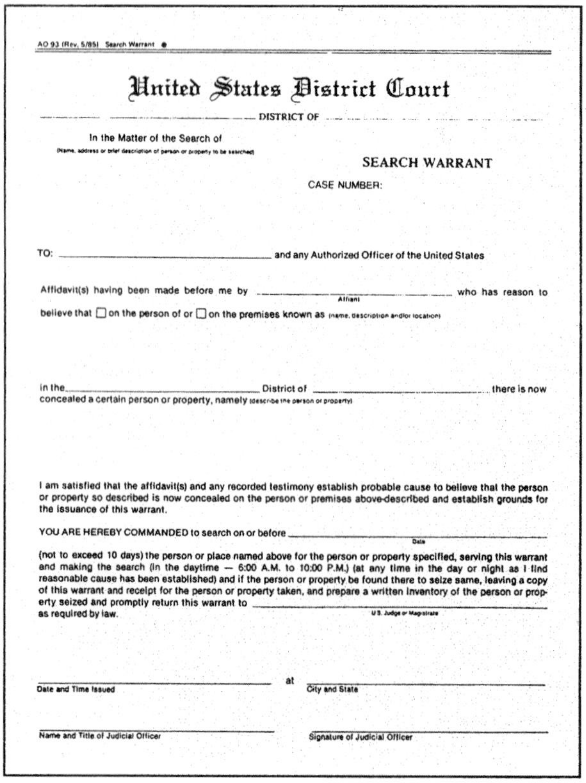

AO 93 (Rev. 5/85) Search Warrant

United States District Court

______ DISTRICT OF ______

In the Matter of the Search of
(Name, address or brief description of person or property to be searched)

SEARCH WARRANT

CASE NUMBER:

TO: ______ and any Authorized Officer of the United States

Affidavit(s) having been made before me by ______ (Affiant) who has reason to believe that ☐ on the person of or ☐ on the premises known as (name, description and/or location)

in the ______ District of ______ there is now concealed a certain person or property, namely (describe the person or property)

I am satisfied that the affidavit(s) and any recorded testimony establish probable cause to believe that the person or property so described is now concealed on the person or premises above-described and establish grounds for the issuance of this warrant.

YOU ARE HEREBY COMMANDED to search on or before ______ (Date)

(not to exceed 10 days) the person or place named above for the person or property specified, serving this warrant and making the search (in the daytime — 6:00 A.M. to 10:00 P.M.) (at any time in the day or night as I find reasonable cause has been established) and if the person or property be found there to seize same, leaving a copy of this warrant and receipt for the person or property taken, and prepare a written inventory of the person or property seized and promptly return this warrant to ______ (U.S. Judge or Magistrate) as required by law.

______ Date and Time Issued at ______ City and State

______ Name and Title of Judicial Officer ______ Signature of Judicial Officer

How is the right to privacy
different today from what
it was when the Framers
wrote the Constitution?

Amendment's language does refer only to "persons, houses, papers, and effects,"
and for many years the Supreme Court gave those words a literal interpretation.

Today, however, the Court gives the Amendment a broader interpretation and
extends the Amendment's coverage to wiretapping, "bugging," and other forms of
eavesdropping. The courts have stated in these cases that persons, not places, are to
be protected and, therefore, wiretapping can only occur after a warrant is issued.

History of the Fourth Amendment

We inherited from British history the saying that "a man's home is his castle." The
right to privacy and its importance to a free society have been understood for generations. English common law protected the right to privacy by prohibiting judges
from giving law enforcement officials general warrants that did not describe in detail
the places to be searched and the things or persons to be seized. General warrants
have been referred to as open-ended "hunting licenses" authorizing government
officials to search people, their businesses, homes, and property indiscriminately.

Despite the common law, royal commissions and Parliament had sometimes authorized the use of general warrants by government officials. At times these searches were
directed at violent criminals. Often they were used to harass and persecute individuals
who were critical of the government or who dissented from the Church of England.

As early as 1589, in a case involving a general search of Puritans and their property,
English lawyers argued that the Magna Carta protected the personal privacy of individuals. Nevertheless, in 1662, Parliament passed a law that permitted general warrants called writs of assistance. These writs gave government officials the power to
search for goods that had entered the country in violation of custom laws.

Officials did not need to convince a judge that they had reason to suspect an individual of committing a crime or that illegal goods were being hidden in a particular place. Without having to show good reason to suspect that a crime had been committed, unscrupulous government officials found it easy to use the writs of assistance to persecute individuals for their political and religious beliefs, or often, just to seek revenge against someone for personal reasons.

In the eighteenth century, Parliament again passed laws that authorized writs of assistance. These were used by British authorities in the American colonies to enforce the Trade Acts that taxed and limited the colonists' right to trade with other nations. Writs of assistance were generally used to collect taxes and to recover stolen goods, including enslaved Africans.

Colonial legislatures tried unsuccessfully to outlaw the writs by requiring warrants specifying who and what was to be searched and why. During the time just before the Revolution, the writs were used more and more frequently against colonists who were critical of British policy. They also were used against those believed to be violating the British restrictions on trade by smuggling tea and other products into Massachusetts and other colonies. The colonists' strong objections to the trade laws and writs of assistance contributed to the American Revolution.

The British were not entirely wrong in suspecting the colonists of smuggling. Some famous Americans violated the trade restrictions. For example, John Hancock's father had made a great deal of money smuggling tea into Boston. A writ of assistance enabled the British to discover that John Hancock himself was smuggling wine. As you can imagine, there was more than one reason why the Founders protested against such general warrants.

After the Revolution, many state declarations of rights outlawed unreasonable searches and seizures. Anti-Federalists later criticized the Constitution for not placing similar limitations on the federal government. A delegate to the Massachusetts ratifying convention said, "There is no provision made in the Constitution to prevent . . . the most innocent person . . . being taken by virtue of a general warrant . . . and dragged from his home." It was in response to such concerns that the Fourth Amend-

What is the importance of the right to be secure in one's home from unreasonable searches and seizures?

ment was included in the Bill of Rights. Today every state constitution contains a clause similar to the Fourth Amendment.

Controversies Raised in the Interpretation and Application of the Fourth Amendment

Three of the most important questions raised by the Fourth Amendment are:

- **When is a warrant not required?**
- **What is probable cause?**
- **How can the Fourth Amendment be enforced?**

We will look briefly at the first two questions. The last question requires a more careful examination, as it has been a constant source of controversy. The next two sections focus on that issue.

When Is a Warrant Not Required?

Whenever there is time to do so, law enforcement officers must convince a judge that they have probable cause to justify a search or arrest. If the judge accepts the officers' facts and reasoning, the judge will issue a warrant for an arrest, a search, or both.

There are times, however, when law enforcement officers cannot wait for a warrant. For example, police may be on the scene of a violent crime or a robbery in progress. If they do not arrest the suspect immediately, the person might injure a police officer or bystanders, or escape. Under these emergency circumstances, it is necessary for officers to be able to arrest a person or search property without a warrant. Later, however, the officers must convince a judge that they had probable cause and did not have time to obtain a warrant.

What Is Probable Cause?

What evidence must law enforcement officers have to justify a search or seizure of a person or property? Generally, at the moment a law enforcement officer decides to

What are some situations when police officers should be able to make an arrest without a warrant?

arrest a person, he or she must have reliable knowledge that the suspect either has already committed a crime or is doing so at the time of arrest.

The specific criteria for probable cause are constantly being refined by the Supreme Court in the light of experience. This process reveals a commitment to protecting the rights of individuals while at the same time protecting society from those who break the law.

Evaluating, Taking, and Defending a Position on Probable Cause

Consider the following situations which are based on actual incidents. Read the Fourth Amendment in reference to probable cause.

1. Tom Alvin was suspected of being an armed and dangerous drug dealer. The entrance to his apartment was by a very narrow staircase over which video cameras were installed. Police officers armed with a search warrant decided it was too dangerous to enter the apartment by normal means. Therefore, they placed ladders against the side of the building, climbed up to Alvin's apartment, smashed in the windows, entered, searched for, and seized cocaine.

2. A consumer organization is lobbying Congress to pass a law to prohibit the selling of a phone gadget which reveals the caller's phone number. They claim that using the product is an unlawful invasion of privacy.

3. Lucy Briggs was laid off her job as a flight attendant as the result of testing positive for drug use. The test was part of a new company policy requiring all airline employees to undergo surprise drug tests. Lucy claims that the mandatory urine test violates the "right of the people to be secure in their persons."

4. Acting quickly before a murder suspect could wash his hands, the police seized him and took skin scrapings from beneath his fingernails. They say the warrant-less search was legal because there was no time to get a warrant before the suspect destroyed the evidence.

5. A student completed certain forms to apply for a government college loan. The confidential, personal information was stored on a computer network. It was later accessed by a different government agency and used without the student's knowledge or permission as part of a survey on college-age Americans.

Means of Enforcing the Fourth Amendment

We must give law enforcement officers enough power to protect us from criminals. This means that we must trust them with the power, in certain situations, to limit some of our most valuable rights. Under certain circumstances, law enforcement officers have the power to:

- **Stop and question us**
- **Use force, if necessary, to restrain us**
- **Search our person, homes, cars, garbage cans, and other property**
- **Arrest us and place us in jail**
- **Question us while we are in jail**

These powers are easily open to abuse. The question is how to keep law enforcement officials from violating constitutional rights. The following are brief descriptions of several policies that are being used to check the abuse of power by police officers.

- *Departmental discipline.* Some law enforcement agencies have a board of officers responsible for investigating claims that an officer has violated a due process right. The board conducts a hearing and, if it finds the officer guilty, takes appropriate action to prevent that person from breaking the law again.

- *Civilian review boards.* Law enforcement agencies are sometimes supervised by a civilian review board appointed by local government. This board has the authority to investigate charges against officers accused of breaking the law or violating rules and procedures. It also has the responsibility to provide the officer a fair hearing. If the board reaches the conclusion that the officer is guilty, it recommends appropriate action to the law enforcement agency or suggests criminal prosecution.

- *Civil suits.* Civilians who think their rights have been violated by law enforcement officers sometimes have the right to sue individual officers and the agency for damages in a civil court or under the Civil Rights Act.

- *Exclusionary rule.* Any evidence gained by law enforcement officers as a result of breaking the law may not be used as evidence in court against the defendant. This evidence is said to be "excluded" by the judge at the trial.

Significance of the Exclusionary Rule

Perhaps the most controversial of these policies is the **exclusionary rule.** The rule is most often used to exclude evidence attained from illegal searches and seizures. It also is used to exclude evidence gathered in violation of the Fifth Amendment **right against self-incrimination** and the Sixth Amendment right to counsel.

The exclusionary rule was created by judges to discourage law enforcement officers from breaking the law. The courts have argued that it is the most effective way of preventing violations of individual rights.

The exclusionary rule has been used since 1914 to limit the powers of federal law enforcement agencies such as the F.B.I. It was not until 1961, however, that the Supreme Court applied the exclusionary rule to criminal prosecutions at the state and local levels in the case of Mapp v. Ohio. Since that time there has been continual controversy about its use.

Purpose of the Fifth Amendment Provision against Self-Incrimination

The right against self-incrimination is a protection of both the innocent and the guilty alike from the potential abuse of government power. The Fifth Amendment provides that, "No person . . . shall be compelled in any criminal case to be a witness against himself." Its primary purpose is to prohibit the government from threatening, mistreating, or even torturing people to gain evidence against them or their associates.

A confession is powerful evidence. If a prosecutor or police can obtain a confession from a suspect, it often eliminates the need for a costly or careful search for other evidence. The Framers were aware of the problems that could arise from the "third degree" and other forms of improper pressure.

Key Note Terms

exclusionary rule—a rule that forbids the introduction of illegally obtained evidence in a criminal trial

right against self-incrimination—granted by the Fifth Amendment, allows a person to refuse to answer questions or give other evidence that would subject him or her to criminal prosecution

Refusing to testify by "taking the Fifth" is one of the most familiar provisions of the Bill of Rights. It is controversial because many people see the refusal to testify as a right that only benefits those who are guilty. The right not to testify against oneself, however, is essential to uphold the principle that a person is presumed innocent until proven guilty beyond a reasonable doubt. This clause of the Fifth Amendment protects persons accused of crimes. It also protects witnesses from being forced to incriminate themselves.

Examining Issues of Self-Incrimination

This exercise provides you an opportunity to examine both a historical and a contemporary case involving the right against self-incrimination. Your entire class should compare the cases and discuss your views using the following questions as a guide:

- In what ways are the two cases similar or dissimilar?

- What values and interests are involved in each case?

- Under what conditions, if any, should the right against self-incrimination be applied and limited?

Commonwealth v. Dillon (1791). On the 18th of December, Dillon, a twelve-year-old Philadelphia apprentice, was arrested for arson, a crime punishable by death. He was accused of burning several stables containing hay and other goods. According to court records, the boy was visited by his minister, master, and other "respectable citizens." They urged him to confess for the good of his "mortal body and soul." He said he was not guilty.

The inspectors of the prison . . . "[then] carried him into the dungeon; they displayed it in all its gloom and horror; they said that he would be confined in it, dark and cold and hungry, unless he made full disclosure [confession]; but if he did . . . he would be well accommodated with room, fire, and victuals [food], and might expect pity and favour from the court."

Dillon continued to deny his guilt, even when kept in the dungeon without heat, food, or water. After about forty-eight hours, however, the boy confessed in front of the mayor, his master, and law enforcement officials.

When the case came to trial, Dillon's attorney argued that the charges should be dismissed. He said that the main evidence against Dillon was his confession, which was forced by keeping him in the dungeon, threatening him, and promising him he could expect pity and good treatment by the court. He claimed that such confessions were unreliable and illegal.

The state's attorney, however, argued that the confession was freely made in public. Therefore, it could be used as evidence at his trial. The attorney admitted that the interference of the inspectors at the prison was slightly irregular, but the way in which Dillon was encouraged to confess was not threatening. Therefore, his confession was not forced and should not be excluded at the trial. To do so would be to excuse the fact that he had committed a serious crime. The boy had confessed to a crime which had endangered lives and destroyed the property of others.

The state's attorney said that confessions freely given, as everyone knows, are the best evidence of guilt. The point to be considered was whether Dillon falsely accused himself of a crime. If there was any possibility that he had done so, he should not be executed. But since Dillon had never retracted his statement, he should be found guilty.

Fulminante v. Arizona (1991). The Arizona police lacked enough evidence to prove that Orestes Fulminante, a convicted child molester, had murdered his eleven-year-old stepdaughter. He was sent to prison on a weapons charge. The murder case, however, remained unsolved. In prison, Fulminante was threatened by several inmates who had heard rumors that he was a child killer. A fellow inmate, with a reputation for mob connections, offered to protect him. But first, the inmate insisted on knowing the details of the murder.

Fearing for his life, Fulminante admitted that he had driven the young girl to the desert. There he abused her, forced her to beg for her life, and then shot her twice in the head. What Fulminante didn't know was that his fellow inmate was an FBI informer. After being freed on the gun charge, Fulminante was arrested, tried, and convicted of murder. The main evidence against him was his confession to the inmate and a similar confession made to the informant's fiancée at a later date.

Fulminante's attorney appealed the conviction. He argued that the prison confession was forced. Its use to convict Fulminante was a violation of the Fifth Amendment right against self-incrimination. Since the confessions were the only real evidence against Fulminante, he deserved a new trial with a jury that would not hear about the confessions.

The state's attorney argued that even if the first confession was forced, the second was not forced. It was freely made. At most, introducing the confession as evidence should be considered a harmless error, made in good faith by officers and prosecutors in a brutal child sexual assault and murder case.

These two cases illustrate how issues involving the right against self-incrimination have been debated for centuries. In 1791, the judge ruled that because arson was a crime punishable by death, benefit of the doubt should be given to twelve-year-old Dillon. The arson charge was dropped and he was retried on a **misdemeanor** charge, a less serious crime. The judge said:

"Though it is the province [of the court] to administer justice, and not to bestow mercy; and though it is better not to err at all . . . in a doubtful case, error on the side of mercy if safer . . . than error on the side of rigid justice."

In 1991, the Supreme Court also sent back the Fulminante case for retrial. The majority of justices said that the confession in prison was made under a believable threat of physical violence. Thus it was the product of coercion and was the main evidence against Fulminante. Without the confession, the prosecution probably would not have had enough evidence to get a conviction. Therefore, Fulminante was entitled to a new trial.

Key Note Term

misdemeanor—a minor offense (crime) for which punishment may be a fine and/or imprisonment in a local rather than state institution (and generally for terms less than a year)

How Protections against Self-Incrimination Developed

There are a number of contemporary issues involving the right against self-incrimination. Originally, the right was limited to proceedings during a trial and did not limit the power of law enforcement officers to question persons they had arrested. This allowed the police to force people to confess or give evidence against themselves.

After hearing numerous cases in which the right against self-incrimination had been violated, the Supreme Court ruled, in Miranda v. Arizona (1966), that law enforcement officers must warn suspects that they may remain silent and that they have the right to have an attorney with them when being questioned. Suspects must also be told that anything they say can and will be used against them and that if they cannot afford an attorney, one will be appointed for them. This warning has become known as the "**Miranda Rights** warning." The Court has ruled, however, that the right to remain silent does not mean that officers cannot take a voluntary statement from the accused.

Key Note Term

Miranda Rights—a written or oral statement advising a suspect at the time of arrest of that person's rights against self-incrimination and to consult an attorney

What are common limitations on the right against self-incrimination?

Courtesy of the Center for Civic Education.

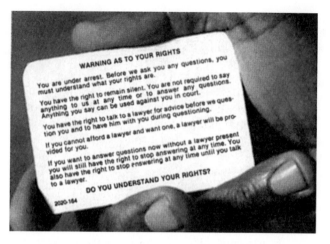

The exercise of the right against self-incrimination is, however, subject to some limitations. For example:

- **Personal right.** Because the right against self-incrimination is intended to protect individuals, it cannot be used to protect organizations such as businesses or trade unions. Nor may someone refuse to testify if the testimony would incriminate a friend or family member. Witnesses, as well as defendants, may refuse to answer questions if their answers might incriminate them personally.

- **Immunity.** Under certain circumstances, a person may be compelled to testify if the court offers immunity. For example, if the court states that nothing the person says can be used in a trial against him or her, the person must testify or be charged with contempt of court.

Key Note Term

immunity—a special exemption, as from laws, taxes, military service, and so on

Chapter 6

Lesson Review

Conclusion

In this lesson, you learned how the Fourth Amendment limits the powers of law enforcement officials to enter and search people's houses or to stop and search someone without reasonable cause. You also learned that the Fifth Amendment contains several other important protections. You learned the importance of protecting individuals from being forced to confess to a crime, and you examined the history of these rights and their importance to the Framers.

Lesson Review

1. How would you define the "right to privacy"? How does the Fourth Amendment protect this right?

2. How would you explain the term "probable cause"? Why does the Fourth Amendment require "probable cause" before a warrant can be issued?

3. Why does the Fourth Amendment generally require a warrant before a search can be conducted? Why does the Fourth Amendment require warrants to "particularly describ[e] the place to be searched, and the persons or things to be seized"? Under what circumstances is a warrant not required? Why?

4. How would you explain the right against self-incrimination? What purposes does this right serve?

Lesson 6

Protection of Rights within the Judicial System

Key Terms

acquitted
bail
capital punishment
cruel and unusual punishment
double jeopardy
felony
indicted
right to counsel

What You Will Learn to Do

- Compare positions on capital punishment to rights protected in the Fifth through Eighth Amendments

Linked Core Objectives

- Do your share as a good citizen in your school, community, country, and the world

- Apply critical thinking techniques

Skills and Knowledge You Will Gain Along the Way

- Identify how provisions in the Fifth Amendment protect your rights after arrest

- Explain how the Sixth Amendment is intended to provide fair hearing for accused criminals

- Look at issues and controversies over the right to counsel

- Examine historic and current positions pertaining to types of punishment

- Define key words contained in this lesson

Chapter 6

Introduction

In this lesson, you will examine how provisions of the Fifth through Eighth Amendments protect the rights of people accused of crimes and put on trial. You will review the importance and history of each right and learn about the right to counsel and its role in the American judicial system. Additionally, you will take a close look at the Supreme Court rules concerning the death penalty and issues involved in allowing capital punishment.

Provisions of the Fifth Amendment Protect an Individual's Rights after Arrest

After a person has been arrested for a crime, the next step is usually to charge the person formally in a judicial proceeding. In the federal system, anyone who is to be tried for a crime must be **indicted** by a grand jury. The military, however, is an exception to this rule. (The following lesson takes a look at military justice.) A grand jury, unlike a trial jury, does not decide whether someone is innocent or guilty, but instead decides whether there is enough evidence to go to trial. This is an important safeguard, because it ensures that the government cannot bring formal charges against people on the basis of weak evidence, or no evidence. A similar purpose lies behind the **double jeopardy** provision of the Fifth Amendment.

The government cannot wear someone out with repeated charges and trials. Usually, someone who is **acquitted** by a jury may not be tried for that crime again.

Limitations the Sixth Amendment Place on the Government

The Sixth Amendment contains a number of additional procedural rights that are part of due process of law. Almost all the protections of the Sixth Amendment have been incorporated into the Fourteenth Amendment, making them applicable to the states. The amendment's provisions are intended to provide a fair hearing in court for persons accused of crimes. Briefly examine each of these provisions before looking at their history and focusing on the **right to counsel.**

- **Speedy trial. The federal government cannot hold you in jail for a long period of time without bringing you to trial if you demand that the trial be held as soon as possible.**

- **Public trial. The government cannot try you in secret. Your trial must be open to the public and there must be a public record of the proceedings.**

- **Impartial jury. The government must try you before a jury. It cannot try you before a jury that is prejudiced. For example, if you were on trial for a drug-related crime and jurors admitted to having angry and violent reactions because they had been victims of similar crimes, the jury could not be impartial.**

- **Location of the trial.** The government must try you in the state, district or community where the crime was committed. You may, however, have the right to have the trial moved if you can show that the community is prejudiced.

- **Information on charges.** The government cannot arrest you and hold you for trial without telling you why it is doing so. Government lawyers also must present in open court enough evidence to justify holding you for trial.

- **Confronting witnesses.** You and your lawyer have the right to confront and cross-examine all witnesses against you. The government cannot present the testimony of secret witnesses who do not appear in court against you.

- **Favorable witnesses.** The government cannot prevent you from presenting witnesses who might testify for you. In fact, if such witnesses do not want to testify and you want them to, the court must force them to appear.

- **Assistance of counsel.** The government cannot prevent you from having a lawyer defend you from the time you are named as a suspect. If you are charged with a serious crime and cannot afford a lawyer, the government must provide one free of charge.

The Right to Counsel

The American criminal justice system is an adversary system as opposed to the inquisitorial system used in some other countries. In an adversary system there are two sides that present their positions before an impartial third party—a jury, a judge, or both. The prosecuting attorney presents the government's side; the defense attorney presents arguments for the accused person.

The complexity of our adversary system requires the use of lawyers to represent defendants. Even well-educated people as well as many lawyers who do not specialize in criminal law, are not competent to conduct an adequate defense in today's courts.

In the twentieth century, the Supreme Court and Congress have extended the right to counsel to people to whom it had not been provided in the past. This right is now interpreted to guarantee that:

- **Every person accused of a felony may have a lawyer**

- **Those too poor to afford to hire a lawyer will have one appointed by the court**

The right also has been extended by decisions in such cases as Miranda v. Arizona (1966) to apply not only to criminal trials, but to other critical stages in the criminal justice process, such as questioning of suspects by police.

Key Note Term

felony—a crime for which the punishment in federal law may be death or imprisonment for more than one year

Why is the right to counsel so important?

Courtesy of F.P.G. International, Ron Chapple.

Enforcing the Rights of the Sixth Amendment

Imagine you are tried in a criminal court, found guilty, and imprisoned. You believe that one or more of your Sixth Amendment rights have been violated by the government during your trial. For example, suppose you believe that the jury was prejudiced against you.

The right to appeal your case to a higher court is available to you if you can show that your constitutional rights have been violated. Each state has a system of appellate courts, and so does the federal government, with the Supreme Court being the highest court of appeals in the nation. If, after reviewing the trial record, an appellate court decides the trial has been unfair, it can overturn the lower court's verdict. If that happens, the prosecution can usually choose whether or not to retry the case.

Limitations the Eighth Amendment Place on the Government

Key Note Term

bail—money or property in the hands of the government to ensure that the accused will appear in court rather than forfeit it

The Eighth Amendment protects people accused of crimes and awaiting trial, and people found guilty of crimes. Its protections, incorporated by the Fourteenth Amendment, limit the powers of the judicial and legislative branches of federal and state government in the following ways:

- **Limitations on the judiciary. Judges usually have the power to decide whether a person arrested for a crime should be held in jail or set free on *bail* while awaiting trial. They also have the right to decide how much bail should be required. This amendment says that judges cannot require excessive bail.**

- **Limitations of the legislature.** Congress and state legislatures establish the range of punishments for breaking laws. This amendment says legislatures cannot pass laws that impose excessive fines or inflict **cruel and unusual punishments.** The power of judges and juries to decide punishments is limited by the laws passed by the legislatures that, in turn, are limited by the Eighth Amendment.

Key Note Term

cruel and unusual punishment—the power of judges and juries to decide punishments is limited by the laws passed

Examining Early Positions on Punishment

The French philosopher Montesquieu greatly influenced Americans' views on law and punishment. The following is a quotation from his writings followed by an excerpt from a letter by Thomas Jefferson. Read the selections and answer the questions that follow.

Experience shows that in countries remarkable for the leniency of their laws the spirit of the inhabitants is as much affected by slight penalties as in other countries by severer punishments. . . . Mankind must not be governed with too much severity . . . if we inquire into the cause of all human corruptions, we shall find that they proceed from the impunity [exemption from punishment] of criminals, and not from the moderation of punishments. . . . It is [also] an essential point, that there should be a certain proportion in punishments. . . . It is a great abuse amongst us to condemn to the same punishment a person that only robs on the highway and another who robs and murders.

Baron de Montesquieu, "Of the Power of Punishments," The Spirit of the Laws, 1748

The fantastical idea of virtue and the public good being sufficient security to the state against the commission of crimes, which you say you have heard insisted on by some, I assure you was never mine. It is only the sanguinary [bloodthirsty] hue of our penal laws which I meant to object to. Punishments I know are necessary, and I would provide them, strict and inflexible, but proportioned to the crime. . . . Let mercy be the character of the law-giver, but let the judge be a mere machine. The mercies of the law will be dispensed equally and impartially to every description of men.

Thomas Jefferson to Edmund Pendleton, August 26, 1776

1. What position does Montesquieu take on the effects of lenient and severe punishments?

2. What does Montesquieu say is a major cause of crime?

3. In what ways do Montesquieu and Jefferson appear to be in agreement?

4. What idea is expressed in Jefferson's statement that is not in Montesquieu's?

5. Do you agree or disagree with the positions stated by Montesquieu and Jefferson? Explain your position.

The Purposes of the Eighth Amendment Rights

The following sections take a look at the purposes of Eighth Amendment rights. These include the right to be free on bail pending trial, the right to be free from excessive fines, and the right to be free from cruel and unusual punishment.

The Right to Be Free on Bail Pending Trial

Although persons accused of crimes have the right to a speedy trial after they have been arrested, there are usually delays while both the prosecution and defense prepare for trial. Since a person is presumed innocent until proven guilty, one might argue that suspects should go free until the time of their trial. Not all suspects can be trusted to appear in court when they are supposed to. Some suspects may be dangerous, and it is reasonable to think that those accused of crimes for which there are severe penalties might not appear.

The government's main responsibility in this regard is to make sure suspects appear in court to be tried. This may be accomplished by one of two ways:

- **Keeping suspects in jail while awaiting trial**
- **Having them place bail—money or property—in the hands of the government to ensure that they will appear in court rather than forfeit it**

The right to bail allows suspects to be free while preparing their defense, which is often difficult to do from jail. It also avoids punishing suspects by holding them in jail before they are found guilty or innocent. This is particularly important for innocent persons who would otherwise suffer unfair punishment while awaiting trial. The sentencing of persons found guilty takes into account how much time they have spent in jail awaiting trial.

Problems arising from the implementation of the right to bail include the following:

- *Unfair treatment of the poor.* **Wealthy people can afford bail; the poor often cannot. Therefore, the poor are more likely to remain in jail awaiting trial, lose income, and not be able to do as much to prepare for their defense.**
- *Punishment of innocent poor.* **Poor people who are innocent and cannot afford bail are kept in jail and then released after their trial. This means that innocent people**

How does the right to bail help protect an accused person's due process right?

are punished by imprisonment and rarely compensated for the time they have lost or the wrongs done to them.

- *Increased chances of conviction and more severe sentences.* Studies have shown that being held in jail prior to a trial seems to have a negative influence on judges and juries. It results in a greater possibility of convicting such people of crimes and giving them more severe sentences.

One remedy for the inequitable aspects of the bail system is to release defendants without bail on their own recognizance, that is, on their promise to return to court for trial. This procedure is being used more and more when defendants have families or other ties to the community that would make it unlikely they would flee. It is used when a suspect's release would not seem to present a danger to the community.

The Right to Be Free from Excessive Fines

The purpose of this provision is to require courts to levy fines that are reasonable in relation to whatever crime has been committed. If a fine was extremely high in proportion to the seriousness of the crime, a person could claim the excessive fine violates his or her rights under the Eighth Amendment.

The Right to Be Free from Cruel and Unusual Punishment

This right is based on the belief that the law should treat even the most horrible criminal with dignity. Punishments should not violate society's standards of decency. The question raised by this right is to determine what is meant by the terms "cruel" and "unusual."

What the Framers meant by "cruel and unusual punishments" is not at all clear. Part of the problem is that what is considered cruel and unusual has changed over the years. The most difficult issues, however, have been raised by the issue of the death penalty.

What are the major arguments for and against the death penalty?

Courtesy of AP/Wide World Photos.

The History of Capital Punishment in the United States

Capital punishment has been used in the United States from colonial times to the present, and the Supreme Court has never held that it is prohibited by the Eighth Amendment. The Constitution appears to accept the legitimacy of the death penalty.

> ### Key Note Term
>
> **capital punishment—** the death penalty

Figure 6.6.1: Some exercise their right to protest by letting their feelings about the death penalty be known.

Courtesy of F. Carter Smith/ Corbis Sygma.

Both the Fifth and Fourteenth Amendments forbid the government to deprive someone of "life" without due process of law. These clauses seem to suggest that if due process is provided, people may be deprived of their lives by the government.

At one time, execution was the automatic penalty for murder or other serious crimes. By the early twentieth century, most states developed laws that allowed juries a choice between the death penalty and other forms of punishment. In most states, however, the juries were not given much guidance in making these decisions. This policy of allowing juries' unguided discretion was common until 1972.

Opposition to the Death Penalty

Executions of murderers and rapists were common in the United States until the 1960s when moral and political opposition developed because of a number of factors:

- **Information on how the death penalty was chosen revealed that juries often acted randomly and capriciously in deciding who should be executed and who should not**
- **Studies showed that the race of the defendant and the victim appeared to be the most important factors in whether a jury inflicted the death penalty**
- **Studies did not confirm the belief that capital punishment deterred crime**
- **Often, the cost of capital punishment, considering appeals, is more expensive than sentencing a person to life in prison without parole**

Many oppose the death penalty on moral and ethical issues, too. At most executions, members of society will protest this form of punishment (see Figure 6.6.1).

Issues Involved in Allowing Capital Punishment

Studies indicating unfairness in the imposition of the death penalty led to widespread debate and increasing opposition to its use. Courts and legislatures faced growing pressure to develop clear, reasonable, and fair standards to be used by juries in making their decisions.

Chapter 6   The Bill of Rights

Since 1972 the Supreme Court and legislatures have been attempting to develop such standards. This process resulted from a decision made by the Court in the case of Furman v. Georgia (1972). In that case, a five-to-four majority struck down a statute giving juries' unguided discretion in the imposition of the death penalty.

The Furman decision did not result in the prohibition of the death penalty. The majority argued that while the death penalty was constitutional, state laws permitting unguided discretion were unconstitutional. The result of this decision was that all executions in the United States were suspended. State legislatures were faced with the task of developing new laws with standards to avoid the arbitrary and discriminatory imposition of the death penalty, which was characteristic of the past.

Some states attempted to solve the problem by going back to the practice of automatic death penalties for certain serious crimes. Others developed new guided discretion laws. These laws called for juries or judges to decide whether to impose life or death sentences at a hearing held for this purpose after the trial in which a person was found guilty.

In 1976, the Supreme Court heard five cases on the new state laws. It upheld the new practice of guided discretion and declared that the automatic sentencing law was unconstitutional. Thus, the Court upheld the constitutionality of the death penalty once again. No clear standards were set to implement the policy of guided discretion, however. As a result, the courts have been flooded with appeals of death penalty sentences claiming that unfair standards have been used.

Recent studies have found that, despite the efforts of state legislatures and the courts to develop fair and reasonable standards, the system may still result in inconsistent and racially biased sentences.

Murderers of whites are far more likely to be sentenced to death than murderers of blacks. Such studies have given new impetus to the question of the constitutionality of the death penalty. It is important to note that whether or not the Supreme Court says the Constitution prohibits the death penalty is an altogether different issue from the question of whether or not society ought to execute individuals who have committed certain kinds of crimes. Even if the death penalty is constitutional, states are free to abolish it. It is quite possible to argue that while the Constitution does not prevent the government from imposing the death penalty, the government should not use it.

Procedural Justice and a Republican Form of Government

The Framers had personal experience with arbitrary government. They understood that rights would not be secure if the government had an unlimited ability to investigate people, accuse them of crimes, and hold them in jail or punish them in some other way. They also understood that republican or popular governments were capable of acting just as arbitrarily as monarchies. Thus the Framers addressed the Bill of Rights to all three branches of the federal government. The Framers set out a careful process by which the innocence or guilt of a person could be decided.

It is important to remember that procedural due process is designed to protect the innocent. In doing their job, they also can be used as "loopholes" by those who are guilty. Many have argued that this is a small price to pay for the protection we often take for granted. Above all, they argue, it is a reminder of our commitment to the idea that the actions of the government must be limited by the rule of law.

Conclusion

In this lesson, you examined how provisions of the Fifth through Eighth Amendments protect the rights of people accused of crimes and put on trial. After a brief examination of some provisions of the Fifth Amendment, you surveyed the Sixth Amendment and took a close look at the right to counsel. In addition, you looked at the Eighth Amendment, which protects people who are being held for trial, and protects persons convicted of crimes from receiving unjust treatment. Finally, you examined the continuing controversy about whether the death penalty should be prohibited under the Eighth Amendment.

In the following lesson, you will take a look at the military justice system. You will learn about the differences to as well as the similarities with non-military justice.

Lesson Review

1. **What are some of the procedural rights contained in the Sixth Amendment? How do these rights help guarantee a fair trial for people accused of crimes?**

2. **How would you explain the right to counsel? Why is this right important in an adversary system of justice?**

3. **What is "bail"? Why are people charged with crimes allowed to remain free on bail before trial?**

4. **How would you explain the Eighth Amendment right to be free from "cruel and unusual punishment"?**

Lesson 7

Military Justice System

Key Terms

admissible
admonition
Article 15
censure
coerced
general, special, and summary court-martials
UCMJ

What You Will Learn to Do

- Justify the differences between the military and civilian justice systems

Linked Core Abilities

- Communicate using verbal, non-verbal, visual, and written techniques
- Apply critical thinking techniques

Skills and Knowledge You Will Gain Along the Way

- Identify the four factors that determine whether a crime is service-connected
- Identify the rights of an accused person under the military justice system
- Explain the procedures for administering and imposing nonjudicial punishment under Article 15 of the UCMJ
- Differentiate between the three levels of court-martial as they pertain to court composition and the types of cases heard by each level
- Define key words contained in this lesson

Chapter 6

Introduction

Military personnel do not have the same basic national rights and freedoms as civilians. For the armed forces to function efficiently, military personnel must give up some of their personal liberties and conform to military standards. Although most of them do not have a problem with the strict discipline of military life, the issue of basic rights becomes extremely important in a military court of law, especially because many of the military justice procedures are different from those used in civilian (federal and state) courts.

The Uniform Code of Military Justice (UCMJ)

Key Note Term

UCMJ (Uniform Code of Military Justice)—the basis for all military law in the U.S. Armed Forces; established by Congress in 1951

The Uniform Code of Military Justice (**UCMJ**) is the basis of all military law in the United States Armed Forces. It describes all of the procedures that should be followed when a member of the armed forces is accused of committing a military offense. In addition, it protects the accused by listing their rights and ensuring that they receive a fair trial. The purpose of the UCMJ is to recognize the different needs of the military while still ensuring justice for all military personnel.

History of the UCMJ

Until 1951, the U.S. Army and Navy had their own court-martial systems. The Army Articles of War dated back to the Revolutionary War; they were borrowed from the British Articles of War with very few changes. Congress occasionally revised the Articles over the years, but the military justice system remained basically the same through World War II.

Under the Articles of War, the commander who initiated a court-martial had almost complete control over the outcome of the trial. The commander brought the charges, appointed officers to the court, and reviewed the proceedings, verdict, and sentence—all without approval from anyone with higher authority.

After World War II, there were many public objections to the military justice system. Congress responded to the complaints by carefully reviewing the Articles of War. The result of this effort was the UCMJ, which introduced several major reforms. These reforms brought military justice closer to civilian justice.

- **The UCMJ established a U.S. Court of Military Appeals composed of three civilian judges appointed for 15-year terms by the President (with the consent of the Senate)**

- **The UCMJ also provided for a law officer, similar to a judge, who would ensure a fair and orderly trial**

- **A third major reform provided by the UCMJ was that enlisted personnel could sit as members of the court if the accused was an enlisted person**

Since 1951, the Court of Military Appeals has undergone several changes. There are now five civilian judges who each serve for 15-year terms. A chief judge serves for five years and is succeeded by the next senior judge on the court. Additionally, in 1994, the name of the court was changed to the U.S. Court of Appeals for the Armed Forces.

Types of Military Offenses

Before 1969, all soldiers accused of crimes could be court-martialed simply because of their military status; however, the Supreme Court case of O'Callahan vs. Parker limited the use of courts-martial to "service-connected" offenses. Factors that determine whether an offense is service-connected include the relationship of the offense to military duties, the presence of a threat to military personnel, abuse of military status or the location of the crime on a military base. Except in a few cases, a soldier can only be court-martialed if the offense in some way affects the military or its personnel.

One exception is a drug-related offense. Because an immediate, serious threat to the military is inherent in drugs, a drug offense is service-connected even if it occurs off-base. Violations of federal or state laws are another exception to the "service-connected" rule. According to Article 134 of the UCMJ, a soldier who violates a federal or state law can be court-martialed and can be tried by a federal or state court for the same offense.

Rights of the Accused

Even though the military justice system functions differently from the civilian justice system, the accused still has similar rights:

- **The right to a speedy trial**
- **The right against self-incrimination**
- **The right to counsel**
- **The right of due process**

Speedy Trial

An accused soldier must be brought to trial within 120 days after receiving notice of the charge. If the soldier is confined, the period is 90 days. A trial must occur within these time limits, or the charges will be dismissed.

The government is accountable for the time required to process a case and must explain any delays. Some delays are acceptable, as long as the government can show special circumstances that caused the delay.

Self-Incrimination

The Fifth Amendment to the Constitution and Article 31 of the UCMJ protect soldiers against **coerced** statements. As in civilian arrests or questioning, the accused must receive a Miranda warning (see Figure 6.7.1). For any statement to be used in a court-martial, the statement must be voluntary. If the prosecutor cannot prove that a military person's admission to an offense was voluntary, the statement cannot be used. In addition, any evidence that comes from a coerced statement will not be considered valid.

Key Note Term

coerced—the act, process, or power of forcing someone to act or think in a given manner, such as by using force or threats as a form of control

Figure 6.7.1: Military personnel receive a Miranda warning, similar to civilians.

Courtesy of Kim Kulish/ Corbis Images.

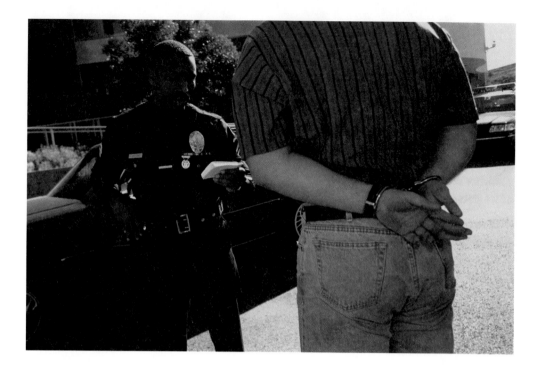

The Miranda Warning

In 1963, Ernesto Miranda was accused of kidnapping and raping an 18-year-old, mildly retarded woman. He was brought in for questioning, and confessed to the crime. He was not told that he did not have to speak or that he could have a lawyer present. At trial, Miranda's lawyer tried to get the confession thrown out, but the motion was denied. In 1966, the case came in front of the Supreme Court. The Court ruled that the statements made to the police could not be used as evidence, since Miranda had not been advised of his rights.

Since then, before any pertinent questioning of a suspect is done, the police have been required to recite the Miranda warning. The statement, reproduced below, exists in several forms, but all have the key elements: the right to remain silent and the right to an attorney. These are also often referred to as the "Miranda rights." When you have been read your rights, you are said to have been "Mirandized."

The Miranda warning reads a follows:

You have the right to remain silent. Anything you say can and will be used against you in a court of law. You have the right to be speak to an attorney, and to have an attorney present during any questioning. If you cannot afford a lawyer, one will be provided for you at government expense.

Counsel

Similar to civilians, military personnel have the right to consult a lawyer both before and during questioning (see Figure 6.7.2). The accused may have a civilian lawyer, a military lawyer, or both. A civilian lawyer is at the military person's expense, but a military lawyer is free.

Due Process

If the government obtains evidence by using unlawful methods, the evidence cannot be used. For example, obtaining evidence by pumping a suspect's stomach or taking a urine sample is a violation of due process; however, a suspect can be required to step in plaster molds of footprints, make a handwriting sample, or submit to fingerprinting.

Searches and Seizures

The Fourth Amendment of the Constitution protects all citizens, including soldiers, against unreasonable searches and seizures; however, a "reasonable" search in the military may not be considered "reasonable" in civilian life. Before most civilian searches can begin, a judge must issue a search warrant based on a probable cause to search.

In the military, a commander can authorize a search without obtaining a warrant as long as there is probable cause. Although the commander can authorize the search orally, a written authorization stating the reasons for the search is preferred. Whether the authorization is oral or written, the commander must specify the place to be searched and the items to be seized; then, the commander cannot conduct the search personally. He or she can be present at the time of the search, but someone else must actually conduct it (such as the Military Police).

Commanders have the right and duty to inspect their troops to make sure they are prepared to accomplish the unit's mission. Inspections are not the same as searches. During an inspection, the commander looks at the overall status of the unit and does not focus attention on any particular person. A search, on the other hand, singles out individuals and looks for particular evidence.

If a commander finds illegal drugs, weapons, or other incriminating evidence during a routine inspection, the evidence is **admissible** in a court-martial. However, commanders cannot conduct a search under the pretense of an inspection. Any evidence seized during an unlawful inspection cannot be used in a trial.

Nonjudicial Punishment—Article 15 of the UCMJ

All commanders may impose nonjudicial punishment under **Article 15** of the UCMJ on members within their command for offenses they consider minor; however, they also have the option of referring the matter to their immediate commander when a higher form of punishment may be more suitable for the offense committed. As one would expect, field grade officers have more punishment power than do company grade officers.

Because the decision to administer discipline under Article 15 is a personal responsibility of each commander, a commander's superior cannot specify when to use an Article 15 or what the punishment should be. However, a superior can withhold or limit a subordinate commander's authority to impose Article 15 punishment.

All commanders can impose any combination of up to four different types of punishment under Article 15. Again, this decision is a personal responsibility made by the commander based on the nature of the offense (after the commander has made a thorough investigation of the incident), prior record of the individual, recommendations made on the individual's behalf by other personnel, and so on.

- **Censure, admonition,** *or reprimand.* **These types of punishment are generally in the form of an oral or written warning; however, if the offense is repeated, a harsher punishment may occur.**

- *Loss of liberty.* **Military personnel can be punished by correctional custody, arrest in quarters, extra duty, or restriction.**

- *Forfeiture of pay.* **Military personnel can lose a portion of their basic pay, sea pay, or foreign duty pay for a specified period of time.**

- *Reduction in grade.* **This punishment is the most severe nonjudicial punishment. It affects the rate of pay and results in a loss of privileges and responsibilities.**

Service Member's Options

When nonjudicial punishment is being considered against a member of the Armed Forces, that individual has the right to:

- **Consult with a judge advocate or other legal expert after receipt of the charges from the commander**

- **Request an open hearing, which would be held in an informal and non-adversarial way**

- **Have a spokesperson present at the hearing**

- **Have witnesses testify on his or her behalf at the hearing**

- **Present evidence**

- **Demand a court-martial instead of accepting punishment under Article 15; if this happens, the Article 15 proceedings stop and the commander decides whether to bring court-martial charges against that person**

Military personnel who are punished under Article 15 have the right to appeal the punishment. The appeal first goes to the officer who imposed the punishment; then, if disapproved, to the next higher authority. Either officer may suspend or reduce the punishment.

Court-Martial Proceedings

Whenever possible, commanders use Article 15 punishment to avoid the time and expense of a court-martial; however, serious crimes require formal proceedings and the more severe punishment that accompanies a court-martial. There are three levels of courts-martial that handle cases ranging from relatively minor offenses to capital crimes. The levels, from lowest to highest are **summary, special,** and **general court-martial.**

Summary Court-Martial

The summary court-martial is designed to discipline enlisted personnel who commit relatively minor offenses. The court is composed of one commissioned officer who acts as a judge, jury, and counsel for both sides. In a summary court-martial, the accused is not entitled to a detailed military counsel (although the accused is entitled to consult with military counsel prior to the court-martial); however, this person may be represented by a civilian attorney at no expense to the government.

No accused may be tried by a summary court-martial if he or she objects; however, the case may then be referred to a higher court.

Because the summary court-martial handles only minor offenses, its punishments are similar to Article 15 punishment. The maximum punishments allowed for a summary court-martial for enlisted personnel in the pay grades of E-1 to E-4 are forfeiture of two-thirds of one month's pay; confinement for one month, hard labor without confinement for 45 days, or restriction for two months; and/or reduction to the lowest enlisted grade. Enlisted personnel in the grades of E-5 to E-9 may be reduced only one grade and may not be confined or placed in hard labor without confinement. Officers cannot be tried by a summary court-martial.

Special Court-Martial

A special court-martial may try any offense not punishable by death. The special court may consist of at least three members and a military judge or a military judge alone if the accused so requests and the judge grants the request. The accused has the right to be represented by a military lawyer or a civilian lawyer at no expense to the government. An accused enlisted member can also request that the court consist of one-third enlisted personnel.

A special court-martial can order a maximum punishment of confinement for six months, forfeiture of two-thirds of a month's pay for six months, and reduction to the lowest enlisted grade. If a punitive discharge is specifically authorized, a special court-martial can impose a bad-conduct discharge on enlisted members in addition to the other punishments. Although officers can be tried by a special court-martial, they cannot be confined or dismissed.

Key Note Terms

summary court-martial—the lowest level of trial courts in the military justice system, which provides for the disposition of minor offenses under a simple procedure when non-punitive measures and punishment are inappropriate or ineffective; it may try only enlisted personnel; its punishment is less severe for senior enlisted personnel; and it does not have the authority to impose a dishonorable discharge of any kind

special court-martial—the intermediate level of trial courts in the military justice system, which tries offenses not punishable by death; if convened by a general court-martial convening authority and a punitive discharge is specifically authorized, it has the authority to impose a bad-conduct discharge to enlisted members. It does not have the authority to dismiss or confine commissioned officers

general court-martial—the highest level of trial courts in the military justice system, which tries the most serious kinds of cases with authority to impose a dishonorable discharge or capital punishment

General Court-Martial

The highest level of trial courts in the military justice system is the general court-martial. General courts try military personnel for the most serious crimes, such as treason and murder. A general officer ordinarily convenes a general court-martial, and each case must have a formal pre-trial investigation.

A general court-martial usually consists of a military judge and at least five members. Except in a capital case, the accused may request that the court consist of a military judge alone. The rules regarding composition of the court and the accused's attorney rights are generally the same for a special court-martial. A general court-martial can impose a dishonorable discharge, dismissal, confinement for life or a lesser term, forfeiture of all pay and allowances, and in capital cases, death.

Court-Martial Appeals

Following a trial, the convening authority has the sole power and responsibility to approve that part of the findings and sentence that he/she finds correct in law and in fact. The convening authority may also approve or set aside, in whole or in part, the findings of guilty and the sentence, but may not change not guilty findings to guilty or increase the severity of the adjudged sentence.

All court-martials are reviewed by an attorney for legal sufficiency. Findings from a general court-martial or a special court-martial which imposed a bad-conduct discharge are sent to the Court of Military Review for a formal appeal after the convening authority has taken action. Some convictions may also be appealed to the U.S. Court of Appeals for the Armed Forces. This court's jurisdiction is worldwide, but it encompasses only questions of law arising from trials by court-martial where:

- **A death sentence is imposed**
- **A case is certified for review by the Judge Advocate General**
- **The accused, who faces a severe sentence, petitions and shows good cause for further review**

The Supreme Court has jurisdiction to review decisions of the U.S. Court of Appeals for the Armed Forces and of military appellate courts in which the U.S. has taken an appeal from rulings by military judges during trials by court-martial.

Case Studies: A Comparison

How does military justice compare to federal justice? Would a case involving a civilian accused of a crime be handled in the same way if a military person were accused of the same crime, or vise versa? The best way to answer these questions is to compare the two systems; therefore, the remainder of this lesson presents three case studies for you to examine. Be prepared to discuss your views about them or to write your views in your journal.

Article 15 for Insubordination

The duty roster read, "Private Breck—cleaning detail." When Cathy Breck reported to her platoon sergeant, SFC Lancaster, he told her, "Your assignment is to clean the extra rifles before the inspection."

"But I already cleaned my rifle," Private Breck protested. "I shouldn't have to clean the rifles that I didn't even fire."

"It is your turn on the duty roster," replied SFC Lancaster. "I don't want to hear any more complaints. Report to the arms room."

"Well, I didn't make those rifles dirty, so I'm not going to clean them," responded Breck.

"Private Breck, this unit can't function properly with this kind of insubordination. If you refuse to complete this assignment, I'll have no choice but to recommend you for an Article 15. This incident will go on your record."

Private Breck still refused to perform her duty and the company commander administered her an Article 15. She was restricted for 15 days, required to forfeit one-third of her pay for one month, and directed to clean all the rifles as well as the entire arms room. She appealed the punishment, but the company commander stuck with the original decision and the battalion commander did not grant her appeal.

United States vs. Garwood

PFC Robert R. Garwood, shown in Figure 6.7.3, did not return from the Vietnam War until 1979, 14 years after he had been taken a prisoner of war (POW) by the North Vietnamese. Major Thomas Hamilton conducted an investigation of this incident while Garwood was assigned to Camp Lejeune, NC. Hamilton discovered that Garwood had accepted a position in the North Vietnamese Army, acted as a guard for other American prisoners, worked as a questioner for the Vietnamese Communists, struck an American without reason, and encouraged Americans to throw down their weapons and refuse to fight. In February of 1980, Hamilton recommended that Garwood be court-martialed on the charges of:

- **Soliciting an act of misbehavior before the enemy (authorized a maximum punishment of ten years confinement at hard labor)**
- **Unauthorized absence without leave (this charge was combined with Charge #3)**
- **Desertion in time of war (authorized the maximum punishment: the death penalty, confinement at hard labor for life, total forfeiture of pay and allowances, reduction to the lowest enlisted grade, and/or dishonorable discharge)**
- **Collaborating with the enemy (authorized the same punishment as Charge #3)**
- **Maltreatment of prisoners of war (authorized the maximum punishment, but not the death penalty)**

Although Major Hamilton recommended that the death penalty not be precluded as a punishment and that while the alleged offenses were serious in nature, it was his opinion this case be referred as a non-capital offense—unless the ordering officer

considered the death penalty to be appropriate punishment if adjudged. Major Hamilton further recommended that if the case was referred as non-capital, then the maximum punishment would be limited to confinement to hard labor for life, forfeiture of all pay and allowances, reduction to the lowest enlisted grade, and/or dishonorable discharge.

After a thorough review, Brigadier General David Barker ordered a general court-martial for Garwood as a non-capital case.

In the only prosecuted case of this kind arising from the Vietnam War, Garwood was found guilty on February 5, 1981 of collaborating with the enemy while a POW in Vietnam in 1967. Because Garwood had presumably been a captive of the North Vietnamese from 1965 to 1979, the court did not sentence him to prison. Instead, he was reduced in rank and given a dishonorable discharge.

Schenck vs. United States

Charles R. Schenck was a civilian who opposed the United States' involvement in World War I. In 1917, he mailed pamphlets to thousands of young men, urging them to refuse the draft. According to the Espionage Act of 1917, it was illegal to interfere with the war effort. A U.S. District Court convicted Schenck for his actions.

Schenck's lawyers appealed his case to the Supreme Court, stating that the Espionage Act violated Schenck's First Amendment right to freedom of speech. The Court unanimously decided that what a person has the right to say during peace-time is different from what a person can say when the nation is at war. According to this Court, Schenck's words presented a "clear and present danger" to the U.S., and his acts were not protected by the Constitution.

Conclusion

Before and during World War II, the Army and Navy had separate disciplinary codes, but the creation of the Air Force after that war led to the enactment of a criminal law system that would be uniformly applied by all the services. Since Congress enacted the Uniform Code of Military Justice (UCMJ) in 1951, it has become the basis for the criminal law system for the military. Over the years since its creation, the UCMJ has evolved to the extent that it now balances the need to maintain discipline in the armed forces while giving military members who are accused of crimes rights that closely parallel those of accused persons in the civilian sector.

This lesson concludes the chapter, "The Bill of Rights." In the next chapter, "Citizen Roles in American Democracy," you will learn about the roles that you have as a citizen of the United States as well as new citizenship and Constitutional issues.

Lesson Review

1. **What is the UCMJ? Explain its purpose.**
2. **In a military justice system, what are the rights of the accused?**
3. **Explain the three types of court martial proceedings.**
4. **What is Article 15? What does it provide?**

Citizen Roles in American Democracy

Lesson 1

Roles of Citizens

Key Terms

civility
civil rights
common good
commonwealth
empowerment
melting pot
nation of nations

naturalized citizen
orthodoxy
political action
political rights
resident alien
social action
spirit of association

What You Will Learn to Do

- Determine your role as a citizen of a constitutional democracy

Linked Core Abilities

- Communicate using verbal, non-verbal, visual, and written techniques
- Do your share as a good citizen in your school, community, country, and the world

Skills and Knowledge You Will Gain Along the Way

- Explain the relationship between self-interest and the common good
- Describe the differences between citizens and resident aliens
- Explain how citizenship in a constitutional democracy differs from citizenship in a totalitarian state
- Explain how citizens can exercise their rights and responsibilities in a constitutional democracy
- Define key words contained in this lesson

Introduction

In this lesson you will examine the American citizenship and its relationship to the natural rights philosophy, republicanism, and constitutional democracy. You will examine the characteristics of effective citizenship, explore the rights and responsibilities of citizenship, and determine the qualities citizens need to develop to become effective citizens in our society.

Citizenship

From its beginnings, America was strongly influenced by the ideals of classical republicanism. The early American colonies of the seventeenth century were political communities in which civic virtue could be exercised. Many of these colonies were called **commonwealths,** a word that meant something like a republic, that is, self-governing communities of equals whose members were expected to help serve the good of all. In the Mayflower Compact, the Pilgrims declared their intent to "covenant and combine themselves together into a civil body politic."

The American Founders admired the civic virtue of the ancients and the classical models of republican government. They also were influenced by the natural rights philosophy of John Locke (see Figure 7.1.1). The natural rights philosophy conflicted in several important ways with the ideals of classical republicanism. Instead of the **common good,** it stressed the importance of individual rights and self interest.

Society and government, according to Locke, were established to protect the rights of the individual. Human communities did not exist for their own sake, but rather to protect the individuals belonging to them, each of whom is free to pursue his or her own interest so long as it does not interfere with the interests of others.

Figure 7.1.1: John Locke.

Courtesy of Bettmann/Corbis Images.

The Founders were influenced by both these theories of government. They had to compromise in adapting this intellectual inheritance to the conditions in America. They established a limited government of checks and balances that allowed civic virtue to flourish, but also could prevent abuses of self-interest when it did not.

The Founders realized that the classical republicanism of the ancient city states could not be easily adapted to a country as large and diverse as America. They also recognized that republican self government required a greater measure of civic virtue than did other forms of government. Civic virtue, therefore, was essential. But how was civic virtue to be promoted in this new experiment in republican self-government?

In general, the Founders looked to two solutions: religion and education. The Founders themselves had different religious beliefs. Many were wary of the dangers that religious **orthodoxy** posed to individual freedom. At the same time, however, they acknowledged the value of organized religion in promoting virtue. Virtuous behavior, which enabled people to control their passions, would produce upright, responsible citizens.

The second solution that the Founders recognized was the importance of education to good citizenship. For the American experiment in republican self-government to succeed, each of its citizens had to be schooled in the ideals and principles upon which that experiment was based.

Formal schooling, together with a free press, became a priority in the early years of the new republic. Public or "common schools" developed rapidly to prepare Americans not only as workers in a growing economy, but also as citizens committed to the principles of self-government. As nineteenth-century American educator Horace Mann observed, "schoolhouses are the republican line of fortifications."

Tocqueville and Good Citizenship

Alexis de Tocqueville was a young French aristocrat who visited the United States in the 1830s, at a time when the spirit of Jacksonian democracy was helping to bring about greater equality and more widespread participation in the nation's political life. He was curious about and impressed by America's experiment in democracy and how well it worked. After finishing his tour of the United States, he recorded his impressions in a very influential book, *Democracy in America.*

Tocqueville found much to admire and criticize as he traveled the country. Though impressed by the equality of opportunity in the American democracy, he wondered how a society so devoted to materialism and the pursuit of individual self-interest could produce the civic spirit needed for self government. He believed the answer was to be found in the qualities he admired in American democracy: traditions of local self-government and habits of free association.

The New England townships were tiny models of classical republicanism, where the habits of citizenship were developed. Tocqueville observed that a citizen of one of these American towns takes part in every affair of the place; he practices the act of government in the small sphere within his reach . . . and collects clear practical notions on the nature of his duties and the extent of his rights.

This tradition of local self-government also encouraged voluntary association. Nothing so impressed de Tocqueville about America as the fondness American citizens had for banding together to address problems of common interest. While Europeans would prefer to let government address all public problems, Americans preferred to do it themselves, as citizens. This **spirit of association** remains a distinctive characteristic of American society today.

Town meeting in Laguna Niguel, California

How does the tradition of local self-government embody Tocqueville's concept of "spirit of association"?

Courtesy of F.P.G. International, Spencer Grant.

Such traditions of local self-government and habits of free association, Tocqueville concluded, provided a way for teaching citizenship in the American democracy. He wrote, "The most powerful and perhaps the only means that we still possess of interesting men in the welfare of their country is to make them participate in the government. At the present time civic zeal seems to be inseparable from the exercise of **political rights.**"

Similar to the Founders, Tocqueville realized that the civic virtue of the ancients was not practical in the United States. Democratic citizenship, he believed, would have to depend upon something else. He did not believe there had to be a contradiction between self-interest and civic-mindedness. In a land of equality and widespread participation in political life, each citizen could see a connection between self-interest and the common good. American citizens are willing to devote themselves to public ends, Tocqueville believed, because they realize that the fulfillment of their private ambitions depends in large part on the success of the democratic society. Good citizenship for Tocqueville, therefore, was nothing other than enlightened self-interest.

Points to Ponder

1. Some people claim that the best way to achieve the common good is for each person to work for his or her self-interest. Do you agree? Why or why not?

2. The common good is a principle originally practiced in relatively small and homogeneous societies. Do you think there is a common good in a nation as large and diverse as the United States? Why or why not?

3. What should voters do if their representative votes for a bill that is good for the entire country but damages their particular interest?

Defining Who Is a Citizen

In our country, anyone who is born in the United States, or is born to citizens of the United States, is a citizen. The term used for non-citizens who legally reside in the United States is **resident aliens.** By satisfying certain requirements, resident aliens may become **naturalized citizens.** Both resident aliens and citizens who live in the United States must obey the laws of the United States. They also receive the protection of those laws. Resident aliens are guaranteed most of the rights possessed by citizens. If they are tried in a court of law, for example, they are guaranteed the same rights to due process that are provided for citizens in the Constitution.

There are two important rights, however, that citizens have and aliens do not: the rights to vote and to hold public office. Possessing these rights, many people have argued, is what distinguishes the citizen from the non-citizen. Some people also argue that in possessing these important rights, citizens also have special responsibilities toward their country that non-citizens do not.

Evaluating, Taking, and Defending a Position on Extending the Right to Vote for School Board Members to Resident Aliens

Your class should be divided into four groups—two for the issue and two against. Each group should choose a spokesperson to present the group's views to the class. Groups on the same side of the issue should compare ideas and not make duplicate points. After the four presentations are made the class should vote on whether to pass the proposed legislation.

In some communities in our nation, there is growing interest in extending to resident aliens the right to vote in local school board elections. Proponents of such a law argue that resident aliens pay state and local taxes to support public education and that all taxpayers should have a representative voice influencing policies that directly affect them or their children. In addition, resident aliens have met all the criteria for being in this country legally. Opponents argue that because resident aliens are not citizens, they lack a long-term interest in the welfare of the community, and granting them voting rights in school board elections blurs the distinction between rights of citizens and non-citizens. It is the first step, they argue, in the demise of meaningful citizenship.

1. Do you think that resident aliens who must pay taxes and obey the government's laws should have a voice in local government by being permitted to vote? Why or why not?

2. Do you think that resident aliens should have the right to serve as elected members of local government?

3. What political obligations or responsibilities should resident aliens or non-citizens have? Explain your position.

American Citizenship and Our Diverse Society

From its beginnings, America has been what the poet Walt Whitman called a **"nation of nations,"** populated by millions of immigrants of different races, religions, languages, and ethnic backgrounds.

One of the greatest challenges to the American experiment in republican government has been to form a common bond out of such diversity. That common bond is provided by the ideal of American citizenship and a commitment to the Constitution and its ideals and principles. Though they could not foresee how diverse the immigration to this country would become, many of the Founders recognized that the new country would continue to take in people of different origins. For them, becoming American was primarily a matter of allegiance to the political ideals of the new land. In the early nineteenth century, Congress established five years as the minimum time required for immigrants to learn these ideals and to become naturalized citizens.

As George Washington told the members of the Touro Synagogue of Newport, Rhode Island, in 1790,

> *Happily, the government of the United States that gives to bigotry no sanction, to persecution no assistance, requires only that they who live under its protection should demean themselves as good citizens in giving it their effectual support.*

For Washington and other Founders, good citizenship meant responsible conduct and acceptance of the nation's political principles.

For much of our nation's history, becoming an American meant something more. It represented a fresh start, a new beginning, leaving the injustices and prejudices of the old world behind.

"What then is this American, this new man?" asked Crevecoeur, the eighteenth-century French immigrant to America. Americans, Crevecoeur believed, had left the values and lifestyles of their different origins behind to become "a new race of men." Perhaps the most famous metaphor for this ideal of Americanization was expressed by Israel Zangwell in his 1908 play, *The Melting Pot,* "America is God's crucible, the great **melting pot** where all the races of men are melting and reforming."

Has America been a melting pot? Not entirely. Throughout our history the assimilation of different people into a new American identity has been only partially successful in achieving the classical republican ideal of a common culture. Many immigrants to the new land were reluctant to give up the heritages they brought with them. They were proud of both their "Americaness" and the cultural inheritance they carried to the New World.

As a nation of immigrants we have come to appreciate the benefits of the great mixture

How can you apply the phrase "to give to bigotry no sanction" to your daily life?

Courtesy of MPI/Stringer/ Hulton Archive/Getty Images.

Key Note Term

melting pot—a term used to describe a society made up of diverse cultures or races which have merged or "melted" into each other

How can America be a "nation of nations" and still have a common civic culture?

Courtesy of AP/Wide World Photos.

of heritages transplanted to America. They have enriched American life in many ways. The diversity of the nation's cultural inheritance also has placed a heavy responsibility on our ideal of citizenship. The unity of American society depends very largely on the ability of that ideal—the civic culture all Americans, whatever their particular origins, share in common—to hold us together as a nation.

Throughout our history there has been tension between the diversity of backgrounds and the common ideal of citizenship. The need to balance unity with diversity remains a challenging goal for your generation.

Evaluating the Relationship between the Ideals of Classical Republicanism and Contemporary American Citizenship

Some observers of American society today are worried about the future health of America's experiment in self-government. They believe we have inherited too much of the self-interest of the natural rights philosophy and not enough of the public spirit of classical republicanism. These critics see contemporary America as a fragmented society, in which individuals are preoccupied with the pursuit of economic self-interest. Some feel that government is disconnected from people's lives. Americans see fewer opportunities to exercise their responsibilities as citizens than they did in the past.

Some critics believe a return to the principles of classical republicanism is the solution to this problem. The nation's schools, they say, should improve civics education, and our democratic institutions must create new ways to involve citizens in public affairs. Work in small groups to develop positions on the following questions. Be prepared to present and defend your positions before the class.

1. Do you think the observations in the exercise about contemporary American society are accurate? Explain your position.

2. Do you think the classical republican sense of community is possible in American society today? What forces work against it? What resources might encourage its development?

3. What ways can you think of to involve citizens in public affairs? What reforms would you propose to the political process? To the Constitution? To our education system?

How Citizens in a Constitutional Democracy Differ from Those in a Dictatorship or Totalitarian State

Citizenship has meant different things at different times in history and in different places. Totalitarian states and dictatorships also refer to those they govern as citizens—though they may lack the rights and responsibilities associated with American citizenship. Your role as a citizen of a constitutional democracy differs in fundamental respects from the role of a citizen living under unlimited or arbitrary government. While passive obedience and unquestioning loyalty are demanded by unlimited regimes, the citizen of a constitutional democracy is expected to be a critical and participating member of the political community. Citizens of constitutional democracies should have a reasoned loyalty and obedience to law not based on unquestioning deference to authority.

Criticism of one's government may carry with it a right, and perhaps even a duty, to disobey laws you believe are unjust laws. The **civil rights** movement provides a contemporary example.

Key Note Term

civil rights—these rights protect us in our private lives from the arbitrary and unfair actions of government

Is it possible to generate reasoned loyalty and obedience in a system that demands unquestioned deference to authority? Why?

More Points to Ponder

1. Is civil disobedience ever a justified form of political participation? Give two examples to support your position.

2. Under what circumstances do you think a citizen in a representative democracy has a right to violate a law? Explain your position.

3. What would be a proper response of the government to someone, who for reasons of conscience breaks a law?

4. Do you agree with Thomas Jefferson that "a little rebellion" now and then is healthy for the political system? If so, what form might a little rebellion take?

Rights and Responsibilities of Citizens

As you consider the rights of citizenship, it is important to distinguish between civil rights and political rights.

- **Civil rights protect us in our private lives from the arbitrary and unfair actions of government**
- **Political rights allow us to participate in our own governance**

Because non-citizens living in this country are granted the same civil rights that citizens enjoy, political rights are to a large extent what define our status as citizens. You must be a citizen to exercise the rights to vote or serve in government.

Many of our rights suggest a corresponding obligation. In exercising our rights as individuals, we must respect other citizens' use of those same rights. Some obligations are legal, imposed by laws commonly agreed upon. For example, we have an obligation to obey the law, including those laws that require us to pay taxes, serve on juries, and meet the other responsibilities that help government operate.

Most of us would agree that we also have certain moral obligations as citizens. For example, some argue we have a duty, as well as a right, to vote. Even though the law no longer requires American citizens to perform military service, many Americans believe it is a duty to defend one's country or to assist it in other emergencies.

What Do You Think?

1. How does Voltaire's statement "I may detest what you say, but will defend to the death your right to say it," relate to the responsibilities of citizenship?

2. Why is it important to speak up for the rights of others even if your own rights are not endangered?

Does U.S. citizenship carry with it an obligation to perform national service? Explain.

Courtesy of AP/Wide World Photos.

Being Effective Citizens

The natural rights philosophy and classical republicanism provide different answers to this question. The natural rights philosophy emphasizes the elective nature of citizenship. Each citizen has a choice whether to remain a citizen of the United States. Each citizen possesses certain natural rights and it is the primary purpose of government to protect these rights. In choosing a government to protect these rights, citizens follow their self-interest in making sure that government does its job.

We pay attention to how well the people we choose to govern us are doing their jobs. We participate as citizens, therefore, to ensure that government complies with its contractual obligations to us as individuals.

The classical republican philosophy, on the other hand, emphasizes our obligation to the society into which we were born or naturalized. Classical republicanism emphasizes the common good and the obligation of each citizen to serve the good of the whole community. Citizenship requires that we put this general good before our own self-interest, especially when the two conflict.

In practice, of course, the American civic tradition includes both concepts of citizenship. One of the enduring challenges you face as a citizen is sorting out for yourself the conflict between them in many different situations.

Reconciling the Common Good and Individual Self-Interest

Your class will be divided into small groups to discuss the issue of conflict between the good of the whole society and individual self-interest. Discuss and take a position on the questions at the end of the exercise. Be prepared to share your opinions with the class.

The conflict between the common good and self-interest is not the only problem you face as citizens. Sometimes it is difficult to determine what the common good or your own self-interest actually is. In some situations the common good may be quite clear as, for example, the need to protect the community from criminals, foreign enemies, and air pollution. In other situations, however, citizens strongly disagree about what the common good is and what policies are needed to serve it. For example, some would argue that laws strictly limiting human activity in environmentally sensitive areas are necessary to preserve the future well-being of our natural resources. Others claim that such restrictive policies can endanger the economy and may violate property rights.

It is not always easy to know how our individual interests are served. What may appear to be self interest in the short-run might not be in our best long-term interest. Some aspects of this problem are raised in the following questions.

1. Is the common good the greatest happiness of the greatest number? If so, what does that phrase mean? Should the measurement of the greatest number be a minimum of 51 percent or should the percentage be higher? What would be the danger in determining the common good according to this principle?

2. Is the common good the goals that all people in the nation share? If so, how do we find out what those goals are?

3. If you find that you and your fellow citizens cannot agree on what the common good is, should you just pursue your own interests and forget about what is good for all? What alternatives might there be?

However defined, the effective use of rights and responsibilities in a constitutional democracy requires certain beliefs, commitments, and skills.

Civic Values

These express our most fundamental beliefs about the purpose of government within a society and the goals that we expect a government to achieve. They are ideals expressed or implied in some of the nation's founding documents, including the Declaration of Independence and the Preamble to the Constitution. They include such ideals as the dignity of the individual, equality, and justice. Though we as citizens might disagree about the meaning and relative importance of each specific value, we share a broad agreement about their significance in defining the ultimate ends of the society we have established.

Civic Principles

These can be defined as those principles of government that best enable society to realize its civic values. Included among these essential principles would be the rule of law, popular sovereignty, and freedom of expression. Such principles define our commitment to constitutional government and democracy.

Civic Skills

These describe the abilities we need as individuals to help realize civic values and make civic principles work. To be effective citizens we must have knowledge of our government's history and how it operates. We also must develop our intellectual abilities: analytical skills for the solving of problems, and communication skills to express our opinions and understand the opinions of others.

Civic Dispositions

Effective citizenship is not possible if we do not adopt those dispositions or qualities of behavior that sustain a civic culture in a free society. Such a culture depends on tolerance, fairness, a respect for the opinions of others, and a commitment to truth. The word **civility** suggests the decency and integrity that are essential to a constitutional democracy.

> **Key Note Term**
>
> **civility**—suggests the decency and integrity that are essential to a constitutional democracy

Town meeting in Charlotte, Vermont

How does participation in public affairs "empower" citizens?

Courtesy of AP/Wide World Photos.

Understanding Empowerment

By developing an informed commitment to the values, principles, and dispositions of our civic culture and by acquiring the knowledge and skills necessary to play a role in it, we become "empowered" as citizens. **Empowerment** is a word we sometimes use today to describe the ability to "make one's voice heard" in public affairs. With empowerment, each of us knows that we have the potential to be effective as citizens when the need and opportunity arise.

You have more empowerment than you may realize. In 1991, at the time our country was celebrating the 200th anniversary of the Bill of Rights, a group of high school students in North Carolina discovered that their state had never ratified the Twenty-fourth Amendment, which abolished the poll tax and other taxes that had been used to discriminate against African Americans.

As a project, the students investigated the legal requirements for ratification. They then petitioned the North Carolina state legislature to formally ratify the amendment. The students visited the state capitol and lobbied their legislators. After the legislature complied, the students carried the official notice of ratification to Washington, D.C., where they presented it to the Archivist of the United States. Through this school project, the students demonstrated their empowerment as citizens.

Becoming Effective Citizens

Citizenship in a free society is not always easy. Freedom requires us to live as self-reliant individuals, to think for ourselves, to solve our own problems, to cope with uncertainty and change, and to assist and respect others.

Citizens are made, not born. Similar to the ancient Greeks and Romans, the Founders placed great importance on the role of education in preparing each generation for citizenship. Your education will help provide you with the knowledge and skills to function effectively as citizens of a constitutional democracy. Practical experience has been as important as formal schooling in preparing Americans for citizenship. Americans learn the skills of citizenship through the many opportunities to participate in public affairs.

We begin the process of learning to be citizens in early childhood. At home and in the classroom, we begin to think for ourselves, to express our own opinions, and to respect the opinions of others.

Through such activities as student government, school projects, sports, and community and club activities, we begin to acquire the skills of teamwork, organization, and debate. In short, many of the qualities that we need for citizenship begin to develop early in our lives.

Exercising Rights and Responsibilities as Citizens

In dealing with the problems of our communities and the nation, we have different possibilities. We may engage in **social action** or we may engage in **political action.** We may, of course, choose to engage in both. For example, in dealing with the

Key Note Terms

social action—organize other members of the community

political action—an organized attempt to influence the political process, from lobbying legislators to seeking the election (or defeat) or particular candidates

Does citizenship obligate a person to participate in social and political actions? Why?

Courtesy of AP/Wide World Photos, F.P.G. International, Paul Conklin.

problems of crime in the community, we might join a neighborhood watch. Alternatively, we might organize other members of the community to present the problem to the city council in an effort to get more police officers on the streets. The first is an example of social action, the second an example of political action. These two courses of action are not mutually exclusive. We might decide to engage in both at the same time.

One of the issues we must decide as citizens is how a particular problem is most effectively solved. The decision we make depends on our analysis of the problem, our estimate of the possible solutions, and our own values. Making these decisions lies at the heart of the practice of responsible citizenship.

Examining the Responsibilities of Citizenship and Deciding on How They Can Be Fulfilled

In contemporary urban and rural America, violence by and against young people is receiving increased social and political attention, as well as daily coverage on television and in newspapers. Statistically, the incidence of youth violence has not increased during the last decade, the deadliness of it has. More young people carry guns or other weapons and use them as a means of settling disputes or intimidating others.

Conclusion

In previous units you were asked to focus on the history and nature of our legacy as a constitutional democracy. In this lesson you examined what this legacy means for us as individual citizens. You should be able to explain how Americans have viewed citizenship and its rights and responsibilities. You also should be able to distinguish between a citizen and a resident alien. Finally, you should be able to explain the special importance the idea of citizenship has in America as a land of immigrants from many nations.

You also examined the characteristics of citizenship in a constitutional democracy. Citizens sometimes disagree about what their role should be. It is your right in a free society to decide how you want to exercise the rights and responsibilities of citizenship. What you have learned in this text and elsewhere about your heritage of constitutional democracy will help you in making this decision. How you conduct yourself as a citizen also will depend on your own interests and abilities.

In the next lesson, you will learn about new citizenship and constitutional issues. This lesson will explore three trends that may impact citizenship in the future: the increasing diversity of American society, the impact of modern technology, and America's growing interdependence with the rest of the world.

Lesson Review

1. What responsibilities, if any, do you as a citizen have to promote sound political and social policies designed to decrease or prevent the problem of violence?

2. What social actions can you, as a citizen of your school and community, become involved in to help prevent the problem?

3. What values and interests do you think are important for you as a citizen to promote in connection with prevention of violence by and against young people?

4. How did the Founders expect to promote civic virtue in a country as large and diverse as the United States?

Lesson 2

New Citizenship and Constitutional Issues

Key Terms

E Pluribus Unum
global village
judicial restraint
plebiscite
teledemocracy

What You Will Learn to Do

- Predict how increased diversity, technological changes, closer international relationships, and current constitutional issues are likely to affect your life as an American citizen over the next 10 years

Linked Core Objectives

- Communicate using verbal, non-verbal, visual, and written techniques
- Do your share as a good citizen in your school, community, country, and the world

Skills and Knowledge You Will Gain Along the Way

- Describe developments taking place in the world that have the potential to have an impact on the future of American citizenship
- Explain the impact of increased diversity in society on the political system
- Describe the potential impact of increasingly sophisticated technology on representative democracy
- Explain how changes in the complexity of American society create new constitutional issues
- Describe constitutional issues currently being raised in American society
- Describe unenumerated rights and the controversies raised by the Ninth Amendment
- Define key words contained in this lesson

Introduction

In this learning plan you explore three trends that may impact citizenship in the future: the increasing diversity of American society; the impact of modern technology; and America's growing interdependence with the rest of the world. In addition, you examine some constitutional issues facing the United States. Finally, you predict how these issues and trends might affect your life as an American citizen over the next 10 years.

World Developments Affecting the Future of American Citizenship

Three developments promise to shape the future of American citizenship in important ways. These developments are:

- **The increasing diversity of American society**
- **The impact of modern technology, especially the computer and electronic telecommunications**
- **America's growing interdependence with the rest of the world**

You know how Americans have adapted the idea of citizenship to a nation of immigrants, people from many lands and cultures, bound together by a commitment to a common set of political values. The American ideal of **E Pluribus Unum** has usually been able to balance the benefits of a diverse society with the unifying influence of a common civic culture. One of the major challenges you face as an American citizen is to sustain that balance in a society that is becoming far more diverse and complex.

America in the founding era was a nation of 3.5 million inhabitants—3 million free whites and half a million enslaved Africans. Most of the white population was northern European in ancestry. The young republic also was overwhelmingly Protestant. Today America is a microcosm of the world. It has become one of the most ethnically diverse countries on earth. You may see evidence of this diversity in your school (see Figure 7.2.1). More than 100 languages are spoken by students in the Los Angeles

Key Note Term

E Pluribus Unum—
Latin, meaning "out of many, one"

What strengths can immigrants bring to a society? What problems can arise as a result of large-scale immigration?

Courtesy of AP/Wide World Photos.

Figure 7.2.1: The United States' open-door policy on immigration has enabled America to become a microcosm of the world.

Courtesy of Jose Luis Pelaez, Inc./Corbis Images.

school district alone. The results of recent immigration to this country have been dramatic. Of the 14 million immigrants since 1965, 85 percent have come from non-European countries. During the 1980s, immigrants to the United States came from 164 different lands. By the turn of the century, one in every four Americans will be Hispanic, African American, or Asian. By the year 2030, one-half of the country's population will belong to one minority group or another. In a sense, there will no longer be a traditional majority group. In 1995 only 15 percent of Americans identify themselves as descendants of British immigrants, who once comprised a large majority of the population. The faces of "We the People" have changed considerably in the course of 200 years and will continue to change during your lifetime.

How Diversity Changes U.S. Society

Americans today disagree about how diversity changes our society. To some the diversity brought about by recent immigration is no different from what has happened throughout American history. The mix of people has strengthened American society and reaffirmed our commitment to ideals that are the property of all humanity, not a particular ethnic group. As with their predecessors, most recent immigrants have adapted to American society, enriching the nation's economic life, culture, and educational institutions.

Others worry that there are limits to how much diversity the country can absorb without losing the common bonds that unite us. They fear that in an increasingly diverse society, self-interests may prevail over the common good. A challenge for your generation as for all previous generations is balancing the unum with the pluribus in America.

How Citizenship Is Changed by Technology

Modern technology has expanded the possibilities for participatory citizenship. Audio and video teleconferencing has become a familiar way for citizens to discuss issues of common concern. So has talk radio. Some state legislatures have begun to use such telecommunications on a regular basis as a way of staying in touch with their constituents. Advocacy groups of all kinds use the internet, databases, and electronic mail to inform and organize their members.

Some futurists—theorists who consider possibilities for the future based on current information and trends—see revolutionary implications in this technology. They envision the possibility of a **teledemocracy** in the years ahead. This term means a new version of direct democracy, where citizens can participate to a much greater extent in the affairs of government with less reliance on their elected representatives.

National **plebiscites** also have become a practical option. By use of online computerized voting, each citizen could register his or her views on particular issues, with the results instantly tabulated. "Going to the polls," as seen in Figure 7.2.2, could become an outmoded custom. Citizens could exercise their political rights from a computer work station at home or in public facilities like libraries or the post office.

The Framers believed that classical republicanism in its purest form was impractical in a country as large and diverse as the American republic. Some people believe that teledemocracy overcomes many of these

Key Note Terms

teledemocracy—the futurist view of a direct democracy using telecommunications to provide greater opportunities for participation in government

plebiscite—an expression of the people's will by direct vote

Does modern technology help or hinder American citizenship?

Courtesy of H. Armstrong Roberts.

Figure 7.2.2: In the near future, American voters might not have to leave their homes or offices to cast their votes.

Courtesy of Rick Wilking/ Reuters/Corbis Images.

impracticalities. The computer makes possible an electronic city-state in which citizens scattered across the country can join together to participate more effectively in public affairs.

Whatever its potential implications, the computer is forcing us to reexamine the most basic principles and institutions in our constitutional democracy.

Role Playing James Madison in the Third Century of Government under the Constitution

Imagine, for a moment, that you are James Madison, brought back to life in the year 2000. What would be your assessment of teledemocracy and the electronic city-state? To help develop your position, answer the following questions.

1. What are the dangers of direct democracy? Why did the Framers of the Constitution distrust it? Why did they prefer representative democracy instead?

2. To what extent is "public opinion" synonymous with the "will of the people"?

3. What should be the role of political leadership in a democracy? To what extent should leaders influence and to what extent should they be influenced by popular opinion? Can government in a democracy be too much in touch with the sentiments of the people?

4. In what ways is computer technology a threat to individual liberty as well as a tool on its behalf?

5. What expectations does teledemocracy place on citizens? To what extent are those expectations realistic?

6. The advancements of technology show us what we have the capability of doing, not what we necessarily have to do or should do. What other considerations about citizenship and civic culture might argue against the creation of teledemocracy?

In what ways does the internationalization of business affect tradition and culture?

Courtesy of Shepard Sherbell/Corbis SABA.

How Internationalism Affects American Citizenship

One important consequence of the communications revolution has been America's increased interaction and interdependence with the rest of the world. Issues of national importance in the United States have an impact beyond our borders. Conversely, events and developments elsewhere in the world are becoming more significant in the lives of American citizens.

The achievements of modern technology are turning the world into a **global village,** with shared cultural, economic, and environmental concerns. National corporations have become international. Economic decisions made in Tokyo or London affect the things Americans buy and the jobs they seek. Environmental concerns also transcend national boundaries. Entertainment—music, sports, and film—command worldwide markets. The culture that we live in is becoming cosmopolitan, that is, belonging to the whole world.

The movement of people, as well as information, has helped bring about global interdependence. Improved transportation has been a key factor in increased immigration to the United States. People go where there is economic opportunity and they can go more easily and much farther than in the past. The movement of people across national borders will continue to increase. Such migrations help to reduce cultural and other differences that have historically divided nations. They also create new problems for governments which have the responsibility for providing for the well-being of citizens and other residents.

Citizenship in modern history has been defined largely in terms of nation-states. The idea of being a citizen, however, developed in many different political contexts throughout history, from tiny city-states to large empires. In the American experience, citizenship has changed in its patterns of allegiance and loyalty. Before the

> ### Key Note Term
>
> **global village**—term used to define achievements of modern technology that indicate shared worldwide cultural, economic, and environmental concerns

Civil War, many Americans would have defined their citizenship in terms of loyalty to their respective states rather than to the United States.

Although national citizenship is likely to remain fundamentally important in the future, the issues confronting American citizens are increasingly international. Issues of economic competition, the environment, and the movement of peoples around the world require an awareness of political associations that are larger in scope than the nation-state.

What Do You Think?

1. In The Federalist essays Madison argued that two conditions would help to prevent a tyranny of the majority in America. One was the diversity of interests in the new nation. The other was geographic distance making it difficult for these different interests to combine. As you evaluate the significant changes now taking place in American society, do you think the threat of such a democratic tyranny has increased or decreased? What trends may have increased the danger? What trends decreased it?

2. In his observations about American democracy, Tocqueville warned of the danger of individual isolation in a society where everyone was equal. Democracy, he said, "throws [each individual] back forever upon himself alone and threatens in the end to confine him entirely within the solitude of his own heart." Has computer technology made such individual isolation more or less likely today? Explain your answer.

3. What advantages might be offered by world citizenship? What disadvantages? Do you think that world citizenship will be possible in your lifetime?

Why the Constitution Has Been Changed Infrequently

Some critics believe the system of government created by the Framers for the world of the eighteenth century has proven itself unsuited for the more complex, faster-paced world of the twenty-first century. Others, however, respond by noting that any system that has managed to adapt itself to the changes of 200 years deserves the benefit of the doubt. Tampering with the Constitution, they say, should always err on the side of caution.

Americans have never been reluctant to tinker with the Constitution. More than 10,000 constitutional amendments have been introduced; but only 33 have been approved by Congress and submitted to the states for ratification; and only 27 of these have been adopted. Changing the Constitution has proven to be difficult, which is what the Framers intended when they outlined the requirements for amendment in Article V. After all, it took two centuries for the Twenty-seventh Amendment to the Constitution to be adopted.

The Framers wanted the Constitution to remain the nation's fundamental law, not to be confused, as a result of frequent changes, with ordinary laws and regulations. Because it has proven difficult to amend, the Constitution remains one of the oldest and shortest written constitutions, with a total of 7,591 words.

Constitutional Rights Issues Raised by Changes in American Society

Progress and change have created new issues for the Constitution. Their complexity challenges the nation's historic commitment to resolve its problems through constitutional means. Among the issues likely to be important in the years ahead are:

- **Group rights**
- **Right to life and death**
- **Right to privacy**
- **Rights of the individual and providing for the common good**
- **Rights of citizens and rights of resident aliens**

Group Rights

America's increasingly pluralistic society and the nation's ongoing commitment to equality have forced Americans to recognize the differences that exist between groups. How far should constitutional guarantees go, for example, in providing for favored treatment of historically excluded groups? In a multilingual society to what extent should the government be obliged to provide ballots, income tax returns, and other government forms in languages other than English?

Right to Life and Death

The accomplishments of modern science in sustaining life before full-term pregnancy and into old age have made our society reexamine both the legal and ethical meaning of life itself. To some, high tech life support systems have created a distinction between life and existence. When does life begin? When does it end? Does an individual have a right to take his or her own life? Does an individual have the right to assist someone else's suicide?

Right to Privacy

Electronic communications pose new potential threats to individual privacy. Federal, state, and local governments now keep vast computer databases on individual citizens. In the computer age, to what extent do the constitutional protections of personal "papers and effects" under the Fourth Amendment extend beyond one's home into these government files? Who has access to these records and for what purposes?

Moreover, Fourth Amendment protections do not apply to the actions of the private sector of our society. Corporations, hospitals, and other private agencies also keep computer records. Both private and public institutions can invade the privacy of individuals through "electronic snooping"—using video cameras, audio "bugs", and microwave technology to spy on individuals. The constitutional limitations on such activity have yet to be developed.

Rights of the Individual and Providing for the Common Good

The enduring tension between these two conflicting values in our constitutional democracy is being tested once again by environmental and other issues in modern society. How will our constitutional arrangements balance the rights of the individual to property and pursuit of happiness with the responsibility to provide for the general good of the larger society by guaranteeing such things as clean air and the preservation of natural habitats? Controversies surrounding the protection of old-growth forests, preservation of the spotted owl, and the effects of cigarette smoking exemplify this tension.

Right of Citizens and Rights of Resident Aliens

The increasing movement of peoples across national borders is likely to raise new constitutional issues regarding the meaning of citizenship and the status of aliens in the United States. Aliens enjoy many of the civil rights that the Constitution accords to "persons" as distinguished from citizens. These include most provisions of the Bill of Rights and freedom from arbitrary discrimination. Aliens are subject to the laws of the United States and must pay taxes. If immigration continues in future years new issues are likely to arise regarding the rights of both citizens and aliens under our Constitution.

Unenumerated Rights

The perplexing constitutional issues of modern life have not only prompted reinterpretations of well established rights, they also have given new importance to a largely unexplored frontier of our Constitution—unenumerated rights. Unenumer-

How can government agencies best mediate the conflict between legitimate individual rights and the common good?

Photos courtesy of AP/Wide World Photos, F.P.G. International, Kenneth Garrett.

ated rights are rights possessed by every American that are not listed or enumerated in the Constitution. They are unspecified rights.

One of the principal objections to a federal bill of rights was that such a document could not possibly list all the rights of the people. Leaving some rights unlisted, or unenumerated, might imply that they did not exist. Omission also could be interpreted to mean that such rights, even if they did exist, were not important.

It was probably as a result of these concerns that the Ninth Amendment was included in the Bill of Rights. It says:

> *The enumeration in the Constitution of certain rights shall not be construed to deny or disparage others retained by the people.*

The Ninth Amendment embodies that great principle that can be traced back through the history of constitutional government to the Magna Carta—the principle that there exist certain fundamental rights that we take for granted, not just those rights that happen to be specified in a particular document. Justice William O. Douglas stated, "It well may be that guarantees which must be written are less secure than those so embedded in the hearts of men that they need not be written."

Power to Identify Unenumerated Rights

Who should decide what is an unenumerated right protected by the Constitution? There are differences of opinion on how this question should be answered. At issue is a basic principle of constitutional government that requires the powers of all the agencies of government be limited by law.

The Supreme Court has the power according to the principle of judicial review to decide whether a legislative act or executive order violates a right protected by the Constitution. This task is difficult enough with issues involving rights explicitly

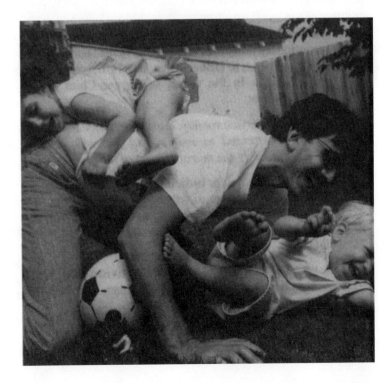

Who should determine which matters of personal privacy should remain free from government regulation?

Courtesy of the Center for Civic Education.

listed in the Constitution, such as the rights to a writ of habeas corpus or protection against unlawful entry by the authorities. The task becomes even more difficult when the issue involves unenumerated rights. What standard, if any, can justices use to avoid reading their own prejudices into the Constitution?

Critics of judicial power have claimed that anyone can find any right they want through a subjective interpretation of the Constitution. These critics often refer to the language of the majority opinion in Griswold v. Connecticut (1965), written by Justice Douglas. The case involved a Connecticut law that prohibited the use of contraceptives in all circumstances. A physician had been arrested for giving information on contraception to a married couple.

Douglas's opinion claimed that the Connecticut law violated the right of marital privacy. This right is not specifically referred to anywhere in the Constitution. In his opinion, however, Douglas argued that the right was protected by "penumbras, formed by emanations" from other enumerated rights, specifically those in the First, Third, Fourth, and Fifth Amendments. By this, he meant that some provisions of the Bill of Rights implied a right to marital privacy. In terms of his colorful metaphor, unenumerated rights were to be found in the shadows cast by the light of enumerated rights.

Should judges be given the freedom to decide what rights are to be discovered in the shadows of the Constitution's emanations? Some critics believe that to allow such latitude gives the Court almost unlimited power, not only to interpret the law but by doing so to create new law. There has been, and will continue to be, disagreement about the role judges should play in a constitutional democracy. There is disagreement about how the Constitution should be interpreted, with some believing in a strict construction, adhering as closely as possible to the original intent of the Framers. Others believe in broad construction, giving judges considerable leeway in applying the words of the Constitution to the circumstances of a changing world.

There also is disagreement about the degree to which judges should intercede in the activities of the legislative and executive branches. Some believe in a philosophy of **judicial restraint,** which places strong limitations on the discretionary powers of judges and relies instead on the political process to influence legislators to pass laws that protect rights. In the words of former Chief Justice Warren Burger, "In a democratic society, legislatures, not courts, are constituted to respond to the will, and consequently the moral values, of the people."

Others have argued for judicial activism by pointing out that the nation's courts, as watchdogs of the Constitution, have always had a special role to play in the identification, definition, and protection of individual rights. It was an advocate of judicial activism and broad construction, Justice William J. Brennan, who said:

> *"We current Justices read the Constitution in the only way we can, as Twentieth Century Americans. We look to the history of the time of framing and to the intervening history of interpretation. The ultimate question must be, what do the words of the text mean for our time? For the genius of the Constitution rests not in any static meaning it might have had in a world that is dead and gone, but in the adaptability of its great principles to cope with current problems and current needs."*

In a sense, what Justice Brennan said applies to every citizen called on to make sense of the Constitution—we cannot escape altogether the context and perspective of our own time. The challenge, as always, will be to apply the principles of the Constitution to changing circumstances without losing its basic principles in the process.

Conclusion

This lesson looked to the future. You focused on some major developments taking place in our society that are likely to affect the very nature of citizenship during your lifetime. You learned how the increased diversity of our society, technological progress, and closer international relationships are likely to affect your life as a citizen. You also learned how diversity has challenged our civic culture, how the computer and modern telecommunications are expanding the possibilities of citizenship, and how our nation's greater interdependence with the rest of the world is changing the pattern of civic loyalties.

This lesson focused on some constitutional issues being raised by our changing roles as citizens and the influence of many developments in modern society. You examined how these issues have challenged our understanding of group rights, the rights to life and to privacy, and the conflict between individual rights and the general good.

Lesson Review

1. How would you describe the challenges and opportunities created by the increasing diversity of American society?

2. How might modern technology expand the opportunities for direct participation by citizens in self-government?

3. How would you describe "strict construction" and "broad construction" of the Constitution?

4. What is meant by "judicial restraint"? What is meant by "judicial activism"? What arguments have been made in support of these two approaches to fulfilling the responsibilities of being a judge?

Lesson 3

Constitutionalism and Other Countries

Key Terms

civil and political rights
European Convention
of Human Rights
federalism
Four Freedoms
human rights
independent judiciary

negative rights
positive rights
prime minister
rights of solidarity
social and economic rights
Universal Declaration
of Human Rights

What You Will Learn to Do

- Illustrate similarities and differences between the American view of human rights and the views held by other constitutional governments

Linked Core Objectives

- Communicate using verbal, non-verbal, visual, and written techniques
- Do your share as a good citizen in your school, community, country, and the world

Skills and Knowledge You Will Gain Along the Way

- Describe the influence of American ideas about government and individual rights have had on other nations of the world
- Describe how constitutional democracy in other nations differs from constitutional democracy in the United States
- Describe the differences between the Bill of Rights and the Universal Declaration of Human Rights and between negative and positive rights
- Defend positions on what rights, if any, in the Universal Declaration of Human Rights should be established in the United States
- Define key words contained in this lesson

Introduction

We often examine constitutionalism primarily within the context of the American experience. By itself this perspective is too narrow, especially in today's world. In this lesson you will look at other traditions of constitutional government and at the many experiments in constitutionalism now taking place in the world. You will examine the historical impact of American constitutionalism on other countries and compare the American view of human rights with the views held by the international community.

How America Influences the World

America's constitutional ideals are perhaps this country's greatest contribution to the world. Few historic documents have had the impact of the Declaration of Independence and the U.S. Constitution, whose words have been copied and paraphrased in numerous other charters of freedom.

The American republic, product of the world's first democratic revolution, influenced many other countries during the first decades of its existence. The French Revolution of 1789 was inspired by the American Revolution and the French Constitution of 1791 copied many elements from America's first state constitutions. The world's second-oldest written constitution, the Polish Constitution of 1791, also was influenced by the American example. When Latin American countries won their independence from Spain in the early nineteenth century, they looked to the U.S. Constitution as a model for republican government. In 1825 the first demands for constitutional government in Russia, though unsuccessful, were inspired by American ideals.

The influence of American constitutionalism has expanded in this century because of the position of the United States as a world power. During the American occupation of Japan and Germany after World War II, a committee of Americans drafted the Japanese Constitution of 1947, and similarly, the new German Constitution of 1949 incorporated elements from the American model.

As the United States celebrated the bicentennial of its Constitution in 1987–1991, other nations were writing new chapters in the history of constitutional government. The 1980s and early 1990s saw the collapse of Soviet Communism and the emergence of democratic governments in Eastern Europe (see Figure 7.3.1). In 1989 students in China staged a challenge to totalitarian government. These dramatic developments could signal the beginning of a new era of constitutionalism with important implications for American citizens.

There has been renewed interest in the heritage of American ideals in the aftermath of the Cold War, as many former Communist states have begun to experiment with their own forms of constitutionalism. Some of the most eloquent tributes to our Constitution's bicentennial were expressed by the leaders of these newly independent countries. The president of Czechoslovakia, Vaclav Havel (see Figure 7.3.2), remarked in a speech before the U.S. Congress in 1990, "Wasn't it the best minds of your country . . . who wrote your famous Declaration of Independence, your Bill of Human Rights, and your Constitution? . . . Those great documents . . . inspire us all; they inspire us despite the fact that they are over 200 years old. They inspire us to be citizens."

Figure 7.3.1: Fall of the Berlin Wall, 1989.

Courtesy of Alain Nogues/Corbis Sygma.

Figure 7.3.2: Vaclav Havel addressing the United States Congress.

Courtesy of Bettmann/Corbis Images.

American Constitutionalism in Other Countries

As the world's first written framework of national government, the U.S. Constitution established an important precedent. Nearly all countries today either have or are in the process of drafting written constitutions. Totalitarian systems also felt it necessary to produce written constitutions, although in no way did they restrict the real exercise of power. The process by which the U.S. Constitution was drafted and adopted also established a precedent—the use of constitutional conventions and popular ratifications.

Key principles of the U.S. Constitution were spread throughout the world by The Federalist, America's greatest contribution to political thought. Many of these principles have been adopted in other constitutions.

Perhaps the most widely admired and imitated feature of the U.S. Constitution, after the Bill of Rights, has been the establishment of an **independent judiciary.** An inviolate—secure from outside influence—judicial branch acts as the watchdog of the Constitution and prevents the executive and legislative branches of government from disregarding it. The judicial branch helps to ensure that the words of the Constitution will be obeyed by the government.

Another aspect of American constitutionalism that is of great interest in the world today is **federalism.** By combining a central government with a large measure of autonomy for the states, the Framers were able to solve the problem of how to establish effective national and local governments in a large country. America's federal system has interested the former Communist states of Eastern Europe, where decades of centralized control all but destroyed local government. Federalism also has influenced the democracies of Western Europe in their creation of a European union.

Key Note Terms

independent judiciary—an inviolate judicial branch that serves to protect the U.S. Constitution and prevents the executive and legislative branches from disregarding

federalism—the distribution of power in an organization (as a government) between a central authority and the constituent units

What Do You Think?

1. What responsibilities, if any, do Americans have to promote representative democracy and constitutional government in other nations? Explain your reasoning.

2. What responsibilities, if any, do Americans have to promote respect for human rights in other nations? Explain your position.

Other Constitutional Democracies Differ from the American Model

The U.S. Constitution, however, is not the world's only source of ideas about constitutional democracy. Nations have looked to other traditions and to their own particular circumstances and historical legacies to find a form of constitutionalism that will be effective for them. However much we value our own political ideals and institutions, we must realize that they cannot always be transplanted.

Some elements in the U.S. Constitution have been adopted by other nations only with substantial modification; other elements have been rejected altogether in favor of different constitutional models. For example, the office of the presidency was another of the great innovations of the Framers. It was their solution to the need for a strong executive to replace a monarchy. Elected independently of the legislature, the president possesses those powers described in the Constitution itself.

The title of "President" to describe the constitutional chief executive has been widely adopted since that time, though usually not with the same powers and responsibilities U.S. presidents have. Because of their own historical experiences, many countries have been fearful of a strong executive. Freed from Communist dictatorships, the countries in the former Soviet bloc have provided for weak executives in their new constitutional arrangements, much like some of the first state constitutions in this country.

Perhaps the most distinguishing characteristic of the American system of government has been its separation and sharing of powers among three co-equal branches. Few other constitutional democracies, however, use that system today. Its critics consider our arrangement of divided powers inefficient and undemocratic. Most of the world's democracies have adopted instead some form of parliamentary government.

How Parliamentary Government Differs from Our Constitutional System

The Framers were very much influenced by the British constitution, even though it differed in important respects from the model they eventually adopted. The British constitution featured a system of checks and balances, but its executive, legislative, and judicial branches were not separated. Parliament, for example, was considered an instrument of the Crown, rather than an independent branch of government.

During the last two centuries a system of government modeled on the British constitution has been widely imitated, not only in Britain's former colonies but in many other countries as well. In a parliamentary system, government ministers are also members of the legislature. The head of the executive branch, usually called a **prime minister** (see Figure 7.3.3), is determined by whatever party or combination of parties has a majority in the parliament or legislature.

Unlike the American system, in a parliamentary arrangement the majority in the legislative branch decides who will head the executive branch. Many nations prefer the parliamentary system because they see the closer linkage of the executive and legislative branches as a more efficient form of government and one that is more reflective of the popular will.

Key Note Term

prime minister—the highest ranking member of the executive branch of a parliamentary government as in great Britain and Japan

Figure 7.3.3: British Prime Minister Tony Blair speaking in Parliament.

Courtesy of Reuters/Corbis Images.

The Bill of Rights' Influence on Other Constitutional Governments

Probably the single greatest contribution of American constitutionalism to the world has been its example of incorporating fundamental guarantees of individual rights into a written constitution. Nearly all national constitutions adopted since have included similar guarantees. The inspiring model of the U.S. Bill of Rights has become especially important during the latter half of this century, when interest in basic rights has increased around the world. As President Jimmy Carter observed in 1977, "The basic thrust of human affairs points toward a more universal demand for fundamental human rights."

Before this century, individual rights were generally regarded as an internal matter, to be left to each nation to decide. The world-wide economic depression of the 1930s, and the unprecedented crimes against humanity committed by totalitarian governments before and during World War II, gave the issue of human rights a new importance.

It was an American president, Franklin D. Roosevelt, who anticipated a new era in the history of basic rights. In a speech to Congress in 1941, the president defined the **Four Freedoms** worth fighting for: freedom of speech and expression, freedom of worship, freedom from want, and freedom from fear (see Figure 7.3.4). The charter that founded the United Nations in 1945, and subsequently led to the United Nations Universal Declaration of Human Rights of 1948, followed President Roosevelt's example.

The Declaration and the charter proclaimed universal standards of basic rights, called **human rights,** because they were considered essential to the dignity of each human being. In the decades since, the concern for human rights has become an issue of importance in the relations among nations. Regional agreements have expanded the United Nations Declaration. For example, in 1950 the countries of Western Europe agreed to a **European Convention on Human Rights.** They established a European Court to which the citizens of these countries could appeal when they believed their rights had been violated.

Increasingly, the protection of rights is also an important diplomatic issue among nations. The United States, for example, has sometimes restricted trade with countries considered to be violating human rights. In recent years our relations with the Republic of South Africa were influenced to a large extent by the issue of rights violations in that country.

Other National Bill of Rights

As fundamental and lasting as its guarantees have been, the U.S. Bill of Rights is a document of the eighteenth century, reflecting the issues and concerns of the age in which it was written. The rights guaranteed to Americans are **civil and political rights.** They express a fear of government power. They protect the individual from wrongful acts by government and provide each citizen with ways to participate in public affairs.

Key Note Terms

Four Freedoms—the four basic rights that Franklin Roosevelt declared worthy of fighting a war to preserve: freedom of speech and expression, freedom of worship, freedom of fear, and freedom of want

human rights—basic rights and freedoms assumed to belong to all people everywhere

European Convention on Human Rights—established a European Court to which the citizens of these countries could appeal when they believed their rights had been violated

civil and political rights—rights that protect the individual from wrongful acts by government and provide each citizen with ways to participate in public affairs

Figure 7.3.4: Four Freedoms by Norman Rockwell.

Freedom of Speech *(February 20, 1943),* Freedom from Fear *(March 13, 1943),* Freedom of Worship *(February 27, 1943),* Freedom from Want *(March 6, 1943), from* Saturday Evening Post. *Courtesy of The Norman Rockwell Art Collection Trust, The Norman Rockwell Museum at Stockbridge, Massachusetts. Reproduced by permission of the Norman Rockwell Family Agency. Copyright © 1943 the Norman Rockwell Family Entities.*

Other national guarantees of rights also reflect the cultures that created them. Many of these cultures have values and priorities different from our own. In many Asian countries, for example, the rights of the individual are secondary to the interests of the whole community. Islamic countries take their code of laws from the teachings of the Koran, the book of sacred writings accepted by Muslims as revelations made to the prophet Muhammad by God.

In some countries freedom of conscience is considered less important than it is in the United States and other Western democracies. What constitutes cruel and unusual punishment, which is forbidden by our Eighth Amendment, differs greatly from country to country, depending on its particular history and culture.

Contemporary charters of basic rights also reflect the changes that have taken place in government and society during the last 200 years. Many guarantees of rights adopted since World War II have been modeled on the United Nations' Universal Declaration of Human Rights. They include many of the civil and political rights represented in our Bill of Rights. Most go further to include **social and economic rights.**

Key Note Term

social and economic rights—examples of social and economic rights would be the right to choose a career, secure employment, health care, and education

Examples of social and economic rights would be the right to choose a career, secure employment, health care, and education. Others might include certain societal rights, such as the right to responsible management of nonrenewable resources or a clean environment. The inclusion of such provisions in guaranteed rights reflects a change in the role government plays in society and the expectations its citizens place on it.

The Founders considered the role of government in people's lives to be very limited, as indeed it was in the eighteenth century. Governments play a much larger role today and that role has expanded the meaning of basic rights in most societies. The people in the former Communist states of Europe, for example, may appreciate their newfound civic and political rights, but many are reluctant to give up the economic security and social rights their former Communist governments provided.

Negative and Positive Rights

In the natural rights tradition, which provides the foundation of the United States Constitution, rights are seen as restraints on the power of government. They are sometimes called **negative rights** because they prevent government from acting in a certain way. The Bill of Rights generally requires the government not to act. For example, the First Amendment says, "Government shall make no law . . ."

The social, economic, and solidarity rights (**rights of solidarity**) included in the United Nations' Universal Declaration of Rights, and in many national guarantees of rights adopted since, are what are sometimes called **positive rights.** Instead of preventing the government from acting, they require it to act, to ensure such things as economic security, health care, and a clean environment for its citizens.

There are other important differences between negative and positive rights. Negative rights prevent the government from taking away something its citizens already possess, for example, freedom of expression. Many positive rights, on the other hand, describe certain benefits that citizens should have. These rights express the objectives worthy of any just society.

Key Note Terms

negative rights—these rights are seen as restraints on the power of government

rights of solidarity—Solidarity rights included in the United Nations' Universal Declaration Of Rights, and in many national guarantees of rights adopted since, are what are sometimes called positive rights

positive rights—instead of preventing the government from acting, they require it to act, to ensure such things as economic security, health care, and a clean environment for its citizens

Examining the Universal Declaration of Human Rights

Review the **Universal Declaration of Human Rights** found in the Reference Section and answer the following questions:

1. What rights does the Universal Declaration of Human Rights proclaim that are in the U.S. Constitution and Bill of Rights?

2. What rights in our Constitution and Bill of Rights are not included in the Universal Declaration of Human Rights? Why do you suppose they are not included?

3. What appears to be the purposes of the rights in the Universal Declaration of Human Rights that are not protected by our Constitution or Bill of Rights?

4. Examine each of the rights in the Universal Declaration of Human Rights that is not protected specifically in our Constitution. Is the right you have identified protected in the United States by other means, such as civil rights legislation; civil or criminal law contracts between private parties; labor and management agreements on employment benefits, vacation pay, and sick leave; custom or tradition; other means not listed above?

5. What rights, if any, in the Universal Declaration of Human Rights should be established in the United States? How should they be established? Explain your position.

6. How do the rights listed in the Universal Declaration of Human Rights appear to reflect the history and experiences of the time in which it was written?

Conclusion

We often examine constitutionalism primarily within the context of the American experience. By itself this perspective is too narrow, especially in today's world. In this lesson you looked at other traditions of constitutional government and at the many experiments in constitutionalism now taking place in the world. You examined the historical impact of American constitutionalism on other countries. The lesson focused on the subject of human rights and its increasing importance in current international affairs.

You learned why some aspects of the U.S. Constitution have been adopted by emerging democracies while others have not. You also learned about the differences between the United States' form of constitutional government and other forms of constitutional government, such as parliamentary systems. Finally, you learned the differences between the American understanding of constitutional rights and rights guarantees as they have been developed in other parts of the world.

Lesson Review

1. Which aspects of American constitutional democracy have been particularly influential in other countries?

2. How would you describe the important features of a parliamentary form of government?

3. What is the difference between civil and political rights, on one hand, and social and economic rights, on the other? How is this difference related to the difference between "negative rights" and "positive rights"?

4. What are some important differences between the Bill of Rights and the Universal Declaration of Human Rights?

Lesson 4

Defending Fundamental Principles

Key Terms

diversity
freedom
liberty
principle
sovereignty

Chapter 7

What You Will Learn to Do

- Justify your opinion about a contemporary issue that presents a conflict among competing fundamental constitutional principles (such as personal freedom vs. social order)

Linked Core Objectives

- Communicate using verbal, non-verbal, visual, and written techniques
- Apply critical thinking techniques

Skills and Knowledge You Will Gain Along the Way

- Explain in what ways the American experience in self-government can be called an "adventure in ideas"

- Explain how differences in opinion about fundamental principles are resolved in the U.S. system of government

- Compare positions on issues related to the fundamental principles and values of government and individual rights in American society

- Define key words contained in this lesson

Introduction

Founder George Mason said, "No free government, or the blessings of liberty can be preserved to any people, but by frequent recurrence to fundamental principles." In this concluding lesson, you have the opportunity of relating some fundamental principles and ideas of our government to contemporary issues.

The format of this lesson differs from the others. Critical Thinking Exercises present a series of quotations representing many great ideas and principles that have shaped our constitutional heritage. Some of these ideas contradict each other.

American constitutional history has witnessed many conflicts between competing principles of equal merit, for example, the conflict between majority rule and minority rights, between sovereign power and fundamental rights, liberty and order, unity, and diversity. You encounter once again some of these conflicts in the following exercises. In each case you are asked to apply the principles and ideas suggested in the quotations to a contemporary issue, to work through the issue on your own, or in small groups, and to reach your own conclusions. In so doing, you use the skills of citizenship—observation, analysis, and value judgments—to reach an opinion, to express that opinion, and to be prepared to defend it. The exercises provide practice for the responsibilities you will encounter in the years ahead.

Why Fundamental Principles Are Important

You will remember that this book began with the observation that the American experiment in self-government was an adventure in ideas. The individuals who founded our government cherished and respected ideas. They were excited about them. Ours is a nation that was created by ideas. It is not the product of a common culture or geography or centuries of tradition. The United States began as an experiment to see if certain ideas about government—never before tried on such a scale and in such a way—would work.

The English economist, John Meynard Keynes, once remarked that "in the long run it is ideas and not men who rule the world." If the upheavals of this century have taught us anything, it is that ideas have consequences, sometimes for good, sometimes for evil. We like to believe that in the end, good ideas will prevail over bad. Whatever the case, ideas do matter. One of the Twentieth century's most compelling images comes from the Chinese student uprising of 1989. It was the photograph of a young man (see Figure 7.4.1), armed only with the moral authority of his cause, confronting a column of armored tanks. The picture moved and inspired the world.

The Soviet dictator, Joseph Stalin, once disparaged the influence of religion by asking, "How many divisions does the Pope have?" It is one of the great ironies of this century that the fall of Stalin's Communist empire began in Poland, in a revolution inspired in large part by the religious faith of the Polish people and supported throughout by the moral influence of the papacy. "An invasion of armies can be resisted," said the French novelist Victor Hugo, "but not an idea whose time has come."

Figure 7.4.1: Do you have an obligation as a citizen and a human being to exercise your moral authority when injustice occurs?

Courtesy of AP/Wide World Photos.

What the Founders Meant by Returning to First Principles

When George Mason spoke of the importance of a frequent recurrence to fundamental principles, he was invoking an old idea associated with republican government. The ancient Greeks and Romans believed that a government established with the purpose of serving the public good and involving the participation of all citizens could not survive unless each generation was reminded of that government's reason for being and the **principles** by which it operated.

"If a nation means its systems, religious or political, shall have duration," said another of the Founders, "it ought to recognize the leading principles of them in the front page of every family book. What is the usefulness of a truth in theory, unless it exists constantly in the minds of the people and has their assent?"

It is doubtful that these Founders had in mind an uncritical acceptance of the "wisdom of the past." In revisiting these principles, each generation must examine and evaluate them anew. Indeed, it is probable that the Founders would be somewhat surprised at the reverence in which they and their writings have been held by subsequent generations of Americans.

The Founders, themselves, were vigorous critics of the wisdom they inherited and the principles in which they believed. They were articulate, opinionated individuals who loved to examine ideas, to analyze, argue, and debate them. They expected no less of future generations. They would expect no less of you. To go back in thought or discussion to first principles requires us to make principled arguments and ground our opinions in ideas of enduring value. It is what citizenship in a free society is all about.

Critical Thinking Exercise #1: Liberty v. Order

One of the most enduring and important challenges in our constitutional system of government is how to balance order with **liberty.** Today, this challenge is focused on the issue of crime. Violent crime is widespread in the nation's inner cities, but few areas of our society feel safe. Violence even has become a problem for our schools. Recently, in response to the crime problem in a housing project of one of the nation's largest cities, officials in that city proposed large-scale police "sweeps" of apartments to search for illegal weapons. These searches would not use a search warrant or provide evidence of probable cause. After a judge struck down the proposal as an unconstitutional violation of the Fourth Amendment, the city then proposed a new policy: requiring prospective tenants in public housing projects to waive their Fourth Amendment rights as a condition of their leases.

Critics of this proposal doubt its constitutionality and worry about the consequences of a policy that would require a citizen to give up any of the liberties protected by the Bill of Rights. Those supporting the proposal point to the dangerous conditions that such tenants must live in. What's the point of worrying about procedural rights in a world that has, in effect, become a lawless state?

Government's first obligation, they say, is to provide the security of an orderly society. What is your position on this issue? Justify it in terms of the situation itself and in terms of constitutional principles.

> ### Key Note Term
>
> **liberty**—the state of a free person; exemption from subjection to the will of another claiming ownership of the person or services; freedom; opposed to slavery, serfdom, bondage, or subjection

1. **How do the following statements apply to this situation? What principles and ideals are implied in each statement? How, if at all, do these principles conflict with each other?**

   a. **"The right of the people to be secure in their persons, houses, papers, and effects, against unreasonable searches and seizures, shall not be violated, and no warrants shall issue, but upon probable cause . . ." Fourth Amendment**

   b. **"The good of the people is the highest law." Cicero**

   c. **"Authority without wisdom is like a heavy axe without an edge, fitter to bruise than polish." Anne Bradstreet**

   d. **"For a man's house is his castle." Edward Coke**

   e. **"They that can give up essential liberty to obtain a little temporary safety deserve neither liberty nor safety." Benjamin Franklin**

   f. **"Since the general civilization of mankind, I believe there are more instances of the abridgment of the freedom of the people by gradual and silent encroachments of those in power, than by violent and sudden usurpation." James Madison**

   g. **"Every successful revolution puts on in time the robe of the tyrant it has deposed." Barbara Tuchman**

   h. **"Liberty, too, must be limited in order to be possessed." Edmund Burke**

   i. **"The great and chief end, therefore, of men's uniting into Commonwealths, and putting themselves under Government, is the preservation of property [i.e., life, liberty, and estate]." John Locke**

2. **Which, if any, of these statements do you find most persuasive? Why?**

3. **What is your position on this issue? Explain the reasons for your position in terms of the situation itself and in terms of the principles involved.**

Critical Thinking Exercise #2: Rights of the Accused

Americans are worried about the drug problem. A recent poll indicated that a substantial percentage of American citizens would be willing to give up some protections of the Bill of Rights in order to control illegal drug use.

Several years ago Congress passed a law authorizing federal authorities to confiscate the property of individuals suspected of trafficking in drugs. Such property could be seized on mere suspicion. Individuals whose property had been seized could appeal and seek a return of their property, but the burden of proof rested on them to prove their innocence.

Advocates of this law argued its constitutionality on the grounds that the government was not acting against the suspected individuals, only against their property. Because only individuals, and not property, enjoy the protection of the Bill of Rights, they said, the law did not violate the Constitution.

Since going into effect the law has proved controversial. Congress may repeal it. Do you think it should be repealed? Even if the constitutionality of such a law is upheld, should the government have such power? How would you determine the circumstances in which protections guaranteed by the Constitution should be curtailed by the government?

1. **How do the following statements apply to this situation? What principles and ideals are implied in each statement? How, if at all, do these principles conflict with each other?**

   a. **"No person shall be . . . deprived of life, liberty, or property, without due process of law. . . ." Fifth Amendment**

   b. **"It is better that ten guilty persons escape than one innocent person suffer." William Blackstone**

   c. **"Man's capacity for justice makes democracy possible, but man's inclination to injustice makes democracy necessary." Reinhold Niebuhr**

   d. **"The mood and temper of the public in the treatment of crime and criminals is one of the most unfailing tests of civilization of any country." Winston Churchill**

2. **Which, if any, of these statements do you find most persuasive? Why?**

3. **What is your position on this issue? Explain the reasons for your position in terms of the situation itself and in terms of the principles involved.**

Critical Thinking Exercise #3: Unity v. Diversity

Key Note Term

diversity—having various forms or qualities; differing from one another

Is a common language essential to the survival of American democracy? One of the most controversial aspects of **diversity** in America has to do with language. Throughout our history English has been the principal language of the country. For millions of immigrants, learning English was an important first step to becoming a U.S. citizen.

Schools must teach immigrant children who speak languages other than English. Educators differ about how best to accomplish their tasks. Moreover, a large percentage of recent immigrants use Spanish as their first language. In certain areas of the country Spanish is as commonly spoken as English. We are becoming, many believe, a bilingual nation.

1. How do the following statements apply to this situation? What principles and ideals are implied in each statement? How, if at all, do these principles conflict with each other?

   a. "America is God's crucible, the great melting pot where all the races of Europe are melting and re-forming!" Israel Zangwell

   b. "Immigrants are not refuse; rather, they are the sinew and bone of all nations. . . . Education is the essence of American opportunity, the treasure that no thief could touch, not even misfortune or poverty." Mary Antin

   c. "Our political harmony is therefore concerned in a uniformity of language." Noah Webster

   d. "We have room for but one language here, and that is the English language, and we intend to see that the crucible turns our people out as Americans, and not as dwellers of a polyglot boardinghouse." Theodore Roosevelt

   e. "In world history, those who have helped to build the same culture are not necessarily of one race, and those of the same race have not all participated in one culture." Ruth Fulton Benedict

   f. "We have become not a melting pot but a beautiful mosaic. Different people, different beliefs, different yearnings, different hopes, different dreams." Jimmy Carter

   g. "America is not a melting pot. It is a sizzling cauldron." Barbara Mikulski

   h. "Unless you speak English and read well, you'll never become a first-class citizen . . . but when you say 'official,' that becomes a racial slur." Barbara Bush

   i. "The individual. . .does not exist for the State, nor for that abstraction called 'society,' or the 'nation,' which is only a collection of individuals." Emma Goldman

2. Which, if any, of these statements do you find most persuasive? Why?

3. Is a common language necessary to American citizenship? Explain your position in terms of the principles involved.

Critical Thinking Skill #4: Individual Rights v. the Sovereignty of the People

One of the great conflicts of principles you have encountered in reading this text is that which exists between fundamental rights on the one hand and sovereign power on the other. This conflict was an important factor in the American Revolution and in the Civil War. A fundamental right, as you remember, is one that cannot be revised or taken away by any power. **Sovereignty** is that power within a state beyond which there is no appeal—whoever has the sovereign power has the final say.

> ### Key Note Term
>
> **sovereignty**—self-governing; independent; a chief of state in a monarchy; freedom from external control, a government's power to exercise supreme authority to rule within a certain territory

In 1990, the Supreme Court ruled in Texas v. Johnson that the burning of an American flag as a political protest, however distasteful an act to many Americans, was protected under the free speech provision of the First Amendment. The Court's decision prompted demands for a constitutional amendment prohibiting the desecration of "Old Glory." President George Bush publicly endorsed such an amendment.

Were the proposed amendment adopted, it would have added to the Constitution for the first time the prohibition of a particular form of expression. It would also have represented a limitation on one of the essential **freedoms** guaranteed in the Bill of Rights.

This incident reminds us that it is within the sovereign authority of the American people to revise or abolish entirely the Bill of Rights. What do you think the incident suggests about the protection of rights in a constitutional democracy? Does it suggest that the theory of fundamental rights is irrelevant? What does it suggest about the relevance of the natural rights philosophy?

1. **How do the following statements apply to this situation? What principles and ideals are implied in each statement? How, if at all, do these principles conflict with each other?**

   a. **"We the People of the United States. . .do ordain and establish this Constitution. . . ."** Preamble to the Constitution

   b. **"Congress shall make no law . . . abridging the freedom of speech."** First Amendment

   c. **"All lawful authority, legislative, and executive, originates from the people. Power in the people is like light in the sun, native, original, inherent, and unlimited by any thing human."** James Burgh

   d. **"No written law has ever been more binding than unwritten custom supported by popular opinion."** Carrie Chapman Catt

   e. **"You have rights antecedent to all earthly governments; rights that cannot be repealed or restrained by human law; rights derived from the Great Legislator of the Universe."** John Adams

   f. **"The people made the Constitution and the people can unmake it. It is the creature of their own will, and lives only by their will."** John Marshall

   g. **". . . No one cause is left but the most ancient of all, the one, in fact, that from the beginning of our history has determined the very existence of politics, the cause of freedom versus tyranny."** Hannah Arendt

   h. **"When I refuse to obey an unjust law, I do not contest the right of the majority to command, but I simply appeal from the sovereignty of the people to the sovereignty of mankind."** Alexis de Tocqueville

2. **Which, if any, of these statements do you find most persuasive? Why?**

3. **What is your position on this issue? Explain the reasons for your position in terms of the situation itself and in terms of the principles involved.**

Critical Thinking Exercise #5: The Dangers and Benefits of Energetic Government

One of the major issues of the 1990s is health care reform. In addition to the many, complex aspects of health care itself, there is also a constitutional aspect to this issue: the benefits and dangers of government power. A national health care plan would mean a substantial expansion of the federal government's involvement in the private sector. Health care services now comprise about one-seventh of the nation's economy.

Advocates of comprehensive health care reform argue the need for government to take charge of what has become a serious problem in contemporary America. They would point to precedents such as the Social Security System, which was created in 1935 as part of the New Deal. Critics of a national health care plan, on the other hand, express concern about any substantial increase in government bureaucracy. A national health care system administered by the government, they believe, constitutes a potential threat to individual liberty.

With the complexities and demands of modern American society, what are the proper limits to an energetic government? What criteria should the citizen employ in evaluating the benefits and dangers of government regulation?

1. **How do the following statements apply to this situation? What principles and ideals are implied in each statement? How, if at all, do these principles conflict with each other?**

   a. "... [to] promote the general Welfare." Preamble to the Constitution

   b. "To make all Laws which are necessary and proper for carrying into Execution the foregoing Powers." Constitution, Article I, Sec. 7

   c. "If, my countrymen, you wait for a constitution which absolutely bars a power of doing evil, you must wait long, and when obtained it will have no power of doing good." Oliver Ellsworth

   d. "A government ought to contain in itself every power requisite to the full accomplishment of the objects committed to its care, and to the complete execution of the trusts for which it is responsible, free from every other control, but a regard to the public good and to the sense of the people." Alexander Hamilton

   e. "I own I am not a friend to a very energetic government. It is always oppressive." Thomas Jefferson

2. **With the complexities and demands of modern American society, what are the proper limits to an energetic government?**

3. **Which, if any, of these statements do you find most persuasive? Why?**

4. **What is your position on this issue? Explain the reasons for your position in terms of the situation itself and in terms of the principles involved.**

Critical Thinking Exercise #6: Capital Punishment and the Constitution

With the exception of the issue of separation of church and state, no issue has focused so sharply the question of constitutional interpretation and the role of the judiciary in making such interpretation as the death penalty. Shortly before his retirement in 1994, Justice Harry Blackmun announced that he would no longer vote in favor of implementation of the death penalty. While he did not exactly say that capital punishment was unconstitutional, his remarks suggested that because the death penalty had become so repugnant to him, he would no longer have anything to do with its enforcement.

Justice Blackmun's remarks were controversial, in part because of the strong opinions on the death penalty issue in the United States. They also were controversial because of what they suggested about how the words of the Constitution should be interpreted and the degree to which a judge's subjectivity should influence that interpretation.

Is the death penalty constitutional? Its opponents say no. They maintain that the penalty itself violates the "cruel and unusual punishment" of the Eighth Amendment—both the manner of taking life and the long delays that usually accompany it. Opponents also have argued that implementation of capital punishment violates the equal protection clause of the Fourteenth Amendment, since its application falls disproportionately on the poor and minorities.

Other citizens, including some who are opposed to the death penalty as a policy, say it is constitutional. The text of the Constitution, they argue, makes clear that the Framers clearly intended to allow for capital punishment. It is up to the people through their representatives and not to judges to decide on whether or not to employ this option.

If you were a justice on the Supreme Court, how would you approach this issue? What outlook and criteria would you use to interpret the words of the Framers? What would you consider to be the proper role of judges in addressing this issue? Would you take a different position if you were a legislator?

1. **How do the following statements apply to this situation? What principles and ideals are implied in each statement? How, if at all, do these principles conflict with each other?**

    a. **". . . nor cruel and unusual punishments inflicted." Eighth Amendment**

    b. **"No punishment has ever possessed enough power of deterrence to prevent the commission of crimes." Hannah Arendt**

    c. **"No person shall be . . . deprived of life, liberty, or property, without due process of law . . ." Fifth Amendment**

    d. **"Then thou shall give for a life, eye for eye, tooth for tooth. . . ." Exodus, 21:23-24**

    e. **"Thou shalt not kill" Exodus, 20:13**

2. **What is the difference between the constitutional principles, a and c, and the passages from the Bible, d and e? What is it about these ideas that allows people to reach opposing points of view? Because something is legal, does that make it moral?**

3. **Which, if any, of these statements do you find most persuasive? Why?**

4. **What is your position on this issue? Explain the reasons for your position in terms of the situation itself and in terms of the principles involved.**

Conclusion

This lesson concludes Chapter 7, "Citizen Roles in American Democracy," as well as the "We The People" part of your education in citizenship. In the following chapter, you will have a chance to put some of the theories and information you have learned into practice as you go through "Critical Thinking in Citizenship."

Lesson Review

1. What did the Founders mean by returning to first principles?

2. Explain the term "rights of the accused."

3. Define the term "sovereignty."

4. What is capital punishment? What is your opinion on capital punishment and why do you hold that opinion?

Chapter 8

Critical Thinking in Citizenship

Leadership Choices, Decisions, and Consequences

Key Terms

After Action Review
contingency

What You Will Learn to Do

- Investigate how leadership choices and decisions can lead to good and/or bad consequences

Linked Core Abilities

- Communicate using verbal, non-verbal, visual, and written techniques
- Apply critical thinking techniques

Skills and Knowledge You Will Gain Along the Way

- Translate how the 11 principles of leadership apply to decision making
- Apply the decision-making process to leadership decisions
- Define key words contained in this lesson

Chapter 8

Introduction

Leaders must be able to decide confidently on what action to take under the most critical conditions. If a leader delays or avoids making a decision, the result might be a lost opportunity, loss of confidence, confusion, and failure of a project. In this lesson you will examine strategies to use when considering decisions as a leader. You will also analyze the impact of actions that involve decisions made at a leadership level.

The Decision-Making Process

When learning how to make sound, rational, and informed decisions, you need to have a basic understanding of the ways decisions are made. Most decision-making rests on two assumptions: that leaders have access to all the information they need to make a decision, and that leaders make decisions by choosing the best possible solution to a problem or response to an opportunity. According to this method, a decision maker should choose how to respond to opportunities and problems by engaging in the following four steps:

1. **Listing all alternatives from which a choice will be selected: These alternatives represent different responses to the problem or the opportunity.**

2. **Listing the consequences of each alternative: The consequences are what would occur if a given alternative were selected.**

3. **Considering his or her own preferences for each alternative or set of consequences and then ranking the sets from most preferred to least preferred.**

4. **Selecting the alternative that will result in the most preferred set of consequences.**

The assumption that decision makers have all the information needed to make optimal decisions bears little resemblance to the conditions facing most situations. Even if the decision makers did have all necessary information, they probably would not be able to use it all because the cognitive abilities of decision makers are limited; often they cannot take into account the large quantities of information available to them.

One way to consider the difficulties of this decision-making process is to compare the four steps described previously to actual decision making in any given situation. With regard to the first step, decision makers often *do not know all the alternatives from which they can choose.* One of the defining features of this process is that is involves an extensive search for information. Even after this search is complete, however, it is likely that decision makers are aware of only some of the possible alternatives.

In the second step of this decision-making process, decision makers list the consequences of each alternative. As in the first step, however, decision makers often *do not know all of the consequences* that will ensue if they choose a given alternative. One reason it's hard to make decisions is that the decision maker often does not know what will happen if a given course of action is chosen.

As the third step in this process, decision makers must consider their own preferences for sets of consequences. Once again, this assumes that decision makers are able to rank sets of consequences and know their own preferences. However, decision makers *don't always know for sure what they want*. Stop and think about some of the important and difficult decisions you have had to make. Sometimes these decisions were difficult to make precisely because *you weren't sure what you wanted*. For example, a graduating senior with an accounting degree from the University of Wisconsin might find it hard to choose between a job offer from a Wisconsin bank and one from a major accounting firm in New York City because he doesn't know whether he prefers the security of staying in Wisconsin, where most of his family and friends are, to the excitement of living in a big city and the opportunity to work for a major firm. Because of the problems with the first three steps in this decision-making model:

- **It is often impossible for a leader to make the best possible decisions**
- **Even if they make a good decision, the time, effort, and cost that were spent making it might not be worthwhile**

Incomplete information and the decision maker's cognitive abilities and psychological makeup affect decision making. Consequently decision makers often choose *satisfactory*, not optimal, solutions.

One key to decision making is to follow the 11 Principles of Leadership, both for yourself as well as for your team. Each principle can help you make the best, most timely and optimal decisions and choices available.

Applying the 11 Principles of Leadership to Decision Making

As discussed in Chapter 1, Lesson 4, "Principles and Leadership," the 11 principles of leadership are critical to effective decision making. As a review, these principles include:

- **Perform a self-evaluation**
- **Be technically proficient**
- **Seek and take responsibility for your actions**
- **Make sound and timely decisions**
- **Set the example**
- **Know your personnel and look out for their welfare**
- **Keep your followers informed**
- **Develop a sense of responsibility in your followers**
- **Ensure each task is understood, supervised, and accomplished**
- **Build a team**
- **Employ your team in accordance with its capabilities**

Take a look at each principle and see how it relates to the decision-making process.

Figure 8.1.1: Make an honest self-evaluation to determine your strengths and weaknesses.

Courtesy of John Henley/ Corbis Images.

Perform a Self-Evaluation

Through self-evaluation (see Figure 8.1.1), you can determine your strengths and weaknesses; you can take advantage of your strengths, and work to overcome your weaknesses. Self-knowledge is crucial towards gaining confidence in your decision-making skills and your ability to lead effectively. When you know who you are and recognize your leadership qualities, making sound, informed, and timely decisions becomes less intimidating. You know exactly what you want, gain courage from your convictions, and confidently adhere to what you think is right. When you don't work on self-knowledge, you can come across to your team members as an uncertain and insecure leader, and this can lead to fear and confusion within the team.

Be Technically Proficient

Being technically proficient means you can show your teammates that you are qualified to lead and perform all tasks associated with any job or assignment, and you are capable of training teammates to carry out those assignments. By knowing what it takes to accomplish each job or task that you ask of your followers, you can base your leadership choices and decisions on the abilities of your support team. If a team member feels that you don't understand the job that they are being asked to do, they might resent the responsibility you've given them and not perform to the best of their abilities.

Seek and Take Responsibility for Your Actions

Leading always involves responsibility, and leaders are always responsible for the choices and decisions they make. As you make your decisions, ensure that you possess the competence necessary to make sound and timely choices. If you feel you need more input or information before making a decision for which you will take full responsibility, get feedback from your superiors or from your team members, or find other ways to gain knowledge. When a leader does not take responsibility for decisions, or takes credit for success when it was not due, or refuses to admit when mistakes have been made, team members can lose confidence in their leadership.

Make Sound and Timely Decisions

Leaders must be able to reason under pressure and decide quickly what action to take. To delay or avoid making a decision may cause a project to fail. When circumstances require a change in plans, prompt reaction builds confidence in your team members. Too, you can encourage your teammates to participate in the planning process. Always consider their advice and suggestions before making a decision.

Figure 8.1.2: By setting a good example, team members are more willing to follow your lead.
Courtesy of US Army JROTC.

Set the Example

A leader must be a good example for his or her team. This is a weighty responsibility, but as a leader, you have no choice. If you expect honor, integrity, loyalty, and respect from your followers, you must demonstrate the same (see Figure 8.1.2). When you're assured that your team has picked up on your courage and convictions, you can make choices and decisions by knowing your team is 100 percent behind you. Without that cohesiveness, any project is doomed to failure.

Know Your Personnel and Look Out for Their Welfare

As a leader, you must know and understand each member of your unit. You must know them as individuals—their interests, values, attitudes, strengths, and weaknesses. Never ask a team member to do something for which they are not qualified, and always use team members to the fullest of their abilities. When you recognize what makes each member "tick," you can encourage them to be their best, and help them eliminate their weaknesses. In making choices and decisions, knowing your team members is crucial to the success of any project.

Keep Your Followers Informed

Each member of your team will do their best if they understand why they are doing something. Keeping your unit informed of any situation and explaining the reasons behind each decision you make helps your team to understand why you are making certain choices and decisions, and helps your team members comprehend their role in each project. Too, by keeping your followers informed, you stay on top of the most current information available.

Develop a Sense of Responsibility in Your Followers

When you develop a sense of responsibility in each team member, you indicate that you trust them. As a leader and instructor, you are responsible for helping each team member meet their potential by giving them the opportunities and challenges you know they can handle; then giving them more responsibility when you feel they're ready. By encouraging them to take initiative and work towards a goal, you let each teammate feel as if they have some amount of ownership in a project. And by developing this ownership or sense of responsibility, you can make decisions knowing that your team will do their best.

Ensure Each Task Is Understood, Supervised, and Accomplished

Your followers must understand what you expect from them. They need to know how and when you want a specific task accomplished, and what the standard is for that task. By supervising each member of your unit, you have the opportunity to let them know what you want done, show them how you want it done, and be available to answer questions. By knowing that each team member understands their job and responsibilities, you can make choices and decisions with the knowledge that each individual is competent in their task.

Build a Team

Leaders must develop team spirit that motivates members to work with confidence and enthusiasm. Team spirit works in two ways—the group as a whole gives its members a feeling of accomplishment, security, and recognition; then each team member gives their best back to the team. Your group becomes a team only when the members can trust and respect you as their leader and each other as trained, supportive professionals. As a leader, this gives you the confidence to make decisions knowing your group can function as a team.

Employ Your Team in Accordance with Its Capabilities

When you serve as a leader, you constantly have choices regarding the course of action you can take. Your decisions can lead to success or failure, but you need to develop sound decision-making techniques that you can use in any situation. Most times, these decisions will need to be made quickly, so knowing how to "hit the ground running" will benefit you and those you lead. The following two historical studies demonstrate how the actions taken after a decision-making process can lead to vastly different consequences. The first shows how the lack of sufficient knowledge and mistaken perceptions resulted in a tragedy that could have been avoided. The second shows how one leader took what could have been a negative situation, used most of the 11 principles of leadership, and changed it to one of the most positive outcomes of the Civil War.

The Battle of Little Big Horn

In the annals of American history, probably no battle has achieved such a legendary status, or has been so misrepresented as the Battle of Little Big Horn. The basic facts are simple. On June 22, 1876, George Armstrong Custer, Commander of the 7th Cavalry (see Figure 8.1.3), led 655 Indian fighters into the Black Hills of the Dakotas. Their mission was to seek out and kill or capture the Sioux, Cheyenne, and Arapaho responsible for the Battle of Rosebud Creek five days earlier. For the first time, the Indian tribes had united against the encroachment of American gold seekers and the

U.S. Army, and in a fight lasting over six hours, 1500 Native Americans fiercely defended their sacred ground against 1000 U.S. troops. The news of Indian resistance reached Washington, and General William T. Sherman, the Commander in Chief of the U.S. Army, proclaimed "only a severe and persistent chastisement [of the Indians] will bring them to a sense of submission." Custer and over 220 of his men never returned from the Black Hills. They were slaughtered by a far superior force led by Chiefs Sitting Bull and Crazy Horse.

The disaster of Custer's Last Stand, as it is also known, resulted from a series of mistakes. At the highest level was a miscalculation of Indian resistance to white settlement of the Black Hills. For the Lakota Sioux, particularly, this territory was consecrated ground where young men experienced manhood rites of passage, and medicine men conferred with ancestral spirits. When gold was discovered in 1874 near the present town of Deadwood, South Dakota, the U.S. government offered the unheard of sum of six million dollars to the Sioux if they would relinquish their claims to the land that had been established by the Laramie Treaty of 1860. The Sioux refused.

Little Big Horn Survivor

After the Battle of Little Big Horn, only one horse, with seven arrows in his body, was found alive in a thicket. The horse, named Comanche, was a gelding ridden by Captain Keogh, one of Custer's slain officers.

At an intermediate level, General Philip Sheridan, who had been charged with dealing with the "Indian problem," underestimated the capacity of his Native American adversaries to mount a combined effort against the U.S. Army. He understood the Battle of Rosebud Creek to be a fluke. After all, these enemies were only "savages." Sheridan ordered a three-pronged attack led by Generals Gibbon, Terry, and Crook.

Almost immediately, General Gibbon was attacked by Crazy Horse, and Gibbon retreated to the closest U.S. garrison, Fort Fetterman. General Terry directed Custer to lead a forward scouting mission to determine the strength of the Indian forces.

On June 25, 1876, Custer discovered a huge Indian encampment, whose numbers were so large, that even with spyglasses no one could produce an accurate estimate. Today, historians believe there were as many as 15,000 Indians present in the valley of the Little Big Horn. Custer made a fatal mistake for him and for his troops. He chose to ignore the standing orders to wait for the arrival of Terry and Crook, and launched an attack against the camp. Worse, he split his small force into three separate units in order to mount the assault from three different directions. Two of those units, led respectively by Captain Benteen and Major Reno survived the onslaught, though not without casualties. Oddly enough, Custer's battalion was not only outmanned but outgunned. Over 4000 Sioux, Cheyenne, and Arapaho warriors overwhelmed Custer's men with Winchester repeating rifles provided them by the U.S. government for hunting. Custer's troops had obsolete carbines, and Custer had left behind Gatling guns at Fort Fetterman in the interest of rapid movement.

President Ulysses Grant, in the aftermath of the Battle of Little Big Horn, expressed what was probably the most accurate assessment Custer's leadership during the engagement. In an interview with the *New York Herald* Grant stated, "I regard Custer's Massacre was a sacrifice of troops, brought on by Custer himself, that was wholly unnecessary."

The Story of Colonel Chamberlain

When Colonel Joshua Lawrence Chamberlain (see Figure 8.1.4) assumed command of the 20th Maine Regiment, it badly needed replacements. Illness and fighting had drained the combat power of the regiment to a dangerously low level.

One month before the Battle of Gettysburg, however, 120 mutineers (soldiers who had taken part in a mutiny) from the 2nd Maine Regiment were brought to Chamberlain's unit by guards with fixed bayonets. General Meade, the Corps Commander, ordered them to be attached to the 20th Maine Regiment as replacements and ordered Chamberlain to shoot them if they did not do their duty.

Chamberlain decided to find out why they were mutineers. When they enlisted at the outbreak of the war, the 2nd Maine Regiment had been formed to serve for three months. During those three months, the Maine Legislature authorized raising ten regiments to serve for two years; it included the 2nd Maine as one of those ten regiments.

Somehow, a foul-up occurred in the enlistment papers for the soldiers of the 2nd Maine. Two-thirds of the members signed up for two years; the other one-third signed up for three years. After two years passed, the men who enlisted for two years had completed their obligation and departed for home. The other one-third (the 120 mutineers) were ordered to remain on duty. Believing that the order was a gross injustice, they refused to serve, and awaited court martial and possible execution for desertion.

Chamberlain believed that if these stubborn men were willing to face death because of their conviction of being treated unfairly, they would be of infinitely more value to the Union Army facing the Confederate Army than a firing squad. Chamberlain desperately needed seasoned veterans of strong will, and knew that executing these men was not the correct course of action. He asked for and received permission from General Meade to handle them in his own way.

Chamberlain returned to his unit and met with the angry soldiers, who were still under guard. Upon learning that they had not eaten in three days, he made sure

Figure 8.1.4: Colonel Joshua Lawrence Chamberlain.

Courtesy of AP/Wide World Photos.

that they were fed. He then broke their group spirit by splitting them up and assigning them to different companies.

He told them that he would treat them as soldiers with all the rights of soldiers. He also assured them that he would look into their case and do what he could to help them. In the meantime, he indicated that he would appreciate it if they would do duty with the 20th Maine Regiment. All but six went along with Chamberlain's suggestion. The six who refused were held for court-martials.

Chamberlain's actions and honesty turned away the anger of these soldiers and showed how the right word, spoken quietly and firmly at the right time, can persuade subordinates to perform. By treating these rebellious soldiers with fairness and respect, he rekindled their motivation to fight. Without their help, the 20th Maine Regiment would probably have been overwhelmed in their defensive position at Little Round Top, which might have resulted in a Union loss at the Battle of Gettysburg—and even the loss of the war. As you can see by this example, respect builds trust and it is an essential part of being an effective leader.

Contingency Plan

Good leaders recognize the importance of having a **contingency** plan. This is a plan of action you can call up or rely on when your original decision isn't working as you had planned. Contingency plans can be considered "Plan B," and are necessary to keep your leadership flow running smoothly.

A good leader looks ahead and plans for the unexpected. By developing a contingency plan, you and your followers will never be caught off guard.

Key Note Term

contingency—a plan to cope with events whose occurrence, timing and severity cannot be predicted

After Action Review

When your decisions are made, plans implemented, orders carried out, and actions completed, you should always perform an **After Action Review.** This gives you a chance to look over your decisions and see what worked well and what needs improvement. An After Action Review can take place in the form of a meeting with superiors or team members, or you can study your decisions and plans by yourself to determine strengths and weaknesses in your leadership abilities. After Action Reviews should always cast a critical eye on the actions performed, and it should be understood that even negative feedback can be useful and constructive.

Key Note Term

After Action Review—a review of decisions, orders, and actions implemented after the actions are carried out

Conclusion

Leadership brings with it great responsibility. By applying the 11 principles of leadership, along with logic and reasoning, you can develop sound decision-making techniques that will be respected by your followers as well as your peers. Contingency plans are always necessary to safeguard against the unexpected, and After Action Reviews can tell you what worked, what didn't, and where your strengths and weaknesses lie.

Lesson Review

1. What are the 11 principles of leadership?

2. Choose one principle of leadership and discuss it in relation to the decision-making process.

3. What can you learn from an After Action Review? Why is it important?

4. Why is it important to have a contingency plan? What might happen if there wasn't a contingency plan?

Case Study

Exercise: Leadership Case Study to discuss the events and impact of a significant leadership decision.

- **Explanation of issue or problem**
- **Choices available to the leader**
- **Consequences of those decisions**
- **Opinion about the effectiveness of the leader's decision**
- **What might have happened if the leader had made a different decision?**

Is Iraq Another Vietnam?

In April 2004, a rising tide of insurgency prompted Senator Ted Kennedy to venture the comparison "Iraq is George Bush's Vietnam." Indeed, the wave of rebellion sweeping across Iraq a year after the conclusion of major combat operations drew many parallels to the 1968 Tet Offensive marking the turning point to the American conflict and its eventual loss in Vietnam. Is Iraq another Vietnam?

The U.S. became embroiled in Vietnam as part of its policy of containing communism during the Cold War. American military personnel began deploying to South Vietnam in 1954 to strengthen the country against communist North Vietnam. In 1960, Ho Chi Minh formed the National Liberation Front to undermine and defeat the government of South Vietnam. Citing a reported North Vietnamese attack against U.S. destroyers in the Gulf of Tonkin, in 1964, Congress authorized President Lyndon Johnson to take "all necessary measures" to win in Vietnam. Drafting all eligible males, the U.S. began a military buildup that placed some 525,000 troops in the region by 1968. Despite mounting casualties against an intractable enemy, Gen. William Westmoreland confidently assured Congress in October 1967, that "We have got our opponents almost on the ropes." Six weeks later, the Viet Cong shocked the world by launching the Tet Offensive involving simultaneous uprisings by communists living undercover in 39 of the 44 provincial capitals of South Vietnam. U.S. forces succeeded in suppressing the rebellion and restoring order at a cost of 34,000 Viet Cong killed, compared to 2,500 Americans. Technically it was a military victory, but Tet precipitated a crisis of confidence in the Johnson administration prompting the President to not seek re-election. President Richard Nixon rode into office promising "peace with honor" and began the drawdown that eventually lost Vietnam.

The U.S. went to war in Iraq as part of its global war on terrorism. American military personnel deployed to the region in 1990, to defend Saudi Arabia against Iraqi aggression in Kuwait. In 1991, Saddam Hussein was defeated by the combined forces of a U.S. led coalition and made to withdraw from Kuwait. The U.S. maintained a military presence in the region to deter future Iraqi aggression at the hands of Saddam Hussein. Disaffected by his government's actions, Osama bin Laden, a rich Saudi businessman, formed al Qaeda to dislodge American forces in the Middle East.

Operating from protected bases in Afghanistan, al Qaeda bombed two U.S. embassies in Africa, raided the U.S. destroyer Cole in Yemen, and mounted direct attacks against the U.S. on September 11, 2001. President Bush swiftly mounted Operation ENDURING FREEDOM eliminating the Taliban government and eradicating state sponsored terrorism in Afghanistan. A year later he turned his sights towards Iraq. In October 2002, President Bush made his case to America that Iraq presented an imminent threat: "Iraq could decide on any given day to provide a biological or chemical weapon to a terrorist group or individual terrorists. Alliance with terrorists could allow the Iraqi regime to attack America without leaving any fingerprints." Despite the absence of indisputable evidence Saddam Hussein possessed weapons of mass destruction, President Bush made his case that "we cannot wait for the final proof—the smoking gun—that could come in the form of a mushroom cloud." On March 20, 2003, U.S. led forces struck out from Kuwait into Iraq. Twenty-six days later Saddam Hussein's regime collapsed and American soldiers were sitting in his palaces in Baghdad. One-hundred-and-seventy-two Americans were killed during Phase III of Operation IRAQI FREEDOM. Casualties continued to mount as the U.S. switched to Phase IV Stability Operations. To the chagrin of many, no evidence of weapons of mass destruction ever surfaced. In April 2004, dissident factions in Fallujah staged an uprising killing 40 American soldiers in a week of the bloodiest fighting since President Bush dramatically announced the "end of major combat operations" a year earlier.

Is Iraq another Vietnam? Analysts disagree. They cite obvious evidence to the contrary including:

- **Vietnam started as a guerrilla war and then escalated into a conventional war; Iraq started as a conventional war and now it's deteriorated into a guerrilla war.**

- **The Vietnam War lasted more than a decade and took 58,000 American lives; the U.S. death toll in Iraq after 13 months was less than 700.**

- **President Johnson said Vietnam was fought to stop the spread of communism in Southeast Asia; President Bush called Iraq part of a war against a network of terrorists who have targeted the U.S.**

- **American forces in Vietnam were subject to forced conscription under the draft; American forces in Iraq are all volunteers.**

Other, evidence seems to support the comparison:

- **President Johnson escalated the war in Vietnam on flimsy proof U.S. destroyers were twice attacked in the Gulf of Tonkin; no weapons of mass destruction have been found in Iraq.**

- **President Johnson suffered a "credibility gap" after Tet soundly disproved the optimistic predictions of Gen. William Westmoreland; Vice President Dick Cheney was harshly criticized following the uprisings in Fallujah for predicting U.S. forces would be greeted as "liberators."**

All analysts agree, however, that it's too early to tell how events will unfold in Iraq, yet the comparison is worth examining. According to Susan Page of *USA Today*, "The comparison has power because, 30 years after it ended, the war in Vietnam continues to stand as a symbol of foreign policy gone awry."

References

"Vietnam War," Infoplease, www.infoplease.com/ipa/A0001292.html

"Vietnam War," www.spartacus.schoolnet.co.uk/VietnamWar.htm

"Kennedy: 'Iraq is George Bush's Vietnam,'" Brad Wright and Jennifer Yuille, CNN Washington Bureau, CNN.com

"Is Iraq Becoming Another Vietnam?" Susan Page, USA TODAY, www.usatoday.com

"Vietnam's 1968 Tet Offensive Offers Parallels for Today," A. J. Langguth, Common Dreams News Center, www.commondreams.org

"President Bush Outlines Iraqi Threat," Office of the Press Secretary, October 7, 2002, www.whitehouse.gov

"President Bush Addresses the Nation," Office of the Press Secretary, March 19, 2003, www.whitehouse.gov

"American Soldier, General Tommy Franks," Malcolm McConnell, Harper-Collins Publishers Inc., New York, NY, 2004.

1. **Explanation of issue or problem. Will the war in Iraq go the same way as the Vietnam War?**

Contrary Evidence:

Vietnam started as a guerrilla war and then escalated into a conventional war; Iraq, started as a conventional war and now it's deteriorated into a guerrilla war.

The Vietnam War lasted more than a decade and took 58,000 American lives; the U.S. death toll in Iraq after 13 months was less than 700.

President Johnson said Vietnam was fought to stop the spread of communism in Southeast Asia; President Bush called Iraq part of a war against a network of terrorists who have targeted the U.S.

American forces in Vietnam were subject to forced conscription under the draft; American forces in Iraq are all volunteers.

Supporting Evidence:

President Johnson escalated the war in Vietnam on flimsy proof U.S. destroyers were twice attacked in the Gulf of Tonkin; no weapons of mass destruction have been found in Iraq.

President Johnson suffered a "credibility gap" after Tet soundly disproved the optimistic predictions of Gen. William Westmoreland; Vice President Dick Cheney was harshly criticized following the uprisings in Fallujah for predicting U.S. forces would be greeted as "liberators."

2. Choices available to the leader.

A. Iraq: Delay military action, continue economic and political efforts to isolate and dismantle the threat posed by Saddam Hussein.

B. Vietnam: Avoid military involvement in Vietnam.

3. Consequences of those decisions.

A. "Iraq could decide on any given day to provide a biological or chemical weapon to a terrorist group or individual terrorists. Alliance with terrorists could allow the Iraqi regime to attack America without leaving any fingerprints . . . we cannot wait for the final proof—the smoking gun—that could come in the form of a mushroom cloud."

B. To justify support for South Vietnam, President Dwight Eisenhower and Vice President Richard Nixon put forward the "Domino Theory." It was argued that if the first domino is knocked over then the rest will topple in turn. Applying this to Southeast Asia, President Eisenhower argued that if South Vietnam was taken by communists, then the other countries in the region such as Laos, Cambodia, Thailand, Burma, Malaysia, and Indonesia would follow.

4. Opinion about the effectiveness of the leader's decision.

5. What might have happened if the leader had made a different decision?

Lesson 2

Ethical Choices, Decisions, and Consequences

Key Term

ethical dilemma

What You Will Learn to Do

- Illustrate how ethical choices and decisions can lead to good or bad consequences

Linked Core Abilities

- Communicate using verbal, non-verbal, visual, and written techniques
- Apply critical thinking techniques

Skills and Knowledge You Will Gain Along the Way

- Differentiate between ethical and unethical behavior
- Examine ethics codes
- Explore how circumstances impact an ethical dilemma
- Discuss the consequences of ethical and unethical decisions
- Define key word contained in this lesson

Chapter 8

Introduction

As a leader, you are responsible for making decisions that affect others within and outside your organization. You need to consider the consequences before deciding on a course of action. As you learned in an earlier lesson, leaders have three ethical responsibilities: to be a good role model; to develop followers in an ethical manner; and to lead in such a way to avoid ethical dilemmas. In this lesson you will examine ethical dilemmas. You will form opinions about the decisions and consequences associated with ethical dilemmas.

Ethical, Moral, Unethical, Immoral

In ordinary language, the words *ethical* and *moral* and *unethical* and *immoral* are frequently used interchangeably; that is, we speak of the ethical or moral person or act. On the other hand, we speak of codes of ethics, but only infrequently do we mention codes of morality. Some reserve the terms moral and immoral only for the realm of sexuality and use the words *ethical* and *unethical* when discussing how the business and professional communities should behave toward their members or toward the public. More commonly, however, we use none of these words as often as we use the terms *good, bad, right,* and *wrong.* What do all of these words mean, and what are the relationships among them?

Ethics comes from the Greek *ethos,* meaning character. *Morality* comes from the Latin *moralis,* meaning customs or manners. Ethics, then, seems to pertain to the individual character of a person or persons, whereas morality seems to point to the relationships between human beings. Nevertheless, in ordinary language, whether we call a person ethical or moral, or an act unethical or immoral, doesn't really make any difference. In philosophy, however, the term *ethics* also is used to refer to a specific area of study: the area of morality, concentrates on human conduct and human values.

When we speak of people as being moral or ethical, we usually mean that they are good people, and when we speak of them as being immoral or unethical, we mean that they are bad people. When we refer to certain human actions as being moral, ethical, immoral, and unethical, we mean that they are right or wrong. The simplicity of these definitions, however, ends here, for how do we define a right or wrong action or a good or bad person? What are the human standards by which such decisions can be made? These are the more difficult questions that make up the greater part of the study of morality, and they will be discussed in more detail in later chapters. The important thing to remember here is that *moral, ethical, immoral,* and *unethical,* essentially mean *good, right, bad,* and *wrong,* often depending upon whether one is referring to people themselves or to their actions.

Characteristics of Good, Bad, Right, Wrong, Happiness, or Pleasure

It seems to be an empirical fact that whatever human beings consider to be good involves happiness and pleasure in some way, and whatever they consider to be bad involves unhappiness and pain in some way. This view of what is good has traditionally been called "hedonism." As long as the widest range of interpretation is given to these words (from simple sensual pleasures to intellectual or spiritual pleasures and from sensual pain to deep emotional unhappiness), then it is difficult to deny that whatever is good involves at least some pleasure or happiness, and whatever is bad involves some pain or unhappiness.

One element involved in the achievement of happiness is the necessity of taking the long-rather than the short-range view. People may undergo some pain or unhappiness to attain some pleasure or happiness in the long run. For example, we will put up with the pain of having our teeth drilled to keep our teeth and gums healthy so that we may enjoy eating and the general good health that results from having teeth that are well maintained. Similarly, people may do very difficult and even painful work for two days to earn money that will bring them pleasure and happiness for a week or two (see Figure 8.2.1).

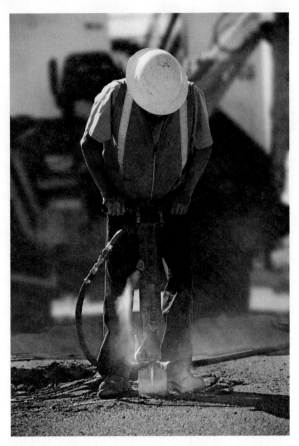

Figure 8.2.1: Enduring hard labor affords workers a living wage.

Courtesy of Bruce Burkhardt/Corbis Images.

Furthermore, the term *good* should be defined in the context of human experience and human relationships rather than in an abstract sense only. For example, knowledge and power in themselves are not good unless a human being derives some satisfaction from them or unless they contribute in some way to moral and meaningful human relationships. They are otherwise nonmoral.

What about actions that will bring someone some good but will cause pain to another, such as those of a sadist who gains pleasure from violently mistreating another human being? Our original statement was that everything that is good will bring some person satisfaction, pleasure, or happiness of some kind, but this statement does not necessarily work in the reverse—that everything that brings someone satisfaction is necessarily good. There certainly are "malicious pleasures."

Excellence

William Frankena states that whatever is good will also probably involve "some kind or degree of excellence." He goes on to say that "what is bad in itself is so because of the presence of either pain or unhappiness or of some kind of defect or lack of excellence." Excellence is an important addition to pleasure or satisfaction in that it makes "experiences or activities better or worse than they would otherwise be." For example, the enjoyment or satisfaction gained from hearing a concert, seeing a fine movie, or reading a good book is due, to a great extent, to the excellence of the creators and presenters of these events (composers, performers, directors, actors, writers). Another and perhaps more profound example of the importance of excellence is that if one gains satisfaction or pleasure from witnessing a well-conducted court case and from seeing and hearing the judge and the lawyers perform their duties well, that satisfaction will be deepened if the judge and the lawyers are also excellent people; that is, if they are kind, fair, and compassionate human beings in addition to being clever and able.

Whatever is good, then, will probably contain some pleasure, happiness, and excellence, whereas whatever is bad will probably contain their opposites: pain, unhappiness, and lack of excellence. This is to say that only *some* of these elements are present. For example, a good person performing a right action might not be particularly happy and might even find what he or she is doing painful; nonetheless, the recipients of the right action might be made happy by it and the right action also might involve excellence.

Harmony and Creativity

There are two other attributes of "good" and "right" that may add to our definition; they are harmony and creativity on the "good" side and discord, or disharmony, and lack of creativity on the "bad" side. If an action is creative or can aid human beings in becoming creative and, at the same time, help to bring about a harmonious integration of as many human beings as possible, then we can say it is a right action. If an action has the opposite effect, then we can say that it is a wrong action.

For example, if a person or a group of people can end a war between two nations and create an honorable and lasting peace, a right or good action has been performed. It can allow members of both nations to be creative rather than destructive and can create harmony between both sides and within each nation. On the other hand, causing or starting a war between two nations will have just the opposite effect. Lester A. Kirkendall stresses these points and also adds to what was stated earlier in this lesson about the necessity of placing the emphasis on what is good or excellent in human experience and relationships:

> *Whenever a decision or a choice is to be made concerning behavior, the moral decision will be the one which works toward the creation of trust, confidence, and integrity in relationships. It should increase the capacity of individuals to cooperate, and enhance the sense of self-respect in the individual. Acts that create distrust, suspicion, and misunderstanding, that build barriers and destroy integrity are immoral. They decrease the individual's sense of self-respect and rather than producing a capacity to work together they separate people and break down the capacity for communication.*

Amoral

Amoral means having no moral sense, or being indifferent to right and wrong. This term can be applied to very few people. Certain people who have had prefrontal lobotomies tend to act amorally after the operation; that is, they have no sense of right and wrong. Arid there are a few human beings who, despite moral education, have remained or become amoral. These tend to be found among certain criminal types who can't seem to realize they've done anything wrong. They tend not to have any remorse, regret, or concern for what they have done.

One such example of an amoral person is Gregory Powell, who, with Jimmy Lee Smith, gratuitously killed a policeman in an onion field south of Bakersfield, California. A good description of him and his attitude can be found in Joseph Wambaugh's book, *The Onion Field*. Another such example is Colin Pitchfork, another real-life character. Pitchfork raped and killed two young girls in England and was described by Wambaugh in his book, *The Blooding*. In that book Wambaugh, also quotes from various psychologists speaking about the amoral, psychopathological, sociopathological personality, which is defined as "a person characterized by emotional instability, lack of sound judgment, perverse and impulsive (often criminal) behavior, inability to learn from experience, amoral and asocial feelings, and other serious personality defects." He describes "the most important feature of the psychopath . . . as his monumental irresponsibility. He knows what the ethical rules are, at least he can repeat them parrot-like, but they are void of meaning to him." He quotes further: "No sense of conscience, guilt, or remorse is present. Harmful acts are committed without discomfort or shame." Amorality, then, is basically an attitude that some—luckily only a few—human beings possess.

All of this doesn't mean that amoral criminals should not be morally blamed and punished for their wrongdoings. In fact, such people are even more dangerous to society than those who can distinguish right from wrong because usually they are morally uneducable. Society, therefore, needs even more protection from such criminals.

Nonmoral

The word nonmoral means "out of the realm of morality altogether." For example, inanimate objects such as cars and guns are neither moral nor immoral. A person using the car or gun may use it immorally, but the things themselves are nonmoral. Many areas of study (for instance, mathematics, astronomy, and physics) are in themselves nonmoral, but because human beings are involved in these areas, morality also may be involved. A mathematics problem is neither moral nor immoral in itself, however, if it provides the means by which a hydrogen bomb can be exploded then moral issues certainly will be forthcoming.

The immoral person knowingly violates human moral standards by doing something wrong or by being bad. The amoral person may also violate moral standards because he or she has no moral sense. Something that is nonmoral can neither be good nor bad nor do anything right or wrong simply because it does not fall within the scope of morality.

Codes of Conduct

As a guideline for ethical and moral behavior, many organizations offer a code of conduct. Similar to an organization's mission statement, this code outlines how employees, volunteers, and so on are expected to conduct themselves. The following is part of the Code of the U.S. Fighting Force, and clearly explains the obligation and actions of Army soldiers as well as defines the responsibilities the Army has towards its fighting forces.

A. **As a member of the armed forces of the United States, you are protecting your nation. It is your duty to oppose all enemies of the United States in combat or, if a captive, in a prisoner of war compound. Your behavior is guided by the Code of Conduct, which has evolved from the heroic lives, experiences and deeds of Americans from the Revolutionary War to the Southeast Asian Conflict.**

B. Your obligations as a U.S. citizen and a member of the armed forces result from the traditional values that underlie the American experience as a nation. These values are best expressed in the U.S. Constitution and Bill of Rights, which you have sworn to uphold and defend. You would have these obligations—to your country, your service and unit and your fellow Americans—even if the Code of Conduct had never been formulated as a high standard of general behavior.

C. Just as you have a responsibility to your country under the Code of Conduct, the United States government has an equal responsibility—always to keep faith with you and stand by you as you fight for your country. If you are unfortunate enough to become a prisoner of war, you may rest assured that your government will care for your dependents and will never forget you. Furthermore, the government will use every practical means to contact, support and gain release for you and for all other prisoners of war.

D. To live up to the code, you must know not only its words but the ideas and principles behind those words.

Later in the Code, it states how a soldier is to behave if captured by the enemy.

A. I will never surrender of my own free will. If in command, I will never surrender the members of my command while they still have the means to resist.

B. As an individual, a member of the armed forces may never voluntarily surrender. When isolated and no longer able to inflict casualties on the enemy, the American soldier has an obligation to evade capture and rejoin friendly forces.

C. Only when evasion by an individual is impossible and further fighting would lead only to death with no significant loss to the enemy should one consider surrender. With all reasonable means of resistance exhausted and with certain death the only alternative, capture does not imply dishonor.

D. The responsibility and authority of a commander never extends to the surrender of a command to the enemy while the command has the power to fight and evade. When isolated, cut off or surrounded, a unit must continue to fight until relieved or able to rejoin friendly forces through continued efforts to break out or evade the enemy.

Ethical Dilemmas

Key Note Term

ethical dilemma—a situation where you must weigh the consequences of your actions before making a decision or taking action

Have you ever been faced with a situation where you have two choices? One choice is morally right but would result in bad consequences; the other choice is morally wrong but would lead to good consequences. If doing what is right produces something bad, or if doing what is wrong produces something good, the force of moral and ethical obligation may seem balanced by the reality of the good end. You can have the satisfaction of being right, regardless of the damage done; or you can aim for what seems to be the best outcome, regardless of what wrongs must be committed. This is called an **ethical dilemma.** And in these situations, many times what you actually do is quite different from what you should do.

Take, for example, this situation:

You run an orphanage and have had a hard time making ends meet. A car dealership offers you a new van worth $15,000 for free if you will falsely report to the government that the dealership donated a van worth $30,000. You really need the van and it will give you an opportunity to make the children happy. Do you agree to take the van?

Of course, you know that taking the van under the condition of lying on a tax form is not only illegal, but unethical as well. But the van would help so very much to get the children to school, to medical appointments, and so on. At the same time, if the Internal Revenue Service found out, you could face losing your orphanage. The ethical decision to make here is to not take the van under these circumstances. Aside from the legal issues, the negative potential consequences to taking the van far outweigh the positive potential consequences.

Or how about this: You are shopping and notice a woman stuffing a pair of socks into her purse. Do you report her? You've always been told it's not right to "tattle" on someone when they do something wrong, and you might think that she's not really hurting anyone by stealing these socks. You know, however, that stealing is wrong. Should you confront her about her actions? Would you tell a sales clerk? Would you ignore the situation? In this case, what would you do? What is your responsibility?

Sometimes personal circumstances can influence or impact the way you resolve an ethical dilemma. For example, it would be much easier to make an ethical decision about the woman stuffing socks in her purse if you didn't know the woman. But change the situation and imagine the woman is someone you know, maybe a classmate. How would that change your behavior and your decision to act?

More for You to Consider

A 31-year-old twice-convicted robber became the first California state prisoner (and likely the first in the U.S.) to receive a heart transplant. He suffered from a viral infection that had damaged his heart valves. Should 1 million dollars of taxpayer money be spent on a convict who was imprisoned for a violent felony?

As another example, scientists would argue that without the ability to use animals for experimentation, humans would have to be used and sometimes harmed or killed in the search for medical cures. These scientists would also argue that animals have much less value than human beings, so it is morally correct to use them for experimentation. Animal rights activists would counter by saying that animals are thinking, feeling beings that suffer pain to the same degree as humans, and that it is immoral to put an animal through suffering just so humans can make medical and scientific progress. What do you think?

Questions to Ask Yourself

When trying to resolve an ethical dilemma, it helps to ask specific questions. These questions include:

- **Am I being fair and honest?**
- **Would I like to be treated this way?**
- **Will my decision stand the test of time?**
- **How will I feel about myself afterwards?**
- **How would it look if reported in the newspaper?**
- **Will I sleep soundly tonight?**
- **How would I feel if my family, friends, and neighbors knew what I was doing?**

Your answers to these questions will guide you towards making good, ethical decisions.

Ethical Decision Making

One criterion of a satisfactory decision is that the decision and subsequent action be *ethical.* Ethical decisions promote well-being and do not cause harm to members of an organization or to other people affected by an organization's activities. Although it is easy to describe what an ethical decision is, sometimes it is difficult to determine the boundary between ethical and unethical decisions in an organization. Is it ethical, for example, for a pharmaceutical company to decide to charge a high price for a lifesaving drug, thus making it unaffordable to some people?

On the one hand, it can be argued that the drug is costly to produce and the company needs the revenues to continue producing the drug as well as to research ways to improve its effectiveness. On the other hand, it can be argued that the company has a moral or ethical obligation to make the drug available to as many people as possible. In 2004, for example, *Sheering Plough* raised the price of its best-selling AIDS prevention drug by 500 percent, causing an uproar among doctors and patients who claimed that this would lead to great hardship for patients, many of whom would no longer be able to afford it. *Sheering Plough* simply said that it had been charging too low a price for its valuable drug and that it had the right to increase its price.

Some people deliberately make unethical decisions to benefit themselves or their organizations, but even decision makers who strive to be ethical are sometimes faced with difficult choices or ethical dilemmas. Under these circumstances, making acceptable decisions that are ethical can be difficult. One example of blatantly unethical decision making by pharmaceutical companies occurred in 1999, when six of them admitted they had conspired to artificially raise the price of vitamins, such as vitamins A, B2, C, E, and beta carotene. Swiss giant Hoffman-La Roche agreed to pay $500 million in criminal fines, and German Company BASF paid a $225 million fine; the others were also fined large amounts. How could this happen?

Senior managers from each of these companies' vitamin divisions jointly made the decision to inflate their division's profits and to act unethically at the expense of consumers. In several meetings around the world, they worked out the details of the plot, which went undiscovered for several years. Many of the top managers involved have been prosecuted in their home countries, and all have been fired. BASF, for example, completely replaced its worldwide management team. What has been the end result of this fiasco for these companies? All have agreed to create a special "ethics officer" position within their organizations. The ethics officer is responsible for developing new ethical standards with regard to how decisions are made. The ethics officer is also responsible for listening to employees' complaints about unethical behavior, training employees to make ethical decisions, and counseling top managers to prevent further wrongdoing.

Making the Decision

When making a decision regarding an ethical dilemma, it's best to have set criteria from which to work. Answering the following questions might be helpful when confronted by an ethical dilemma.

- **What options do you see are available to resolve this dilemma?**
- **Which options are the most compelling? Why?**
- **How would you resolve the dilemma?**
- **What values did you rely on to make your decision?**
- **What consequences (if any) do you see your decision has on the others involved?**
- **Could you personally live with this decision? If not, examine other options to your dilemma.**

Figure 8.2.2: One option is to turn and walk away.

Courtesy of Anthony Redpath/Corbis Images.

What Are Your Options?

In any situation, there are a variety of options available to you. Some of these are good and reasonable; others can produce short- and long-term negative effects. Going back to the example of the woman and the socks, your options include:

- **Turning away and forgetting that you saw anything (see Figure 8.2.2)**
- **Telling a cashier**
- **Confronting the woman yourself**

Out of these three options, which are the most compelling?

Which Options Are Most Compelling?

You've determined your available options. Now it's time to figure out which ones would work best in this specific situation. Doing nothing is one option. You can figure that it's none of your business, and even though you know stealing is wrong, this pair of stolen socks really doesn't concern you. But then you remember that the store might have to raise its prices on various items to cover the cost of shoplifted merchandise, so this does directly affect you. You might decide that doing nothing is not a compelling option.

Telling a cashier is another option. You've been told your entire life that "tattling" is wrong, but you feel that the cashier would probably know how to handle this situation. She most likely would call a security person who is trained in dealing with circumstances like this, would probably speak to the woman and get the socks back from her, or have her pay for the items. This seems like a compelling option.

Your third option is to confront the woman yourself. But what if the woman told you that she was going to pay for the socks before she left the store, and that this is none of your business? What would you do then? Or what if she yelled at you, or shoved you? This doesn't seem like a good option.

How Would You Like to Resolve the Dilemma?

When making ethical decisions, you need to look down the road and imagine how you'd like the situation resolved. In most cases, you don't want to see anyone hurt. You don't want to damage friendships and other relationships. You just want to do the right things for the right reasons. In this case, you feel that doing nothing will not resolve the problem to the best end. And confronting the woman isn't an option. All you want is for the woman to pay for the socks or return them to the store.

What Values Did You Rely on?

Values are taught to us at a very early age. Some values you have learned from your family, such as The Golden Rule ("do unto others as you'd have them do unto you"). Some you have learned from your church, such as those found in The Ten Commandments. Others you have learned from your friends and the situations you've lived through, such as to have a friend you need to be a friend. One of your values is that stealing is wrong, but hurting an individual is also wrong. So you decide that telling a cashier is the best course of action.

What Are the Consequences to Your Actions?

You tell the cashier and a security person arrives to speak with you. You point out the woman with the socks, and the security person talks with her. She is embarrassed, but as the customer and security person talk, she realizes that she needs to pay for the merchandise, or be arrested for shoplifting. She pays for the socks and vows to never try shoplifting again.

Can You Live with Your Decision?

In this case, the decision you made and the course of action you took is very easy to live with. The store didn't lose money on the merchandise; the woman learned a lesson and has decided to never shoplift again; and you know you did the right thing.

Not all ethical decisions are that easy, however. Sometimes your personal values are different from others. Sometimes you need to understand where your values come from, and be open to change or adjust your thinking in different situations. And sometimes doing the right and ethical thing can be hard, especially when the consequences of your action are different from how you'd like to see a situation resolved.

Setting the Example

When making an ethical decision and taking action on it, sometimes things just don't turn out as well as you might have liked. As discussed in the previous lesson, leaders must know themselves through self-evaluation and stand on their convictions. They must take responsibility for their actions and set an example for their team. One way to avoid dealing with ethical dilemmas within your unit is to lead by example and develop followers in an ethical manner. Set high standards, be loyal, be morally and ethically courageous, establish principles and stand by them, and develop convictions within your followers that you are the best role model for them.

Being the best role model you can possibly be is crucial to avoiding ethical problems, dilemmas, and situations within your team. Your followers will follow your example, so if you expect honor, integrity, courage, loyalty, respect, and ethical behavior from your team members, you must demonstrate these traits yourself. Your personal example affects people more than any amount of instruction or form of discipline. This might seem like a heavy responsibility, but remember that no aspect of leadership is more powerful than the example you set.

Conclusion

Ethical dilemmas can occur in any setting, whether it's a personal or professional arena. But one of the best ways to avoid ethical dilemmas within your leadership role is to set the example for those whom you lead. Your followers will imitate you and your actions, so by being the best, showing sound and fair decision-making skills, and treating your followers with respect and dignity, you instill ethical behavior in them.

When faced with an ethical dilemma, ask yourself what options are available to you, how you would like to see the situation resolved to everyone's benefit, and whether your decision is something you can live with.

In the following lesson, you will learn about global citizenship and what it takes to be a good global citizen. You will also learn about global choices, decisions, and consequences.

Lesson Review

1. Define the term "ethical dilemma."

2. Refer back to the scenario of the woman stealing the socks in the store. Which option would you choose? Why?

3. Have you ever been faced with an ethical dilemma? How did you solve it?

4. You discover Bill Gates' wallet lying on the street. It contains $10,000.00 in cash. Do you send it back to him?

Case Study

Exercise: Ethical Case Study—Participate in a discussion about the **ethical choices and consequences** of an assigned case study. Develop a multi-flow map to illustrate the **motives and consequences** of the decisions that were made. Discuss how the consequences had a **positive or negative impact.**

The Decision to Drop the Atomic Bomb in World War II

World War II erupted in Europe when Hitler invaded Poland, September 1, 1939. Concerned that Nazi Germany might develop an atomic weapon of unimaginable destruction, Albert Einstein wrote to President Roosevelt, warning him of the danger. Sufficiently alarmed, the United States embarked on a top secret project, code named "Manhattan," to develop an atomic bomb. At $2,000,000,000, the Manhattan Project was the riskiest and most expensive program ever undertaken by the U.S. Government up to that time.

The United States was drawn into World War II after Japanese forces attacked the Pacific Fleet at Pearl Harbor Hawaii, December 7, 1941 (see Figure 8.2.3). American forces were immediately rushed to the European and Pacific theaters to fight the combined Axis Powers of Germany and Japan. Believing Hitler was the bigger threat, the Allies, led by the United States, Great Britain, and Soviet Union, agreed on a "Europe First" policy, focusing their attention against the Nazis. Germany was defeated May 5, 1945, before either side could build an atomic bomb. A top secret report concluded that neither Germany nor Japan was capable of producing an atomic bomb, yet the Manhattan Project continued working to build one.

Figure 8.2.3: Pearl Harbor was attacked by the Japanese on December 7, 1941.

Courtesy of The Granger Collection, New York.

On July 16, 1945, American scientists successfully detonated the first atomic device at Trinity Site near their secluded laboratories in Los Alamos, New Mexico. The United States was still at war with Japan. Harry S. Truman was President of the United States, having succeeded Roosevelt who died in office April 16, 1945. While war raged in Europe, American and British forces slugged their way across the Pacific in their drive towards Tokyo. The Soviet Union had not participated in the Pacific campaign, choosing to remain neutral with Japan while fighting for survival against Germany. Truman was in Potsdam meeting with Churchill, trying to enlist the aide of Stalin, when he learned of the atomic test at Trinity. Truman was troubled by the mounting casualties in the Pacific as Allied forces drew nearer the Japanese home islands. Driven by the Bushido warrior code, the Japanese were prepared to resist to the last, and more willing to die than surrender. Over 207,000 Japanese gave their lives while exacting a huge toll on American forces invading Okinawa. The Joint Chiefs told Truman to expect over 1,000,000 American casualties and even larger number of Japanese dead in the pending attack on the home islands. Truman appointed a committee to evaluate using the atomic bomb. The committee examined many options, including a demonstration in Tokyo Bay, but Los Alamos was uncertain the device would detonate. Rather than lose a valuable war asset, and to emphasize its destructive power, the committee recommended dropping the atomic bomb on a city. By August 1945, the United States had two nuclear bombs in its arsenal.

On August 6, 1945, the Enola Gay dropped the first atomic bomb on Hiroshima. Over 140,000 Japanese were killed in the blast, and an uncounted number died from the lingering effects of radiation. On August 9, 1945, a second atomic bomb was dropped on the city of Nagasaki. The next day, August 10, 1945, Japan indicated its willingness to surrender.

References

http://www.me.utexas.edu/~uer/manhattan/debates.html

http://www.nuclearfiles.org/etinternationallaw/granoff-nuclearweaponsethicsmoralsandlaw.htm

Borman, Stu, "Chemists Reminisce on 50th Anniversary of the Atomic Bomb," *Chemical & Engineering News* (July 17, 1995).

Dyson, J.D., "Documentation and Diagrams of the Atomic Bomb," http://neutrino.nuc.berkeley.edu/neutronics/todd/nuc.bomb.html (Berkeley: Todd's Atomic Homepage, March 1997).

Fermi, Rachel, and Samara, Esther, *Picturing the Bomb* (Japan: Harry N. Abrams, Inc., 1995), pp. 96–122.

Kraus, Joe, "Enola Gay Perspectives: Scientists," http://www.glue.umd.edu/~enola/dvel (College of Library and Information Services at the University of Maryland, College Park, May 1996).

Moody, Sid, and Kincaid, Cliff, "The Manhattan Project," *American Legion Magazine,* vol. 139 (August 1995), pp. 30–32.

Parshall, Gerald, "Shockwave," *U.S. News & World Report* (July 31, 1995), pp. 49–54.

Rhodes, Richard, *The Making of the Atomic Bomb* (New York: Simon & Schuster, Inc., 1986).

Seidel, Robert, "Groves Takes Command," http://bang.lanl.gov/video/history/lanl50th/9-18-92.html (Los Alamos National Laboratory, March 1997).

Stoff, Michael B.; Fanton, Jonathan F.; and Williams, R. Hal, *The Manhattan Project* (New York: McGraw-Hill, Inc., 1991).

"The Manhattan Project," http://www.needham.mec.edu/NPS_Web_docs/High_School/cur/mp/project.html (Nick Heinle, March 20, 1997).

Ann Fagan Ginger, ed. *Nuclear Weapons Are Illegal: The Historic Opinion of the World Court and How It Will Be Enforced*, Apex Press, New York, 1998.

John Burroughs, *The (Il)legality of Threat or Use of Nuclear Weapons, A Guide to the Historic Opinion of the International Court of Justice*, Munster, London, 1997.

UN (document A/51/218, 15 October 1996), UN Publications, 2 UN Plaza, DC2-853, NY, NY 10017, 212-963-8302.

International Association of Lawyers Against Nuclear Arms (IALANA) website http://www.ddh.nl/org/ialana.

Ethical Choices	Consequences	Impact
Should the U.S. have continued producing the atomic bomb after it knew Germany and Japan couldn't?	The U.S. has already invested $2,000,000,000 into the program, and the project was in full production	Could it have delayed the onset of the Cold War and a nuclear arms race with the Soviet Union?
Should the U.S. have invaded the home islands of Japan?	Estimated 1,000,000 Americans and many more Japanese killed.	Does the President have an obligation to reduce American casualties at the expense of the enemy?
Should the destructive power of the atomic bomb have been demonstrated in Tokyo Bay?	Los Alamos scientists uncertain if device would work.	The U.S. could lose a valuable war asset.
Should the U.S. drop atomic bombs on inhabited cities?	Over 210,000 Japanese killed from the blast; untold number killed or maimed from lingering effects of radiation.	The U.S. is the only country in history to use nuclear weapons in war.
Why are nuclear weapons considered so frightening?	Overwhelming destructive power and lingering radiation effects.	Nuclear weapons have the potential to destroy human civilization.

Lesson 3

Global Citizenship Choices, Decisions, and Consequences

Key Terms

aggression
deterrence
diplomacy
foreign policy
intelligence
terrorism
nationalism
sanctions
standard of living
summit meeting

What You Will Learn to Do

- Predict how American choices and decisions can affect those in other countries differently from the way in which they affect Americans

Linked Core Objectives

- Apply critical thinking techniques

Skills and Knowledge You Will Gain Along the Way

- Compare characteristics of developed and developing nations

- Summarize the main goals of American Foreign Policy

- Discuss ways that nations can cooperate to solve global problems

- Examines ways that American political, military, and humanitarian choices affect other nations

- Define key words contained in this lesson

Chapter 8

Introduction

Have you ever considered how your actions affect people outside of your community? Your actions often have an impact on your family, friends, and neighborhood. The actions and choices made by you and other Americans can also impact people outside your neighborhood and even outside the country. In this lesson you will examine the ways that American choices can impact other nations, and the importance of being a global citizen.

Global Citizenship

A global citizen can be defined as a person who feels a need to tackle injustice and inequality on worldwide scale, and who possesses a desire and ability to work actively to do so. Global citizenship requires seeing the Earth's inhabitants as precious and unique, and safeguarding the future for those generations coming after us no matter their origin. It is a way of thinking and behaving, an outlook on life, and a belief that you can make a difference beyond the confines of your particular community or nation.

A global citizen can be described as someone who:

- **Is an individual with rights and responsibilities**
- **Bases actions on his/her developing beliefs and values**
- **Is aware of the world and has a sense of their own role in it**
- **Respects and values diversity**
- **Has an understanding of how the world works economically, politically, socially, culturally, technologically, and environmentally**
- **Is outraged by social injustice**
- **Participates in and contributes to the community at a range of levels from local to global**
- **Is willing to act to make the world a more sustainable place**
- **Is in relationship with others within interdependent local, national, and global communities**
- **Takes responsibility for their actions**

It takes hard work to become a global citizen. You need to have a knowledge and understanding of beliefs and teachings, practices, processes, and lifestyles at local, national, and global levels. You also need to have a basic understanding of economic and political institutions, as well as values in countries other than the United States. Everyone has the potential to be a global citizen, and in a world of increasing interdependence, it is a necessity for those who wish to lead. For those willing to take up the challenge, all you need is courage and commitment.

Being a global citizen requires you to examine how actions in your community affect those in other communities. In this case, imagine that the United States is your "community." You need to recognize that what U.S. decision makers do can have widely rippling effects throughout the world. To begin with, an understanding of American foreign policy is necessary.

American Foreign Policy

The United States is one nation among many in the world. One of the main duties of any government is making a plan for relating to other nations. A government's **foreign policy** is a plan that outlines the goals it hopes to meet in its relations with other countries (see Figure 8.3.1). Foreign policy also sets forth the ways these goals are to be met.

Key Note Term

foreign policy—of or involving the relations of one country with another

Goals of Foreign Policy

What do Americans hope for in relations with other countries? To think about that question, you might ask yourself what we, as individual Americans, want in our relations with the people around us.

First of all, we want to be respected. We want others to treat us as equals. We would like to live in a safe place, free from the fear of harm. As adults, we would like to be able to earn a living.

Figure 8.3.1: President Bush meets with Russian President Vladmir Putin in an effort to further American foreign policy.

Courtesy of Brooks Kraft/ Corbis Images.

These goals are like the goals we have as a nation. In general, the foreign policy goals of the United States are to protect citizens' safety, to promote prosperity, and to work for peace and democracy in other countries.

- **National Security.** Government leaders naturally try to protect the interests of their country. Acting in the national interest involves making sure the nation is safe. National security, or the ability to keep the nation safe from attack or harm, is the chief goal of American foreign policy. Because war is the greatest danger to any nation, national security mainly focuses on the threat of war.

- **World Peace.** A second goal of American foreign policy is to get countries to work together as a way to keep out of war. In today's world, wars anywhere can be a threat to people everywhere. People fear that other countries may be drawn into the fighting. They fear that nuclear weapons may be used and the world destroyed.

- **Trade.** Increasing trade is a third goal of United States foreign policy. Trade is good for the United States economy. Trade creates markets for American goods and services, earning profits for our businesses. It also brings us goods from other countries.

  Trade also brings greater interdependence and therefore cooperation. Maintaining good trading relations helps the United States meet its goals of national security and world peace. The profit and products nations gain from trade give them a good reason to avoid war with their trading partners.

- **Human Rights and Democracy.** Another goal of American foreign policy is to encourage all countries to respect the human rights of freedom, justice, and equality. Americans believe that democracy, in which citizens have the final say in their government, is the best way to protect human rights. Thus, they want to help people in other countries who are trying to form or keep democratic governments.

History shows that countries in which human rights are denied can be a threat to world peace. When citizens do not have the right to take part in their own government, revolutions and civil wars are likely to break out, and other countries are likely to be drawn in. Therefore, encouraging human rights and democracy is also a way to meet our foreign policy goals of peace and security.

Tools of Foreign Policy

How does a country go about meeting its foreign policy goals? The United States uses several tools, such as defense, alliances, diplomacy, trade measures, and intelligence, in its relations with other nations.

Defense

Defense is an important tool of American foreign policy. It helps the government maintain national security. American armed forces, with modern weapons, aircraft, and ships, are the means by which we defend ourselves against **aggression.**

A key part of United States foreign policy has been **deterrence.** In the arms race between the United States and the Soviet Union, both sides claimed that they were building weapons as deterrence against aggression.

Sometimes it is not clear whether a nation is using its armed forces for defense or aggression. When the Soviets sent their army into Afghanistan in 1979, they said they were just helping the Afghan government defend against anti-communist forces. The United States accused the Soviets of aggression—of using its military power to take over an independent nation.

Key Note Terms

aggression—an attack or threat of attack by another country

deterrence—keeping a strong defense to discourage aggression by other nations

In 1989, when American forces overthrew Panama's dictator, Manuel Noriega, Latin American leaders accused the United States of aggression. President Bush said the invasion's purpose was to protect American interests, especially the Panama Canal, and to help Panama get rid of a corrupt leader.

Alliances

The United States also meets its foreign policy goals by forming military, political, or economic alliances with other countries. North Atlantic Treaty Organization members (NATO), a military alliance created to protect Western Europe from Soviet aggression, pooled military forces into one army in order to better defend themselves if attacked.

An example of a political alliance is the Organization of American States (OAS), made up of countries in North, Central, and South America. The OAS helps its members work together peacefully, trying to settle disputes before they become violent. The OAS also reports on human rights in its member countries and helps to keep elections fair and honest.

The United States is a member of several economic alliances. One is the Organization for Economic Cooperation and Development (OECD). The 27 members of the OECD, mostly Western European countries, agree to help each other's economic well-being through trade. They also work together in giving aid to developing nations.

Foreign Aid

Another tool used to meet foreign policy goals is foreign aid. After World War II the United States gave aid to European countries to help them rebuild factories, farms, cities, and homes destroyed in the war. Since the end of World War II, the United States has given or loaned almost $500 billion in foreign aid to over 100 countries.

Foreign aid can support American policy goals by strengthening governments and political groups that are friendly to the United States. In some cases this military aid has helped countries that are trying to put down rebellions within their borders. Sometimes the United States has sent weapons to rebels who are struggling against governments considered unfriendly to American interests.

Economic aid takes many forms. The United States might help pay for a hospital, or a dam to control floods or produce electricity. Aid might be loans or grants to help a country start a new industry, or to help rebuild nations that are devastated by natural disasters, as shown in Figure 8.3.2.

Developed or Developing Nations

There is a striking difference between nations that are considered *developed*, and those that are considered *developing*. These differences must be taken into account when applying the tools of foreign policy to these nations. A developed nation can be defined as one that is capable of world focus. A developing nation, on the other hand, has its focus on internal matters. Too, a developed nation does not base its wealth solely on natural resources, such as diamonds, oil, or raw materials, but rather on a post-industrial economy. Developed nations generally operate under a stable form of republic government; developing nations generally suffer under a

Figure 8.3.2: Part of the U.S. foreign aid policy is to help countries in time of dire need, such as Indonesia after the tsunami of 2004.

Key Note Term

standard of living— social conditions established by authority as a fixed rule, measure, or model

dictatorship with tribal warfare being considered common. In general, the **standard of living** is better in developed nations rather than in developing. Developed nations include England, France, Germany, Japan, and Australia. Developing nations include many of the countries in Africa, South America, and some in the Middle East.

Sending experts and teachers to work in developing countries is also a form of aid. The United States also sends aid in a crisis such as a flood or earthquake. Aid helps nations' economies to grow and is seen as a way to reduce the chance of revolution and war.

Foreign aid has caused bitter debates in Congress and the nation. Americans disagree over how much and what kind of aid to give. Some say that giving help to other countries is our duty as a rich and powerful country. They say that if we do not give aid, poorer nations will turn to other governments—governments that are not necessarily friendly to the United States—for help. Another argument for economic aid is that it helps the United States. Countries that receive our aid can then buy American products.

Those who oppose aid do so for two main reasons. Some say that we should solve problems at home first and not send so much money out of the country.

Other critics say that the kind of aid we give does more harm than good. They charge that our military aid has sometimes helped governments that violate human rights. Just because a group is friendly to the United States, they say, is not a good reason to give it money and weapons. Critics also believe that some kinds of economic aid give the United States too much control over how other countries develop.

Trade Measures

Another tool of foreign policy is trade measures, or the terms under which the United States trades with other countries. One trade measure is a quota, which states how much of a foreign product can be sold in the United States. Another measure is a tariff, a tax on foreign products sold in the United States. Trade measures also include limits on what products United States firms can sell abroad, such as weapons, or whether untested foreign products, such as drugs, can be brought into the United States.

In recent years a foreign policy tool has been **sanctions.** In 1998, for example, India and Pakistan conducted underground nuclear weapons tests. To demonstrate its disapproval of the tests, the United States imposed economic sanctions on both nations.

The United States has two main goals in regulating trade with other countries. One is to get other countries to buy American goods. The other is to get our trading partners to support us in other foreign policy goals, such as stopping human rights violations and reducing possible threats to peace.

Intelligence

Information about another country and what its government plans to do is called **intelligence.** Most countries work hard to gather intelligence in order to help them meet the goal of national security.

The Central Intelligence Agency (CIA) and other agencies gather information for the United States government. The CIA focuses mostly on countries it thinks might be unfriendly, and tries to learn what the governments of these countries intend to do. It also tries to predict how these governments will react to what the United States does.

Much of intelligence is secret. Information is sometimes gathered by spying. Sometimes intelligence agencies have helped overturn the government of a country. In Chile in 1973, for example, the CIA took part in overthrowing the government of Salvador Allende. The United States government thought Allende was not favorable to our national interest. Like defense, diplomacy, foreign aid, and trade measures, intelligence is an important tool of foreign policy.

Diplomacy

Can you remember settling a disagreement with someone by talking it out? In a similar way, the American government tries to settle disagreements with other countries peacefully. To do so, it depends mostly on another tool of foreign policy, diplomacy. **Diplomacy** is the relations and communications carried out between countries. When countries disagree, they send representatives called diplomats to talk about the issues.

The United States uses diplomacy not only to settle disagreements but also to accomplish tasks such as building a canal or space station. Alliances and trade agreements are also made through diplomacy. Diplomacy often results in formal agreements known as treaties.

Usually, diplomacy is carried out by members of the Department of State. Sometimes, however, there is a **summit meeting,** a meeting at which the President talks about important issues with heads of other governments. In 1999, President Clinton traveled to China for a summit meeting with Chinese President Jiang Zemin (see Figure 8.3.3) at which the two leaders discussed military and economic issues.

Key Note Term

sanctions—measures to stop or limit trade with another nation in order to change its behavior

Key Note Term

intelligence—information, not always available in the public domain, relating to the strength, resources, capabilities and intentions of a foreign country or domestic groups that can affect the lives and the safety of citizens

Key Note Term

diplomacy—relations and communications carried out between countries

Key Note Term

summit meeting—a meeting between heads of state

Figure 8.3.3: Summit meetings are held between heads of nations.

Courtesy of AP/Wide World Photos.

The Importance of Diplomacy

Diplomacy deals with the influence of public attitudes on the formation and execution of foreign policies. It encompasses dimensions of international relations beyond traditional negotiations; the cultivation by governments of public opinion in other countries; the interaction of private groups and interests in one country with those of another; the reporting of foreign affairs and its impact on policy; communication between those whose job is communication, as between diplomats and foreign correspondents; and the processes of intercultural communications.

When you engage in successful diplomatic efforts, you:

- **Compare and contrast the political, economic, and military components of foreign policy decision making and analyze the impact of foreign policy on domestic decisions**

- **Draw conclusions about the implications of foreign policy as it is currently applied to various regions of the world**

- **Evaluate the national interest and how it is formulated, assess alternatives to current policies, and examine their likely impact on the United States, its allies, and other nations**

- **Examine the theory, nature, and causes of war and their relationship to diplomacy; assess the contributions of diplomacy to accomplishment of war objectives**

When diplomacy is carried out correctly, a volatile situation can be managed and diffused. Take, for example, the incident between the U.S. and China when an American military plane was crippled and forced to land on Chinese soil. Had it not been for the expert diplomatic efforts of Brigadier General Neal Sealock and his team, this situation might have ended very differently.

BG Sealock and his team engaged in several aspects of diplomacy. As you read the following account of the China incident, you will see how intercultural communications played a major role in negotiations. You will also see how this team evaluated the impact of the situation on the U.S. and other nations of the world. Had the U.S. responded to this event by not taking into account the difference in cultures and foreign policies, the U.S. might have been viewed by other nations in a less than favorable light. And the situation could have escalated into something much more dangerous.

BG Sealock and his team also engaged in global citizenship by:

- **Being aware of the world and the U.S. role in it**
- **Respecting and valuing the culture of China**
- **Understanding how the world (especially China and the Far East, in this case) works economically, politically, socially, culturally, technologically, and environmentally**
- **Respecting and understanding the different political system in China and working with it rather than against it**

Diplomacy, an understanding of foreign policy, and global citizenship worked together to diffuse a critical situation, and work it through to a peaceful and mutually satisfactory conclusion.

The China Incident

In the early months of 2001, relations between the United States and China had reached a low point. The newly elected President George W. Bush and the U.S. Congress had under consideration a proposal for additional weapons sales to Taiwan, the island nation off the coast of China that had been established by Chinese opponents to Mao Zedong in the aftermath of the successful Communist revolution of 1949. Until 1978, the United States had recognized Taiwan as the official government of China; however, as the result of a long-standing effort beginning with the Nixon administration to defuse tensions between our government and the most populous nation on Earth, we withdrew our official recognition of Taiwan and granted it to the People's Republic of China (PRC) with the understanding that China would not use military force to impose its sovereignty over Taiwan. To underscore U.S. determination to protect the Taiwanese from mainland China's aggression, the U.S. Congress passed the Taiwan Relations Act in 1979, obligating the United States to provide Taiwan with defensive weapons. In 2001, Taiwan requested an arms deal that would include such sophisticated weapons platforms as Arleigh Burke destroyers, air to air and surface to air missiles, and electronic tracking systems. The PRC viewed these discussions with intense suspicion, suggesting these weapons were not defensive but offensive, and that further discussions between the U.S. and Taiwan regarding the sale of these weapons would damage or destroy the relationship between China and the United States.

Coupled with this dispute, China still harbored resentment over an incident that had taken place in Belgrade, Yugoslavia, two years before. On May 7, 1999, during the NATO Allied Force operation against Yugoslavian Slobodan Milosevic's genocidal government, American aircraft had mistakenly bombed the Chinese embassy, killing three Chinese journalists and wounding 20 staff members. China did not fully accept the U.S. explanation that the error was caused by reliance on old databases and out of date maps, and instead suggested the bombing came as a result of China's opposition to NATO's intervention in the Balkans.

With these events as a backdrop, the mid-air collision between a U.S. Navy reconnaissance aircraft and a Chinese fighter jet on April 1, 2001, threatened to escalate into an event with global consequences. Were it not for the training and discipline of the Navy flight crew and the chief negotiator for the United States, Army Brigadier General Neal Sealock, the outcome might have been far different. The details of this incident illustrate the importance of diplomatic skills and awareness of international relationships for those who strive to acquire global citizenship.

For Lt. Shane Osborn, mission commander for the reconnaissance flight, the day had been routine. He and his 23-member crew had awakened at 0300 for a 0400 preflight briefing and a take-off at 0500 from Kadena Air Force Base on Okinawa, Japan, to conduct an eight-hour electronic surveillance mission in international airspace over the western Pacific. The EP-3E ARIES II aircraft, a four-engine turboprop, had performed nominally, and four hours into the flight, the heading was changed for the long flight back to Kadena at their cruising altitude of 24,500 feet and cruising speed of 180 knots. Because of the complexity of the aircraft, most of the EP-3E flights were conducted on auto-pilot. As the plane headed home, Lt. Osborn experienced a sense of relief that the usual "escort" of Chinese mach speed jet aircraft had not joined them. Commonly, Chinese pilots, based on the island of Hainan, would fly in tandem with the EP-3E reconnaissance flights at some point during the mission as a means of harassment and a way to signal their mastery of the international airways. Normally the Chinese jets maintained a safe distance, but in recent months, there had been a number of close calls as the high speed jets slowed far below what was safe for their aircraft to match the relative snail's pace of the reconnaissance aircraft, and flew within 50 feet of American planes.

Shortly after changing course, Lt. Osborn's fears were realized. Two Chinese jet fighters approached at great speed, and then, slowing almost to a stall, began to weave back and forth and around the EP-3E. In horror, the flight crew watched as one of the Chinese pilots approached within ten feet, removed his oxygen mask, and mouthed fierce angry words while gesturing with his hand. Just as Lt. Osborn warned the intelligence specialists in the rear of plane, who without windows were unaware of the unfolding drama, the unthinkable happened. The Chinese pilot lost control of his plane. It collided with the American aircraft with such force that the nose cone dislodged, the fuselage was punctured in several places, and the high strength propeller blades of one of the left engines were shredded. Immediately, the EP-3E plunged into a vertical inverted dive following in slow motion the now bisected Chinese jet's descent to the South China Sea.

Four years of intensive training in jets and multi-engine aircraft preparing for every imaginable emergency paid off for Lt. Osborn and his crew. Before the air speed indicator malfunctioned, it registered 450 knots, almost twice the maximum safe speed

Figure 8.3.4: The damaged U.S. Navy EP-3E surveil-lance plane parked at Lingshui base on China's Hainan Island in this April 3, 2001 photo, released by China's official Xinhua news agency.

Courtesy of AP/Wide World Photos.

for the EP-3E. Osborn, his co-pilot, and flight engineer managed to right the aircraft, and then level it off at an altitude of 8000 feet. After verifying the good condition of all of his crew and telling them to put on their parachutes, Osborn quickly calculated the options available considering the overwhelming damage to the plane. He could order the crew to bail out through the rear hatch into shark infested waters, thereby guaranteeing his death and at least one other member of the flight crew because two people had to remain at the controls to ensure a fairly level flight and the safe evacuation of the rest of the crew. Or he could attempt to land the crippled aircraft at the closest airfield, Lingshui Air Base on Hainan Island, the home base of the two pilots who had caused the disaster. The crew had already begun Emergency Destruction procedures of all the classified and sensitive equipment and documents aboard the plane. At least three direct radio broadcasts to Hainan had been made to alert the airfield of the emergency though there had been no audible response. Osborn made the decision to save as many of his crew as possible and set course for Lingshui Air Base in the People's Republic of China (see Figure 8.3.4).

Very shortly, China announced that 24 American military personnel were being detained as "guests" while an investigation of the accident proceeded. However, the Chinese made clear that a preliminary assessment of the situation indicated an act of deliberate aggression on the part of the American air crew, the illegal encroachment upon Chinese airspace and sovereign territory, and espionage against the People's Republic of China.

The United States responded by sending two Arleigh Burke destroyers, and one Spruance class anti-submarine destroyer to patrol the waters off Hainan Island. President Bush, in a brief statement on the evening of April 1, called for immediate access to the crew by American officials, and the prompt return of our personnel and the EP-3E. To expedite these demands, Ambassador Prueher directed a three person diplomatic crew to travel by commercial flight from Beijing to Hainan Island to gain first-hand knowledge of the situation, establish contact with the crew, and direct negotiations with the Chinese holding the air crew and the reconnaissance plane.

Brigadier General Sealock, the senior member of the American delegation, brought formidable qualifications and experience to the task at hand. During his 28-year Army career, BG Sealock had acquired an extensive knowledge of Chinese culture that included fluency in Mandarin Chinese, a familiarity with military aviation during his career as an attack helicopter pilot, and an in-depth understanding of U.S. foreign policy and intelligence analysis through formal education at Command and Staff College and practical participation at domestic and foreign billets. At the time of the mid-air collision, BG Sealock was the senior military attaché to the U.S. Embassy in Beijing, China's capital. Very shortly after his arrival on Hainan Island, BG Sealock and his team had accomplished the most pressing objective, a brief conversation with local authorities indicating our desire to meet with them and arrange for their expeditious departure back to the U.S. They were also able to press for confirmation of the welfare and safety of our American military personnel.

The Right Man . . . Excerpt from Born to Fly, by Shane Osborn

Shane Osborn, pilot of the downed plane, wrote the following in his book, *Born To Fly*. This book chronicles the events that took place during The China Incident from the viewpoint of the crew. Here, Osborn describes meeting BG Sealock for the first time since their capture.

"We saw the glare and shadow of a video lamp and the flash of still camera strobes. In the hubbub, I called to Johnny, 'Let me know if it's a military rep.'

"But I didn't have time to depend on a scout to identify the man who strode through the door. Army Brigadier General Neal Sealock, the U.S. Defense Attaché at our Beijing Embassy, was tall and square-shouldered. The left breast of his green uniform blouse bore multiple rows of decorations and ribbons.

"'Attention on deck,' I ordered the crew. We rose in unison and snapped to attention.

"'At ease,' General Sealock said, his eyes scanning the room.

"U.S. Consular Officer Ted Gomm followed General Sealock. A heavyset Chinese official set off to the right.

"'Take your seats,' General Sealock said. 'We've got to get this going quick because they only gave me 40 minutes to see you. I need some information on papers, your places of birth and dates of birth.'

"As he raised his pen above his open notebook, the Chinese official shook his head. 'No, that is against the rules.'

"General Sealock looked at the man in exasperation. 'This is information you requested. You told me to get it. I'm just writing it down like we negotiated. I'm not passing anything.'

"'Ah, alright,' the official conceded.

"General Sealock looked evenly at the man, and then down at his watch. 'Now you're going to give us back those 60 seconds towards the 40 minutes.'

"We've got the right guy working for us, I realized. It was fantastic for morale to see the U.S. side standing up for us.

"Once he had collected the personal information, General Sealock rose to his full height and looked us all in the eye, one at a time. This is what is known as command presence. It was meant to inspire people, and I can certainly say it did so that night."

On the afternoon of April 3, 2001, President Bush addressed the nation regarding this potentially explosive event and commended BG Sealock for his immediate actions. In his speech, President Bush stated:

"I want to report to the American people, and especially to the families involved, that I've just talked with Brigadier General Sealock, who, earlier today, met with our 24 men and women in China.

"The General tells me they are in good health, they suffered no injuries, and they have not been mistreated. I know this is a relief to their loved ones, and to all Americans.

"Our crew members expressed their faith in America, and we have faith in them. They send their love to their families. They said they're looking forward to coming home, and we are looking forward to bringing them home.

"This is an unusual situation, in which an American military aircraft had to make an emergency landing on Chinese soil. Our approach has been to keep this accident from becoming an international incident. We have allowed the Chinese government time to do the right thing. But now it is time for our servicemen and women to return home. And it is time for the Chinese government to return our plane.

"This accident has the potential of undermining our hopes for a fruitful and productive relationship between our two countries. To keep that from happening, our servicemen and women need to come home."

Meet Brigadier General Gratton O'Neal Sealock, Deputy Commanding General, United States Army Cadet Command

Brigadier General Sealock, shown in Figure 8.3.5, entered the U.S. Army in 1974 upon graduation from Eastern Washington State College as a Distinguished Military Graduate, receiving a Regular Commission in Infantry.

After the Infantry Officer Basic Course, BG Sealock was assigned to the 1st Battalion (Airborne) 508th Infantry, 82d Airborne Division, serving as a rifle platoon leader, weapons platoon leader, and heavy mortar platoon leader before receiving orders to attend flight training. Completing flight school and the AH-1 Cobra Course in 1977, he was assigned to C Company, 3d Aviation Battalion (Combat), Schweinfurt, FRG. He joined the battalion staff in Kitzingen in 1979.

Figure 8.3.5: Brigadier General Gratton O'Neal Sealock.

Courtesy of Reuters/ Corbis Images.

Upon completion of the Infantry Officer Advanced Course in 1981, BG Sealock was assigned to the Army Aviation Center, Fort Rucker, Alabama, as an attack helicopter instructor pilot and flight commander. He served as operations officer for the Hanchey Division and assumed command of 64th Company, 6th Battalion in May 1983.

From late 1984 through 1986, BG Sealock studied Mandarin Chinese at the Defense Language Institute, the Ministry of Defense (UK) Chinese Language School in Hong Kong, and Fudan University in Shanghai, PRC through the Army's Foreign Area Officer Program. He graduated from the Armed Forces Staff College in 1987.

Returning overseas, he served as the executive officer, 4th Squadron, 7th Cavalry at Camp Garry Owen, ROK. Subsequently, BG Sealock was assigned to DIA as the China Country Officer in Washington, D.C. In August 1990, he returned to Hong Kong as the Assistant Army Attache and Director of the China FAO Training Program. From May 1992 through April 1994, BG Sealock commanded the 4th Squadron, 3d Armored Cavalry Regiment, Fort Bliss, Texas.

April 1994–June 1995, as a National Security Fellow at the Kennedy School of Government, Harvard University in lieu of the Army War College. Afterward, he was assigned as the China Desk Officer and the Northeast Asia Branch Chief, Asia Pacific Division in the Directorate for Strategy and Policy, J-5, the Joint Staff from June 1995 through May 1997.

BG Sealock returned to Fort Rucker and assumed command of the 1st Aviation Brigade June 26, 1997, through June 1999.

From August 1999 through May 2000, BG Sealock was assigned as the United States Army Attaché for the United States Embassy, in Australia.

From September 2000 to August 2002, BG Sealock was assigned as the United States Defense Attaché, Defense Intelligence Agency, in Beijing, China.

BG Sealock held the position as Deputy Commanding General, Cadet Command, Fort Monroe, Virginia, August 2002.

For the American crew who had been held incommunicado for over forty-eight hours, the arrival of General Sealock offered an extraordinary boost to their morale. Accompanied by Senior U.S. Consular Officer, Ted Gomm, General Sealock met for forty minutes with the captive Americans, assuring them that the United States was making every effort to secure their release. As Lt. Osborn wrote, his immediate impression was, "We've got the right guy working for us." Not only did General Sealock hold the Chinese to account for the guidelines agreed upon for this initial meeting, he also ensured personal messages to family and friends of the American crew would be transcribed and conveyed.

The difficulties of the team's mission cannot be overstated. Aside from the seriousness of the charges from Chinese officials, heightened further by inflammatory accusations from a Chinese press spurred on by extreme **nationalism,** General Sealock and his team also dealt with the absence of senior civilian Chinese leadership. Many of the leaders were on a trip to Latin America accompanying President Jiang Zemin. One major concern was how to establish productive communications with China's leaders. He was forced to deal directly with representatives from the Chinese Communist Party (CCP) based in Beijing. The People's Liberation Army was not in control of the negotiations; in fact, two separate negotiations had to be conducted—one in Hainan and the other in Beijing by Ambassador (Admiral) Joseph Prueher—and these efforts required coordination. To be effective, General Sealock needed the sophisticated interpersonal skills developed over his professional career including the ability to lead, build a team on the run, listen carefully, interpret the body lan-

Figure 8.3.6: BG Sealock during negotiations in China.

Courtesy of AP/Wide World Photos.

guage of his Chinese adversaries, and employ his understanding of Chinese culture and negotiating techniques. Moreover, the time difference between China and Washington, DC, required members of General Sealock's team to be available at any hour of the day or night. Despite all the possible roadblocks, General Sealock and the U.S. diplomatic corps in China rapidly assembled a negotiations team with the full confidence of the President of the United States, and the authority to act independently to ensure the interests of the U.S. It is interesting to note that every member of the team had prior military experience. Their military backgrounds, training, and education proved invaluable in the direct contact with Chinese counterparts. Negotiations were started, as shown in Figure 8.3.6.

Before BG Sealock had pierced the wall of isolation surrounding the American air crew, these dedicated members of the military had held their own. Unsure of their status, but extremely aware of the hostility and suspicion from their Chinese hosts, they rightly fell back on their own military training, especially the mandatory Survival, Evasion, Resistance and Escape (SERE) instruction, and the military Code of Conduct integrated with SERE indoctrination. All of them recognized the need for cohesion, and for maintaining, within the restrictions of their confinement, the same military discipline expected of them when performing the more routine duties of their military service. The existing chain of command, especially Lt. Osborn and Senior Chief Petty Officer Mellos, provided the leadership to see them through this ordeal. As an example, the crew staged a mini hunger strike after Lt. Osborn was separated from the crew for a lengthy interrogation by the commanding officer of the Lingshui air base, refusing to eat until he rejoined their ranks. They also refused to admit any responsibility for the mid-air collision, insisting that the Chinese pilot, later identified as Wang Wei, had been wholly to blame for his own tragic death. In spite of repeated threats from the Chinese that they might be bound over for trial for espionage and that their families might be in jeopardy, the Americans held steadfast. Their mission commander, Lt. Osborn, through both personal persuasion and strict compliance to military guidelines, bolstered their resolve. Just as his piloting skills had saved their lives, Lt. Osborn's college NROTC lessons and active duty officer schooling in leadership and strategic decision making kept his young crew on a focused and even keel. Subsequently, General Sealock singled out Lt. Osborn and Senior Chief Mellos but praised the professionalism, exuberance, and experience of the entire crew, and credited their behavior as an important element in the successful outcome.

General Sealock also mentioned the positive effect of the Inter-agency and the total support provided through the leadership of the National Command Authority. All Americans can be proud of a system that works in an emergency situation. In this particular case, a relatively new organization, the Joint Personnel Recovery Agency (JPRA), a Department of Defense organization established in 1999, provided outstanding support. They are charged with "shaping the planning, preparation, and execution of personnel recovery for the Department of Defense." In its mission statement the JPRA notes four key goals:

- **To return isolated personnel to friendly control**
- **To deny the enemy a potential source of intelligence**
- **To prevent the exploitation of captured personnel in propaganda programs designed to influence our national interest and military strategy**
- **To maintain morale and the national will**

All of these goals were particularly pertinent to the repatriation of the EP-3E and its crew.

Originally, Chinese officials had demanded four conditions for resolution of the crisis. First, China insisted on an abject apology for the collision with the U.S. taking full blame for the death of Wang Wei. Second, China asked for a complete explanation of the incident, including every detail of the flight of the EP-3E, a demand certain to compromise the classified reconnaissance mission. Third, China required full compensation for their losses. This demand for compensation amounted to one million dollars in U.S. currency. Finally, China called for the halt of all future reconnaissance flights. By April 11, when an agreement was reached for the release of the American crew, then-Secretary of State Colin Powell and President Bush had both expressed regret for the death of the Chinese pilot and the loss of the Chinese aircraft, while making it clear the United States would not proffer a blanket apology. Instead, an agreement was struck to continue discussions about further reconnaissance flights, the return of the EP-3E, and appropriate payment to the Chinese for the expenses associated with the accident. According to the Beijing government, the U.S. acknowledged that the Navy aircraft did violate Chinese airspace, but did so only during the emergency landing procedure. The actual collision happened over international waters.

U.S.-China relations cooled after the incident but gradually improved. Following the September 11, 2001, terrorist attacks in New York City and Washington DC., China offered strong public support for the war on **terrorism** and has been an important partner in U.S. counterterrorism efforts. China and the U.S. have also been working closely on regional issues such as North Korea.

What changed the ferociously adamant stance of the Chinese? For years China had been pressing for membership in the World Trade Organization (WTO), and approval of their inclusion in this prestigious international group depended heavily on the good will of the United States. Moreover, China had bid to be the host nation for the 2008 Summer Olympics, and although the International Olympic Committee claims neutrality when awarding host status, the Chinese could not afford the continuing controversy of holding foreign military personnel hostage. Finally, during the initial furor over the loss of the Chinese jet, the pilot, Wang Wei, had been hailed as a hero and a martyr of the People's Liberation Army. Secret intelligence information possessed by the United States, including photos of Wang Wei flying recklessly close to another American reconnaissance flight, exposed the likely truth of the incident. Wang Wei routinely jeopardized his own safety, and the safety of those around him, including his own wingman.

Ultimately, China was offered $34,567 as payment for goods and services associated with the detention of the EP-3E crew. In July, 2003, the EP-3E was disassembled by U.S. personnel at Lingshui Air Base and flown to the United States aboard a leased Russian cargo plane. It has been completely refurbished and is back with the fleet. Lt. Osborn received the Distinguished Flying Cross for his heroism and leadership. Brigadier General Sealock now serves as the Deputy Commanding General of the United States Army Cadet Command. For General Sealock, it is the culmination of a distinguished career in which he continues to serve his country by developing and encouraging the leaders of tomorrow.

> ### NOTE
>
> In August of 2001, Richard L. Armitage, Deputy Secretary of State, said of BG Sealock, "His talents came to the fore during the EP-3 incident. General Sealock made invaluable contributions to the USG effort to secure release of our service men and women. His timely reports from Hainan Island—in some cases, reporting directly to the President—on the status of the U.S. aircrew and on his interactions with the local PLA provided crucial information to USG decision makers. His meetings with the detained aircrew were also key in helping out service men and women sustain their high morale in a very stressful situation. General Sealock's performance during the incident was nothing short of brilliant."

As mentioned earlier in this lesson, BG Sealock and his team worked intelligently and diligently to take into account the Chinese culture and political system, the world view of the United States, and the places in the world political and economic arenas that China and the U.S. both held. These expert and well-thought-out negotiations led to a satisfactory conclusion that left the relations between the United States and China intact, and prevented other countries from any involvement that could have led to global problems.

Key Note Term

terrorism—the use of threat of violence to spread fear, usually for the purpose of reaching political goals

Conclusion

Global citizenship is mandatory if the United States and the rest of the world is to grow, thrive, and cooperate for the good of all. The ability to look at problems and situations objectively in the world, and predict or determine how choices and decisions can either benefit or injure a world neighbor is crucial in today's society. By understanding how actions, choices, and decisions can lead to good or bad consequences, you understand how those choices and decisions can impact other nations.

American political, military, and humanitarian choices can have tremendous impact on other nations. In the China Incident:

- **Two different political archetypes had to work together to resolve an issue to the benefit of both countries**
- **Although very different in structure, the American and Chinese military cooperated with each other to solve the problem**
- **By recognizing the cultural differences between Americans and the Chinese, and by respecting those cultural differences, the China Incident was resolved without injury to either culture**

In the following lesson, you will examine timelines. You will learn the importance of being able to follow and understand the information given in a timeline, and how history plays a crucial role in the present.

Lesson Review

1. **Why is global citizenship so important?**
2. **Discuss diplomacy and explain how a person can be diplomatic. What is the importance of diplomacy?**
3. **Define the term "sanctions." When and why might they be used?**
4. **What might have happened if BG Sealock had not given the Chinese the time required to resolve the situation? How did his expert diplomatic work keep this from developing into a larger international incident?**

Case Study

Exercise: Examine a case study that involves a series of events that impacted international relations. **Develop a flow map** or multi-flow map to **organize the events of the incident.** Participate in a discussion to compare **how people in and out of the U.S. were impacted** by the decisions and choices made during the case study incident.

- **Illustrate how an American choice affects at least one other country**
- **Summarize the "Who, What, Where, When" of a specific American decision or action that affects those in at least one other country**
- **How did the decision affect Americans and how did it affect those in other countries?**
- **Evaluate the negative and/or positive consequences for Americans and for other countries**
- **Make recommendations for increasing the positive consequences for both Americans and those from other countries**

Recap of the EP-3 Incident with China

On April 1, 2001 at 8:16 p.m., the staff in DIA's Alert Center received a report of a MAYDAY from an EP-3 aircraft heading toward Lingshui, China. To their horror, they learned that an American EP-3 surveillance plane and a Chinese F-8 jet fighter had collided over the South China Seas. Despite an 8,000-foot freefall, the EP-3 made it safely to China's Hainan Island; the F-8 tore apart and crashed, and the pilot Wang Wei was killed. At 8:31 p.m. the Alert Center began notifying key people who would be directly involved in this incident. And by 9:00 p.m., the Alert Center had notified BG Neal Sealock.

The EP-3 ARIES II is a Navy signals intelligence reconnaissance aircraft equipped with sensitive receivers and high-gain dish antennas for collecting electronic emissions deep within targeted territory. China immediately impounded the aircraft and detained the 24-man crew. Deputy Foreign Minister Li Zhaoxign said the Chinese public was outraged both by the resumption of U.S. surveillance flights near China and by U.S. suggestions that the spy plane be flown back from the Chinese military base where it landed after colliding with a Chinese fighter jet. "If we allow such a military plane which had a mission of spying on China to be flown back from a Chinese military airfield, that would further hurt the dignity and sentiments of the Chinese people," said Li. "It would be the cause of strong indignation and opposition from the Chinese people." Spokesman Zhu Bangzao declared: "The United States should take full responsibility, make an apology to the Chinese government and people, and give us an explanation of its actions." U.S. Secretary of State Colin Powell responded with equal bluntness: "We have nothing to apologize for." According to Secretary of Defense Donald Rumsfeld, the United States wasn't spying: "Our EP-3 was flying an overt reconnaissance and surveillance mission in international airspace in an aircraft clearly marked, 'United States Navy.' It was on a well-known flight path that we have used for decades. Many countries perform such flights, including China." Secretary Rumsfeld further accused China of provoking the incident. Later testimony by Navy Lieutenant Shane Osborn, the EP-3 commander, supported this view by stating his aircraft was flying straight and level, on autopilot, heading away from Hainan Island in international airspace when it was subjected to harassment from the Chinese fighter.

Lt. Osborn said that the Chinese jet came within three to five feet of his own aircraft twice, and on the third time, the Chinese pilot apparently misjudged and the F-8's vertical stabilizer contacted the EP-3's number one propeller. Lt. Osborn's initial thought was "This guy just killed us" as the EP-3 dropped 8,000 feet and rolled out of control. Lt. Osborn regained control of the aircraft and declared an in-flight emergency as he turned back towards Chinese airspace, deciding to head towards Hainan Island. The EP-3 made numerous attempts to broadcast Mayday distress signals, but none of them were answered. When they landed, they were greeted with armed troops.

BG Neal Sealock, the U.S. defense attaché to China, was dispatched to Hainan to negotiate the return of the EP-3 aircraft and crew. BG Sealock reported directly to the President and was given authority to act on the Nation's behalf. Tensions mounted as three days into the crisis President Bush declared "It is time for our servicemen and women to return home. It is time for the Chinese government to return our plane." In response, Chinese President Jiang Zemin demanded "The United States must stop these types of flights in the airspace of China's coastal areas." Furthermore, China bluntly rejected U.S. claims that the damaged plane and the advanced intelligence-gathering equipment on board were sovereign U.S. territory and off-limits to inspection or seizure.

As the standoff continued, Republican congressional leaders, including Richard Shelby, chairman of the Senate Select Committee on Intelligence, and Henry Hyde, chairman of the House International Relations Committee, began referring to the spy plane crew as "hostages." All this time, BG Sealock pursued intense negotiations with Chinese representatives in Hainan, coordinating his efforts with the Ambassador in Beijing. Having spent four years as an attaché, BG Sealock had a good background on the Chinese language and culture that helped him understand the implications and possible innuendos as negotiations proceeded. He was aided by a team of inter-agency experts with similar training in Chinese language, culture, and negotiating techniques. These skills proved critical in defusing the situation by persuading Chinese representatives to allow BG Sealock to meet with the EP-3 crew. At the time of his first meeting with the crew, he stated, "My name is Neal Sealock, and I'm here to get you home."

After reporting their apparent good health and safety, Secretary of State Colin Powell assumed a more conciliatory approach saying "I hope this starts us on a road to a full and complete resolution of this matter." The impasse was broken after 11 days of intensive negotiations. Ambassador Joseph Prueher gave a letter to Foreign Minister Tang: "Please convey to the Chinese People and the family of pilot Wang Wei that we are very sorry for their loss . . . We are very sorry the entering of China's airspace and the landing did not have verbal clearance."

Having extracted an 'apology' from Washington, Beijing released the 24 American servicemen. The EP-3 was disassembled and shipped to the United States three months later. President Bush later announced the resumption of EP-3 flights along the Chinese coast.

References

News Transcript, "Secretary Rumsfeld Briefs on EP-3 Collision," 13 April 2001, www.defenselink.mil/transcripts/2001/t04132001_t0413ep3.html

News Special, "EP-3E crew receives medals at Armed Forces Day ceremonies," www.chinfo.navy.mil/navpalib/news/news_stories/ep3-china.html

Washington Post Foreign Service, "U.S. Crew in 'Good Health' as Strain Builds over Plane," Philip P. Pan and John Pomfret, 4 April 2001, www.calguard.ca.gov/ia/China/China-Crew%20in%20good%20health.htm

"Why China Not Allowing EP-3 to Fly Out", www.china.org.cn/english/12478.htm

"Culture Clash? Apologies East and West," Peter Hays Gries and Kaping Peng, *Journal of Contemporary China* (2002), Vol. 11, No. 30, 173–178.

United States Navy Fact File, "EP-3A (ARIES II)," 2 April 2001, www.chinfo.navy.mil/navpalib/factfile/aircraft/air-ep3e.html

Government Fact File, United States Department of State, "China," www.state.gove/r/pa/ei/bgn/18902.htm

"Just War Theory and the Recent U.S. Air Strikes Against Iraq," Mark Edward DeForrest, http://law.gonzaga.edu/borders/documents/deforres.htm

1. **Illustrate how an American choice affects at least one other country.**

"Deputy Foreign Minister Li Zhaoxign said the Chinese public was outraged both by the resumption of US surveillance flights near China and by US suggestions that the spy plane be flown back from the Chinese military base where it landed after colliding with a Chinese fighter jet."

2. **Summarize the "Who, What, Where, When" of a specific American decision or action that affects those in at least one other country.**

Who: **President of the United States**

What: **Chose to conduct surveillance flights of China**

Where: **Hainan Island**

When: **April, 2001**

3. **How did the decision affect Americans and how did it affect those in other countries?**

"If we allow such a military plane which had a mission of spying on China to be flown back from a Chinese military airfield, that would further hurt the dignity and sentiments of the Chinese people," said Li. "It would be the cause of strong indignation and opposition from the Chinese people."

4. **Evaluate the negative and/or positive consequences for Americans and for other countries.**

   Negative

   China: U.S. acquiring military intelligence of their country.

   U.S.: China acquired valuable intelligence on EP-3.

   Positive

   China: Won international support for anti-U.S. stance.

   U.S.: President perceived as strong, without using force.

5. **Make recommendations for increasing the positive consequences for both Americans and those from other countries.**

U.S.–China Relations (U.S. Department of State)

U.S.–China relations cooled after the incident but gradually improved. Following the September 11, 2001, terrorist attacks in New York City and Washington D.C., China offered strong public support for the war on terrorism and has been an important partner in U.S. counterterrorism efforts. China and the U.S. have also been working closely on regional issues like North Korea.

Lesson 4

Historical Timeline: Choices, Decisions, and Consequences

Key Terms

chronological
timeline

What You Will Learn to Do

- Outline how major decisions (leadership, ethical, or global) have led to significant events in American history

Linked Core Abilities

- Apply critical thinking techniques

Skills and Knowledge You Will Gain Along the Way

- Examine ways leadership, ethical, global decisions have impacted history
- Describe how historic events have influenced leadership, ethical, and global decisions
- Investigate historic actions and decisions that have influenced citizens today
- Define key words contained in this lesson

Chapter 8

Introduction

History is a fascinating subject. There is an almost irresistible draw to look at the bigger picture—the overall course of events—in an attempt to glean some insight, or to approach some greater knowledge.

An important aspect in the study of an historical event is an analysis of the significant actions that took place. History is more than memorization of dates, events, and people. History influences the future. What happened yesterday affected events today; what happens today impacts life tomorrow. In this lesson you will assess how major leadership, ethical, and/or global decisions led to significant events in American history. You will examine a timeline to get an idea of how that history played out.

One Thing Leads to Another

Imagine this scenario: You wake up late one morning and miss the bus to school. Because of that, you also miss an important exam in a class. Your instructor will not let you make up the exam, so you get a lower grade then you expected in this class. And that lower grade keeps you from traveling with the debate team to a crucial debate. The team loses.

Now, imagine this: You get up on time to get to school. You take the exam in your class and get an A+. You travel with your debate team to the crucial debate and because of your debating expertise, your team wins. Also, there's someone at the debate from an exceptional university who sees you debate and offers you a full scholarship to this school. You graduate from college with honors and end up becoming President of the United States.

These are two examples of how one event builds on another; how one minor event can greatly influence the future. This concept holds true in American and world history. Try to envision what might have happened if Abraham Lincoln had the flu and couldn't deliver the Gettysburg Address. Or if the Battle of Normandy had never happened? How one event or action is handled can dictate how the future plays out; one thing leads to another.

Examining a Timeline

One way to examine how historical events build on one another to bring us to where we are today is to analyze a **timeline.** A timeline is an account of specific decisions and events, broken down into specific segments of time. Timelines can visually share changes over time in different curriculum areas such as science, social studies, math, and language arts. Timelines can document the events of a person's or character's life, the stages of an animal's life, the sequence of how something occurred, or the events in a time period.

The entries on a timeline are not listed in order of importance; rather, they are shown in the **chronological** order that the events happened. By showing the timing of events, you can see how one incident or event has an effect on another.

Have you ever wondered how Saddam Hussein took control of Iraq? What led to the current situation? The following is one example of a timeline of the history of Iraq from 1920 through 1991.

By examining this timeline, you can ask yourself:

- **What might have happened if Iraq had not received independence from Britain until later?**
- **Would Israel have been different if Iraq had not joined in the 1948 attack of the newly independent state?**
- **How might today's Iraq be different if the Kurds had not violated their peace agreement?**
- **If Al-Bakr had not resigned and Saddam Hussein succeeded him, who might have eventually led Iraq, and how would their politics have changed history?**

Through timelines, you can see where one action influenced how the next action occurred. One historic action caused or had a major impact on another, and the timeline gives you a clear picture of choices, decisions, and consequences from the timing of these events.

Other examples of timelines include the following:

1920	Iraq comes under British mandate after the fall of the Ottoman empire in 1918.
1921	Faisal I becomes king of Iraq (Aug. 23).
1932	Iraq achieves independence from Britain (Oct. 3).
1933	Faisal I dies and is succeeded by his son, Ghazi.
1934	The first of seven military coups over the next five years takes place; King Ghazi is retained as a figurehead.
1939	King Ghazi is killed in an automobile accident; his son, Faisal II, 3, becomes king; Faisal's uncle, Emir Abd al-Ilah, becomes regent.
1940	Anti-British leaders in Iraq side with the Axis powers in the early part of World War II.
1941	Britain defeats Iraq; pro-Axis leaders flee.
1943	Iraq declares war on the Axis countries.
1945	Iraq becomes a charter member of the Arab League.
1948	Iraq and other Arab countries launch an unsuccessful war against Israel, which had declared statehood that year.

1958	A military coup overthrows the monarchy, kills King Faisal II, and declares Iraq a republic. General Abdul Karim Kassem becomes Iraq's leader, and begins reversing the monarchy's pro-western policies (July 14).
1961	The Kurds, located in northern Iraq, revolt and demand autonomy; fighting between the Kurds and the government continues for decades.
1963	Kassem is killed in a coup led by Colonel Abd al-Salam Aref and the military as well as members of the Ba'ath party (Feb. 8). The Ba'ath party, founded in Syria, advocates pan-Arabism, secularism, and socialism. Colonel Aref becomes president, Ahmed Hasan al-Bakr of the Ba'ath Party becomes president. Aref purges the government of Ba'ath party, including President al-Bakr.
1966	Aref dies; his brother, Abdul Rahman Aref, takes over the presidency (Apr. 17).
1968	Ahmad Hasan al-Bakr overthrows Aref in a bloodless coup. The Ba'ath party again dominates (July 17).
1970	A peace agreement is signed between the Iraqi government and the Kurds, granting the Kurds some self-rule (March 11).
1973	Iraq fights in the Arab-Israeli War (The Yom Kippur War) and participates in the oil boycott against Israel's supporters.
1975	Fighting again breaks out with the Kurds, who call for their independence.
1979	Al-Bakr resigns; his vice-president, Saddam Hussein, succeeds him (July 16). Hussein swiftly executes political rivals.
1980	The bloody eight-year Iran–Iraq war begins. The main issue is control of the Shatt al Arab waterway, an essential resource providing for water and transportation that runs along the border of both countries (Sept. 22).
1988	Iraq retaliates against the Kurds for supporting Iran during the Iran–Iraq war, and through "Operation Anfal" slaughters civilians or forces them to relocate. Thousands flee to Turkey (Feb.–Sept.). Iran–Iraq war ends in a stalemate. An estimated 1.5 million died in the conflict (Aug. 20).
1990	Iraqi troops invade Kuwait. Saddam Hussein justifies the attack by blaming Kuwait for falling oil prices that harm the Iraqi economy (Aug. 2). The UN imposes economic sanctions on Iraq (Aug 6). U.S. military forces arrive in Saudi Arabia (Aug. 9). The UN issues a Security Council resolution setting Jan. 15, 1991, as the deadline for Iraq's withdrawal from Kuwait, authorizing the use of "all necessary means" if it does not comply (Nov. 29).

1991	The Persian Gulf War begins when Operation Desert Storm launched by a U.S.-led coalition of 32 countries under the leadership of U.S. Gen. Norman Schwarzkopf. A campaign of air strikes against Iraq begins (Jan. 16–17).
	Ground forces invade Kuwait and Iraq, vanquish the Iraqi army, and liberate Kuwait. President George H. W. Bush declares a cease-fire on the fourth day (Feb. 24–28).
	Shiites and Kurds rebel, encouraged by the United States. Iraq quashes the rebellions, killing thousands (March).
	Formal cease-fire is signed. Saddam Hussein accepts UN resolution agreeing to destroy weapons of mass destruction and allowing UN inspectors to monitor the disarmament (April 6).
	A no-fly zone is established in Northern Iraq to protect the Kurds from Saddam Hussein (April 10).
	UN weapons inspectors report that that Iraq has concealed much of its nuclear and chemical weapons programs. It is the first of many such reports over the next decade, pointing out Iraq's thwarting of the UN weapons inspectors (July 30).
1992	A southern no-fly zone is created to protect the Shiite population from Saddam Hussein and provide a buffer between Kuwait and Iraq (Aug. 26).
	U.S. launches cruise missile on Baghdad, after Iraq attempts to assassinate President George H. W. Bush while he visited Kuwait (June 27).
1994	Iraq drains water from southern marshlands inhabited by Muslim Shiites, in retaliation for the Shiites' long-standing opposition to Saddam Hussein's government (April).
1996	A UN Security Council's "oil-for-food" resolution (passed April 1995) allows Iraq to export oil in exchange for humanitarian aid. Iraq delays accepting the terms for more than 1 year (Dec. 10).
1997	The UN disarmament commission concludes that Iraq has continued to conceal information on biological and chemical weapons and missiles (Oct. 23).
	Iraq expels the American members of the UN inspection team (Nov. 13).
1998	Iraq suspends all cooperation with the UN inspectors (Jan. 13).
	UN secretary-general Kofi Annan brokers a peaceful solution to the standoff. Over the next months Baghdad continued to impede the UN inspection team, demanding that sanctions be lifted (Feb. 23).
	Saddam Hussein puts a complete halt to the inspections (Oct. 31).

1998	Iraq agrees to unconditional cooperation with the UN inspectors (Nov. 14), but by a month later, chief UN weapons inspector Richard Butler reports that Iraq has not lived up to its promise (Dec. 15).
Cont.	The United States and Britain began four days of intensive air strikes, dubbed Operation Desert Fox. The attacks focused on command centers, missile factories, and airfields—targets that the Pentagon believed would damage Iraq's weapons stores (Dec. 16–19).
1999	Beginning in January, weekly, sometimes daily, bombings of Iraqi targets within the northern no-fly zone begin, carried out by U.S. and British bombers. More than 100 air strikes take place during 1999, and continue regularly over the next years. The U.S. and Britain hope the constant barrage of air strikes will weaken Saddam Hussein's grip on Iraq (Jan. 1999–present).

NOTE

To view more timelines, go to *http://ph.infoplease.com/spot/timelinearchive.html*. Another good website for timelines is *http://www2.canisius.edu/~emeryg/time.html*. Both of these websites offer many timelines for you to examine.

Why Study Timelines

There is a saying that those who do not remember history are doomed to repeat it. By studying history through historical timelines, you can make decisions so that history does not repeat itself. Basically, if an action didn't work at one point in time, it is unlikely that it will work now.

Timelines also show how events went from Point A to Point B. By understanding how decisions were made and events unfolded, you have a better idea of the history of any situation, can form knowledgeable opinions, and make decisions based on sound information. For example, check out *http://www2.canisius.edu/~emeryg/time.html* and examine the following timelines:

- **The Berlin Wall (construction and destruction)**
- **The U.S. Civil War**
- **The Holocaust**
- **The Vietnam War**
- **The American Revolution**
- **America's Great Depression**

By looking at these timelines, you can ask and answer:

- **How did leadership, as well as ethical and global decisions impact history?**
- **How did historic events influence leadership, ethical, and global decisions?**
- **How did these historic actions and decisions influence citizens today?**

Figure 8.4.1: The bombing of Japan in World War II is still ethically debated, but the outcome shortened the War.

Courtesy of AP/Wide World Photos.

One example of an ethical decision based on recent history was the bombing of Japan in World War II (see Figure 8.4.1). By understanding the events that led up to that decision and actions, you can get an idea of how and why this event occurred.

Ethical Decisions on a Global Scale

As you learned in Chapter 8, Lesson 2, "Ethical Choices, Decisions, and Consequences," ethical choices can lead to good or bad consequences. When looking at timelines, you can see what lead up to these decisions, and how they influenced history. Take, for example, the U.S. dropping the atomic bomb on Japan in World War II.

NOTE

The word "ethics" comes from the Greek word *ethos,* meaning character, a way of life. Western philosophers transformed the root word to refer to a good way of life appropriate to all human beings in all places in all times. Largely by way of reason, but sometimes by education, every person can understand the rules of ethical behavior. The word "morality" comes from the Latin moralis, meaning customs or manners, and therefore refers to the laws and traditions of particular places and times. To give you an understanding of the difference, almost all societies condemn stealing. This is a matter of ethics. But the penalties for stealing have varied throughout history and national culture. In one of the classics of Western literature, *Les Miserables,* the protagonist, Jean Valjean was condemned to 19 years in prison for stealing a loaf of bread to feed his family. His penalty was a matter of morality. Ethics, then, seems to pertain to the individual character of a person or persons, where morality seems to point to the relationship between human beings. Nevertheless, in ordinary language, whether a person is called ethical or moral, or an act is referred to as unethical or immoral, doesn't really make any difference. In philosophy, however, the term ethics is also used to refer to a specific area of study: morality, which concentrates on human conduct and human values.

Figure 8.4.2: Did the outcome of this action out-
weigh the devastation? A
timeline can help answer
questions such as this.

Courtesy of Corbis Images.

On August 6, 1945, the atomic bomb was dropped on the Japanese city of
Hiroshima. After being released from the Enola Gay, one of the B-29 bombers flying
over the city on that day, it took about a minute for the bomb (nicknamed "Little
Boy") to reach the point of explosion. Little Boy exploded at approximately 8:15 A.M.
(Japan Standard Time) when it reached an altitude of 2,000 feet above the building
that is today called the "A-Bomb Dome."

Little Boy, shown in Figure 8.4.2, generated an enormous amount of energy in terms
of air pressure and heat. In addition, it generated a significant amount of radiation
(Gamma ray and neutrons) that subsequently caused devastating human injuries.

The strong wind generated by the bomb destroyed most of the houses and buildings within a 1.5 mile radius. When the wind reached the mountains, it was
reflected and again hit the people in the city center. The wind generated by Little
Boy caused the most serious damage to the city and people.

On August 9, 1945, another atomic bomb (nicknamed "Fat Man") was dropped on
Japan, this time on the city of Nagasaki. The following day, on August 10th, Japan
surrendered, thus drawing World War II to its conclusion. The following timeline
shows the events from July 16, 1945, when the first atomic bomb was tested in New
Mexico, to the day of Japan's surrender. By examining the following timeline, you
can get an idea of some of the global events that led up to the decision to drop the
bomb on Japan.

Jul 16, 1945	The first U.S. test explosion of the atomic bomb was made at Alamogordo Air Base, south of Albuquerque, New Mexico, equal to some twenty thousand tons of TNT. The bomb was called the Gadget and the experiment was called Trinity. It was conducted in a part of the desert called Jornada del Muerto, (Dead Man's Trail), and measured the equivalent of 18,600 (21,000) tons of TNT. It was the culmination of 28 months of intense scientific research conducted under the leadership of physicist Dr. J. Robert Oppenheimer under the code name Manhattan Project. The successful atomic test was witnessed by only one journalist, William L. Laurence of the New York Times, who described seeing the blinding explosion.
Jul 17– Aug 2, 1945	President Truman, Soviet leader Josef Stalin, and British Prime Minister Winston S. Churchill (and his successor Clement Atlee) began meeting at the Schloss Cecilienhof in Potsdam in the final Allied summit of World War II. It re-established the European borders that were in effect as of Dec 31, 1937.
Jul 23, 1945	French Marshal Henri Petain, who had headed the Vichy government during World War II, went on trial, charged with treason. He was condemned to death, but his sentence was commuted.
Jul 24, 1945	U.S. Navy bombers sank the Japanese battleship-carrier Hyuga in shallow waters off Kure, Japan.
Jul 26, 1945	U.S. cruiser Indianapolis reached Tinian with atom bomb.
Jul 26, 1945	The U.S., Britain, and China issued the Potsdam Declaration to Japan that she surrenders unconditionally. Two days later Japanese Premier Kantaro Suzuki announced to the Japanese press that the Potsdam declaration is to be ignored.
Jul 29, 1945	After delivering parts of the first atomic bomb to the island of Tinian, the USS Indianapolis was hit and sunk by the I-58 Japanese submarine around midnight. Some 900 survivors jumped into the sea and were adrift for 4 days. Nearly 600 died before help arrived.
Jul 30, 1945	The USS Indianapolis, which had just delivered key components of the Hiroshima atomic bomb to the Pacific island of Tinian, was torpedoed by a Japanese submarine. Only 316 out of 1,196 men survived the sinking and shark-infested waters.
Aug 3, 1945	Chinese troops under American General Joseph Stilwell took the town of Myitkyina from the Japanese.
Aug 6, 1945	Hiroshima, Japan, was struck with the uranium bomb, Little Boy, from the B-29 airplane, Enola Gay, piloted by Col. Paul Tibbets of the US Air Force along with 11 other men. The atom bomb killed an estimated 140,000 people in the first use of a nuclear weapon in warfare. Major Thomas Wilson Ferebee was the bombardier. Richard Nelson was the radio operator.
Aug 8, 1945	President Truman signed the United Nations Charter.
Aug 8, 1945	The Soviet Union declared war against Japan.
Aug 9, 1945	The 10,000 lb. plutonium bomb, Fat Man, was dropped over Nagasaki after the primary objective of Kokura was passed due to visibility problems. It killed an estimated 74,000 people. The B-29 bomber plane Bock's Car so named for its assigned pilot, Fred Bock, was piloted by Captain Charles W. Sweeney. Kermit Beahan (d.1989) was the bombardier.
Aug 10, 1945	Japan announced its willingness to surrender to Allies provided that the status of Emperor Hirohito remains unchanged. Yosuke Yamahata photographed the aftermath of the bombing of Nagasaki. He was dispatched by the Japanese military, but did not turn over the pictures to the military authorities.

When thinking of ethical decisions that affected U.S. and world history, try to imagine how history would have been changed if the atomic bomb had not been dropped on Japan during World War II. Would the war have continued much longer? Would the U.S. have been attacked again by the Japanese, as they had been at Pearl Harbor the year before? Because the Soviet Union had declared war on Japan on August 8th, do you think that thousands of Soviet and U.S. soldiers would have lost their lives? By looking at a timeline, how can you predict what might have happened if the decision to drop the atomic bombs had been different?

Ethical Decisions on a Local Level

Historic timelines can also show events on a local level. Take this example: The city of Indianapolis, Indiana, had a problem. Local leaders noted that historically in the summertime when kids were out of school, many disadvantaged children were not eating lunch. When school was in session, a midday meal was supplied by the school system, but this wasn't the case when the schools were closed for summer vacation. This data had been collected and was presented in a timeline spanning several years. These kids still needed lunch, so local Indianapolis leaders set out to solve this problem.

With local government and community support, Indy Parks and Recreation began hosting the Free Summer Lunch Program at park locations and other partnered sites throughout the city. In the summer of 2004, the fifth year this program had been in existence, Indy Park officials expected that more than 70,000 lunches would be served. Free meals were available to children 18 years of age and under, and were provided without regard to race, color, national origin, sex, age, or disability. This program will continue, and will most likely grow larger with each summer, but the city of Indianapolis is prepared to handle it.

This is an example of how local leaders looked at the historic decline of local nutrition, made a decision to solve the problem, and did the ethically correct thing. They provided meals for those who wouldn't otherwise have had food during the day.

Conclusion

One decision or action builds on another, and these events are what comprise not only history but the future as well. To get a clear picture of how events unfolded or how specific decisions caused specific actions, a timeline is an invaluable tool. Timelines break down history into chunks of categorized information, and show how present times came about.

This concludes the chapter, "Critical Thinking in Citizenship." In this chapter, you have examined choices, decisions, and consequences in leadership. You have learned about ethical decision making, and what it takes to be a good global citizen. You also learned the importance of examining historic events in making choices and decisions in the present.

Lesson Review

1. Define the term "timeline."

2. What does a timeline show?

3. Is there a limit to the amount of time a timeline can show? Why?

4. Why is it important to see how decisions were made and events unfolded?

Case Study

Exercise: Historical case study to examine the impact of a **series of events.** Discuss **citizen and global reactions** during and after the events described in the case study. **Classify events** that involved leadership, ethical, or global decisions. **Predict** what might have happened if different choices and decisions were made.

Timeline—a timeline is an account of specific decisions and events, broken down into specific segments of time.

The Spark That Ignited World War I

On June 28, 1914, Gavrilo Princip, a Bosnian Serb and radical nationalist, assassinated Franz Ferdinand, the Archduke of Austria-Hungary and heir to the throne, and his wife, Sophie (see Figure 8.4.3). How could this single act of barbarism engulf over 32 nations and 30,000,000 lives in world war?

Figure 8.4.3: The assassination of Austria's Franz Ferdinand and his wife Sophie was the act that set World War I in motion.

Courtesy of Bettmann/ Corbis Images.

Historians trace the origins of World War I to the end of the Napoleonic era and blame the Congress of Vienna in 1815 for setting conditions for the Franco-Prussian war in 1870 leading to the rise of Germany in 1871. Eager to maintain Germany's new status as a major European power, Chancellor Otto von Bismarck began forming a system of alliances designed to isolate France. In 1872, Bismarck orchestrated the League of the Three Emperors between Kaiser Wilhelm I of Germany, Czar Alexander II of Russia, and Emperor Franz Joseph of Austria. Russia departed the League after Germany sided with Austria over a dispute in the Balkans during the Congress of Berlin in 1878.

In the absence of Russia, Bismarck forged the Dual Alliance with Austria in 1879, and expanded it to include Italy, thus creating the Triple Alliance in 1882. Bismarck made no formal alliance with Britain, but did his best to remain on friendly terms with the traditional enemy of France. For 20 years, Bismarck maintained the peace in Europe by brokering a skillful balance of powers on the continent.

In 1890, Bismarck was dismissed by Kaiser Wilhelm II. The new emperor wanted to make Germany a world power, and commenced a program of colonial and naval expansion. Alarmed by Germany's ambition and suspicious of her ties with Austria, Russia sided with France and formed the Franco-Russian Alliance in 1893. In 1905, the German General Staff formulated the Schlieffen Plan advocating an attack on France in the event of war with Russia. Feeling increasingly isolated, Britain began to seek her own alliances. In 1902, she concluded the Anglo-Japanese Alliance to check Russian expansion in the Pacific.

In 1904, Britain defied expectations by signing the Entente Cordiale expressing friendship with France. In 1907, Britain joined the Triple Entente allying with both Russia and France. The Triple Entente of Britain, France, and Russia now stood in direct opposition to the Triple Alliance of Germany, Austria, and Italy. A single incident could now ignite global conflagration.

In 1912, Italy came into conflict with the Ottoman Empire over holdings in the Adriatic Sea. Serbia took advantage of the weakened Ottoman Empire to attack Bulgaria. Russia sided with Serbia while Austria supported Bulgaria; Britain and Germany urged peace. Russia and Austria were now poised for war. The crisis enraged Serbs against Austria for its support of Bulgaria and its continued occupation of Bosnia-Herzegovina. On June 28, 1914, when Gavrilo Princip assassinated Franz Ferdinand, Austria declared war on Serbia. Russia declared war on Austria. Germany attacked into France, and Europe was plunged into the first world war.

References

World War I (1914–1918) Timeline, www.sparknotes.com/history/european/ww1/htimeline.html

World War I, www.thecorner.org/wwi

The Great War, "Causes of World War I," Suzanne Karpilovsky, Maria Fogel, Olivia Kobelt, www.pvhs.chico.k12.ca.us/~bsilva/projects/great_war/causes.htm

Event	Reaction	Classification
1871—Creation of the German Empire under Kaiser Wilhelm I and Otto von Bismarck.	None	**leadership**—unify independent states into German nation.
1873—Three Emperor's League established between Germany, Austria, Hungary, and Russia.	None	**global**—isolate France.

Event	Reaction	Classification
1874—First Balkan Crisis; revolt in Bosnia-Herzegovina.	**1878**—Congress of Berlin **1879**—Dual Alliance between Germany and Austria-Hungary	**leadership**—Russia resigns from the Three Emperor's League. **global**—Russia forms enmity against Austria.
1882—Triple Alliance between Germany, Austria-Hungary, and Italy.	**1894**—Franco-Russian Alliance	**global**—Franco and Russia unite to contain Germany.
1890—Kaiser Withelm II fires Otto von Bismarck.	**1890**—Germany embarks on colonial and military expansion.	**ethical**—Kaiser Wilhelm interested in the greater glory of an expanded Germany.
1905—Development of Schlieffen Plan in Germany.	None	**global**—War with Russia will provoke an automatic attack against France.
1907—Triple Entente between Britain, France, and Russia.	**1907**—Germany begins military buildup and naval arms race.	**global**—the Triple Entente and Triple Alliance stand in opposition; an attack on one will ignite global conflagration.
1912 to 1913—Third Balkan Crisis.	• Austria and Russia now poised for war. • Serbians hate Austria.	**global**—conditions set to start global war.
June 28, 1914—Gavrilo Princip Assassinates Archduke Franz Ferdinand of Austria.	• Austria declares war against Serbia. • Russia declares war against Austria. • Germany invades France. • Britain declares war against Germany.	**ethical**—Gavrilo Princip attempted to achieve nationalist objectives through illegal and immoral means.

Unit 6: Citizenship in American History and Government
Correlated to:
McRel Standards for Civics, Thinking and Reasoning, Working with Others, Self Regulation and US History

McRel Standards	Unit 6: Citizenship in American History and Government
CIVICS STANDARDS (C) **What is Government and What Should it Do?**	
C 1. Understands ideas about civic life, politics, and government	Citizenship Skills, 8–19; Our Natural Rights, 47–62; Constitution Used to Organize New Government, 184–190; Bill of Rights, 191–198; Rise of Political Parties, 199–207; Judicial Review, 208–216; Division of Power, 217–222; Roles of Citizens, 345–359; New Citizenship and Constitutional Issues, 360–371; Constitutionalism and Other Countries, 372–381; Defending Fundamental Principles, 382–291
C 2. Understands the essential characteristics of limited and unlimited governments	Our Natural Rights, 47–62; Developing Republican Government, 63–79; Constitution Used to Organize New Government, 184–190; Bill of Rights, 191–198; Rise of Political Parties, 199–207; Judicial Review, 208–216; Division of Power, 217–222; First Amendment and Freedom of Expression 286–294; First Amendment and Freedom of Assembly, 295–303
C 3. Understands the sources, purposes, and functions of law, and the importance of the rule of law for the protection of individual rights and the common good	Introduction to Chief Justice, 38–45; Our Natural Rights, 47–62; Developing Republican Government, 63–79; British Origins of American Constitutionalism, 80–93; Colonial Government—Basic Rights and Constitutional Government, 94–113; State Constitutions, 114–125; Constitution Used to Organize New Government, 184–190; Bill of Rights, 191–198; Rise of Political Parties, 199–207; Judicial Review, 208–216; Division of Power, 217–222; Procedural Due Process, 304–311; Military Justice System, 333–343

Copyright © 2004 McREL
Mid-continent Research for Education and Learning
2550 S. Parker Road, Suite 500
Aurora, CO 80014
Telephone: 303/337-0990
www.mcrel.org/standards-benchmarks

McRel Standards	Unit 6: Citizenship in American History and Government
What is Government and What Should it Do?	
C 4. Understands the concept of a constitution, the various purposes that constitutions serve, and the conditions that contribute to the establishment and maintenance of constitutional government	The Preamble, 3–7; Our Natural Rights, 47–62; Developing Republican Government, 63–79; British Origins of American Constitutionalism, 80–93; Colonial Government—Basic Rights and Constitutional Government, 94–113; State Constitutions, 114–125; Articles of Confederation 1781, 127–137; Creating Our Constitution, 138–150; Balancing Power, 151–169; The Debate over the Constitution, 170–182; Constitution Used to Organize New Government, 184–190; Bill of Rights, 191–198; Rise of Political Parties, 199–207; Judicial Review, 208–216; Division of Power, 217–222; Civil Rights Movement, 247–257; First Amendment and Freedom of Religion, 277–285; First Amendment and Freedom of Expression, 286–294; First Amendment and Freedom of Assembly, 295–303; Procedural Due Process, 304–311; Protection against Unreasonable Law Enforcement, 312–322; Protection of Rights within the Judicial System, 323–332
C 6. Understands the advantages and disadvantages of federal, confederal, and unitary systems of government	Articles of Confederation 1781, 127–137; Creating Our Constitution, 138–150; Balancing Power, 151–169; The Debate over the Constitution, 170–182; Constitution Used to Organize New Government, 184–190
C 7. Understands alternative forms of representation and how they serve the purposes of constitutional government	Constitutionalism and Other Countries, 372–381
What are the Basic Values and Principals of American Democracy?	
C 8. Understands the central ideas of American constitutional government and how this form of government has shaped the character of American society	The Preamble, 3–7; Developing Republican Government, 63–79; British Origins of American Constitutionalism, 80–93; State Constitutions, 114–125; Articles of Confederation 1781, 127–137; Creating Our Constitution, 138–150; Balancing Power, 151–169; The Debate over the Constitution, 170–182; Constitution Used to Organize New Government, 184–190; Bill of Rights, 191–198; Rise of Political Parties, 199–207; Judicial Review, 208–216; Division of Power, 217–222; First Amendment and Freedom of Religion, 277–285; First Amendment and Freedom of Expression, 286–294; First Amendment and Freedom of Assembly, 295–303; Procedural Due Process, 304–311; Protection against Unreasonable Law Enforcement, 312–322; Protection of Rights within the Judicial System, 323–332; Roles of Citizens, 345–359; New Citizenship and Constitutional Issues, 360–371; Constitutionalism and Other Countries, 372–381; Defending Fundamental Principles, 382–291

McRel Standards	Unit 6: Citizenship in American History and Government
What are the Basic Values and Principals of American Democracy?	
C 9. Understands the importance of Americans sharing and supporting certain values, beliefs, and principles of American constitutional democracy	The Preamble, 3–7; Citizenship Skills, 8–19; Colonial Government—Basic Rights and Constitutional Government, 94–113; Civil Rights Movement, 247–257; First Amendment and Freedom of Religion, 277–285; First Amendment and Freedom of Expression, 286–294; First Amendment and Freedom of Assembly, 295–303; Procedural Due Process, 304–311; Protection against Unreasonable Law Enforcement, 312–322; Protection of Rights within the Judicial System, 323–332; Roles of Citizens, 345–359; New Citizenship and Constitutional Issues, 360–371; Defending Fundamental Principles, 382–291
C 10. Understands the roles of voluntarism and organized groups in American social and political life	Small Group Meetings, 20–31; Rise of Political Parties, 199–207; Civil Rights Movement, 247–257; First Amendment and Freedom of Assembly, 295–303; Roles of Citizens, 345–359
C 11. Understands the role of diversity in American life and the importance of shared values, political beliefs, and civic beliefs in an increasingly diverse American society	Citizenship Skills, 8–19; Small Group Meetings, 20–31; Representative Group Sessions, 32–37; Colonial Government—Basic Rights and Constitutional Government, 94–113; Civil Rights Movement, 247–257; First Amendment and Freedom of Religion, 277–285; First Amendment and Freedom of Expression, 286–294; First Amendment and Freedom of Assembly, 295–303; Roles of Citizens, 345–359; New Citizenship and Constitutional Issues, 360–371
C 12. Understands the relationships among liberalism, republicanism, and American constitutional democracy	Developing Republican Government, 63–79; British Origins of American Constitutionalism, 80–93
C 14. Understands issues concerning the disparities between ideals and reality in American political and social life	Civil Rights Movement, 247–257; Right to Vote, 258–266; Using the Law to Correct Injustice, 267–276
How Does the Government Established by the Constitution Embody the Purposes, Values, and Principles of American Democracy?	
C 15. Understands how the United States Constitution grants and distributes power and responsibilities to national and state government and how it seeks to prevent the abuse of power	Division of Power, 217–222; Procedural Due Process, 304–311; Protection against Unreasonable Law Enforcement, 312–322; Protection of Rights within the Judicial System, 323–332
C 18. Understands the role and importance of law in the American constitutional system and issues regarding the judicial protection of individual rights	Introduction to Chief Justice, 38–45; Using the Law to Correct Injustice, 267–276; First Amendment and Freedom of Religion, 277–285; First Amendment and Freedom of Expression, 286–294; First Amendment and Freedom of Assembly, 295–303; Procedural Due Process, 304–311; Protection against Unreasonable Law Enforcement, 312–322; Protection of Rights within the Judicial System, 323–332

McRel Standards	Unit 6: Citizenship in American History and Government
What is the Relationship of the United States to Other Nations and to World Affairs?	
C 23. Understands the impact of significant political and nonpolitical developments on the United States and other nations	Global Citizenship Choices, Decisions, and Consequences, 421–442; Historical Timeline: Choices, Decisions, and Consequences, 443–456
What are the Roles of the Citizen in American Democracy?	
C 24. Understands the meaning of citizenship in the United States, and knows the requirements for citizenship and naturalization	Roles of Citizens, 345–359; New Citizenship and Constitutional Issues, 360–371
C 25. Understands issues regarding personal, political, and economic rights	First Amendment and Freedom of Religion, 277–285; First Amendment and Freedom of Expression, 286–294; First Amendment and Freedom of Assembly, 295–303; Procedural Due Process, 304–311; Protection against Unreasonable Law Enforcement, 312–322; Protection of Rights within the Judicial System, 323–332
C 26. Understands issues regarding the proper scope and limits of rights and the relationships among personal, political, and economic rights	Right to Vote, 258–266
C 27. Understands how certain character traits enhance citizens' ability to fulfill personal and civic responsibilities	Ethical Choices, Decisions, and Consequences, 407–420
C 28. Understands how participation in civic and political life can help citizens attain individual and public goals	Right to Vote, 258–266; Roles of Citizens, 345–359; Defending Fundamental Principles, 382–291
C 29. Understands the importance of political leadership, public service, and a knowledgeable citizenry in American constitutional democracy	Roles of Citizens, 345–359; Leadership Choices, Decisions and Consequences, 393–402; Defending Fundamental Principles, 382–291
THINKING AND REASONING STANDARDS (TR)	
TR 1. Understands and applies the basic principles of presenting an argument	Introduction to Chief Justice, 38–45; Defending Fundamental Principles, 382–291; Case Study: Is Iraq another Vietnam?, 403–406
TR 2. Understands and applies basic principles of logic and reasoning	Leadership Choices, Decisions and Consequences, 393–402; Case Study: Is Iraq another Vietnam?, 403–406
TR 3. Effectively uses mental processes that are based on identifying similarities and differences	Developing Republican Government, 63–79; Defending Fundamental Principles, 382–291; Case Study: Is Iraq another Vietnam?, 403–406
TR 5. Applies basic trouble-shooting and problem-solving techniques	Small Group Meetings, 20–31; Representative Group Sessions, 32–37; Leadership Choices, Decisions and Consequences, 393–402

McRel Standards	Unit 6: Citizenship in American History and Government
THINKING AND REASONING STANDARDS (TR)	
TR 6. Applies decision-making techniques	Small Group Meetings, 20–31; Representative Group Sessions, 32–37; First Amendment and Freedom of Religion, 277–285; Leadership Choices, Decisions and Consequences, 393–402; Ethical Choices, Decisions, and Consequences, 407–420; Global Citizenship Choices, Decisions, and Consequences, 421–442; Historical Timeline: Choices, Decisions, and Consequences, 443–456
WORKING WITH OTHERS STANDARDS (WO)	
WO 1. Contributes to the overall effort of a group	Citizenship Skills, 8–19; Small Group Meetings, 20–31; Representative Group Sessions, 32–37; Leadership Choices, Decisions and Consequences, 393–402
WO 2. Uses conflict-resolution techniques	Small Group Meetings, 20–31; Representative Group Sessions, 32–37
WO 3. Works well with diverse individuals in diverse situations	Citizenship Skills, 8–19; Small Group Meetings, 20–31; Representative Group Sessions, 32–37
WO 4. Displays effective interpersonal communication skills	Citizenship Skills, 8–19; Small Group Meetings, 20–31; Representative Group Sessions, 32–37; Introduction to Chief Justice, 38–45
WO 5. Demonstrates leadership skills	Small Group Meetings, 20–31; Representative Group Sessions, 32–37; Protection of Rights within the Judicial System, 323–332; Leadership Choices, Decisions, and Consequences, 393–402
SELF REGULATION STANDARDS	
SR 1. Sets and manages goals	The Preamble, 3–7; Leadership Choices, Decisions, and Consequences, 393–402
SR 2. Performs self-appraisal	Leadership Choices, Decisions, and Consequences, 393–402
SR 3. Considers risks	Ethical Choices, Decisions, and Consequences, 407–420; Global Citizenship Choices, Decisions, and Consequences, 421–442; Historical Timeline: Choices, Decisions, and Consequences, 443–456
SR 4. Demonstrates perseverance	
SR 5. Maintains a healthy self-concept	Leadership Choices, Decisions and Consequences, 393–402
SR 6. Restrains impulsivity	

McRel Standards	Unit 6: Citizenship in American History and Government
US HISTORY STANDARDS (USH)	
USH6. Understands the causes of the American Revolution, the ideas and interests involved in shaping the revolutionary movement, and reasons for the American victory	Our Natural Rights, 47–62
USH6. Understands the impact of the American Revolution on politics, economy, and society	The Preamble, 3–7; Developing Republican Government, 63–79; British Origins of American Constitutionalism, 80–93; State Constitutions, 114–125; Articles of Confederation 1781, 127–137; Creating Our Constitution, 138–150; Balancing Power, 151–169; The Debate over the Constitution, 170–182; Constitution Used to Organize New Government, 184–190; Bill of Rights, 191–198
USH8. Understands the institutions and practices of government created during the Revolution and how these elements were revised between 1787 and 1815 to create the foundation of the American political system bases on the U.S. Constitution and the Bill of Rights	The Preamble, 3–7; Our Natural Rights, 47–62; Developing Republican Government, 63–79; British Origins of American Constitutionalism, 80–93; Colonial Government—Basic Rights and Constitutional Government, 94–113; State Constitutions, 114–125; Articles of Confederation 1781, 127–137; Creating Our Constitution, 138–150; Balancing Power, 151–16; The Debate over the Constitution, 170–182; Constitution Used to Organize New Government, 184–190; Bill of Rights, 191–198; Rise of Political Parties, 199–207; Judicial Review, 208–216; Division of Power, 217–222
USH12. Understands the sources and character of cultural, religious, and social reform movements in the antebellum period	First Amendment and Freedom of Religion, 277–285
USH13. Understands the causes of the Civil War	Constitutional Issues and Civil War, 224–237
USH15. Understands how various reconstruction plans succeeded or failed	Constitutional Issues and Civil War, 224–237; The Fourteenth Amendment, 238–246; Significance of the Plessy v. Ferguson Decision, 248–249; Consequences of Plessy v. Ferguson, 249
USH29. Understands the struggle for racial and gender equality and for the extension of civil liberties	Civil Rights Movement, 247–257; Right to Vote, 258–266

Glossary

A

Absolute veto. The inviolable power to cancel or nullify a legislative act.

Acquitted. To discharge completely.

Admissible. Capable of being allowed or accepted (as in a court of law); worthy of being admitted.

Admonition. Cautionary advice or criticism for a fault; a mild censure.

Adversary system. System of law, generally adopted in common law countries that relies on the skill of the different advocates representing their party's positions and not on some neutral party, usually the judge, trying to ascertain the truth of the case.

Affirmative action. A policy or a program that seeks to redress past discrimination through active measures to ensure equal opportunity, as in education and employment.

After Action Review (AAR). A review of decisions, orders, and actions implemented after the actions are carried out.

Age of Enlightenment. An intellectual movement of the late seventeenth and eighteenth centuries that celebrated human reason and sought to realize its potential in all areas of human endeavor.

Agenda. A list of tasks or a schedule to be followed.

Aggression. An attack or threat of attack by another country.

Aggressive recruitment programs. To obtain replacements for or new supplies of something lost, wasted, or needed.

Agrarian. Characteristic of farmers or their way of life.

Alien and Sedition Acts. Gave the President the power to imprison or deport aliens suspect of activities posing a threat to the national government.

American constitutionalism. Government in which power is distributed and limited by a system of laws that must be obeyed by the rulers.

Anti-Federalist. The early political leaders who were against the ratification of the Constitution because they thought it gave too much power to the national government and did not protect the political rights of the people.

Appellate jurisdiction. The legal authority of a court to hear appeals from a lower court.

Apportioned. The allocation of legislative seats.

Article 15. The least severe and most commonly used punitive measure for minor military offenses. Though called on-judicial punishment, the accused's company or battalion commander (who usually imposes non-judicial punishment) acts in a quasi-judicial capacity.

B

Bail. Money or property in the hands of the government to ensure that the accused will appear in court rather than forfeit it.

Balance. The understanding that there is more than one side to every issue, and having the ability to come to an agreement and resolve differences by using either compromising or harmonizing solutions.

Balance of power. The division of governmental powers in such a way that no one individual or group can dominate or control the exercise of power by others.

Beneficiaries. Those who benefit.

Bills of Attainder. An act of legislature that inflicts punishment on an individual or group without a judicial trial.

Boston Massacre. On March 5, 1770, a mob of colonists harassed British soldiers guarding the tax collector's office in Boston. Soldiers killed five Bostonians.

Boston Tea Party. In an act of rebellion against British authority, and in particular to protest British taxes on tea imported to the colonies, a band of colonists boarded ships in Boston harbor and destroyed thousands of dollars' worth of tea by throwing it overboard.

Broad construction. The idea that judges should be given great leeway in application of the U.S. Constitution in order to adapt to a changing world.

Bureaucracy. Government characterized by specialization of functions, adherence to fixed rules, and a hierarchy of authority.

Burgesses. Wealthy merchants and craftsmen who represented the cities and towns of England.

C

Cantons. A small territorial district; esp. one of the twenty-two independent states which form the Swiss federal republic.

Capitalism. An economic system in which the means of producing and distributing goods are privately owned and operated for profit in a competitive market.

Capital punishment. The death penalty.

Censure. An opinion or judgment that criticizes or condemns sternly.

Charters. Written documents from a government or ruler which grants certain rights to an individual, a group, an organization, or the people in general.

Chief Justice. The highest honor at the end of the game is to become Chief Justice. The game will come to an end and then one law form has reached the level of Supreme Court. The cadets are them asked to confirm a Chief Justice by secret.

Christendom. The Christen world or Christians in general, considered as a single society.

Chronological. A list or arrangement of events in the order they took place.

Civic Virtue. The dedication of citizens to the common good, even at the cost of their individual interests.

Civil and political rights. Rights that protect the individual from wrongful acts by government and provide each citizen with ways to participate in public affairs.

Civil disobedience. The refusal to obey a law, usually on the ground that is morally unjust, or to protest a government policy. Civil disobedience is a form of nonviolent resistance and is aimed at arousing public opinion against the law or policy.

Civil rights. These rights protect us in our private lives from the arbitrary and unfair actions of government.

Civil Rights Act of 1964. An act of Congress designed to protect the rights of individuals to fair treatment by private persons, groups, organizations, businesses, and government.

Civility. Suggests the decency and integrity that are essential to a constitutional democracy.

Classical Republicanism. A theory that holds that the best kind of government is one that promotes the common welfare instead of the interests of one class of citizens.

Clear and present danger. The constitutional ability of the government to restrict First Amendment rights to prevent immediate and severe danger to government interests.

Coerced. The act, process, or power of forcing someone to act or think in a given manner, such as by using force or threats as a form of control.

Commission. An authority, or request, given to another to carry out some act or duty. In particular, a formal written authority given to one party to act in place of another.

Committees of correspondence. Formed to publicize colonial opposition and coordinate resistance throughout the colonies.

Common good. The obligation of each citizen to serve the good of the whole community.

Common law. The body of unwritten law developed in England from judicial decisions based on custom and earlier judicial decisions, which constitutes the basis of the English legal system and became part of American law.

Commonwealth. Something like a republic, that is, self-governing communities of equals whose members were expected to help serve the good of all.

Confederation. A group of confederates, especially states or nations, united for a common purpose; a league.

Consensus. A process by which everyone in a group accepts a decision. It is not necessary for everyone to agree to the decision to reach a consensus, but that everyone accepts the decision or the manner in which it was made, and will not oppose or undermine the result.

Consent. Agreement or acquiescence.

Constituents. The people represented by an elected official.

Constitutional government. A government in which the powers of government are limited in practice by a written or unwritten constitution which they must obey.

Contingency. A plan to cope with events whose occurrence, timing, and severity cannot be predicted

Contracts. Binding agreements between two or more persons.

Cooperation. The art of working together as a group toward a common goal. Cooperation is shown in an attitude of group awareness and willingness to help each other reach a common goal.

Cosmopolitan. Composed of elements from the entire world or from many different parts of the world.

Covenant. A binding agreement made by two or more persons or parties.

Cross examine. To question the witness or opposing side.

Cruel and unusual punishment. The power of judges and juries to decide punishments is limited by the laws passed.

D

Decision making. The process through which a decision is made.

Declaration of Independence. The declaration of the congress of the thirteen United States of America, on the 4th of July, 1776, by which they formally declared that these colonies were free and independent states, not subject to the government of Great Britain.

Delegates. A person chosen to act for or represent others, as at a convention.

Deliberations. A period of time given to a jury to discuss and determine a ruling in a case.

Democracy. A form of government in which political control is exercised by all the people, either directly or through their elected representatives.

Deterrence. Keeping a strong defense to discourage aggression by other nations.

Diplomacy. Relations and communications carried out between countries.

Diversity. Having various forms or qualities; differing from one another.

Double jeopardy. The act of putting a person through a second trial for an offense for which he or she has already been prosecuted or convicted.

Due process. The right to due process.

E

Education Amendment of 1972. No person in the United States shall, on the basis of sex, be excluded from participation in, be denied the benefits of, or be subjected to discrimination under any education program or activity receiving federal financial assistance.

Electoral College. The group of presidential electors that casts the official votes for president after a presidential election.

Electors. A group of persons selected by each state party to vote for that party's candidates for president and vice president if the party's candidates win the popular vote in the general election in that state.

Electronic city-state. The futurist vision of increased citizen participation in public affairs through a telecommunications-based network, or teledemocracy.

Emanations. A specific listing of elements.

Emancipation. The act or an instance of emancipating.

Empowerment. Describes the ability to "make one's voice heard" in public affairs.

Enumerated powers. Those rights and responsibilities of the U.S. government specifically provided for and listed in the constitution.

Enumeration. An act of enumerating.

Epluribus unum. Out of many, one.

Equal Employment Opportunities. Prohibits employment discrimination based on race, color, religion, sex, or national origin.

Equal Pay Act of 1963. To prohibit discrimination on account of sex in the payment of wages by employers engaged in commerce or in the production of goods for commerce.

Equal protection. A requirement of the fourteenth amendment to the U.S. Constitution that state laws may not arbitrarily discriminate against persons.

Equal [state] representation. Each state has the same number of representatives in Congress.

Established church. A church that is recognized by law, and sometimes financially supported, as the official church of a nation.

Established religion. An official, state-sponsored religion.

Establishment clause. A part of the Fourteenth Amendment that forbids Congress from passing laws that violate the "separation of church and state" thus respecting the establishment of religion.

Ethical dilemma. A situation where you must weigh the consequences of your actions before making a decision or taking action.

European Convention of Human Rights. Established a European court to which the citizens of these countries could appeal when they believed their rights had been violated.

Ex Post Facto laws. A criminal law that makes an act a crime that was not a crime when committed, that increases the penalty for a crime after it was committed, or that changes the rules of evidence to make conviction easier.

Exclusionary rule. A rule that forbids the introduction of illegally obtained evidence in a criminal trial.

Executive. Made up of several persons appointed by congress; this branch has the power to administer national laws, appoint other executive officials, and direct all military operations.

Executive departments. Cabinet-level agencies in the federal government.

Executive power. The powers of the executive branch of the federal government.

Existence. The state or fact of having being especially independent of human consciousness and as contrasted with nonexistence.

F

Faction. A party, in political society, combined or acting in union, in opposition to the government, or state: usually applied to a minority, but it may be applied to a majority; a combination or clique of partisans of any kind, acting for their own interest; especially if greedy, clamorous, and reckless of the common good.

Fairness. The act of tempering individual desires with the needs of society as a whole.

Federal district court. A district court of law and equity that hears cases under federal jurisdiction.

Federal system. Of, relating to, or being from a government in which a union of states recognizes the sovereignty of a central authority while retaining certain residual powers of government.

Federalism. The distribution of power in an organization (as a government) between a central authority and the constituent units.

Federalist. The party who supported the ratification of the Constitution, advocated a strong central government, believed in or supported a federal system of government.

Federalist Party. The party, who supported the ratification of the Constitution, advocated a strong central government, believed in or supported a federal system of government.

Felony. A crime for which the punishment in federal law may be death or imprisonment for more than one year.

Fifteenth Amendment. Right of citizens to vote.

First Continental Congress. The body of delegates representing the colonies that first met to protest British rule and that eventually became the government of the United States.

Foreign policy. Of or involving the relations of one country with another.

Forum. A place or opportunity for open discussion and participation.

Four Freedoms. The four basic rights that Franklin D. Roosevelt declared worthy of fighting a war to preserve: freedom of speech and expression, freedom of worship, freedom from fear, and freedom from want.

Framers. The fifty-five delegates who attended the Philadelphia convention.

Franchise. A privilege or right officially granted a person or a group by a government.

Free exercise clause. A clause of the First Amendment of the Constitution that protects the rights of the people to practice (worship), or to abstain from, a religion of their choice.

Freedom. Political independence or immunity from arbitrary exercise of authority; the condition of being without restraints; the capacity to exercise one's choice; exception from unpleasant or onerous conditions.

Fugitive slave clause. Provided that slaves who escaped to other states must be returned to their owners.

Fundamental Orders of Connecticut. Adopted in 1639, this series of laws is the first written constitution in North America.

Futurists. The theorist who considers possibilities for the future based on current information and trends.

G

Gag rule. In U.S. history, any of a series of congressional resolutions that tabled, without discussion, petitions regarding slavery; passed by The House of Representatives between 1836 and 1840 and repealed in 1844.

General warrants. A precept issued by a magistrate authorizing an officer to make an arrest, a seizure, or a search, or do other acts incident to the administration of justice.

General welfare clause. Congress' constitutional authorization to tax and spend is found in Article I, Section 8.1 of the Constitution, which states, "Congress shall have Power to lay and collect Taxes, Duties, Imports and Excises, to pay the Debts and provide for the common Defense and general welfare of the United States."

General, special, and summary court-martials. The lowest level of trial courts in the military justice system, which provides for the disposition of minor offenses under a simple procedure when no punitive measures and punishment are inappropriate or ineffective. It may try only enlisted personnel.

Global village. Term used to define achievements of modern technology that indicate shared worldwide cultural, economic, and environmental concerns.

Goals. What one strives to achieve and attain.

Governor. The manager or administrative head of an organization, business, or institution.

Great Awakening. Swept the English-speaking world, as religious energy vibrated between England, Wales, Scotland, and the American colonies in the 1730s and 1740s.

Ground rules. Rules to ensure that everyone has an equal chance to participate fully and the group works together.

H

Habeas corpus. A judicial mandate to a prison official ordering that an inmate be brought to the court so it can be determined whether or not that person is imprisoned lawfully and whether or not he should be released from custody.

Hierarchical. Organized or classified according to rank, capacity, or authority.

Higher (fundamental) law. As used in describing a legal system, refers to the superiority of one set of laws over another.

House of Representatives. Elected directly by the people of each state.

Human nature. Personality and character traits that all human beings have in common.

Human rights. Basic rights and freedoms assumed to belong to all people everywhere.

I

Immunity. A special exemption, as from laws, taxes, military service, and so on.

Impeach. Charging a public official with a crime in office for which they can be removed from power.

Impeachment. The constitutional process whereby the House of Representatives may "impeach" (accuse of misconduct) high officers of the federal government for trial in the Senate.

Implied. To involve or indicate by inference, association, or necessary consequence rather than by direct statement.

Incorporation. To admit as a member to a corporation or similar organization.

Indentured servant. Voluntary servants who sold their labor for a period of four to seven years in exchange for passage to America.

Independent judiciary. An inviolate judicial branch that serves to protect the U.S. Constitution and prevents the executive and legislative branches from disregarding the Constitution.

Indicted. To charge with a crime by the finding or presentment of a grand jury in due form of law.

Inquisitorial system. A legal system where the court or a part of the court is actively involved in determining the facts of the case.

Intelligence. Information, not always available in the public domain, relating to the strength, resources, capabilities and intentions of a foreign country or domestic groups that can affect the lives and the safety of citizens.

International. Relating to, or constituting a group or association having members in two or more nations.

Intolerable acts. Parliament replied to the "Boston tea party" with the five coercive acts of 1774. the colonists dubbed them the "intolerable acts." They were an important factor contributing to the American revolution.

J

Judeo-Christian. Beliefs and practices which have their historical roots in Judaism and Christianity.

Judge. A high-ranking court officer who supervises and gives a decision on an action or court case.

Judicial. Branch with the power to decide cases involving treaties, trade among the states or with other nations, and the collection of taxes.

Judicial activism. Others have argued for judicial activism by pointing out that the nation's courts, as watchdogs of the constitution, have always had a special role to play in the identification, definition, and protection of individual rights.

Judicial restraint. The belief that the Supreme Court should neither overrule the decisions of elected officials nor make public policy.

Judicial review. The power of a court to adjudicate the constitutionality of the laws of a government or the acts of a government official.

Judiciary Act of 1789. An act to establish the Judicial Courts of the United States.

Jury. A select group of individuals chosen to listen and render a verdict in a court case.

Jury foreman. A person who conducts the jury deliberation and speaks for the jury.

L

Law firm. A group of lawyers.

Law of nature. In natural rights philosophy, the law of nature would prevail in the absence of man-made law, and contains universally obligatory standards of justice.

Legal remedy. Correcting a dispute or problem by a legal means.

Legislative. Branch given the powers of taxes, trade, and control over the states.

Legislative power. The power to write and enact laws.

Legislative supremacy. A system of government in which the legislative branch has the most power.

Legislatures. An officially elected or otherwise selected body of people vested with the responsibility and power to make laws for a political unit, such as a state or nation.

Legitimate. Being in compliance with the law.

Libel. A malicious defamation expressed either in printing or writing or by signs or pictures, tending to blacken the memory of one who is dead, with intent to provoke the living; or the reputation of one who is alive and to expose him to public hatred, contempt.

Liberty. The state of a free person; exemption from subjection to the will of another claiming ownership of the person or services; freedom—opposed to slavery, serfdom, bondage, or subjection.

Life. The period from birth to death

Limited government. In natural rights philosophy, a system restricted to protecting natural rights and that does not interfere with other aspects of life.

Lobby. Communicating with political decision makers to try to influence them on a political matter.

Loyalists. Colonists who remained loyal to Great Britain during the American revolution.

M

Magistrate. A lower-level judicial officer, usually elected in urban areas, who handles traffic violations, minor criminal offenses, and civil suits involving small amounts of money.

Magna Carta. The great charter of freedom granted in 1215 by King John of England by demand of his barons.

Majority rule. A principle of democracy which asserts that the greater number of citizens in any political unit should select officials and determine policies.

Manorialism. The form of economic life of the middle ages, when most people were involved in agriculture and land was divided up into self-contained farms or manors.

Massachusetts Body of Liberties. A document that described the rights of citizens and the authority of public officials.

Mayflower Compact. An agreement signed in 1620 by all adult males aboard the ship Mayflower, before landing in Plymouth, to form a body politic governed by majority rule.

Melting pot. A term used to describe a society made up of diverse cultures or races which have merged or "melted" into each other.

Middle Ages. A period, lasting from the fifth century to the fourteenth century, during which the political, economic, and military structure was characterized by feudalism.

Minutemen. Civilian armies of the American revolution, so called because of their readiness for battle.

Miranda Rights. A written and oral statement advising a suspect at the time of arrest of that person's rights against self-incrimination and to consult an attorney.

Misdemeanor. A minor offense (crime) for which punishment may be a fine and/or imprisonment in a local rather than a state institution (and generally for terms less than a year).

Mixed government. A government composed of some of the powers of a monarchical, aristocratical, and democratical government.

Monarch. A king or queen.

N

National Association for the Advancement of Colored People (NAACP). An interracial group founded in 1909 to advocate the rights of African Americans, primarily through legal and political action.

Nation of nations. America is peopled by millions of immigrants of different races, religions, languages, and ethnic backgrounds.

National government. Manages relationships among the states and unites the states in their relations with the rest of the world.

Nationalism. A sense of national consciousness that exalts one nation above all others.

Nation-state. The modern nation as the representative unit of political organization.

Natural rights. The doctrine of natural rights assumes that human beings had rights in a "state of nature" and create government in order to protect those rights.

Naturalized citizen. An individual who gains full citizenship in a country other than that of their birth.

Necessary and proper clause. The clause in Article I of the U.S. Constitution that gives Congress the power to make all laws that are "necessary and proper" to carry out the powers expressly delegated to it by the Constitution.

Negative rights. These rights are seen as restraints on the power of government.

Neutrality. The state or quality of being neutral; the condition of being unengaged in contests between others; state of taking no part on either side; indifference.

Nineteenth Amendment. Women's suffrage rights.

Nonviolent direct action. Peaceful tactics used as a means of gaining one's civil or political ends.

O

Opening statements. Statements that state the opinion of one side in the beginning of a court case.

Original jurisdiction. The legal authority of a court to be the first to hear a case.

Orthodoxy. A belief or orientation agreeing with conventional standards.

P

Papacy. The office or authority of the pope, the spiritual leader of the Roman Catholic church.

Parliamentary government. A system that gives governmental authority to a legislature or parliament which in turn selects the executive from among its own members.

Patience. The skill of knowing the proper timing for acting on an idea or decision.

Penumbras. A body of rights held to be guaranteed by implication in a civil constitution.

Perpetual union. Lasting for eternity.

Philadelphia Convention. The meeting held in Philadelphia from May 25 through September 18, 1787, at which the Constitution of the United States was drafted.

Plebiscite. An expression of the people's will by direct vote.

Political action. Any organized attempt to influence the political process, from lobbying legislators to seeking the election (or defeat) or particular candidates.

Political guarantees. Guarantee of varied rights.

Political parties. An organization that runs candidates for public office under its label and for directing the policies of government.

Political rights. All of the implicit (constitutionally guaranteed) and implied (by natural laws) rights of a citizen in a free society.

Popular sovereignty. The natural rights concept that ultimate political authority rests with the people.

Positive rights. Instead of preventing the government from acting, they require it to act, to ensure such things as economic security, health care, and a clean environment for its citizens.

Preamble. The basic mission statement for the United States Constitution.

Precedents. Legal principle, created by a court decision, which provides an example of authority for judges deciding similar issues later.

Preferential treatment programs. Preferred.

President's Cabinet. The President's hand picked advisors, each in charge of a different government office or department.

Prime minister. The highest ranking member of the executive branch of a parliamentary government as in Great Britain and Japan.

Primogeniture. The condition of being the first-born child. In law, it refers to the right of the eldest son to inherit all of his parents' estates.

Principle. A fundamental, primary, or general law or truth from which others are derived.

Private domain. Areas of human affairs placed off limits to unreasonable government interference.

Probable cause. Reasonable grounds for belief that an accused person is guilty as charged or that a crime has been committed.

Procedural due process. A course of formal proceedings (as judicial proceedings) carried out regularly, fairly, and in accordance with established rules and principles.

Procedural guarantees of due process. Refers to those clauses in the U.S. Constitution that protect individuals from unreasonable and unfair governmental procedures.

Proportional representation. The electoral system in which the number of representatives of a state in the house of representatives is based on the number of people who live in that state.

Providence. The care, guardianship, and control exercised by a deity.

Provision. That which is stipulated in advance; a condition; a previous agreement; a proviso; as, the provisions of a contract; the statute has many provisions.

Public and private morality. The principles of civic virtue as expressed in Judeo-Christian teachings, as well as fundamental ideas about right and wrong that come from religion, ethics, and individual conscience.

Public forum. An open place for free speech.

Q

Quartering act. Also known as the mutiny act, the law passed by parliament that authorized colonial governors to requisition certain buildings for the use, or "quartering," of British troops.

Quotas and group entitlements. The state of being entitled.

R

Ratification. Formal approval of the U.S. Constitution by the states.

Ratify. To approve and sanction formally.

Realm. A community or territory over which a sovereign rules; a kingdom.

Reasonable doubt. The level of certainty a juror must have to find a defendant guilty of a crime. A real doubt, based upon reason and common sense after careful and impartial consideration of all the evidence, or lack of evidence, in a case.

Redress of grievances. A setting right, as of wrong, injury, or oppression; as, the redress of grievances; hence, relief; remedy; reparation; indemnification.

Referenda. The submission of a proposed public measure or actual statute to a direct popular vote.

Reformation. Sixteenth-century religious movement aimed at reforming the Roman Catholic church and resulting in the establishment of Protestant churches.

Regents of the University of California v. Bakke (1978). Race or ethnic background may be deemed a "plus" in a particular applicant's file, yet it does not insulate the individual from comparison with all other candidates for the available seats.

Remedial programs. Supplying a remedy.

Renaissance. The great revival of art, literature, and learning in Europe during the fourteenth, fifteenth, and sixteenth centuries, based on classical sources.

Representation. The state or condition of serving as an official delegate, agent, or spokesperson.

Representative democracy. The system of government in which power is held by the people and exercised indirectly through elected representatives.

Representative group session. One of two types of citizen action groups in which small groups elect representatives to discuss and decide on issues in front of a class or other gathering.

Representative group session agenda. A list of tasks or a schedule to be followed during a representative group session.

Republic. A form of government in which the supreme political power resides in the electorate, and administration is exercised by representatives who are responsible to the people.

Republican. One of the two major political parties in the United States.

Resident alien. A foreign-born inhabitant.

Respect. Accepting the differences in others and honoring those differences.

Responsible parties. Those who take responsibility to ensure goals are met.

Reverse discrimination. Discrimination against members of a dominant or majority group, especially when resulting from policies established to correct discrimination against members of a minority or disadvantaged group.

Revolution of 1800. The election of 1800 where the Republicans took control of both houses and Thomas Jefferson became President and Aaron Burr became Vice President.

Right against self-incrimination. Granted by the Fifth Amendment; allows a person to refuse to answer questions or give other evidence that would subject him or her to criminal prosecution.

Right of association and right of petition. To associate with anyone you desire and to deliver a petition.

Right of revolution. It is the foundation of consent of the governed and guarantees that you can take matters into your own hands if you must.

Right to assembly. The right to meet together in groups.

Right to counsel. The government cannot prevent you from having a lawyer defend you from the time you are named as a suspect. If you are charged with a serious crime and cannot afford a lawyer, the government must provide one free of charge.

Right to privacy. To be secure in your own person and belongings.

Rights of Englishman. Basic rights, established over time, that all subjects of the English monarch were understood to have.

Rights of solidarity. Solidarity rights included in the United Nations' Universal Declaration of Rights, and in many national guarantees of rights adopted since, are sometimes called positive rights.

Rule of law. Implies that government authority may only be exercised in accordance with written laws, which are adopted through an established procedure.

S

Sanctions. Measures to stop or limit trade with another nation in order to change its behavior.

Secession. The act of seceding.

Sectionalism. Excessive devotion to local interests and customs.

Secular governments. A system of political power not exercised by ecclesiastical bodies or the clergy.

Sedition Act of 1798. An act for the punishment of certain crimes against the United States.

Seditious libel. Of or pertaining to sedition; partaking of the nature of, or tending to excite, sedition; as, seditious behavior; seditious strife; seditious words.

Selective incorporation. A theory or doctrine of constitutional law that those rights guaranteed by the first eight amendments to the U.S. Constitution that are fundamental to and implicit in the concept of ordered liberty are incorporated into the Fourteenth Amendment's due process clause.

Self-improvement. A desire to continually learn new skills and improve on others so that citizens can better serve themselves and those around them.

Senate. The upper house of the U.S. Congress, to which two members are elected from each state by popular vote for a six-year term.

Separate but equal doctrine. "The argument, once upheld by the Supreme Court, that separate public facilities were constitutional if the facilities were of equal quality."

Separated powers. The division of powers among different branches of government.

Separation of church and state. Principle is part of our historical, legal and political social heritage and preserves and protects our religious liberties.

Seven Years War. A series of dynastic and colonial wars between England and France; the American phase, fought between 1754 and 1763, is known as the French and Indian war.

Simple majority. Show of hands in the voting process.

Small group leader. Leads a small group meeting.

Small group meeting. One of two types of citizen action groups where a small group of five to nine persons meets periodically to discuss and decide on various issues and actions.

Small group representatives. A member of a small group who is elected to represent the group at the representative group session.

Social action. Organize other members of the community.

Social and economic rights. Examples of social and economic rights would be the right to choose a career, secure employment, health care, and education.

Social contract. The agreement among all the people in a society to give up part of their freedom to a government in return for the protection of their natural rights by that government.

Sons of Liberty. An organization of radicals created in 1765 in the American colonies to express colonial opposition to the stamp act.

Sovereignty. Supremacy of authority or rule as exercised by a sovereign or sovereign state.

Spirit of association. The fondness American citizens had for banding together to address problems of common interest.

Stamp Act Congress. A meeting in New York in 1765 of twenty-seven delegates from nine colonies, the congress was the first example of united colonial action in the developing struggle against Great Britain.

Standard of living. Social conditions established by authority as a fixed rule, measure, or model.

State declarations of rights. The citizens to be governed by these new constitutions possessed certain basic rights that existed prior to government and that no constitution or government could take away.

State of nature. The basis of natural right philosophy, state of nature is the hypothetical condition of people living together in a society.

Strength. The willingness of citizens to stand up for what they believe in, to denounce what's wrong, and to admit when they've made a mistake.

Strict construction. A narrow interpretation of the U.S. Constitution's provisions, in particular those granting power to government.

Substantive due process. Requirement that laws and regulations must be related to a legitimate government interest (as crime prevention) and may not contain provisions that result in the unfair or arbitrary treatment of an individual.

Suffrage. The right to vote. A vote cast in deciding a disputed question or in electing a person to office.

Summit meeting. A meeting between heads of state.

Supremacy clause. Article VI, Section 2 of the U.S. Constitution, which states that the Constitution, laws passed by Congress, and treaties of the United States "shall be the supreme law of the land" binding on the states.

T

Tea Act. The act by parliament that conferred upon the East India company a monopoly importation of tea into the mainland colonies, thus eliminating the profits of the colonial importer and shopkeeper.

Telecommunications. The science and technology of sending messages over long distances, especially by electronic means.

Teledemocracy. The futurist view of a direct democracy using telecommunications to provide greater opportunities for participation in government.

Tenets. An opinion, doctrine, or principle held as being true by a person or especially by an organization.

Terrorism. The use of threat of violence to spread fear, usually for the purpose of reaching political goals.

The Great Compromise. Adopted at the Philadelphia convention n, this plan provided for equal representation of the states in the Senate and House of Representatives according to population.

The Laws and Liberties. Code that abolished the laws of primogeniture and provided more humane treatment of criminals.

Timekeeper. An individual who keeps track of the time at a small group meeting.

Timeline. A linear representation of important events in the order in which they occurred; a schedule; timetable.

Time-place-and manner restrictions. A statute or government action that restricts the time, place, or manner of speech.

Token integration. A show of accommodation to the principle of racial integration by small, merely formal concessions.

Treason. In the U.S. Constitution, treason is "giving aid and comfort" to the enemy during wartime.

Trials. Examinations of facts and law in a court of law.

Twenty-fourth Amendment. The right of citizens of the United States to vote in any primary or other election for President or Vice President, for electors for President or Vice President, or for Senator or Representative in Congress, shall not be denied or abridged by the United States or any state by reason of failure to pay any poll tax or other tax.

Twenty-sixth Amendment. An amendment to the U.S. Constitution, ratified in 1971, lowering the voting age to 18.

U

UCMJ. The basis for all military law in the U.S. armed forces; established by congress in 1951.

Unalienable (inalienable). Fundamental rights of the people that may not be taken away.

Unconstitutional. Not in keeping with the basic principles or laws set forth in the Constitution of a state or country, especially the Constitution of the United States.

Unenumerated rights. Rights which are not specifically listed in the U.S. Constitution or Bill of Rights, but which have been recognized and protected by the courts.

Unitary governments. Have only one source of power, the central or national government.

United Nations. An organization created as a result of a multilateral treaty that serves as a constitution for the United Nations Organization.

Universal Declaration of Human Rights. The declaration and the charter proclaimed universal standards of basic rights, called human rights, because they were considered essential to the dignity of each human being.

Unlimited government. A government in which those who govern are free to use their power as they choose, unrestrained by laws or elections.

V

Vassal. In feudal times, a person granted the use of land by a feudal lord in return for military or other service.

Verdict. The decision rendered by a judge or jury in a court case.

Veto. The constitutional power of the president to refuse to sign a bill passed by Congress, thereby preventing it from becoming a law.

Virginia Declaration of Rights. The first state declaration of rights, which served as a model for other state declarations of rights and the Bill of Rights.

Virginia Plan. The plan traced the broad outlines of what would become the U.S. Constitution: a national government consisting of three branches with checks and balances to prevent the abuse of power.

W

Warrant. In law, written order by an official of a court directed to an officer.

Writ of Assistance. A document giving a governmental authority the power to search and seize property without restrictions.

Writ of Mandamus. It is a command issuing in the name of the sovereign authority from a superior court having jurisdiction, and is directed to some person, corporation, or inferior court, within the jurisdiction of such superior court, requiring them to do some particular thing therein specified, which appertains to their office and duty, and which the superior court has previously determined, or at least supposes to be consonant to right and justice.

Index